# Formal Assessment

W9-ATT-868

## McDougal Littell

# THE LANGUAGE OF
# LITERATURE

### GRADE NINE

## McDougal Littell
A HOUGHTON MIFFLIN COMPANY
**Evanston, Illinois • Boston • Dallas**

# Acknowledgments

**Ballantine Books:** Excerpt from *The Hanging Tree* by Dorothy M. Johnson. Copyright 1950 and renewed © 1978 by Dorothy M. Johnson. Reprinted by permission of Ballantine Books, a division of Random House, Inc.

**Virginia Kidd Agency, Inc.:** "The Wife's Story," from *The Compass Rose* by Ursula K. Le Guin. Copyright © 1982 by Ursula K. Le Guin. Reprinted by permission of the author and the Virginia Kidd Agency, Inc.

ISBN 0-395-96801-1

# Contents

**To the Teacher** . . . . . . . . . . . . . . . . . . . . . . . . . . . . . . . . . . . . . . . . . . . . . . . iv

**Tests for *The Language of Literature***

    Contents . . . . . . . . . . . . . . . . . . . . . . . . . . . . . . . . . . . . . . . . . . . . . . 1

    To the Teacher . . . . . . . . . . . . . . . . . . . . . . . . . . . . . . . . . . . . . . . . 4

    Selection and Part Tests, Unit One . . . . . . . . . . . . . . . . . . . . . . . 7

    Selection and Part Tests, Unit Two . . . . . . . . . . . . . . . . . . . . . . 41

    Selection and Part Tests, Unit Three . . . . . . . . . . . . . . . . . . . . 67

    Mid-Year Test . . . . . . . . . . . . . . . . . . . . . . . . . . . . . . . . . . . . . . . . 93

    Selection and Part Tests, Unit Four . . . . . . . . . . . . . . . . . . . . . 101

    Selection and Part Tests, Unit Five . . . . . . . . . . . . . . . . . . . . . 125

    Selection and Part Tests, Unit Six . . . . . . . . . . . . . . . . . . . . . . 147

    End-of-Year Test . . . . . . . . . . . . . . . . . . . . . . . . . . . . . . . . . . . . 169

**Additional Test Generator Questions**

    Contents . . . . . . . . . . . . . . . . . . . . . . . . . . . . . . . . . . . . . . . . . . 179

    To the Teacher . . . . . . . . . . . . . . . . . . . . . . . . . . . . . . . . . . . . . 179

    Additional Questions . . . . . . . . . . . . . . . . . . . . . . . . . . . . . . . 180

**Writing Assessment**

    Contents . . . . . . . . . . . . . . . . . . . . . . . . . . . . . . . . . . . . . . . . . . 211

    To the Teacher . . . . . . . . . . . . . . . . . . . . . . . . . . . . . . . . . . . . . 212

    Holistic Scoring Guide . . . . . . . . . . . . . . . . . . . . . . . . . . . . . . . 213

    General Rubric . . . . . . . . . . . . . . . . . . . . . . . . . . . . . . . . . . . . . 215

    Writing Prompts for Assessment Practice . . . . . . . . . . . . . . . 216

**Standardized Test Practice**

    Contents . . . . . . . . . . . . . . . . . . . . . . . . . . . . . . . . . . . . . . . . . . 221

    To the Teacher . . . . . . . . . . . . . . . . . . . . . . . . . . . . . . . . . . . . . 222

    To the Student . . . . . . . . . . . . . . . . . . . . . . . . . . . . . . . . . . . . . 223

    Test Practice . . . . . . . . . . . . . . . . . . . . . . . . . . . . . . . . . . . . . . . 225

**Answer Key**

    Contents . . . . . . . . . . . . . . . . . . . . . . . . . . . . . . . . . . . . . . . . . . 259

    *The Language of Literature* Test Answers . . . . . . . . . . . . . . . 260

    Standardized Test Practice Answers . . . . . . . . . . . . . . . . . . . . 323

# To the Teacher

This Formal Assessment booklet contains the materials described below. For more detailed information, turn to the front of each section.

## Tests for *The Language of Literature*

- **Selection Tests.** A Selection Test is provided for each selection or group of selections in the Pupil's Edition. Each Selection Test may use graphics, multiple-choice items, or essay questions to test students' understanding of vocabulary words, content, major issues, and the literary concepts taught with each selection. Selection Tests should be administered after students have discussed the selection and completed the Responding Options.

- **Part Tests.** Part Tests are open-book tests. Students are directed to answer multiple-choice or short essay questions and complete graphics that require them to discuss or compare a number of selections in terms of themes, characters, and literary concepts.

- **Mid-Year and End-of-Year Tests.** The Mid-Year and End-of-Year Tests are open-book tests designed to check students' understanding of the concepts and skills that were taught in the units preceding the tests. These two tests are similar in format, although the End-of-Year Test is somewhat longer than the Mid-Year Test. Each test consists of a short reading passage followed by several series of multiple-choice questions and short-answer, open-ended questions. These questions test the students' basic understanding of the passage as well as the literary elements and techniques used to write the passage. The writing portion of the tests includes a prompt, which calls for the students to write a short essay applying at least one taught concept or skill. Finally, there is a short activity testing the students' editing and revising skills.

## Additional Test Generator Questions

This section contains a bank of additional questions for each selection, which you can use to create customized tests for your classes. The items in this section of the book are duplicated on the Test Generator software. You are encouraged to scan these items and select the ones that would be most useful for your classes. You can then use the Test Generator software to create tests to suit your students' needs.

## Writing Assessment

This section contains several tools to help you conduct holistic evaluations of students' writing, including a general evaluation form and writing assessment prompts to help students prepare for essay tests.

## Standardized Test Practice

This section provides opportunities for students to develop strategies for performing well on standardized tests. Practice items are included for areas typically found on standardized tests. Each section of practice items explains the purpose for those particular items, provides an example, and describes specific strategies students can use to be successful.

## Answer Key

This section includes answer keys for Selection Tests, Part Tests, Mid-Year and End-of-Year Tests, and the Standardized Test Practice.

# Tests for *The Language of Literature*

## Contents

To the Teacher . . . . . . . . . . . . . . . . . . . . . . . . . . . . . . . . . . . . . . . . . . 4

| | Tests* | Additional Test Generator Questions |
|---|---|---|

### Unit One: The Power of Storytelling

**Part One: Crisis and Conflict**

| | | |
|---|---|---|
| The Necklace | 7 | 180 |
| The Most Dangerous Game | 9 | 180 |
| Where Have You Gone, Charming Billy? | 11 | 180 |
| Marigolds | 13 | 181 |
| Two Kinds | 15 | 181 |
| *from* The Perfect Storm | 17 | 182 |
| The Wreck of the Hesperus | 19 | 182 |
| Unit One, Part One Test | 21 | |

**Part Two: Suspense and Surprise**

| | | |
|---|---|---|
| O What Is That Sound | 23 | 183 |
| Incident in a Rose Garden | 25 | 183 |
| The Gift of the Magi | 27 | 184 |
| The Sniper | 29 | 184 |
| The Possibility of Evil | 31 | 184 |
| The Censors | 33 | 185 |
| Annabel Lee/The Bells | 35 | 185 |
| The Cask of Amontillado | 37 | 186 |
| Unit One, Part Two Test | 39 | |

### Unit Two: Passages

**Part One: Journeys of Discovery**

| | | |
|---|---|---|
| Life Without Go-Go Boots | 41 | 187 |
| *from* Angela's Ashes | 43 | 187 |
| Unfinished Business | 45 | 187 |
| A Christmas Memory | 47 | 188 |
| Song of the Open Road/The Road Not Taken | 49 | 188 |
| American History | 51 | 189 |
| Unit Two, Part One Test | 53 | |

*Answer Key for Selection, Part, Mid-Year, and End-of-Year Tests begins on page 260.

|  | Tests* | Additional Test Generator Questions |
|---|---|---|

**Part Two: Rites of Passage**

The Beginning of Something . . . . . . . . . . . . . . . . . . . . . . . . . 55 . . . . . . . . . . 189
Young/Hanging Fire . . . . . . . . . . . . . . . . . . . . . . . . . . . . . . 57 . . . . . . . . . . 190
The Seven Ages of Man . . . . . . . . . . . . . . . . . . . . . . . . . . . . 59 . . . . . . . . . . 190
Brothers Are the Same . . . . . . . . . . . . . . . . . . . . . . . . . . . . . 61 . . . . . . . . . . 191
Through the Tunnel . . . . . . . . . . . . . . . . . . . . . . . . . . . . . . . 63 . . . . . . . . . . 191

Unit Two, Part Two Test . . . . . . . . . . . . . . . . . . . . . . . . . . . . 65

# Unit Three: Voices of Experience

**Part One: Speaking Out**

The Devil and Daniel Webster . . . . . . . . . . . . . . . . . . . . . . . 67 . . . . . . . . . . 192
I Have a Dream/Glory and Hope . . . . . . . . . . . . . . . . . . . . . 69 . . . . . . . . . . 192
The United States vs. Susan B. Anthony . . . . . . . . . . . . . . . . 71 . . . . . . . . . . 193
Theme for English B/The Writer . . . . . . . . . . . . . . . . . . . . . 73 . . . . . . . . . . 193
*from* I Know Why the Caged Bird Sings . . . . . . . . . . . . . . . . 75 . . . . . . . . . . 194
New Directions . . . . . . . . . . . . . . . . . . . . . . . . . . . . . . . . . 77 . . . . . . . . . . 194
Encounter with Martin Luther King, Jr. . . . . . . . . . . . . . . . . 79 . . . . . . . . . . 195

Unit Three, Part One Test . . . . . . . . . . . . . . . . . . . . . . . . . . 81

**Part Two: Facing Limits**

To Build a Fire . . . . . . . . . . . . . . . . . . . . . . . . . . . . . . . . . . 83 . . . . . . . . . . 195
*from* Into Thin Air . . . . . . . . . . . . . . . . . . . . . . . . . . . . . . 85 . . . . . . . . . . 195
The Sharks/A narrow Fellow in the Grass . . . . . . . . . . . . . . . 87 . . . . . . . . . . 196
My Wonder Horse/Mi Caballo Mago . . . . . . . . . . . . . . . . . . 89 . . . . . . . . . . 196

Unit Three, Part Two Test . . . . . . . . . . . . . . . . . . . . . . . . . . 91

Mid-Year Test . . . . . . . . . . . . . . . . . . . . . . . . . . . . . . . . . . 93

# Unit Four: All in the Family

**Part One: Family Ties**

The Scarlet Ibis . . . . . . . . . . . . . . . . . . . . . . . . . . . . . . . . . 101 . . . . . . . . . . 198
Lineage/The Courage That My Mother Had . . . . . . . . . . . . . 103 . . . . . . . . . . 198
My Papa's Waltz/Grape Sherbet . . . . . . . . . . . . . . . . . . . . . 105 . . . . . . . . . . 199
Marine Corps Issue . . . . . . . . . . . . . . . . . . . . . . . . . . . . . . 107 . . . . . . . . . . 199

Unit Four, Part One Test . . . . . . . . . . . . . . . . . . . . . . . . . . 109

**Part Two: Declarations of Independence**

*from* Black Boy . . . . . . . . . . . . . . . . . . . . . . . . . . . . . . . . 111 . . . . . . . . . . 200
Daughter of Invention . . . . . . . . . . . . . . . . . . . . . . . . . . . . 113 . . . . . . . . . . 200
A Voice/The Journey . . . . . . . . . . . . . . . . . . . . . . . . . . . . . 115 . . . . . . . . . . 201
Only Daughter . . . . . . . . . . . . . . . . . . . . . . . . . . . . . . . . . 117 . . . . . . . . . . 201
*from* The House on Mango Street . . . . . . . . . . . . . . . . . . . 119 . . . . . . . . . . 202
On Writing The House on Mango Street . . . . . . . . . . . . . . . . 121 . . . . . . . . . . 202

Unit Four, Part Two Test . . . . . . . . . . . . . . . . . . . . . . . . . . 123

*Answer Key for Selection, Part, Mid-Year, and End-of-Year Tests begins on page 260.

|  | Tests* | Additional Test Generator Questions |
|---|---|---|

# Unit Five: A World of Mysteries

## Part One: Criminal Minds

| | | |
|---|---|---|
| Full Circle | 125 | 203 |
| Wasps' Nest | 127 | 203 |
| Trifles | 129 | 203 |
| The Great Taos Bank Robbery | 131 | 204 |
| Unit Five, Part One Test | 133 | |

## Part Two: Illusion and Reality

| | | |
|---|---|---|
| The Open Window | 135 | 204 |
| Sorry, Right Number | 137 | 205 |
| Beware: Do Not Read This Poem | 139 | 205 |
| In the Family | 141 | 206 |
| A Very Old Man with Enormous Wings | 143 | 206 |
| Unit Five, Part Two Test | 145 | |

# Unit Six: The Classic Tradition

## Part One: The Odyssey

| | | |
|---|---|---|
| Book 9 *from the* Odyssey | 147 | 207 |
| Book 10 *from the* Odyssey | 149 | 207 |
| Book 12 *from the* Odyssey | 151 | 208 |
| Books 21, 22, and 23 *from the* Odyssey | 153 | 208 |
| Unit Six, Part One Test | 155 | |

## Part Two: The Tragedy of Romeo and Juliet

| | | |
|---|---|---|
| The Tragedy of Romeo and Juliet: Act One | 157 | 208 |
| The Tragedy of Romeo and Juliet: Act Two | 159 | 209 |
| The Tragedy of Romeo and Juliet: Act Three | 161 | 209 |
| The Tragedy of Romeo and Juliet: Act Four | 163 | 210 |
| The Tragedy of Romeo and Juliet: Act Five | 165 | 210 |
| Unit Six, Part Two Test | 167 | |
| End-of-Year Test | 169 | |

*Answer Key for Selection, Part, Mid-Year, and End-of-Year Tests begins on page 260.

# To the Teacher

This section contains Selection Tests, Part Tests, the Mid-Year Test, and the End-of-Year Test. The following charts indicate the types of questions and the tested concepts for each type of test in this section. Administer Selection Tests after students have discussed the selection and completed the postreading activities. Tests for poetry should be open-book.

## Selection Tests

| Section | Type of Item | Tested Concepts and Skills from the Selection |
|---------|--------------|-----------------------------------------------|
| A | graphic device (table, chart, diagram, etc.) | selection content or the introduced literary concept |
| B | multiple-choice questions | selection content or the introduced literary concept |
| C* | multiple-choice questions | vocabulary words |
| D** | essay questions | introduced literary concepts |
| E | essay question | how introduced concept relates to student's personal experience |
| F*** | optional | optional |

* If a selection has no vocabulary words, the item types and tested elements will move up one section. In some tests, a graphic exercise testing a major concept from the selection is inserted in Section C. In this case, the vocabulary questions and/or other items are moved down one section.
** The student chooses one of two essay questions to answer.
*** If a graphic exercise is used in Section C and vocabulary is tested in Section D, the remaining sections may be moved down. In this case, Section F is necessary.

## Part Tests

| Section | Type of Item | Tested Concepts and Skills from the Part |
|---------|--------------|------------------------------------------|
| A | multiple-choice or short answer questions | content of selections in the part or the literary concepts that were introduced in those selections |
| B | graphic device (table, chart, diagram, etc.) | compare/contrast elements from one or more selections; analyze elements within a single selection |
| C* | essay questions | students' personal reactions to selections; major ideas, characters, themes, literary concepts |
| D** | graphic device (table, chart, diagram, etc.) | compare/contrast elements from one or more selections; analyze elements within a single selection |

* The student chooses two of three to four essay questions to answer.
** Included whenever space permits; uses a different graphic device and tests other elements than Section B.

# Mid-Year and End-of-Year Tests*

| Section | Type of Item | Tested Concepts and Skills |
|---------|--------------|----------------------------|
| 1 | multiple-choice questions | basic comprehension of the reading passage |
| 2 | multiple-choice questions | how the literary concepts and skills taught in the preceding units relate the reading passage |
| 3 | short, open-ended essay questions | how the literary concepts and skills taught in the preceding units relate the reading passage |
| 4 | multiple-choice questions | ability to analyze and critically evaluate the reading passage in terms of literary concepts and skills |
| 5 | short, open-ended essay questions | ability to analyze and critically evaluate the reading passage in terms of literary concepts and skills |
| 6 | essay question | writing ability (organization and mechanics) |
| 7 | multiple-choice questions | revising and editing ability (organization and mechanics) |

* Reading passages for these tests are included in this book.

All questions appearing in this Formal Assessment book, as well as the quizzes printed in the URB, can be found electronically on the Test Generator software.

# The Necklace (page 26)

# Selection Test

**A.** Think about the events in the plot of this story. In the chart below, write notes describing what happens in each stage of the plot: the **rising action,** which includes the main conflict and complications; the **climax,** or turning point; and the **falling action,** which includes the resolution. (8 points each)

| |
|---|
| **1. Rising Action** |
| **2. Climax** |
| **3. Falling Action** |

**B.** Write the letter of the best answer. This exercise is continued on the next page. (6 points each)

_____ 1. At the beginning of the story, Mme. Loisel's unhappiness is due to a contrast between
    a. what she has and what she wants.
    b. what she once had and what she has now.
    c. what she wants and what her husband wants.
    d. what she's been promised and what she's received.

_____ 2. What makes Mme. Loisel so happy at the party?
    a. the way other people react to her
    b. the opportunity to be among friends
    c. the fact that she is making her husband proud
    d. the fact that Mme. Forestier has trusted her with the necklace

_____ 3. The events of the story suggest that what Mme. Loisel fears **most** is
    a. poverty.
    b. boredom.
    c. humiliation.
    d. the loss of her beauty.

4. Mme. Loisel decides, at last, to tell Mme. Forestier the whole story mainly because she
   a. is angry at Mme. Forestier.
   b. is proud of having paid the debts.
   c. wants Mme. Forestier to feel sorry for her.
   d. thinks that confession is good for the soul.

**C.** On the line, write the name of either M. Loisel or Mme. Forestier. Then, note how that minor character contrasts with Mme. Loisel. (12 points)

**Character** _____

**D. Words to Know.** Write the letter of the best answer. (4 points each)

_____ 1. An <u>exorbitant</u> price for a new car would be
   a. $100.          b. $10,000.          c. $100,000.

_____ 2. Which is **most** likely to leave you <u>aghast</u>?
   a. running a mile     b. eating a big meal     c. finding a dead body

_____ 3. You are **most** likely to cause <u>vexation</u> in a person who is
   a. happy.          b. irritable.          c. hypnotized.

_____ 4. Which are you **most** likely to find <u>askew</u>?
   a. a train on a track     b. a picture on a wall     c. a skyscraper in a city

_____ 5. Which is **most** likely to receive <u>adulation</u>?
   a. a movie star     b. a truck driver     c. a homeless person

**E.** Answer one of the following questions based on your understanding of the story. Write your answer on a separate sheet of paper. (10 points)

1. What effects do you think the news that the necklace is fake has on Mme. Loisel? Describe an immediate effect and a long-term effect.

2. What flaws in Mme. Loisel's character do you think lead to her troubles? Explain your answer.

**F. Linking Literature to Life.** Answer the following question based on your own experience and knowledge. Write your answer on a separate sheet of paper. (10 points)

Do you think that having a great deal more money would make you happier? Explain your answer.

# The Most Dangerous Game (page 38)

# Selection Test

**A.** Think about how suspense is created in the story. Choose **three** suspenseful moments and make notes in the boxes below to describe them. (24 points)

| Uncertain or suspenseful moment | How is the suspense resolved? |
|---|---|
| | |

| Uncertain or suspenseful moment | How is the suspense resolved? |
|---|---|
| | |

| Uncertain or suspenseful moment | How is the suspense resolved? |
|---|---|
| | |

**B.** Write the letter of the best answer. This exercise is continued on the next page. (6 points each)

_____ 1. The sailors on the yacht suspect that "Ship-Trap Island" is a place where
    a. people are hunted.
    b. treasure is buried.
    c. undefined evil exists.
    d. marked channels are deceiving.

_____ 2. Zaroff is glad Rainsford has come to the island because he thinks Rainsford will
    a. be an exciting quarry.
    b. teach him something about hunting.
    c. help him find some good people to hunt.
    d. become a longtime companion for him.

_____ 3. Which of the following statements would Rainsford and Zaroff fail to agree about?
    a. The greatest sport is hunting.
    b. The world is made up of hunters and the hunted.
    c. Animals do not have the capacity to reason and understand.
    d. Animals do not offer sufficient challenge to be interesting prey.

_____  4. Zaroff responds to Rainsford's criticism of his activities as if he finds it
   a. insulting.              c. dangerous.
   b. amusing.                d. worth thinking about.

_____  5. What does Rainsford refuse to do?
   a. resort to violence
   b. resort to deceit and trickery
   c. keep Zaroff's activities secret
   d. become the prey in Zaroff's hunt

_____  6. At the end of the story, the fact that Rainsford is sleeping in Zaroff's bed
   indicates that
   a. Zaroff has admitted defeat.
   b. Rainsford has killed Zaroff.
   c. Rainsford has scared Zaroff off.
   d. Rainsford has decided to join Zaroff's activities.

**C. Words to Know.** Write the letter of the best answer. (4 points each)

_____  1. Which of the following is tangible?
   a. an idea          b. an orange          c. a shadow

_____  2. If you were droll, people would **most** likely consider you to be
   a. funny.          b. athletic.          c. rude.

_____  3. You would be **most** likely to need stamina to
   a. cook dinner.          b. read a book.          c. run a marathon.

_____  4. If something is imperative, it is
   a. gracious.          b. immoral.          c. required.

_____  5. People try to elude each other in the game of
   a. tag.          b. tug of war.          c. tennis.

**D.** Answer **one** of the following questions based on your understanding of the story. Write your answer on a separate sheet of paper. (10 points)

1. How does Zaroff justify his hunting of humans? What would you say to argue against his position?

2. Do you think that Rainsford's view of hunting animals is changed by his experience as the hunted? Why or why not?

**E. Linking Literature to Life.** Answer the following question based on your own experience and knowledge. Write your answer on a separate sheet of paper. (10 points)

Do you support hunting animals as a sport? Why or why not?

# Where Have You Gone, Charming Billy? (page 62)

## Selection Test

**A.** In this selection, you learn many things about the character Paul Berlin. The story tells about the events of his first day in the war. But you also learn about his thoughts, and from his thoughts you can infer things about him and his family. In the boxes on the left, list three things you can infer about Paul and his relationship with his family. In the boxes on the right, give evidence from the story for each of your inferences. (10 points each)

| Inference About Paul Berlin | Evidence from the Story |
|---|---|
| **1.** | |
| **2.** | |
| **3.** | |

**B.** Write the letter of the best answer. This exercise is continued on the next page. (5 points each)

_____  1. To help himself feel less afraid, Paul
      a. thinks about avoiding land mines
      b. pictures Billy Boy's face
      c. counts his steps
      d. talks about his fears

_____  2. When Toby talks with Paul, he conveys an attitude of
      a. indifference.      c. scorn.
      b. sympathy.      d. anger.

_____  3. What did Billy Boy do when he stepped on the land mine?
      a. He sat down casually.
      b. He passed out.
      c. He rolled on the ground, screaming in agony.
      d. He began laughing uncontrollably.

_____ 4. What did Paul fear most of all?
   a. land mines and booby traps
   b. being so terribly afraid again
   c. mortar fire from the enemy
   d. dying of a heart attack

**C. Words to Know.** Write the letter of the best answer. (4 points each)

_____ 1. If your thoughts are <u>diffuse</u>, they are
   a. contradictory.　　　b. unfocused.　　　c. resolute.

_____ 2. A bird in flight at night is most likely to be <u>silhouetted</u> against
   a. a tree.　　　b. the moon.　　　c. a nest.

_____ 3. A person who does something <u>casually</u> is
   a. awkward.　　　b. hostile.　　　c. unconcerned.

_____ 4. Words of <u>consolation</u> are intended to offer
   a. comfort.　　　b. practical advice.　　　c. praise.

_____ 5. To <u>execute</u> a stunt is to
   a. eliminate it.　　　b. attempt it.　　　c. perform it.

**D.** Answer **one** of the following questions based on your understanding of the selection. Write your answer on a separate sheet of paper. (15 points)

1. At the end of the story, a soldier says to Paul, "You got to stay calm, buddy. Half the battle, just staying calm." Relate this quotation to the internal struggles of Paul and to the death of Billy Boy. Do you think Paul will win this "half the battle"? Explain why or why not.

2. Irony is a situation in which the result is very different from what one would have expected. Why did Billy Boy's death seem ironic to his companions? What impact did this ironic death have on Paul?

**E. Linking Literature to Life.** Answer the following question based on your own experience and knowledge. Write your answer on a separate sheet of paper. (15 points)

   How do you think you would feel about being a soldier in a war? Would the reason for the war make a difference? Explain.

# Marigolds (page 74)

# Selection Test

**A.** Think about the setting of this story and how it influences the narrator's experiences and her perceptions of what happens. In the chart below, write notes describing each element of the setting. Then, write notes describing how each element influences the narrator's actions or her feelings about the events and characters. (12 points each)

| Description of Setting | How It Influences the Narrator's Actions or Feelings |
| --- | --- |
| 1. The town | |
| 2. The time | |
| 3. Miss Lottie's | |

**B.** Write the letter of the best answer. (6 points each)

_____ 1. Miss Lottie's reaction to Lizabeth's destroying the marigolds is one of
   a. blind rage.
   b. extreme relief.
   c. sorrowful defeat.
   d. complete indifference.

_____ 2. Which of the following is **not** a reason that the marigold incident stands out in the narrator's memory?
   a. It was a turning point in her life.
   b. It marked the end of troubles in her life.
   c. It marked the end of her childhood innocence.
   d. The realization that she gained from it is still important to her.

**C. Words to Know.** Write the letter of the best answer. (4 points each)

_____ 1. What would a person's <u>stoicism</u> cause him or her to do while watching
a funny movie?
a. laugh               b. cry                    c. keep a straight face

_____ 2. An act of <u>bravado</u> is **usually**
a. admirable.          b. showy.                c. sweet.

_____ 3. People who live in <u>degradation</u> are **most** likely to feel
a. bored.              b. proud.                c. humiliated.

_____ 4. What do **all** <u>impotent</u> people lack?
a. power               b. education             c. maturity

_____ 5. When you show <u>compassion</u>, you reveal an awareness of the existence of
a. good and evil.      b. suffering.            c. future opportunities.

**D.** Answer **one** of the following questions based on your understanding of the story.
Write your answer on a separate sheet of paper. (16 points)

1. Why do you think Lizabeth destroys Miss Lottie's marigolds? Why do you think she
   immediately regrets doing it? Support your answers with details from the story and
   your own ideas.

2. The marigold incident signals a change in Lizabeth. Is that also true of Miss Lottie?
   Support your answer with details from the story and your own ideas.

**E. Linking Literature to Life.** Answer the following question based on your own
experience and knowledge. Write your answer on a separate sheet of paper. (16 points)

The narrator says of the children in her town, "Perhaps we had some dim notion of
what we were, and how little chance we had of being anything else. Otherwise why
would we have been so preoccupied with destruction?" Do you agree that lack of
hope and opportunity motivates people to destructiveness? Explain your answer.

# Two Kinds (page 88)

# Selection Test

**A.** Think about each of these statements made by the mother or the daughter/narrator in this story. In the chart below, write notes describing what each statement reveals about the character's beliefs and how the statement relates to the overall theme of the story. (8 points each)

| Character's Statement | What the Statement Reveals |
|---|---|
| 1. Mother: "You can be best anything." | |
| 2. Daughter: "Why don't you like me the way I am? I'm *not* a genius!" | |
| 3. Mother: "Only two kinds of daughters . . . those who are obedient and those who follow their own mind! Only one kind of daughter can live in this house. Obedient daughter!" | |
| 4. Daughter/Narrator: And after I played them both a few times, I realized they were two halves of the same song. | |

**B.** Write the letter of the best answer. This exercise is continued on the next page. (6 points each)

_____  1. Which of the following does the daughter do to rebel against her mother?
    a. try to predict daily temperatures
    b. practice her curtsy for the talent show
    c. watch Shirley Temple movies on television
    d. count the foghorn bellows during her mother's tests

...................................................................................................................................

_____ 2. After which of the following events does the daughter decide to stop trying
to be a prodigy?
a. the talent show
b. the mother's death
c. the first piano lesson
d. the Shirley Temple haircut

_____ 3. As an adult, the daughter believes that she has grown to be
a. simply herself.
b. the best person she could possibly be.
c. the worst person she could possibly be.
d. the genius that her mother always wanted her to be.

**C. Words to Know.** Write the letter of the best answer. (4 points each)

_____ 1. An <u>indignity</u> is something that causes you to lose your
a. memory.          b. honor.          c. freedom.

_____ 2. People usually <u>lament</u> actions that
a. cause them pain.     b. interest them.     c. make them happy.

_____ 3. You would be deserving of <u>reproach</u> if you were
a. at fault.          b. apologetic.          c. guiltless.

_____ 4. If your party is a <u>fiasco</u>, it is a
a. surprise.          b. failure.          c. success.

_____ 5. An act of <u>betrayal</u> should be taken as a sign of
a. shyness.          b. acceptance.          c. disloyalty.

**D.** Answer **one** of the following questions based on your understanding of the story.
Write your answer on a separate sheet of paper. (15 points)

1. In what ways are the daughter's internal conflicts reflected in the two contrasting
songs—"Pleading Child" and "Perfectly Contented"?

2. Why do you think the mother wants the daughter to be a prodigy? What does she
hope this will achieve for her daughter? What do you think she hopes it will achieve
for herself?

**E. Linking Literature to Life.** Answer the following question based on your own
experience and knowledge. Write your answer on a separate sheet of paper. (15 points)

What do you think are some important differences between a parent who guides and
one who controls?

## *from* **The Perfect Storm (page 112)**

# Selection Test

**A.** Think about how this selection, like a fiction adventure story, builds suspense—a feeling of tension and excitement about what is going to happen. In each numbered box below, write notes describing a moment of crisis or high suspense. Then, in the boxes below, describe how each crisis is resolved. (10 points each)

| 1. Moment of Crisis: | 2. Moment of Crisis: | 3. Moment of Crisis: |
|---|---|---|
| Resolution: | Resolution: | Resolution: |

**B.** Write the letter of the best answer. This exercise is continued on the next page. (5 points each)

_____ 1. When the people on the *Satori* first understand that they will be rescued, how does Ray Leonard react?
a. He feels enormous relief.
b. He is giddy with excitement.
c. He takes charge of the situation.
d. He does not wish to cooperate.

_____ 2. Helicopters have an advantage over Falcon jets in a sea rescue mission because they can
a. cover longer shifts.
b. take people out of the water.
c. fly faster.
d. relay messages between ships.

_____ 3. Leaving the *Satori* is harder for Leonard than for his crew because
   a. the *Satori* is his home.
   b. he is not as good a swimmer.
   c. his pride is wounded.
   d. he is convinced he will die.

_____ 4. Dave Moore can best be described as
   a. worried and hesitant.
   b. bold and reckless.
   c. grim and hard-working.
   d. friendly and competent.

**C. Words to Know.** Write the letter of the best answer. (4 points each)

_____ 1. Someone who acts <u>incredulously</u> is filled with
   a. disbelief.          b. regret.          c. grief.

_____ 2. Fish that <u>flail</u> are
   a. disappearing.          b. moving steadily.          c. thrashing about.

_____ 3. Which of these would be considered a <u>maelstrom</u>?
   a. a tornado          b. a sandy beach          c. an island

_____ 4. A swimmer who is <u>hypothermic</u> is very
   a. strong.          b. cold.          c. wet.

_____ 5. An <u>amalgam</u> is **most** like a
   a. solution.          b. mixture.          c. resignation.

**D.** Answer **one** of the following questions based on your understanding of the selection. Write your answer on a separate sheet of paper. (15 points)

1. During the rescue attempt, many things went wrong. Describe at least **two** unexpected mishaps, and explain why the rescue attempt was successful in the end.

2. Ray Leonard and Dave Moore experienced the rescue of the *Satori* crew in very different ways. Compare and contrast their experiences and views of the event. Why were they so different?

**E. Linking Literature to Life.** Answer the following question based on your own experience and knowledge. Write your answer on a separate sheet of paper. (15 points)

   If a captain wishes to go down with his ship, do you think the Coast Guard should insist on rescuing him? Should the Coast Guard have the right to make such a decision? Why or why not?

# The Wreck of the Hesperus (page 124)

## Selection Open-Book Test

**A.** "The Wreck of the Hesperus" is a narrative poem with characters, setting, and plot. In the boxes on the left, write notes describing each of the two main characters, the setting, and the plot. In the boxes on the right, write one or more lines from the poem that support your description. (10 points each)

| Description | Supporting Lines from the Poem |
|---|---|
| **1. Character: The Skipper** | |
| **2. Character: The Skipper's Daughter** | |
| **3. Setting** | |
| **4. Plot** | |

**B.** Write the letter of the best answer. (5 points each)

_____ 1. The skipper could **best** be described as
   a. cautious.          c. overconfident.
   b. cruel.             d. heroic.

_____ 2. The words used to describe the skipper's daughter emphasize her
   a. innocence.         c. fear.
   b. nervousness.       d. wisdom.

_____ 3. The mood of the poem could **best** be described as
   a. hopeful.           c. angry.
   b. comforting.        d. woeful.

**C.** Answer **one** of the following questions based on your understanding of the selection. Write your answer on a separate sheet of paper. (25 points)

1. "The Wreck of the Hesperus" has two main characters and two minor characters. Explain how each character contributes to the story.

2. In what ways do poetic devices contribute to the telling of the story? Think about the ways in which the structure and language of poetry differ from that of prose. Explain how those differences affect the experience of reading this disaster story.

**D. Linking Literature to Life.** Answer the following question based on your own experience and knowledge. Write your answer on a separate sheet of paper. (20 points)

   Throughout history, disasters have inspired books, poetry, songs, movies, and visual art. Why do you think disasters are a popular subject? What do these stories tell us about ourselves and others? Use examples from the shipwreck stories you have just read or from other disaster stories you know.

# Unit One: The Power of Storytelling

# Part One Open-Book Test

**A.** Write the answer to each question on the lines. (5 points each)

1. In "The Necklace," what does the necklace symbolize for Mme. Loisel—before she loses it and after she loses it?

   _____

   _____

2. In "Where Have You Gone, Charming Billy?" why can't Paul Berlin stop giggling about Billy Boy?

   _____

   _____

3. What is the meaning of the title of Amy Tan's story "Two Kinds"?

   _____

   _____

4. How is the selection from *The Perfect Storm* different from all the other selections in this part?

   _____

   _____

**B.** In many of the selections in this part, there are symbols—people, places, or things that stand for something else. Choose symbols from **two** different selections. In the boxes below, write the title of each selection you choose and the symbol you wish to discuss. Then explain what the symbol represents in the selection. (20 points)

| **Selection:** | **Selection:** |
| --- | --- |
| **Symbol:** | **Symbol:** |
| **What the Symbol Represents:** | **What the Symbol Represents:** |

**C.** Answer **two** of the following questions based on your understanding of the selections. Write your answers on a separate sheet of paper. (20 points each)

1. Choose any **two** characters in this part and compare the conflicts they face and the ways in which they handle them. Are the conflicts internal or external? Are they resolved?

2. Many of these selections concern the idea of loss. Choose **two** selections in which one or more things are lost, given up, or left behind. What is lost in each selection? Is any one loss greater than the others? Support your answers with details from the selections.

3. Choose any **two** minor characters from two different selections. Explain how their actions, beliefs, or words add to another character's understanding of the situation.

**D.** The power of storytelling can reveal important lessons about life and human nature. Choose **two** characters from this part who learned important or interesting lessons about life. Write their names and the names of the selections in the two boxes. For each character, write notes explaining the lesson that the character learned and how that lesson was learned. (20 points)

| **Selection:**<br><br>**Character:** | **Selection:**<br><br>**Character:** |
|---|---|
| What lesson did the character learn? | What lesson did the character learn? |
| How did the character learn the lesson? | How did the character learn the lesson? |

# O What Is That Sound (page 141)

## Selection Open-Book Test

**A.** Think about the rhythm of this poem and the various purposes it serves. Then, in the box on the left, jot down some words or phrases that describe the rhythm. In the box on the right, note one thing that the rhythm accomplishes. (15 points each)

| 1. The rhythm is . . . | 2. The rhythm makes . . . |
| --- | --- |
|  |  |

**B.** Write the letter of the best answer. (15 points each)

_____    1. Which of the following best describes the second speaker's apparent
            attitude toward the soldiers at the beginning of the poem?
            a. shocked
            b. frightened
            c. disapproving
            d. unconcerned

_____    2. What is the main feeling that grows in the first speaker as the poem
            progresses?
            a. dread
            b. hatred
            c. courage
            d. curiosity

**C.** Answer **one** of the following questions based on your understanding of the poem.
Write your answer on a separate sheet of paper. (20 points)

  1. Why do you think the soldiers are coming to the speakers' home? What might
     explain why the second speaker leaves? Support your ideas with reference to
     the poem.

  2. What effects does the poet achieve by dividing each of the first eight stanzas
     between the first speaker and the second speaker? Who do you think is the
     speaker in the last stanza? Support your answers.

**D. Linking Literature to Life.** Answer the following question based on your own
experience and knowledge. Write your answer on a separate sheet of paper. (20 points)

  What are some ways in which the lives of men and women might be affected
differently by war? Support your ideas.

# Incident in a Rose Garden (page 146)

# Selection Open-Book Test

**A.** Think about the reactions of the gardener and the master toward Death. In the middle boxes below, jot down words or phrases that describe each character's attitude toward Death. In each box on the right, write notes explaining why you think the character has that attitude. (16 points each)

| Character | Attitude | Reasons for His Attitude |
|---|---|---|
| **1. The Gardener** | | |
| **2. The Master** | | |

**B.** Write the letter of the best answer. This exercise is continued on the next page. (8 points each)

_____ 1. The master addresses Death as if Death were
a. a welcome guest.
b. an unwelcome stranger.
c. an object or a thing.
d. an old friend of his father's.

_____ 2. The phrase "thin as a scythe" is an example of
a. metaphor.
b. personification.
c. alliteration.
d. simile.

_____ 3. Which quotation from the poem contains an example of metaphor?
a. "And held that out in greeting, / A little cage of bone"
b. "A connoiseur of roses"
c. "... his eyes lit up / With the pale glow of those lanterns ..."
d. "Dressed like a Spanish waiter."

_____ 4. The speaker compares the light of Death's eyes to the "pale glow" of workmen's lanterns at dusk. This image suggests that

    a. there is a ray of hope for the master.

    b. Death mistakes the master for a workman.

    c. it is "dusk" for the master; his life is near its end.

    d. Death itself will soon fade away.

**C.** Answer **one** of the following questions based on your understanding of the selection. Write your answer on a separate sheet of paper. (20 points)

1. What is ironic about the plot of "Incident in a Rose Garden"? What theme, or main idea, does that irony help to express? Explain.

2. Do you think the poet meant this poem to be scary? Funny? Thought-provoking? Or did he have more than one purpose in mind? Explain. Use examples from the poem to defend your position.

**D. Linking Literature to Life.** Answer the following question based on your own experience and knowledge. Write your answer on a separate sheet of paper. (16 points)

Which character in this poem seemed better prepared for his own death? To what extent do you think people should think about and prepare for their own deaths? Explain.

# The Gift of the Magi (page 151)

# Selection Test

**A.** Think about the ironies in this story. In the box next to each event below, write notes explaining why that event was ironic. (8 points each)

| Event | Why It Was Ironic |
|-------|-------------------|
| 1. Della bought Jim a watch fob. | |
| 2. Della yearned for a particular set of tortoise-shell hair combs. | |
| 3. Jim had to comfort his sobbing wife. | |

**B.** Write the letter of the best answer. This exercise continues on the next page. (5 points each)

_____ 1. The narrator implies that Jim's full name was ironic because
a. he used only a short nickname.
b. it gave the impression of wealth.
c. he had no middle name.
d. it made him seem old.

_____ 2. When the narrator says that after Della sold her hair, two hours "tripped by on rosy wings," he means that she
a. felt very happy.
b. was very worried.
c. was not thinking clearly.
d. had ups and downs.

_____ 3. The watch fob that Della bought was
a. beautifully decorated.
b. secondhand.
c. the latest fashion.
d. made of precious metal.

_____ 4. Della is best described as
    a. a miserly penny pincher.
    b. unconcerned about appearances.
    c. generous and loving.
    d. reckless and wild.

**C. Words to Know.** Write the letter of the best answer. (4 points each)

_____ 1. A person who <u>instigates</u> an event is one who
    a. prevents it.    b. provokes it.    c. controls it.

_____ 2. A person with <u>prudence</u> is known for
    a. good judgment.    b. greed.    c. generosity.

_____ 3. A <u>coveted</u> object is something
    a. deeply resented.    b. depended on.    c. wanted badly.

_____ 4. If something is <u>inconsequential</u>, it is not
    a. desirable.    b. polite.    c. important.

_____ 5. An <u>agile</u> dancer is
    a. clumsy.    b. graceful.    c. tireless.

**D.** Answer **one** of the following questions based on your understanding of the selection. Write your answer on a separate sheet of paper. (20 points)

1. Would you agree that Jim and Della had sacrificed for each other "the greatest treasures of their house"? Why or why not?

2. O. Henry contrasts Jim and Della with people who give "wise" gifts, such as those "bearing the privilege of exchange in case of duplication." Why does he declare Jim and Della to be the wisest? Do you agree with him? Why or why not?

**E. Linking Literature to Life.** Answer the following question based on your own experience and knowledge. Write your answer on a separate sheet of paper. (16 points)

What is the greatest gift you have ever received or given? What made the gift so special?

# The Sniper (page 162)

# Selection Test

**A.** Think about how the level of suspense in this story increases from the beginning to the end. In the chart below, describe six events from the story, in order, that help to create a mounting sense of suspense. (5 points each)

| **The sniper eats a sandwich.** |
| --- |
| **1.** |
| **2.** |
| **3.** |
| **4.** |
| **5.** |
| **6.** |
| **The sniper looks at the face of the man he has killed.** |

**B.** Write the letter of the best answer. This exercise is continued on the next page. (5 points each)

_____ 1. As the story opens, the sniper's mood is one of
   a. dread.                    c. excitement.
   b. exhaustion.               d. anger.

_____ 2. The sniper shot a woman on the street because
   a. she supported his enemies.
   b. he was eager to kill someone.
   c. she was armed and dangerous.
   d. he knew and disliked her.

_____ 3. The sniper needed to kill the man on the opposite roof in order to
   a. overcome his sense of shame.
   b. win the war for the IRA.
   c. find out if the woman was dead.
   d. make his own escape.

_____ 4. The sniper threw down his revolver after shooting his enemy because he
        a. no longer needed it.
        b. was upset by what he had done.
        c. was too weak to hold it.
        d. was celebrating his success.

## C. Words to Know. Write the letter of the best answer. (4 points each)

_____ 1. An ascetic man most often looks
        a. comforting.      b. puzzled.      c. stern.

_____ 2. Which person would most likely use a ruse?
        a. a magician      b. a sailor      c. a musician

_____ 3. A feeling of remorse is one of
        a. forgiveness.      b. regret.      c. enthusiasm.

_____ 4. A person who is reeling is
        a. off balance.      b. graceful.      c. quick.

_____ 5. A city is most likely to be enveloped by
        a. streets.      b. fog.      c. people.

**D.** Answer **one** of the following questions based on your understanding of the selection. Write your answer on a separate sheet of paper. (15 points)

1. At the beginning of the story, the sniper's eyes have "the cold gleam of the fanatic." How do you think the sniper will feel about the war and his role in it on the day following the events of this story? Use evidence from the story to support your answer.

2. What message do you think the author was trying to convey by the surprise ending of this story? How does the ending lend new meaning to other events in the story?

**E. Linking Literature to Life.** Answer the following question based on your own experience and knowledge. Write your answer on a separate sheet of paper. (15 points)

   What kinds of political causes, if any, can justify the sort of violence portrayed in this story? What causes have been used to justify this sort of violence in the past? Do you think this kind of violence could happen today?

# The Possibility of Evil (page 172)

# Selection Test

**A.** Think about the interaction between Miss Strangeworth and Helen Crane. What is revealed about Miss Strangeworth through this one relationship? On the left, write notes describing what happens during the interaction. On the right, explain what the thought or action reveals about Miss Strangeworth's character. (6 points each)

| What Happens When Miss Strangeworth Meets Helen Crane | What This Reveals About Miss Strangeworth |
|---|---|
| 1. What Miss Strangeworth does: | |
| 2. What Miss Strangeworth thinks: | |
| 3. What Miss Strangeworth says: | |
| 4. What Helen says to Miss Strangeworth: | |
| 5. What Miss Strangeworth does later in response to this meeting: | |

**B.** Write the letter of the best answer. This exercise is continued on the next page. (5 points each)

_____ 1. As she observes other people during the day, Miss Strangeworth's thoughts about them are
  a. kind.          c. judgmental.
  b. worried.       d. indifferent.

_____ 2. When you think of Miss Strangeworth's life, which of the following seems ironic?
  a. She always buys tea on Tuesday.
  b. She never uses Mr. Lewis's first name.
  c. Her dining room can seat 22 people.
  d. She sleeps in the room her grandmother slept in.

_____ 3. The messages in Miss Strangeworth's letters are intended to
        a. cause suspicion.          c. solve problems.
        b. stimulate discussion.      d. create fear.

_____ 4. The letter Miss Strangeworth received at the end of the story was
        probably sent
        a. as a practical joke.       c. by mistake.
        b. as an act of revenge.     d. by an evil person.

**C. Words to Know.** Write the letter of the best answer. (4 points each)

_____ 1. A person with a <u>rapt</u> expression probably feels
        a. worried.           b. enchanted.          c. bored.

_____ 2. A <u>potential</u> disaster is one that
        a. can possibly happen.   b. has been averted.     c. has taken many lives.

_____ 3. Which of these is <u>reprehensible</u>?
        a. a job well done      b. a crime          c. a donation to charity

_____ 4. Something that exists <u>unchecked</u> is not
        a. safe.             b: examined.         c. controlled.

_____ 5. A person who acts <u>indulgently</u> is being
        a. tolerant.         b. foolish.          c. nasty.

**D.** Answer **one** of the following questions based on your understanding of the selection. Write your answer on a separate sheet of paper. (15 points)

1. Discuss Miss Strangeworth's relationship to her roses. How does she feel about them? Give at least **three** examples from the story to show how the roses help to reveal Miss Strangeworth's character.

2. How do the letters Miss Strangeworth writes contrast with her appearance and her reputation? Note at least **two** points of contrast, and explain what the letters reveal about her.

**E. Linking Literature to Life.** Answer the following question based on your own experience and knowledge. Write your answer on a separate sheet of paper. (15 points)

   What is your opinion of Miss Strangeworth's anonymous letters? Is she providing a public service, or is she a public menace? What effects might the letters have on the people who receive them? Explain.

# The Censors (page 185)

# Selection Test

**A.** Think about the uses of irony in this story. For each event listed in the chart below, write a note in the middle box to explain why the event is ironic. Then, in the box on the right, note which type of irony is used: verbal, situational, or dramatic. (6 points each)

| Event | Why It Is Ironic | Type of Irony |
|---|---|---|
| 1. Juan was very happy when he got Mariana's new address. | | |
| 2. The chief in the explosives unit claimed a worker was negligent. | | |
| 3. The narrator refers to Juan's work as a noble mission. | | |
| 4. Juan's instincts became so sharp that he could detect antigovernment messages behind any simple phrase. | | |
| 5. Juan finally located the letter he wrote to Mariana. | | |

**B.** Write the letter of the best answer. This exercise is continued on the next page. (5 points each)

_____ 1. Juan applies for a censor's job because he
   a. needs steady work.
   b. wants to catch enemies of the government.
   c. wants to intercept his own letter.
   d. hopes the job will help him find Mariana.

_____ 2. As a censor, Juan
   a. tries to undermine the system.
   b. loses sight of his original goal.
   c. stands up for his beliefs.
   d. causes all sorts of controversy.

_____ 3. By the time he reaches Section E, Juan has become a
   a. hero.                   c. genius.
   b. traitor.               d. fanatic.

_____ 4. Which theme is central to the meaning of this story?
   a. Honest people will recognize their own guilt.
   b. Those who participate in a corrupt system become its victims.
   c. Commitment to the job and hard work are their own rewards.
   d. It is a privilege to sacrifice oneself for the greater good.

**C. Words to Know.** Write the letter of the best answer. (4 points each)

_____ 1. When a person's behavior is <u>irreproachable</u>, it is
   a. faultless.        b. cruel.        c. tiresome.

_____ 2. A person who drops <u>subtle</u> hints is being
   a. obvious.        b. foolish.        c. indirect.

_____ 3. A <u>conniving</u> person is most likely being
   a. dishonest.      b. generous.      c. threatening.

_____ 4. A person described as having <u>staidness</u> is most likely
   a. cheerful.       b. dignified.      c. friendly.

_____ 5. Which is a <u>subversive</u> act in a democracy?
   a. jury service     b. speeding     c. assassination

**D.** Answer **one** of the following questions based on your understanding of the selection. Write your answer on a separate sheet of paper. (15 points)

1. Explain why Juan's attitude toward censorship changes dramatically over the course of the story.

2. Something that is absurd is so clearly unreasonable as to be laughable or ridiculous. What situations in this story are absurd? What does this emphasis on the absurd tell you about the author's point of view?

**E. Linking Literature to Life.** Answer the following question based on your own experience and knowledge. Write your answer on a separate sheet of paper. (15 points)

What is your opinion of censorship in schools and libraries? Does it serve a useful purpose? Are there certain materials that people your age should be kept from reading? Explain.

# Annabel Lee/The Bells (page 198)

# Selection Open-Book Test

**A.** Think about the use of sound devices in these excerpts from "Annabel Lee" and "The Bells." Then, using all three excerpts, find two examples of each sound device: end rhyme, internal rhyme, assonance, and alliteration. Write each example in the box on the right under the name of the sound device it illustrates. (10 points each)

| Excerpt | Examples of Sound Devices |
|---|---|
| "And neither the angels in Heaven above<br>Nor the demons down under the sea<br>Can ever dissever my soul from the soul<br>Of the beautiful Annabel Lee:—" | 1. End Rhyme<br>_____<br>_____ |
| "For the moon never beams without<br>    bringing me dreams<br>Of the beautiful Annabel Lee;<br>And the stars never rise but I feel the bright eyes<br>Of the beautiful Annabel Lee;" | 2. Internal Rhyme<br>_____<br>_____<br><br>3. Assonance<br>_____<br>_____ |
| "Oh, the bells, bells, bells!<br>What a tale their terror tells<br>Of despair!<br>How they clang and clash and roar!<br>What a horror they outpour<br>In the bosom of the palpitating air!" | 4. Alliteration<br>_____<br>_____ |

**B.** Write the letter of the best answer. This exercise is continued on the next page. (5 points each)

_____ 1. What happened to Annabel Lee?
    a. She scorned the speaker's love.
    b. She drowned in the ocean.
    c. She became ill and died.
    d. She disappeared without a trace.

_____ 2. According to the speaker, angels in Heaven reacted to the love he and
Annabel Lee felt for each other with

a. envy.
b. grace.
c. approval.
d. anger.

_____ 3. The poem "Annabel Lee" gives the impression that the speaker

a. is ready to get on with his life.
b. has lost his mind due to grief.
c. is covering up a crime.
d. is comforted by his memories.

_____ 4. "The Bells" is concerned primarily with

a. telling a story.
b. creating mental pictures through description.
c. linking past with present.
d. evoking different moods through sound.

**C.** Answer **one** of the following questions based on your understanding of the selection.
Write your answer on a separate sheet of paper. (20 points)

1. Why does the speaker of "Annabel Lee" find the death of Annabel Lee especially
tragic, and why does he think it happened? Use details from the poem to support
your ideas.

2. What makes poetry different from prose? Identify at least **three** differences and use
examples from these two poems to illustrate your points.

**D. Linking Literature to Life.** Answer the following question based on your own
experience and knowledge. Write your answer on a separate sheet of paper. (20 points)

How did you react to "The Bells"? How did it make you feel? What part of it did you
like best? Explain.

# The Cask of Amontillado (page 207)

# Selection Test

**A.** Think about the verbal irony in this story. Each of Montresor's statements shown below could be considered ironic. In each box on the right, make notes that describe what is ironic about what Montresor says. (8 points each)

| | |
|---|---|
| 1. "Enough, " he said; "the cough is a mere nothing; it will not kill me. I shall not die of a cough." "True—true," I replied . . . "but you should use all proper caution." | |
| 2. "I drink," he said, "to the buried that repose around us." "And I to your long life." | |
| 3. "Once more let me *implore* you to return. No? Then I must positively leave you." | |

**B.** Write the letter of the best answer. This exercise is continued on the next page. (7 points each)

_____ 1. Why does Montresor tell Fortunato that he is going to ask Luchesi to judge the wine?
   a. He wants to insult Fortunato.
   b. He wants Luchesi's opinion as well.
   c. He doesn't want Fortunato to feel obligated to help him.
   d. He knows this will make Fortunato determined to do it himself.

_____ 2. Throughout most of the story, Montresor treats Fortunato with
   a. open hostility.
   b. cold politeness.
   c. great friendliness.
   d. cheerful unconcern.

3. Montresor is able to manipulate Fortunato **mainly** through appealing to Fortunato's
   a. guilt.
   b. pride.
   c. greed.
   d. kindheartedness.

_____ 4. The line at the end of the story, "For the half of a century no mortal has disturbed them," indicates that
   a. the crime has gone unsolved.
   b. the police are still looking for the body.
   c. Montresor fears that God will punish his act.
   d. Montresor has lost track of the time that has passed.

**C. Words to Know.** Write the letter of the best answer. (4 points each)

_____ 1. When you <u>implore</u> someone, you are **most** likely to say
   a. "No way!"          b. "So there!"          c. "Please!"

_____ 2. When a storm <u>subsides</u>, it
   a. builds up.          b. gets weaker.          c. stops suddenly.

_____ 3. If someone were to <u>accost</u> you, he or she would
   a. hit you.          b. confront you.          c. defend you.

_____ 4. Which of the following is **most** likely to be <u>fettered</u>?
   a. a prisoner          b. a mattress          c. a bald eagle

_____ 5. What do people usually do at the <u>termination</u> of an airplane flight?
   a. get on          b. get off          c. make reservations

**D.** Answer **one** of the following questions based on your understanding of the story. Write your answer on a separate sheet of paper. (14 points)

1. Do you think that Montresor, as he is narrating the story, is sane or insane? Explain your answer.

2. Do you think that Montresor feels remorse at any point in the story? Use details from the story to support your answer.

**E. Linking Literature to Life.** Answer the following question based on your own experience and knowledge. Write your answer on a separate sheet of paper. (14 points)

Do you believe that the old saying "revenge is sweet" is true? Should the "punishment fit the crime"? Explain your answers.

# Unit One: The Power of Storytelling

# Part Two Open-Book Test

**A.** Write the letter of the best answer to each question. (5 points each)

_____ 1. In which of these poems is Death personified?
      a. "Annabel Lee"        c. "The Bells"
      b. "O What Is That Sound"    d. "Incident in a Rose Garden"

_____ 2. The title of O. Henry's story "The Gift of the Magi" suggests that Jim
      and Della
      a. will soon become parents.
      b. represent the true spirit of Christmas.
      c. believe in magical powers.
      d. follow religious traditions in observing Christmas.

_____ 3. Which event in "The Censors" is ironic?
      a. Juan writes a letter to his friend Mariana.
      b. Juan's mother tries to help him change his life.
      c. Juan censors his own letter and is executed.
      d. Juan moves from Section F to Section E.

_____ 4. Revenge is the primary motive for the actions of
      a. Montresor in "The Cask of Amontillado."
      b. Juan in "The Censors."
      c. The sniper in "The Sniper."
      d. Miss Strangeworth in "The Possibility of Evil."

**B.** Some of the selections in this part challenge the reader to accept things that are outside of ordinary experience. Write the title of one selection you wish to discuss. In the boxes below, describe something from that selection that you found difficult to believe and explain why it was difficult to believe. (20 points)

**Title:** _____

| Something That Was Difficult to Believe | Reasons It Was Difficult to Believe |
|---|---|
| | |

**C.** Answer **two** of the following questions based on your understanding of the selections. Write your answers on a separate sheet of paper. (20 points each)

1. Choose **one** selection from this part in which the tables are turned—that is, in which people's or characters' fortunes or roles are reversed. Explain how the tables are turned, what results from this reversal, and whether you think that this reversal is deserved.

2. Choose **two** selections from this part—one in which you think justice was served and one in which it wasn't. Explain your views, using details from the selections to support your ideas.

3. Compare and contrast the risks taken by **two** characters or people from different selections in this part. Consider the risks they take, their reasons for taking those risks, and what happens as a result of those risks.

**D.** In many of these selections, people are greatly affected by others. Choose a person from **one** selection you wish to discuss. Write the person's name and the title of the selection. In the boxes below, write notes describing who or what affects the person you chose, how the person is affected, and why the person is affected in that way. (20 points)

**Character and Title:** _____

| **Who or what affects the person?** |
| --- |
| |

| **How is the person affected?** |
| --- |
| |

| **Why is the person affected in that way?** |
| --- |
| |

# Life Without Go-Go Boots (page 236)

## Selection Test

**A.** In this essay, Kingsolver reveals much about herself by expressing her views on women's fashions. Choose **three** adjectives that you think describe Kingsolver's personality. Write each adjective in one of the boxes below. Then, below each adjective, note at least **one** example from the essay that supports your choice of that adjective. (10 points each)

| 1. Descriptive adjective: | 2. Descriptive adjective: | 3. Descriptive adjective: |
|---|---|---|
| Supporting evidence: | Supporting evidence: | Supporting evidence: |

**B.** Write the letter of the best answer. This exercise is continued on the next page. (5 points each)

_____ 1. As a child, the author wanted go-go boots because she wanted to appear
      a. practical.      c. fashionable.
      b. grown-up.     d. unique.

_____ 2. High fashion has "the shelf life of potato salad" because it
      a. isn't good for you.
      b. doesn't last long.
      c. is very satisfying.
      d. won't appeal to everyone.

_____ 3. The author's memories of how she dressed at age 11 are best described as
      a. painful.      c. proud.
      b. sad.        d. disbelieving.

_____ 4. As an adult, the author is happy with her clothes because she
  a. can afford to buy high-fashion clothes.
  b. makes her own clothes.
  c. doesn't go out much.
  d. dresses however she chooses.

**C. Words to Know.** Write the letter of the best answer. (4 points each)

_____ 1. If nothing can <u>compel</u> you, you cannot be
  a. tricked.          b. forced.          c. changed.

_____ 2. An <u>inscrutable</u> person is difficult to
  a. understand.       b. avoid.           c. appreciate.

_____ 3. Parents who <u>indulge</u> their children too much are likely to
  a. punish them.      b. spoil them.      c. ignore them.

_____ 4. Which is a <u>conventional</u> style for American businessmen?
  a. T-shirt and jeans     b. tuxedo       c. suit and tie

_____ 5. An <u>irreparable</u> injury cannot be
  a. described.        b. avoided.         c. undone.

**D.** Answer **one** of the following questions based on your understanding of the selection. Write your answer on a separate sheet of paper. (15 points)

1. According to the author, what are some differences between fashion and style? Why are these differences important to her?

2. Use your own words to explain the "larger truths" that the author learned from analyzing her attitude, and that of her parents, toward fashion.

**E. Linking Literature to Life.** Answer the following question based on your own experience and knowledge. Write your answer on a separate sheet of paper. (15 points)

How important is fashion to you and your friends? How do you react to students whose clothes do not conform to the kinds of things most students wear?

## *from* **Angela's Ashes (page 243)**

# Selection Test

**A.** In this memoir, McCourt brings the reader directly into the world of his youth. In the chart below, answer each question about his world. Then, in the box to the right of each question, write notes to explain ways in which each aspect of McCourt's world affected his childhood. (10 points each)

| McCourt's World | How It Affected Him |
| --- | --- |
| 1. Where did he live? | |
| 2. What was his religion? | |
| 3. What problems did his family have? | |

**B.** Write the letter of the best answer. This exercise is continued on the next page. (5 points each)

_____ 1. The happy moments McCourt remembers from his hospital stay call attention to his
      a. playful nature.      c. interest in history.
      b. scientific mind.      d. love of words.

_____ 2. You can tell that Patricia Madigan was
      a. an intellectual child.      c. shy and reserved.
      b. high-spirited.      d. tense and anxious.

_____ 3. Seamus is unhappy about the book Patricia gives McCourt because
      a. it is not a poetry book.
      b. he thinks McCourt should rest.
      c. it is all about England.
      d. he cannot read it himself.

_____ 4. Because of Patricia and McCourt, Seamus begins to
   a. memorize poetry.
   b. like children.
   c. write letters to the *Limerick Leader.*
   d. learn how to read.

**C. Words to Know.** Write the letter of the best answer. (4 points each)

_____ 1. When a patient has a <u>relapse</u>, his or her condition
   a. improves.          b. is stable.          c. worsens.

_____ 2. A <u>potent</u> medicine is
   a. powerful.          b. useless.          c. harmful.

_____ 3. It is a <u>privilege</u> of democracy to be able to
   a. work.          b. vote.          c. travel.

_____ 4. Someone who is <u>clamoring</u> is making
   a. unfounded claims.     b. loud demands.          c. accusations.

_____ 5. A person who commits an act of <u>perfidy</u> is
   a. treacherous.          b. honest.          c. worried.

**D.** Answer **one** of the following questions based on your understanding of the selection. Write your answer on a separate sheet of paper. (15 points)

1. In what ways did books and poetry affect McCourt's hospital stay? Cite at least **three** ways in which literature was important to McCourt and the people around him.

2. McCourt's father is only a minor character in this selection, yet it is clear that he is very important to McCourt. Discuss McCourt's relationship with his father, using evidence from the selection.

**E. Linking Literature to Life.** Answer the following question based on your own experience and knowledge. Write your answer on a separate sheet of paper. (15 points)

If you were going to write a memoir about your childhood, what important aspects of your world would you be sure to tell about? Why?

# Unfinished Business (page 260)

# Selection Test

**A.** Read each quotation from the interview with Kübler-Ross and think about what advice she is suggesting by her remark. In the box below each quotation, make notes about what you think the advice is. In the box at the bottom, make notes about what you think the main message of the selection is. (8 points each)

| |
|---|
| 1. "If I love somebody, I tell them 'I love you' now, so I can skip the schmaltzy eulogies afterward." |
| |
| 2. "There is a beauty in [dying people] that very few see. And all you have to do is look." |
| |
| 3. "Dying patients literally teach you about life." |
| |

    ↓              ↓             ↓

| |
|---|
| 4. What do you think the main idea, or message, of this selection is? |
| |

**B.** Write the letter of the best answer. This exercise is continued on the next page. (6 points each)

_____    1. What is the **main** feeling that the six-year-old boy expresses about his sister's dying?
         a. guilt about his reactions
         b. fear of what is happening
         c. jealousy over the attention she receives
         d. frustration with delaying what is unavoidable

_____ 2. The dying girl responds to her brother's statement to her by indicating that she sees him as
    a. a partner.        c. an enemy.
    b. a selfish person.      d. an immature person.

_____ 3. Kübler-Ross suggests that the **most** important thing to do in dealing with dying children is to
    a. deal with them honestly.
    b. protect them from conflict.
    c. pretend that their illness is temporary.
    d. ask them to hold on to life as long as they possibly can.

_____ 4. According to Kübler-Ross, grieving for a dying person is something that should be
    a. avoided.        c. started before death.
    b. done in private.     d. saved for the funeral.

**C. Words to Know.** Write the letter of the best answer. (4 points each)

_____ 1. If something is unique, it is completely
    a. finished.      b. unavoidable.      c. unusual.

_____ 2. Which is used to convey something?
    a. a letter      b. a nail      c. a telephone pole

_____ 3. If you transcend your goal, you
    a. meet it.      b. exceed it.      c. fall short of it.

_____ 4. Procrastinating can be expressed by saying,
    a. "I did it."      b. "I'm doing it."      c. "I'll get to it."

_____ 5. A spontaneous activity is one that is
    a. unseen.      b. unplanned.      c. unproductive.

**D.** Answer **one** of the following questions based on your understanding of the selection. Write your answer on a separate sheet of paper. (12 points)

1. Give an example of something that would qualify as "unfinished business," according to Kübler-Ross, and tell why she thinks "unfinished business" is harmful.

2. Why might the statement "I love to work with dying children" be considered a paradox?

**E. Linking Literature to Life.** Answer the following question based on your own experience and knowledge. Write your answer on a separate sheet of paper. (12 points)

How might a person behave if he or she followed Kübler-Ross's advice to view life and death as "a challenge and not a threat"? Explain your answer.

# A Christmas Memory (page 272)

## Selection Test

**A.** Reread the quotation below that Capote wrote at the end of "A Christmas Memory." Then write notes to answer the questions in the boxes. (8 points each)

"And when that happens, I know it. A message saying so merely confirms a piece of news some secret vein had already received, severing from me an irreplaceable part of myself, letting it loose like a kite on a broken string. That is why, walking across a school campus on this particular December morning, I keep searching the sky. As if I expected to see, rather like hearts, a lost pair of kites hurrying toward heaven."

| |
|---|
| 1. What does the phrase "like a kite on a broken string" communicate about Capote's feelings toward his friend's death? |
| 2. What does the phrase "rather like hearts, a lost pair of kites hurrying toward heaven" communicate about Capote's feelings toward his friend? |
| 3. What might kites symbolize to Capote and his friend before they are separated? Briefly explain. |
| 4. What might kites symbolize to Capote after his friend's death? Briefly explain. |

**B.** Write the letter of the best answer. This exercise is continued on the next page. (6 points each)

_____ 1. Which of the following would Capote **most** probably say caused him the greatest grief during his childhood?
   a. God
   b. nature
   c. poverty
   d. those who Know Best

_____ 2. Capote and his friend bake their fruitcakes mostly for
     a. celebrities.
     b. kind strangers.
     c. family members.
     d. close friends and neighbors.

_____ 3. On their last Christmas together, Capote's friend realizes that God shows Himself
     a. in everyday things.
     b. only at Christmas time.
     c. only at the moment of death.
     d. only to children and old people.

**C. Words to Know.** Write the letter of the best answer. (4 points each)

_____ 1. An activity that exhilarates you makes you feel
     a. exhausted.     b. sad and lonely.     c. happy and energetic.

_____ 2. When you squander money, you
     a. waste it.     b. steal it.     c. save it.

_____ 3. Which is the **most** noncommittal answer to a question?
     a. "Yes."     b. "No."     c. "Maybe."

_____ 4. Which is the **best** place to cavort?
     a. a highway     b. a playground     c. a restaurant

_____ 5. When you sever a friendship, you
     a. end it.     b. begin it.     c. continue it.

**D.** Answer **one** of the following questions based on your understanding of the selection. Write your answer on a separate sheet of paper. (15 points)

1. What does "fruitcake weather" mean to Capote as a child? What do you think it means to him, 20 years later, as he records his memories of it? Use details from the selection to support your answers.

2. In what ways does Capote's friend differ from "those who Know Best"? How do you think these differences make her special to him?

**E. Linking Literature to Life.** Answer the following question based on your own experience and knowledge. Write your answer on a separate sheet of paper. (15 points)

   Many people believe that holidays have become more about spending money and meeting obligations than about expressing feelings and sharing experiences. Do you agree? Why or why not?

# Song of the Open Road/The Road Not Taken (page 288)

# Selection Open-Book Test

**A.** Compare and contrast the poems by Whitman and Frost, using the chart below to organize your information. For each poem, write notes in the boxes to answer the questions. (10 points each)

| Question | "Song of the Open Road" | "The Road Not Taken" |
|---|---|---|
| 1. What does the road represent? | | |
| 2. What is the rhyme scheme? | | |
| 3. What force directs the speaker to set out on the road? | | |
| 4. What is the speaker's attitude at the end of the poem? | | |

**B.** Write the letter of the best answer. This exercise is continued on the next page. (5 points each)

_____ 1. As he starts his journey in "Song of the Open Road," the speaker feels
      a. confident.         c. desperate.
      b. cautious.          d. resigned.

_____ 2. In "Song of the Open Road," how does the speaker characterize his previous attitude toward setting out?
      a. fearful           c. impatient
      b. determined     d. reluctant

_____ 3. As he stands looking at two paths in the first stanza of "The Road Not Taken," the speaker seems to feel
      a. enthusiastic.     c. optimistic.
      b. indecisive.      d. sad.

_____ 4. In "The Road Not Taken," the fact that both roads "equally lay /
In leaves no step had trodden black" suggests that no matter
which road he chooses, the speaker must
a. follow where others have gone.
b. make his own way.
c. step lightly.
d. take his time.

**C.** Answer **one** of the following questions based on your understanding of the selection.
Write your answer on a separate sheet of paper. (20 points)

1. The speaker in "The Road Not Taken" says he will someday tell about the two
roads "with a sigh." Why? Was he unhappy with the choice he made? Explain.

2. Both poems are told in first person, but they are told from very different
perspectives. What are these two perspectives, and how do they affect
the tone of each poem?

**D. Linking Literature to Life.** Answer the following question based on your own
experience and knowledge. Write your answer on a separate sheet of paper. (20 points)

As you think about your own future, do you like the idea of taking a road "less
traveled by," or do you think you would prefer to take a well-traveled road? Explain.

## American History (page 293)

# Selection Test

**A.** In the box below, write down notes describing what you think the climax of the story is, and why. Then, to show where the climax occurs in the story, draw a line from the box to the appropriate place on the bar. (20 points)

**Beginning**                                                                                          **End**

**B.** Write the letter of the best answer. This exercise is continued on the next page.
(6 points each)

_____     1. Elena is first attracted to Eugene because he
            a. is shy.
            b. is white.
            c. is intelligent.
            d. lives in the house below her fire escape.

_____     2. Which of the following is **least** likely the reason that Eugene forms a
            friendship with Elena?
            a. Eugene is lonely.
            b. Elena is Puerto Rican.
            c. They have common interests.
            d. They go to the same school and live in the same neighborhood.

_____     3. One essential way in which Elena differs from Eugene as a student is that
            Elena **clearly** isn't
            a. as smart as Eugene.
            b. as motivated as Eugene.
            c. as interested in attending college.
            d. offered the same educational opportunities.

Name _____   Date _____

........................................................................................................................................

_____ 4. Who is **least** upset by the death of President Kennedy?
      a. Eugene's mother
      b. Elena's gym teacher
      c. Elena's mother and father
      d. Elena and the other students at her school

_____ 5. Elena's reaction to Eugene's mother's behavior is **mainly** one of
      a. disbelief.
      b. defiance.
      c. contempt.
      d. embarrassment.

**C. Words to Know.** Write the letter of the best answer. (4 points each)

_____ 1. Which phrase is an example of an <u>abusive</u> statement?
      a. "You're stupid!"    b. "Be careful!"    c. "I'm sorry."

_____ 2. <u>Martyrs</u> are generally considered to be
      a. cautious.      b. heroic.      c. ruthless.

_____ 3. How does a <u>distraught</u> person feel?
      a. inferior      b. numb      c. deeply disturbed

_____ 4. A person who is <u>resigned</u> has
      a. given up.      b. gone away.      c. matured.

_____ 5. <u>Solace</u> is something that people desire when they feel
      a. irritated.      b. hopeful.      c. miserable.

**D.** Answer **one** of the following questions based on your understanding of the story. Write your answer on a separate sheet of paper. (15 points)

1. In what ways are the political and personal events that take place on the day of this story related? In your answer, consider how the political and personal events concern hope, innocence, and prejudice.

2. How do the feelings of Eugene's mother toward the relationship between Elena and Eugene compare and contrast with those of Elena's mother? Use details from the story to support your answer.

**E. Linking Literature to Life.** Answer the following question based on your own experience and knowledge. Write your answer on a separate sheet of paper. (15 points)

Do you think young people should be discouraged from entering into interracial friendships that could blossom into love? Support your opinion with reasons.

# Unit Two: Passages

# Part One Open-Book Test

**A.** Write the answer to each question on the lines. (5 points each)

1. In "Life Without Go-Go Boots," what did go-go boots represent to the author?

_____

_____

2. In the excerpt from *Angela's Ashes,* why don't the nurses allow McCourt and Patricia
   to talk to each other?

_____

_____

3. In what way do the speakers in "Song of the Open Road" and "The Road Not Taken"
   feel the same?

_____

_____

4. What is the climax of the story "American History"?

_____

_____

**B.** In several selections in this part, the writers were moved to describe significant
personal experiences. In the boxes below, write the title of **one** selection from this
part that you want to discuss. Then write notes to describe some specific memories
related by the writer and explain what you think made these experiences memorable
to the writer. (20 points)

| Selection: | |
|---|---|
| **Memories:** | **What made these experiences memorable to the writer?** |
| | |

**C.** Answer **two** of the following essay questions. Write your answers on a separate sheet of paper. (20 points each)

1. Choose **one** of the selections in this part. What insight into life and human nature does the selection express, and how is this insight communicated? Do your life experiences support this insight? Use details from the selection to support your answer.

2. In several of the selections in this part, the writers describe hardships they experienced during childhood. Choose **two** of the selections in this part. In what ways are the writers' attitudes toward the hardships they experienced similar, and in what ways are they different? Do the writers seem to be affected by their experiences with hardship in similar ways? Support your answers with details from the selections.

3. Discuss the importance of love and devotion to family in a character's struggle in any **one** of these selections.

**D.** In the selections in this part, the writers or narrators describe experiences or important realizations that significantly changed them. In the chart below, write the titles of **two** selections from this part that you want to discuss. Then, for each selection, write notes describing who has the experience or important realization, what it is, and how it changes the person. (20 points)

| Selection: | Selection: |
|---|---|
| **Who has the experience or realization, and what is it?** | **Who has the experience or realization, and what is it?** |
| **How does it change the person?** | **How does it change the person?** |

# The Beginning of Something (page 324)

# Selection Test

**A.** Think about Roseanne as a dynamic character who changes as a result of events in the story. The changes she experiences are reflected in the different feelings she has concerning her cousin Melissa. In each box on the left, note a word or phrase that describes one of those emotions. In each box on the right, write notes explaining why Roseanne feels that emotion. (10 points each)

| **1. Emotion** → | **What are some reasons that Roseanne feels that emotion?** |
|---|---|
| | |
| **2. Emotion** → | **What are some reasons that Roseanne feels that emotion?** |
| | |
| **3. Emotion** → | **What are some reasons that Roseanne feels that emotion?** |
| | |

**B.** Write the letter of the best answer. This exercise is continued on the next page. (5 points each)

_____ 1. When Cousin Jessie was still alive, what was Roseanne's attitude toward her mother's friendship with Cousin Jessie?
   a. envy
   b. anger
   c. admiration
   d. annoyance

_____ 2. When Roseanne and Melissa are sitting on the porch before the visitation, Melissa seems
   a. guilty.
   b. angry.
   c. numb.
   d. relieved.

_____  3. Roseanne changes her mind about going to the visitation
because she
   a. feels sorry for Melissa.
   b. wants to impress Travis.
   c. wants to wear her new dress.
   d. doesn't want to stay with her brother.

_____  4. Seeing herself and Melissa in the mirror after the date leads Roseanne to
   a. lose her self-confidence.
   b. change her perception of Melissa.
   c. realize that Melissa will always be her best friend.
   d. realize that she has been right about Melissa all along.

**C. Words to Know.** Write the letter of the best answer. (4 points each)

_____  1. The bereaved at a funeral usually include the
   a. family.              b. coffin.              c. funeral director.

_____  2. A scrapbook of pictures of one's kin would **most** probably include
   a. cousins.             b. classmates.          c. co-workers.

_____  3. An artist in the throes of creation would **most** probably look
   a. calm.                b. in pain.             c. bored.

_____  4. An infernal noise would **most** probably be made by a
   a. furious cat.         b. forest stream.       c. talented pianist.

_____  5. A person who felt remorse would **least** likely
   a. cry.                 b. apologize.           c. brag.

**D.** Answer **one** of the following questions based on your understanding of the story.
Write your answers on a separate sheet of paper. (15 points)

1. Which minor character do you think has most to do with the change in Roseanne's
   feelings for Melissa? Support your answer with details from the story and your own
   ideas.

2. When Roseanne says that kissing Travis is "as private as grief but it doesn't need
   sharing," what do you think she is saying about intimacy and about grief?

**E. Linking Literature to Life.** Answer the following question based on your own
experience and knowledge. Write your answer on a separate sheet of paper. (15 points)

   What experience, besides the experience of another's death, might cause someone
to understand life better? Explain your answer.

# Young/Hanging Fire (page 343)

## Selection Open-Book Test

**A.** Think about the feelings or needs that the speaker reveals in each poem. Then, think about the speaker and the main character. Are they identical, or are they different? In the boxes on the left, jot down a feeling or need of each speaker, and answer each question. In the boxes on the right, write notes giving evidence from the poems to support your conclusions. (10 points each)

| | |
|---|---|
| **1. Feeling or need of speaker in "Young"** | **Evidence:** |
| **2. Are the main character and the speaker identical?** | **Evidence:** |
| **3. Feeling or need of speaker in "Hanging Fire"** | **Evidence:** |
| **4. Are the main character and the speaker identical?** | **Evidence:** |

**B.** Write the letter of the best answer. This exercise is continued on the next page. (5 points each)

_____ 1. In "Young," the "lonely kid" seemed to feel that
a. the summer night was frightening.
b. time was standing still.
c. growing up was exciting and fun.
d. the house itself was like a friend.

_____ 2. The speaker of "Hanging Fire" expresses concerns about all of the following **except**
a. her own death.        c. her mother.
b. her appearance.       d. her father.

_____  3. In "Hanging Fire," the speaker suggests that she isn't on the Math Team
because she
    a. chose not to be.       c. was treated unfairly.
    b. isn't smart enough.     d. didn't work hard enough.

_____  4. The main characters in both poems seem to be
    a. feeling closed off from their parents.
    b. aware of the presence of God.
    c. disappointed in boys.
    d. worried about their appearance.

**C.** Answer **one** of the following questions based on your understanding of the
selections. Write your answer on a separate sheet of paper. (20 points)

1. Compare the speaker's voice in "Young" with the speaker's voice in "Hanging Fire."
How are they different? Then compare the two girls in the poems, showing at least
**three** ways in which they are alike or different.

2. Do you think the poem "Hanging Fire" does a good job of expressing what it is like
to be fourteen? Give at least **three** reasons for your opinion.

**D. Linking Literature to Life.** Answer the following question based on your own
experience and knowledge. Write your answer on a separate sheet of paper. (20 points)

   Compare and contrast what you think are the best and worst things about being
a teenager with what you think are the best and worst things about being an adult.

# The Seven Ages of Man (page 348)

# Selection Open-Book Test

**A.** Think about how Jaques describes each of the seven stages of life. For each stage listed in the boxes below, write an adjective that describes a male at that stage. Then write details from the speech to describe the male further and support your choice of adjective. (5 points each)

| Stage | Adjective | Supporting Details |
|---|---|---|
| 1. Infant | | |
| 2. Schoolboy | | |
| 3. Lover | | |
| 4. Soldier | | |
| 5. Justice | | |
| 6. Pantaloon | | |
| 7. Final Scene | | |

**B.** Write the letter of the best answer. This exercise is continued on the next page. (5 points each)

_____ 1. In the context of the play *As You Like It,* "The Seven Ages of Man" is a dramatic monologue because
a. two characters in the play are interacting.
b. it is a speech spoken by one character to another.
c. a character in the play is thinking out loud.
d. it is a poem that is spoken aloud by a character.

_____ 2. At which stage of life does Jaques see males as most reluctant to do what they are supposed to do?
a. schoolboy          c. soldier
b. lover              d. justice

_____     3. At which stage does man most eagerly seek success?
                a. schoolboy            c. soldier
                b. lover                 d. justice

_____     4. In general, what can you infer about Jaques's attitude toward people?
                a. He is fascinated by them.
                b. He feels great sympathy for them.
                c. He respects their differences.
                d. He finds them tiresome.

_____     5. In telling about the seven ages of man, Jaques most likely wants his
              listener to think of him as a person who
              a. needs cheering up.
              b. is observant and wise.
              c. is making a witty joke.
              d. fits this description perfectly.

**C.** Answer **one** of the following questions based on your understanding of the selection. Write your answer on a separate sheet of paper. (20 points)

1. Choose **three** of the ages described by Jaques in his monologue. What negative thing does Jaques say about each age? How could these same three ages be described as positive times of life?

2. If you were to rewrite this poem as the "Seven Ages of Woman," how would the names of the ages be different? List the Seven Ages of Woman, and describe one of the later five ages. Make your description as negative as the descriptions Jaques gives of the ages of man.

**D. Linking Literature to Life.** Answer the following question based on your own experience and knowledge. Write your answer on a separate sheet of paper. (20 points)

How would you describe yourself at your current age? Using Jaques's speech as a model, describe yourself in negative terms and then in positive terms. Which version best reflects how you generally think of yourself?

# Brothers Are the Same (page 359)

# Selection Test

**A.** In this story, two characters—Temas and Medoto—are in conflict. Think about the actions and feelings that cause the conflict and separate them and those that resolve it and bring them together. Then, make notes in the boxes below to answer the questions. (15 points each)

| 1. What separates Temas and Medoto? |
| --- |
| |

| 2. What brings them together? |
| --- |
| |

**B.** Write the letter of the best answer. This exercise is continued on the next page. (8 points each)

_____ 1. Temas's real battle with the lion is different from that in his dreams in
 a. its outcome.
 b. the reason for it.
 c. how he feels before it begins.
 d. the speed and power of the lion's attack.

_____ 2. What Temas **most** fears is
 a. pain.
 b. death.
 c. humiliation.
 d. losing Kileghen to Medoto.

_____ 3. The lion's attitude toward the young men can **best** be described as
     a. fearful.
     b. scornful.
     c. impatient.
     d. respectful.

_____ 4. Medoto's reason for throwing the pebble was based on a feeling of
     a. hatred.
     b. sympathy.
     c. superiority.
     d. competition.

_____ 5. Temas's success is considered particularly honorable because of the fact that he
     a. saved another from attack.
     b. stood firm during an attack.
     c. fought the lion single-handedly.
     d. killed the lion while being dragged by it.

**C.** Answer **one** of the following questions based on your understanding of the story. Write your answer on a separate sheet of paper. (15 points)

1. How is what young American men face today in "becoming men" similar to and different from what Temas faces in this story?

2. In your opinion, why does Kileghen's smile at the end of the story have "more of triumph in it, and less of wonder, than it might have had"?

**D. Linking Literature to Life.** Answer the following question based on your own experience and knowledge. Write your answer on a separate sheet of paper. (15 points)

  How important a trait is courage? Is it the most important trait a person can have? Explain your answer.

# Through the Tunnel (page 373)

# Selection Test

**A.** Reread the first sentence of the story below. Then write notes to answer the
questions in the boxes. (8 points each)

> "Going to the shore on the first morning of the vacation, the young English boy
> stopped at a turning of the path and looked down at a wild and rocky bay, and
> then over to the crowded beach he knew so well from other years."

| 1. What does the sentence reveal about the setting of the story? | |
|---|---|
| Time | Place |
| | |

| | What greater meaning do the things described in these phrases from the opening sentence come to have in the story? What do they come to symbolize or represent? |
|---|---|
| **2. "at a turning of the path"** | |
| **3. "wild and rocky bay"** | |
| **4. "the crowded beach"** | |

**B.** Write the letter of the best answer. This exercise is continued on the next page.
(6 points each)

_____    1. How does Jerry's mother feel when he tells her he wants to go off
             and explore the bay?
             a. terrified
             b. anxious
             c. abandoned

_____ 2. Why does Jerry's mother agree to allow him to explore the bay despite her feelings?
a. She really wants to be alone.
b. She isn't afraid of anything happening to him.
c. She is worried that she may be overprotecting him.

_____ 3. What is the **most** likely reason that it isn't important to Jerry to return to the bay after he swims through the tunnel?
a. He realizes how foolish his efforts have been.
b. He is afraid that he would fail if he tried the tunnel again.
c. He has accomplished exactly what he set out to do at the bay.

**C. Words to Know.** Write the letter of the best answer. (4 points each)

_____ 1. Contrition makes a person feel
a. anxious.          b. proud.          c. sorry.

_____ 2. A supplication is a special type of
a. request.          b. demand.          c. agreement.

_____ 3. Which would be the most defiant answer to an order?
a. "No!"          b. "Yes!"          c. "Why?"

_____ 4. When you beseech your parents to buy you a car, you are
a. just kidding them.     b. annoying them.     c. begging them.

_____ 5. If you are incredulous, you are
a. easily fooled.     b. disbelieving.     c. cheerful.

**D.** Answer **one** of the following questions based on your understanding of the story. Write your answer on a separate sheet of paper. (15 points)

1. What qualities does Jerry display in the course of achieving his goal of swimming through the tunnel? Use details from the story to support your answer.

2. How and why does Jerry's relationship with his mother complicate his desire to swim through the tunnel?

**E. Linking Literature to Life.** Answer the following question based on your own experience and knowledge. Write your answer on a separate sheet of paper. (15 points)

What are some symbols of maturity and status for people your age? Explain.

# Unit Two: Passages

# Part Two Open-Book Test

**A.** Write the letter of the best answer to each question. (5 points each)

_____  1. The title "The Beginning of Something" refers mainly to
　　　　　　　a. Cousin Jessie's death.
　　　　　　　b. Roseanne's determination that she will marry Travis.
　　　　　　　c. Travis's new job as a lifeguard.
　　　　　　　d. Roseanne's new understanding of Melissa and herself.

_____  2. In "The Seven Ages of Man," Jaques compares a man to
　　　　　　　a. a leopard lost in the jungle.
　　　　　　　b. an actor who plays many parts.
　　　　　　　c. the mouth of a cannon.
　　　　　　　d. a bubble that floats and finally bursts.

_____  3. In "Brothers Are the Same," Medoto proves himself to be
　　　　　　　a. selfish.　　　　　　　　c. honorable.
　　　　　　　b. treacherous.　　　　　　d. cowardly.

_____  4. In "Through the Tunnel," the tunnel represents an obstacle Jerry must overcome in order to
　　　　　　　a. become a man.　　　　　c. impress his friends.
　　　　　　　b. please his mother.　　　　d. escape from his family.

**B.** Think about how symbols are used in this part to convey meaning. Circle the letter of **one** symbol you wish to discuss. In the box on the left, note what you think the symbol stands for. In the box on the right, note reasons or details from the selection that support your answer. (20 points)

　　a. the closed door in "Hanging Fire"　　　c. the lion in "Brothers Are the Same"
　　b. the beach in "Through the Tunnel"　　　d. the beaded belt in "Brothers Are the Same"

| What the Symbol Stands For | Supporting Details |
|---|---|
|  |  |

**C.** Answer **two** of the following essay questions. Write your answers on a separate sheet of paper. (20 points each)

1. Many of the people in these selections struggle to communicate with others. Choose any **two** characters and compare and contrast their communication problems.

2. In "The Seven Ages of Man," Jaques describes the stages of a man's life. In most of the selections in this part, a character moves from one stage in life to another. Choose a character from **one** of the selections in this part. Compare and contrast the character's stage in life with the stages described in Jaques's monologue.

3. The selections in this part describe situations that are emotionally, intellectually, or physically difficult. Choose **two** characters from different selections and compare and contrast the difficulties they face and how they deal with them.

**D.** Think about the rites of passage that the characters in the selections go through. Circle the letter of **one** person or character you wish to discuss. In the boxes below, write notes describing the character and his or her life before the rite of passage, what the rite of passage is, and the effect that the rite of passage has on the character and his or her life. (20 points)

    a. Roseanne in "The Beginning of Something
    b. Jerry in "Through the Tunnel"
    c. Temas in "Brothers Are the Same"

| Before | The Rite of Passage | After |
|--------|---------------------|-------|
|        |                     |       |

Name _____   Date _____

# The Devil and Daniel Webster (page 412)

# Selection Test

**A.** Think about how the dialogue and stage directions reveal information about the plot and the characters. For each character listed below, write notes describing something you have learned about the character and the character's role in the plot of this drama. (6 points each)

| Character | What You Have Learned About the Character | Character's Role in the Plot |
|---|---|---|
| 1. Jabez Stone | | |
| 2. Mary Stone | | |
| 3. Scratch | | |
| 4. Daniel Webster | | |

**B.** Write the letter of the best answer. This exercise is continued on the next page. (6 points each)

_____ 1. The crowd's gossip during the square dance does all of the following
**except**
a. explain Jabez's good fortune.
b. create a feeling of expectation.
c. cast doubt on Jabez's accomplishments.
d. suggest that people may be jealous of Jabez.

_____ 2. When Mary expresses her pride in Jabez, he feels uncomfortable **mainly**
because he
a. doesn't believe her.
b. is a very humble person.
c. is embarrassed by her love.
d. hasn't told her the truth about himself.

_____ 3. The first sign that the devil (Scratch) is at the wedding occurs when
a. the dancing begins.
b. the old couple starts arguing.
c. there is trouble with the fiddle.
d. Daniel Webster walks in the door.

_____ 4. Scratch agrees to a trial when Webster
   a. offers money to break the contract.
   b. offers to let Scratch choose the jury.
   c. says that Scratch isn't an American.
   d. challenges the signature on the contract.

_____ 5. To prove that he is an American, Scratch mentions all of the following
   **except**
   a. slavery.
   b. church beliefs.
   c. the Declaration of Independence.
   d. wrongs that were committed against Indians.

**C. Words to Know.** Write the letter of the best answer. (4 points each)

_____ 1. You would be **most** likely to pay <u>homage</u> to a
   a. cashier.          b. hero.          c. blackmailer.

_____ 2. A smile that was <u>feigned</u> would be
   a. fake.          b. friendly.          c. fierce.

_____ 3. A boat floating <u>placidly</u> would be **most** likely to
   a. tip over.          b. move quickly.          c. move slowly.

_____ 4. <u>Intimidation</u> usually involves
   a. threats.          b. favors.          c. hints.

_____ 5. An <u>oppressor</u> controls people's behavior by using
   a. power.          b. persuasion.          c. reason.

**D.** Answer **one** of the following questions based on your understanding of the play.
Write your answer on a separate sheet of paper. (13 points)

1. Do you think Daniel Webster's speech to the jury would be as appropriate for
   an ordinary criminal as it is for Jabez Stone? Explain your opinion.

2. The writer uses poetic language in the repetition of phrases by the crowd and jury,
   in Scratch's song and his summoning of the jury, in Webster's speech to the jury,
   and so on. How do you think this poetic language contributes to the effect of the
   play? Support your answer with reference to the play.

**E. Linking Literature to Life.** Answer the following question based on your own
experience and knowledge. Write your answer on a separate sheet of paper. (13 points)

   Is there anything that you would trade for your freedom? If so, what would you trade
it for, and why? If not, why not?

# I Have a Dream/Glory and Hope (page 439)

# Selection Test

**A.** Think about the purpose and main idea of each speech. Then write notes to answer the questions in the boxes below. (10 points each)

|  | **"I Have a Dream"** | **"Glory and Hope"** |
|---|---|---|
| **1. What happened in the past?** |  |  |
| **2. What is the current situation?** |  |  |
| **3. What does the speaker call on listeners to do?** |  |  |

**B.** Write the letter of the best answer. This exercise is continued on the next page. (5 points each)

_____ 1. Both Nelson Mandela and Martin Luther King, Jr., use the image of "the valley" to represent
  a. justice.                           c. the future.
  b. bad times.                       d. peace.

_____ 2. Referring to two sources of pain for the South African people under apartheid, Mandela says that the people fought one another and
  a. failed to use resources for economic development.
  b. destroyed the beauty of the environment.
  c. were shunned by the rest of the world.
  d. spoke many different languages.

_____ 3. The main focus of King's speech is on
  a. getting more money for America's black population.
  b. convincing everyone to live in peace and tranquillity.
  c. celebrating the anniversary of the Emancipation Proclamation.
  d. ending segregation and racial injustice in America.

_____ 4. King's "I Have a Dream" speech appeals **mainly** to his listeners'
   a. common sense.
   b. desire for a better future.
   c. sense of guilt.
   d. concerns about America's status among the world's nations.

**C. Words to Know.** Write the letter of the best answer. (4 points each)

_____ 1. A legitimate concern is
   a. false.              b. reasonable.              c. questionable.

_____ 2. If people have a reconciliation, they return to a state of being
   a. friends.            b. prisoners.              c. enemies.

_____ 3. A man who seeks social mobility wants to
   a. convince others.    b. buy a house.            c. improve his situation.

_____ 4. To sustain something is to
   a. diminish it.        b. keep it alive.          c. enclose it.

_____ 5. A pernicious idea is
   a. harmful.            b. creative.               c. practical.

**D.** Answer **one** of the following questions based on your understanding of the selection. Write your answer on a separate sheet of paper. (15 points)

1. Think about King's words, "Again and again we must rise to the majestic heights of meeting physical force with soul force." What did he mean by this? In what ways could his "I Have a Dream" speech help people follow this principle?

2. In what ways are King's dream for America and Mandela's hopes for South Africa the same?

**E. Linking Literature to Life.** Answer the following question based on your own experience and knowledge. Write your answer on a separate sheet of paper. (15 points)

   Which speech did you find more impressive? What was it about the speech that impressed you?

# The United States vs. Susan B. Anthony (page 453)

# Selection Test

**A.** Think about how the author presents a combination of factual details and subjective opinions in her descriptions of Susan B. Anthony and the events Anthony was involved in. For each event listed below, write an example of a factual detail and a subjective opinion from the selection that describes the event or the people involved.
(10 points each)

| Event | Factual Detail | Subjective Opinion |
|-------|----------------|--------------------|
| 1. Susan B. Anthony registers to vote. | | |
| 2. Anthony is arrested. | | |
| 3. Anthony stands trial. | | |

**B.** Write the letter of the best answer. This exercise is continued on the next page.
(4 points each)

_____ 1. The writer of this biography makes it more likely that we will think she is objective about Susan B. Anthony by
a. admitting she didn't like Anthony at first.
b. giving the viewpoint of the court.
c. giving arguments against Anthony's actions.
d. stressing how much research she has done.

_____ 2. The writer changed her mind about Anthony because she detected in her
a. weakness.
b. cowardice.
c. a loss of faith.
d. a sense of humor.

_____ 3. The editorial calling for people to register to vote neglects to mention the
a. days of registration.
b. place of registration.
c. consequences of failing to register.
d. gender of the people who should register.

4. In Anthony's struggle for the rights of women, the court case concerning her voting could be **most** accurately considered
   a. her first step.
   b. her most difficult step.
   c. just one action in a long process.
   d. one last, desperate attempt to win.

5. The court case has value for the suffrage movement for all of the following reasons **except** that
   a. the case results in a Supreme Court victory.
   b. Anthony's speech receives a great deal of publicity.
   c. her lawyer's speech receives a great deal of publicity.
   d. the judge's conduct is seen as an example of injustice.

**C. Words to Know.** Write the letter of the best answer. (4 points each)

1. If you hurt someone inadvertently, you do it
   a. in anger.         b. severely.         c. by accident.

2. One way to concur is to
   a. argue.         b. run away.         c. nod your head.

3. Fortitude would be **most** useful
   a. in a war.         b. at a party.         c. watching television.

4. You might give a tirade about your
   a. pet peeve.         b. dreams.         c. favorite color.

5. Someone who is adamant is
   a. overwhelmed.         b. mistaken.         c. stubborn.

**D.** Answer **one** of the following questions based on your understanding of the selection. Write your answer on a separate sheet of paper. (15 points)

1. What qualities of Susan B. Anthony are revealed in this biographical selection? Support your answer with details from the selection.

2. Based on this selection, do you think Anthony's decision to vote in this situation was the right one? Support your opinion with details from the selection and your own ideas.

**E. Linking Literature to Life.** Answer the following question based on your own experience and knowledge. Write your answer on a separate sheet of paper. (15 points)

Would you vote for a woman to be president of the United States if you believed she was as well qualified as a male candidate? Why or why not?

# Theme for English B/The Writer (page 466)

## Selection Open-Book Test

**A.** Think about the feelings that are associated with the creative process in the poems. Then, in each box on the left, note a feeling that the speaker associates with the creative process. In each box on the right, write notes explaining why the speaker might associate that feeling with the creative process. (14 points each)

### 1. "Theme for English B"

| Feeling | ➡ | Why might the speaker associate this feeling with the creative process? |
|---|---|---|
|  |  |  |

### 2. "The Writer"

| Feeling | ➡ | Why might the speaker associate this feeling with the creative process? |
|---|---|---|
|  |  |  |

**B.** Write the letter of the best answer. This exercise is continued on the next page. (6 points each)

_____ 1. In "Theme for English B," when the instructor says to "let that page come out of you," what does he or she **most** probably mean?
   a. "Try to be the best writer you can be."
   b. "Express your identity in your writing."
   c. "Your writing should always appear effortless."
   d. "Complete this writing assignment on your own."

_____ 2. In "The Writer," the speaker suggests that the process of writing is all of the following **except**
   a. routine.
   b. personal.
   c. worthwhile.
   d. demanding.

_____ 3. Which of the following statements about the lines in the poems is true?
- a. In "Theme for English B," the lines have regular lengths.
- b. In "Theme for English B," the lines are grouped in regular stanzas.
- c. In "The Writer," the lines have many different lengths.
- d. In "The Writer," the lines are grouped in stanzas of three lines each.

**C.** In "The Writer," an extended metaphor is used to convey information about the daughter and her efforts to communicate as a writer. She is compared to the world of ships and sailing, and to a trapped starling. In each box below, note ways in which the daughter's experience is like each of these things. You may note details from the poem and your own ideas. (12 points each)

| 1. The world of ships and sailing | 2. The trapped starling |
|---|---|
|  |  |

**D.** Answer **one** of the following questions based on your understanding of the poems. Write your answer on a separate sheet of paper. (15 points)

1. In "Theme for English B," the speaker says that he or she and the instructor can learn from each other. What do you think these two people might have to teach each other? Explain, using your own ideas or details from the poem.

2. What do you think the speaker of "The Writer" is referring to at the end of the poem when he or she says, "It is always a matter . . . / Of life or death"? Why do you think the speaker wishes even "harder" for the daughter? Explain.

**E. Linking Literature to Life.** Answer the following question based on your own experience and knowledge. Write your answer on a separate sheet of paper. (15 points)

To whom or to what would you compare yourself as a writer? What do you, as a writer, have in common with that person or thing?

## *from* I Know Why the Caged Bird Sings (page 480)

# Selection Test

**A.** As you may have learned, the title of this selection is an allusion to a poem written by Paul Laurence Dunbar. In the poem, the caged bird is described as bruised and sore, and its song is a plea sent from the heart to Heaven. In each box on the left, note three ways in which Marguerite is like this bird. In each box on the right, note three ways in which the visit with Mrs. Flowers frees Marguerite. (15 points each)

| **1. Ways in which Marguerite is like the caged bird** | **2. Ways in which the visit with Mrs. Flowers frees Marguerite** |
| --- | --- |
| | |

**B.** Write the letter of the best answer. This exercise is continued on the next page. (5 points each)

_____ 1. What is Marguerite's attitude toward her grandmother's bad grammar?
   a. tolerant
   b. amused
   c. indifferent
   d. embarrassed

_____ 2. Mrs. Flowers **most** probably views Marguerite's grandmother's bad grammar as a sign of her
   a. wisdom.
   b. ignorance.
   c. lack of self-esteem.
   d. lack of formal education.

_____ 3. What does the visit to Mrs. Flowers mean to Marguerite?
   a. that she is no longer a little girl
   b. that she has more possibilities in her life than she believed
   c. that she will never achieve what Mrs. Flowers has achieved
   d. that she should be more careful about what she says and does

_____ 4. Which of the following is a way in which Mrs. Flowers is like most of the
other people Marguerite knows?
a. She uses proper grammar.
b. She is wealthy.
c. She is formal in dress and behavior.
d. She is looked down upon by the white people of Stamps.

**C. Words to Know.** Write the letter of the best answer. (4 points each)

_____ 1. If a person talks <u>incessantly</u>, he or she is never
a. loud.              b. silent.                c. understood.

_____ 2. <u>Illiteracy</u> is the inability to
a. communicate.     b. speak English.      c. read and write.

_____ 3. Teardrops are often described as <u>cascading</u> because they
a. flow downward.   b. are salty.          c. communicate sadness.

_____ 4. The <u>essence</u> of a person is his or her
a. secrets.          b. appearance.         c. basic qualities.

_____ 5. A <u>sacrilegious</u> action reveals disrespect for
a. religious belief.  b. law and order.       c. people of color.

**D.** Answer **one** of the following questions based on your understanding of the selection.
Write your answer on a separate sheet of paper. (15 points)

1. About the visit with Mrs. Flowers, Angelou writes, "I was respected not as Mrs.
Henderson's grandchild or Bailey's sister but for just being Marguerite Johnson."
What do you think she means by that? Why is it important to her to be respected
"for just being Marguerite Johnson"?

2. What skills and qualities does Mrs. Flowers encourage Marguerite to develop?
Why do you think Mrs. Flowers feels these are important to Marguerite?

**E. Linking Literature to Life.** Answer the following question based on your own
experience and knowledge. Write your answer on a separate sheet of paper. (15 points)

How would you describe the difference between ignorance and illiteracy? What do
you think of Mrs. Flowers's advice to be "intolerant of ignorance but understanding
of illiteracy"?

# New Directions (page 494)

# Selection Test

**A.** Angelou states the major theme of "New Directions" directly in the last paragraph of the selection. In addition to this directly stated theme, there are several minor themes, or insights about life, that can be understood from reading about Annie Johnson. Complete the sentence in each box on the left to state one of the selection's themes. Then, in the box on the right, note evidence from the selection that supports the theme. (10 points each)

| Theme | Evidence from the Selection |
|---|---|
| 1. Each of us has the right and responsibility to | |
| 2. Success in business depends on a person's | |
| 3. When life seems to offer more obstacles than opportunities, then | |

**B.** Write the letter of the best answer. This exercise is continued on the next page. (5 points each)

_____ 1. When Annie Johnson told her husband she was dissatisfied with their marriage, he felt
  a. angry.  c. relieved.
  b. sad.  d. ashamed.

_____ 2. Mrs. Johnson's primary concern in deciding on a job was
  a. using her skills to their fullest.
  b. giving what she could to her community.
  c. making the highest income she could.
  d. being able to care for her young children.

_____ 3. The success of Mrs. Johnson's business was due largely to her
      a. excellent advertising.    c. superb cooking.
      b. patient determination.    d. cheerful friendliness.

_____ 4. Which word would **best** describe Mrs. Johnson in the early years
      of her business?
      a. desperate    c. dependable
      b. enthusiastic    d. lucky

**C.** Answer **one** of the following questions based on your understanding of the selection. Write your answer on a separate sheet of paper. (25 points)

1. How did Mrs. Johnson establish her business and help it continue to grow? Based on what you know from the selection, how would she have gone about adding new products and services for her customers?

2. Describe Mrs. Johnson's approach to life. What problems did she face, and what personal qualities helped her to succeed?

**D. Linking Literature to Life.** Answer the following question based on your own experience and knowledge. Write your answer on a separate sheet of paper. (25 points)

According to Maya Angelou, if you think you are on the wrong road, you must step off and take another direction. If that path also seems wrong, you must be ready to change again "without embarrassment." Think about your own road. Is there a new direction that you need or would like to take? How might Angelou's essay provide some of the help you need?

# Encounter with Martin Luther King, Jr. (page 500)

## Selection Test

**A.** Before Maya Angelou met Martin Luther King, Jr., she already knew a lot about him. But when she encountered him in person, she discovered that he was not exactly as she had expected him to be. In the selection, she reveals aspects of King's character by telling what surprised her. The chart below lists three aspects that she commented on. For each aspect, note what Angelou expected and what she found surprising. (10 points each)

|  | **What Was Expected** | **What Was Surprising** |
|---|---|---|
| **1. Appearance** | | |
| **2. Speech** | | |
| **3. Attitude toward Bailey** | | |

**B.** Write the letter of the best answer. This exercise is continued on the next page. (5 points each)

_____ 1. Maya Angelou did not want to talk about her brother because he
     a. was crippled.         c. had hurt her.
     b. was in prison.       d. was uneducated.

_____ 2. How did King's manner change when Stanley Levison arrived
     on the scene?
     a. He became more relaxed and friendly.
     b. He seemed annoyed and irritable.
     c. He began to use his public voice and manner.
     d. He showed the exhaustion he had been hiding.

_____   3. How had King first become a hero and a leader to Angelou?
          a. He was the head of the organization she worked for.
          b. He was an African-American celebrity.
          c. She enjoyed his sense of humor.
          d. She had been inspired when she heard him speak.

_____   4. What was the most important thing King gave to Angelou in their
        brief meeting?
          a. a job                c. hope
          b. a good story       d. help for Bailey

**C.** Answer **one** of the following questions based on your understanding of the selection. Write your answer on a separate sheet of paper. (25 points)

1. Why do you think King's sense of humor was a little-known aspect of his character? Use this and other examples from the selection to discuss differences between the public and private person.

2. What does King mean when he says, "We must save the Baileys of the world"? What does this tell you about his attitude toward what Bailey did?

**D. Linking Literature to Life.** Answer the following question based on your own experience and knowledge. Write your answer on a separate sheet of paper. (25 points)

    Think about how Maya Angelou felt when she met Martin Luther King, Jr. How do you think you would feel if you met Maya Angelou? What would you want to ask her or tell her? How do you think she might react?

# Unit Three: Voices of Experience

# Part One Open-Book Test

**A.** Write the answer to each question on the lines. (5 points each)

1. How does Daniel Webster win his case in *The Devil and Daniel Webster?*

   _____

   _____

2. In "The United States vs. Susan B. Anthony," why did Anthony refuse to pay the fine imposed on her by Judge Hunt?

   _____

   _____

3. In the excerpt from *I Know Why the Caged Bird Sings,* how was young Marguerite affected by her visit with Mrs. Flowers?

   _____

   _____

4. Based on your reading of "New Directions" and "Encounter with Martin Luther King, Jr.," write a sentence that describes Maya Angelou. What kind of person is she?

   _____

   _____

**B.** In several of these selections, a person has a talent, a goal, or something else that makes him or her unusual. In the boxes below, write the name of the person from **one** of the selections you want to discuss. Then write notes to describe what makes the person unusual and how other people react to the thing that makes the person unusual. (20 points)

| Person and Selection: | |
|---|---|
| **What Makes the Person Unusual** | **How Others React to the Person** |
| | |
| | |
| | |
| | |

**C.** Answer **two** of the following essay questions. Write your answers on a separate sheet of paper. (20 points each)

1. Choose **one** selection in which the writer expresses—either directly or indirectly—a criticism of the society or culture in which he or she grew up. Explain what the writer criticizes in this society or culture, and why.

2. In several of the selections in this part, people struggle to achieve something. Choose **two** of these people and tell what they try to achieve. What are the risks and rewards of their struggles? Use details from the selections and your own views to support your ideas.

3. In "New Directions," Angelou says that we must all be willing to step off "that road" we are traveling and take a different direction. Choose **two** of the selections in this part and explain how this theme applies to the person or people in the selection. What road were they traveling, and what new direction did they take?

**D.** In some of the selections in this part, a man or woman meets a person of great stature and is changed by the experience. In the boxes below, write the titles of **two** selections from this part that you want to discuss. Then, for each selection, write notes describing who meets a person of great stature, who that person is, and how the man or woman is changed by the experience. (20 points)

| Selection: | Selection: |
|---|---|
| **Persons Involved** | **Persons Involved** |
| | |
| **How is the man or woman changed by the experience?** | **How is the man or woman changed by the experience?** |
| | |

Name _____ Date _____

# To Build a Fire (page 517)

# Selection Test

**A.** London uses many images in this story to help the reader experience the bitter cold setting. Choose three images from the story that stand out in your mind, and note them in the three boxes on the left. Then, for each image, write notes describing the sense or senses that the image appeals to and how the image contributes to the mood of the story. (10 points each)

| Image from the Story | Sense(s) Appealed To | How It Contributes to the Mood |
|---|---|---|
| **1.** | | |
| **2.** | | |
| **3.** | | |

**B.** Write the letter of the best answer. This exercise is continued on the next page. (5 points each)

_____ 1. The man wanted the dog to go in front of him so that the dog would
      a. find the trail.        c. set the pace.
      b. test the ice.        d. scare off wild animals.

_____ 2. The man stopped to make a second fire in order to
      a. prepare his lunch.
      b. give his dog a break.
      c. wait out the cold snap.
      d. dry his socks and moccasins.

_____ 3. Why was it so difficult for the man to light the last fire?
      a. The fuel was too cold.
      b. The matches were old.
      c. His hands were frozen.
      d. The firewood was damp.

_____ 4. According to the old-timer on Sulphur Creek, what was the man's biggest mistake?
a. traveling alone
b. stopping for too long at lunch
c. failing to bring extra clothes
d. not watching for hidden springs

**C. Words to Know.** Write the letter of the best answer. (4 points each)

_____ 1. Which of these is an <u>appendage</u> on a dog?
a. its tail
b. its fur
c. its head

_____ 2. Which of these animals moves with an <u>undulation</u>?
a. a hawk
b. a frog
c. a snake

_____ 3. If something is <u>intangible</u>, you cannot
a. change it.
b. remember it.
c. touch it.

_____ 4. A baseball player is most likely to <u>smite</u>
a. the bat.
b. the ball.
c. a base.

_____ 5. Someone who behaves <u>appeasingly</u> is trying to
a. soothe anger.
b. fool someone.
c. cause irritation.

**D.** Answer **one** of the following questions based on your understanding of the selection. Write your answer on a separate sheet of paper. (15 points)

1. How might the man in this story have survived? Think about what happened to him and what he might have done differently. Include at least **three** examples of things he could have done to avoid disaster.

2. Why do you think London never gives the man in this story a name? How does it make you feel about the character? What other aspects of the story support this impression?

**E. Linking Literature to Life.** Answer the following question based on your own experience and knowledge. Write your answer on a separate sheet of paper. (15 points)

Are you a person who would likely do well in a physically challenging situation, such as the one described in the story? Think about the mental, emotional, and physical demands of such a situation, and assess your abilities to deal with it.

# *from* Into Thin Air (page 538)

# Selection Test

**A.** The author's choice of words establishes a tone and tells you something about the author's feelings. Read each passage from the selection below and circle the words or phrases that are most important in establishing the tone. Then, in the box to the right, describe the tone or feelings expressed in the passage. (10 points each)

| Words That Establish the Tone | Author's Tone/Feelings |
|---|---|
| 1. ". . . I left everything in my pack and stayed on top of the world just long enough to fire off four quick shots of Andy Harris and Anatoli Boukreev posing in front of the summit survey marker." | |
| 2. "Some minutes later I was overwhelmed by a disturbingly familiar feeling of suffocation. . . ." | |
| 3. "Fifteen minutes of dicey, fatiguing crampon work brought me safely to the bottom of the incline . . . and another ten minutes after that I was in camp myself. I lunged into my tent with my crampons still on, zipped the door tight, and sprawled across the frost-covered floor. . . ." | |

**B.** Write the letter of the best answer. This exercise is continued on the next page. (5 points each)

_____ 1. What was Krakauer most worried about as he began his descent?
   a. the approaching storm
   b. his dwindling oxygen supply
   c. his weakness from exhaustion
   d. the climbers who were on the way up

_____ 2. As the author tells about his interactions with other people during his descent from the summit, the mood is mainly one of
   a. triumph.                 c. grief.
   b. gratitude.               d. regret.

_____ 3. One reason for Krakauer's failure to recognize that the guide, Andy Harris, might be in trouble was that
   a. Andy's behavior was totally normal.
   b. Krakauer had been told never to question a guide's judgment.
   c. Mike Groom insisted that Andy was fine.
   d. there was no way of proving that what Andy said was wrong.

_____ 4. How did Krakauer feel when Beck Weathers decided to wait for Mike rather than accept his offer of help?
   a. worried              c. relieved
   b. embarrassed          d. puzzled

**C. Words to Know.** Write the letter of the best answer. (4 points each)

_____ 1. If you are cognizant of something, you are
   a. tired of it.          b. aware of it.          c. afraid of it.

_____ 2. A person known for obstinacy is
   a. stubborn.            b. generous.             c. brave.

_____ 3. As a conflict escalates, it becomes
   a. less violent.        b. random.               c. more intense.

_____ 4. A person who takes the initiative is most likely to
   a. avoid conflict.      b. wait for help.        c. begin a task.

_____ 5. If a trail meandered, it went
   a. back and forth.      b. straight.             c. down sharply.

**D.** Answer **one** of the following questions based on your understanding of the selection. Write your answer on a separate sheet of paper. (15 points)

1. On the day Jon Krakauer climbed down from the summit of Mt. Everest, some of the other climbers died. Why did Krakauer survive, and how did he feel about it later? Include at least **three** factors that contributed to his survival.

2. How did the thin air at the top of Mt. Everest affect Krakauer? Be specific. Describe at least **three** ways in which it affected how he felt and what he did.

**E. Linking Literature to Life.** Answer the following question based on your own experience and knowledge. Write your answer on a separate sheet of paper. (15 points)

   Do you think that Krakauer deserves any blame for what happened to the other climbers? Do you think that he feels that he deserves blame? Explain your views.

# The Sharks/A narrow Fellow in the Grass (page 552)

# Selection Open-Book Test

**A.** Words, sounds, and rhythms might establish one consistent mood throughout a poem or might indicate changes in mood. For example, a poem might begin with frightening, scary images and end with a feeling of comforting reassurance. For each of these poems, describe the mood at the beginning, middle, and end. Jot down words or phrases that help to establish each mood. (20 points each)

|  | 1. "The Sharks" | 2. "A narrow Fellow in the Grass" |
|---|---|---|
| **Beginning** | Mood/Words | Mood/Words |
| **Middle** | Mood/Words | Mood/Words |
| **End** | Mood/Words | Mood/Words |

**B.** Write the letter of the best answer. This exercise is continued on the next page. (5 points each)

_____ 1. In lines 8–11 of "The Sharks," the speaker
a. is excited about the future.
b. likes watching the sharks.
c. looks back at happier times.
d. imagines a danger that isn't there.

_____ 2. The time before the sharks' arrival was especially important in the speaker's life because
a. the sea had been clear.
b. she had dared to swim out farther than ever before.
c. the sea had been copper-colored and dark.
d. she had been preparing to leave.

_____ 3. How does the speaker in "A narrow Fellow in the Grass" feel when encountering a snake?

     a. afraid

     b. friendly

     c. confused

     d. hostile

_____ 4. The speaker's encounters with the "narrow Fellow" are best described as

     a. satisfying.

     b. fleeting.

     c. frequent.

     d. imaginary.

**C.** Answer **one** of the following questions based on your understanding of the poems. Write your answer on a separate sheet of paper. (20 points)

1. Suppose that "The Sharks" is about a turning point in a person's life. What might that turning point be? Use evidence from the poem to support your ideas.

2. Each poem describes an encounter with a creature in the wild. In what ways are these two encounters similar? In what ways are they different?

**D. Linking Literature to Life.** Answer the following question based on your own experience and knowledge. Write your answer on a separate sheet of paper. (20 points)

Choose one of the creatures described in these poems or another creature that has significance to you. Explain what the creature is like, your emotional response to the creature, and what the creature might represent if you were to write a poem about it.

# My Wonder Horse/Mi Caballo Mago (page 557)

## Selection Test

**A.** Read each descriptive passage below. In the box to the right of the quotation, note what the passage literally describes. In the box below it, make notes about how the writer's style contributes to the description. (10 points each)

| 1. "A sharp neigh. A far-reaching challenge that soars on high, ripping the virginal fabric of the rosy clouds. Ears at the point. Eyes flashing. Tail waving active defiance. Hoofs glossy and destructive. Arrogant ruler of the countryside." | **What does the passage literally describe?** |
|---|---|

**How does the writer's style contribute to the description?**

| 2. "A frenzy of fury and rage. Whirlpools of light and fans of transparent snow. A rope that whistles and burns the saddletree. Smoking, fighting gloves. Eyes burning in their sockets. Mouth parched. Fevered forehead. The whole earth shakes and shudders. The long, white trench ends in a wide, white pool." | **What does the passage literally describe?** |
|---|---|

**How does the writer's style contribute to the description?**

**B.** Write the letter of the best answer. This exercise is continued on the next page. (8 points each)

_____ 1. **Most** of the stories about the Wonder Horse center on his
    a. speed.
    b. beauty.
    c. courage.
    d. ability to avoid capture.

_____ 2. The narrator's horse is able to catch the Wonder Horse because
    a. the narrator's horse is faster.
    b. the narrator's horse has a head start.
    c. the Wonder Horse has to break the trail.
    d. the Wonder Horse has to protect his mares.

_____ 3. The Wonder Horse is able to escape because the narrator underestimates the horse's
a. speed.
b. determination.
c. ability to jump.
d. magical powers.

_____ 4. At the end of the story, it is clear that the narrator feels
a. guilt.
b. anger.
c. humiliation.
d. mixed emotions.

**C. Words to Know.** Write the letter of the best answer. (4 points each)

_____ 1. A person is **most** likely to feel <u>lethargy</u> after a
a. huge meal.        b. sudden fright.        c. good night's sleep.

_____ 2. During a <u>vigil</u>, one must remain
a. kneeling.        b. calm.        c. awake.

_____ 3. Which of the following could **best** be described as <u>indomitable</u>?
a. a pillow        b. an angry bear        c. a chocolate cake

_____ 4. Sunlight normally <u>wanes</u>
a. at dawn.        b. at midday.        c. in the evening.

_____ 5. A person who gives <u>mandates</u> in a courtroom is a
a. judge.        b. defendant.        c. witness.

**D.** Answer **one** of the following questions based on your understanding of the story. Write your answer on a separate sheet of paper. (14 points)

1. The narrator says, "Every day he became for me more of an ideal, more of an idol, more of a mystery." Why do you think the narrator is so inspired by the Wonder Horse? What does this horse represent for him?

2. How is the narrator changed by his experience with the Wonder Horse? Support your answer.

**E. Linking Literature to Life.** Answer the following question based on your own experience and knowledge. Write your answer on a separate sheet of paper. (14 points)

Do you think it is right to capture a wild animal to keep as a pet? Why or why not?

# Unit Three: Voices of Experience

# Part Two Open-Book Test

**A.** Write the letter of the best answer to each question. (5 points each)

_____   1. "To Build a Fire" focuses on the central theme of
        a. the existence of God.      c. the desire for wealth.
        b. man against nature.       d. love for others.

_____   2. In *Into Thin Air,* Krakauer's main purpose was most likely to
        a. describe the beauty of Mt. Everest.
        b. express his grief over the death of several climbers.
        c. praise the guides who led the expedition.
        d. explain what he did during a tragic climb of Mt. Everest.

_____   3. "The Sharks" and "A narrow Fellow in the Grass" both suggest
        a. fear of a wild creature.     c. a simple, carefree life.
        b. the wonders of nature.     d. a sense of adventure.

_____   4. At the end of "My Wonder Horse," the narrator feels happiness because
        a. his father is pleased.
        b. he is no longer a boy.
        c. the Wonder Horse deserves to be free.
        d. the Wonder Horse is waiting for him.

**B.** Think about the unexpected challenges faced by many of the people and characters in these selections. In the boxes below, write the name of the person or character from **one** of the selections you want to discuss. Then write notes to describe an unexpected challenge faced by that person or character and explain why the challenge was unexpected. (20 points)

| Person or Character/Selection: | |
|---|---|
| **The Unexpected Challenge** | **Why It Was Unexpected** |
| | |

Name _____   Date _____

.......................................................................................................................................

**C.** Answer **two** of the following essay questions. Write your answers on a separate sheet of paper. (20 points each)

1. Of the people in these selections, which **one** do you think faces the most difficult problem or impossible demand? In your answer, describe the problem or demand and tell what makes it so difficult.

2. In several of the selections in this part, people strive to reach an important goal. Choose **two** of these people and tell what goal each one strives for, whether or not the person attains the goal, and how the person feels about the goal afterward. Use details from the selections to support your ideas.

3. In an important sense, every selection in this part focuses on a person's encounters with nature. Choose **two** persons or characters from the selections in this part. Compare and contrast their encounters with nature, how they view the encounters, and how the encounter affects each one.

**D.** In most of these selections, a person or character is influenced by a "voice of experience." In the boxes below, write the titles of **two** selections from this part that you want to discuss. Then, for each selection, write notes describing who the "voice of experience" is and what he or she suggests. Then, explain whether the voice of experience has a positive or negative influence on the person or persons involved, and why. (20 points)

| Selection: | Selection: |
|---|---|
| **Who is the voice of experience and what was the suggestion?** | **Who is the voice of experience and what was the suggestion?** |
| **Is the voice a positive or negative influence?** | **Is the voice a positive or negative influence?** |

# Mid-Year Test

**Directions:** Read the story below. Then answer the questions that follow.

### The Last Boast
*Dorothy M. Johnson*

When the time came for them to die, Pete Gossard cursed and Knife Hilton cried, but Wolfer Joe Kennedy yawned in the face of the hangman.

What he wanted to do was spit, to show he was not afraid, because he knew men would talk about him later and describe the end he made. But even Wolfer Joe could not raise enough saliva for spitting when he had a noose around his neck. The yawn was the next best thing.

Barney Gallagher, the United States deputy marshal, finished adjusting the rope and asked half-admiringly, "Are we keeping you up?"

"Hanging me up, they told me," Wolfer Joe answered.

On a packing box between his companions, he stood glaring out at the crowd of miners, with his lips pulled back from his teeth in the grin that was his trademark. He had foreseen the hour of his death, but not the way of it. He had felt the jar of the bullet, heard the Cheyenne arrow whir, gone down screaming under a grizzly's claws—all these were probabilities for a man who had lived as he had lived, and a man had to die sometime.

But he had always seen himself fighting to the end. He had not dreamed of an end by hanging, helpless, with his hands tied behind him. He would not give his executioners the satisfaction of knowing he was astonished. They were going to get satisfaction enough without that.

Knife Hilton stopped crying and stood drooping on his packing box, snuffling like a baby. Pete Gossard stopped yelling curses, and thinking he had figured out a way to delay the performance, shouted earnestly, "I want a preacher! You wouldn't deny a man a preacher, would you?"

The Vigilanters had thought of that, too, and had a preacher there. They knew, by this time, about all the tricks a man could think of to make delay. Pete Gossard had nothing to say to the preacher, after all, except the frantic plea: "Tell 'em to give me a good drop."

"They will, Pete," the preacher promised. He shivered and added, "They always have. May God have mercy!"

There was still a lot of noise from the crowd of miners—the seven or eight hundred of them who had constituted the jury and had filed solemnly between two wagons to vote. Fourteen men had voted for acquittal, and after four hundred voted "guilty," the Vigilanters had stopped the farce of tallying. The noise was far out on the edge of the crowd, where those who could not see clearly were milling around, but in the center, at the hanging place, there was hardly any sound. Here death was, and the men who would beckon to it had nothing much to say.

The three packing boxes were sturdy; each had a rope tied to it by which it would be pulled away at the signal; the nooses were soundly wound. The Vigilanters, Wolfer Joe recollected, had had plenty of practice.

He felt a shudder coming over him, and to disguise it, he threw back his head and laughed.

He had few illusions about himself. Once he had said, grinning, "Reckon I was born bad." More accurately, he might have said, "I was born outside the law, and mostly I've stayed outside it." He had kept moving westward to places where the law was not. And what caught up with him at last was not law but anger. The angry men at the diggings could not wait for the law to catch up; they set up the Vigilance Committee to enforce ruthless justice.

Barney Gallagher frowned at that laugh. He stepped down from the box, wiping his hands on his pants, and said reflectively, "I was wondering—did you ever do one good thing in your life?"

Wolfer Joe looked into his eyes and answered with his lips pulled back from his teeth, "Yeah. Once. I betrayed a woman."

At the hangman's signal, men pulled the ropes on the packing box.

The word love was in the language he used with women, but its meaning was not in his understanding when he met Annie. Even when he left her, he was not sure he knew the meaning, and after that he never had much chance to find out.

She stood with her arms outspread, her hands touching the barn wall, trembling, withdrawing not so much from Wolfer Joe as from life itself pressing toward her.

"You don't really like me," he insisted. "Bet you don't."

"Maybe I do," Annie answered, breathless. "I got to go in now." She could have ducked under his arm, but she only glanced up at him with a scared smile. She was seventeen years old. Wolfer Joe was twenty-nine.

"You go in now," he said, "and I'll know you don't love me." He said the word lightly; he had said it before. The shape of it was easy in his mouth.

She looked away desperately, and the color rose on her neck. "I do so l-love you," she said. "You could just as well stay here, instead of going on."

Oh, no, not at twenty-nine. He could not stay in the settlements for long at a time. The law was creeping westward too fast. He was not sure what the law was, but he knew that he and his like had better keep ahead of it.

"Nothing here to keep me," he said. The words hurt her as he had meant them to hurt, and she drew back. "I got to go on," he said. He added boldly, suddenly seeing a dream, "Going to move on and settle down somewheres. Where I'm going, a girl like you wouldn't go. You wouldn't go with me."

She was pressed tight against the barn wall. "Maybe I would, if I wanted to."

"Your pa wouldn't let you," he scoffed.

"Pa couldn't stop me. Now let me be—let me go!" She struggled against him, but his arms were an iron cage, and his heart pounded against hers.

"Tonight at the fork of the trail," he said when he let her go, when he loosed her arms from their clinging. "Wait for me there.—But you won't come."

"I will!" she said. "Because I l-love you."

That was the last thing she ever said to him.

"I believe you mean it," he answered, and found his voice was hushed with wonder. "I guess you really do," he said, trying to laugh.

The wonder was still on him when he waited where the trail forked. But Doubt hovered there too, and roosting on his shoulder, Suspicion watched the trail with cold, yellow eyes.

If she came, he could take her west and build a soddy,[1] get a bunch of cattle started—he knew how to swing a long loop on someone else's beef. He had done it before, for pay.

"What makes you think she'll come?" hooted Doubt, circling over him.

"What reason would she have if she did?" croaked Suspicion, with claws sharp in his shoulder.

"There's no reward out for me around here," argued Wolfer Joe. "Supposing she does come, her reason's her own business. It's her I want, not her reasons. I'll settle down somewheres. If she comes."

He watched the trail from up above, belly-down on a flat rock. He jerked when he saw her ride to the meeting place and look anxiously around. She had a little bundle of clothing tied to the saddle. He saw her dismount and look around again. But she didn't call out or say a word. She simply sat down to wait.

He was furious, with an unreasoning anger. "Damn little fool!" he whispered. "Running off with a man she don't hardly know! What she'll get is no more'n she's got coming."

He remembered that he himself was the man, and he lay there grinning at his own nonsense.

He would wait a while. When she gave up, he would appear and accuse her: "I knowed it was just a notion. You never meant what you said. You start but you can't finish."

Then he would let her go home weeping—or on with him, to do her crying later, when she knew what a fool she was.

But she did not give up. When darkness came, she built a little fire to keep the night away. With his heart pounding, with his lips pulled back from his teeth, Wolfer Joe lay on the flat rock, watching her. She had come so far; she had been so faithful. How long would she wait there for him? How far could he trust her?

Suspicion whispered, "There'll come a day when she'll go crying to the law and say, 'I know where Wolfer Joe is if you want him.'"

He answered, "You don't know my Annie."

He watched her head bend forward on her knees as she waited and dozed. He saw it snap up again when a night sound scared her. After a while the fire burned low, and he knew she was sleeping. She awoke and fed it, and it blazed.

Then he knew he wasn't going down there. He saw not the girl but her patience. He saw not the red glow of the fire but faith abiding.

He saw love by the fire, and he could not endure looking for fear he might see it end, during that night or some year to come.

He crept back off the rock and slid silently into the darkness to where his horse was waiting.

He lived for fourteen years after that. He was said to have seventeen notches on his gun, but that wasn't true. He never notched his gun butt for anything he did.

He was justly sentenced to hang for helping to murder two miners whom he and Pete Gossard and Knife Hilton had dry-gulched[2] when the miners tried to take their gold out.

Wolfer Joe made an ending that earned him grim respect, and he left Barney Gallagher puzzling about how betraying a woman could be a thing a man might boast of with the last words he ever had a chance to speak.

1. **soddy:** a sod house.
2. **dry-gulched:** killed from ambush.

**A.** The following items test your understanding of the selection. Circle the letter of the response that best completes the sentence or answers the question.

1. As he stood on the packing box, Wolfer Joe wanted to show that he
   a. felt sorry for his actions.
   b. was not afraid.
   c. did not care about anyone.
   d. was proud of himself.

2. Wolfer Joe and his two companions were going to be hanged for
   a. stealing cattle.
   b. robbing a bank.
   c. stealing horses.
   d. murdering two miners.

3. As used in this story, the word *farce* means
   a. a ridiculous situation.
   b. an official election.
   c. a large group of men.
   d. a voting booth.

4. Fourteen years earlier, who was Wolfer Joe supposed to meet at the fork in the trail?
   a. Barney Gallagher
   b. Annie
   c. Pete Gossard
   d. Knife Hilton

5. The story says that Wolfer Joe had foreseen
   a. how he would die.
   b. the man who would execute him.
   c. where he would die.
   d. the time of his death.

6. At the end, who was the only man who won "grim respect" for the way he died?
   a. Wolfer Joe
   b. Barney Gallagher
   c. Knife Hilton
   d. Pete Gossard

**B.** The following items check your understanding of the way in which the selection is written. Circle the letter of the response that best completes the sentence.

7. This story takes place in the
   a. South during the Civil War.
   b. West during the 1800s.
   c. southern part of Texas.
   d. colonies during the American Revolution.

8. "Suspicion watched the trail" is an example of
   a. irony.
   b. personification.
   c. simile.
   d. metaphor.

9. "Snuffling like a baby" is an example of
   a. hyperbole.
   b. irony.
   c. simile.
   d. personification.

10. Pete Gossard called for a preacher because he
   a. wanted to delay the hanging.
   b. was a religious man.
   c. had a plan to escape.
   d. wanted to be forgiven.

**C.** The following items check your understanding of the way in which the selection is written. Write your response after each item.

11. Describe the mood in the first half of the story and tell how it changes during the second half.

_____

_____

_____

_____

12. How does Barney Gallagher react to Wolfer Joe's behavior as Wolfer Joe waits to hang?

_____

_____

_____

_____

13. What kind of person is Wolfer Joe? Describe his character.

_____

_____

_____

_____

**D.** The following items check your ability to analyze and evaluate the selection. Circle the letter of the response that best completes the sentence or answers the question. This exercise is continued on the next page.

14. Wolfer Joe was "astonished" that he was going to hang because
    a. he never thought he would get caught.
    b. Annie had promised she would not reveal where he was.
    c. his friends had always saved him before.
    d. he had always expected to fight until the end.

15. The main purpose of the Vigilance Committee was to
    a. enforce the law.
    b. hold elections.
    c. govern the town.
    d. protect the mines.

16. What was the most important reason why Wolfer Joe could not stay in the settlements with Annie?
    a. He was much older than she was.
    b. She did not really love him.
    c. He had to stay ahead of the law.
    d. Her father would have him arrested.

17. Which saying best states a theme expressed in the first part of this story?
    a. "A penny saved is a penny earned."
    b. "Good things come to those who wait."
    c. "Crime doesn't pay."
    d. "Waste not want not."

**E.** The following items check your ability to analyze and evaluate the selection. Write your response after each item.

18. How did Doubt and Suspicion influence Joe's decision to leave Annie?

_____

_____

_____

_____

19. In Wolfer Joe's view, what kind of person was Annie? Use details from the story to support your ideas.

_____

_____

_____

_____

20. Why do you think Wolfer Joe boasted that he had once "betrayed a woman"? Why was this act worth boasting about?

_____

_____

_____

_____

**Writing Exercise** The following activity is designed to assess your writing ability. The prompt asks you to give an opinion. Think of your audience as being any reader other than yourself.

When scorers evaluate your writing, they will look for evidence that you can:

- respond directly to the prompt;

- make your writing thoughtful and interesting;

- organize your ideas so that they are clear and easy to follow;

- develop your ideas thoroughly by using appropriate details and precise language;

- stay focused on your purpose for writing by making sure that each sentence you write contributes to your composition as a whole; and

- communicate effectively by using correct spelling, capitalization, punctuation, grammar, usage, and sentence structures.

Prompt: Do you think Wolfer Joe Kennedy did the right thing when he left Annie behind? Write an opinion statement telling whether or not he did the right thing and why you think so.

Use the bottom of the page to organize your ideas. Then write your essay on a separate sheet of paper.

_____

_____

_____

_____

_____

_____

_____

_____

_____

_____

_____

_____

_____

_____

Name _____    Date _____

...............................................................................................................................

**Revising/Editing** The purpose of the following exercise is to check your ability to proofread and revise a piece of writing in order to improve its readability and presentation of ideas. Read the following paragraph. Then, for each underlined section, circle the letter of the revision below that most improves the writing. Or, if the section is best left as it is, circle letter *d*.

Between 1850 and 1890, many thousands of Americans moved

from the crowded eastern cities to the open lands of the West.

The miners was one of the first groups, they went west to search for
      1.                            2.

gold. Next came the ranchers, which settled on the Great Plains to
                           3.

raise cattle. Homesteaders and farmers followed. Also, those
                  4.                 5.

homesteaders who settled on the prairies lived hard lives. There

weren't no trees on the prairie, so they found no wood for building
      6.

houses. Many of the homesteaders built houses with bricks of sod.

1. a. The miner was
   b. The miners were
   c. The miners are
   d. Correct as is

2. a. groups. They
   b. groups, they
   c. groups; They
   d. Correct as is

3. a. ranchers, that
   b. ranchers, where
   c. ranchers, who
   d. Correct as is

4. a. Homesteaders also farmers followed.
   b. Homesteaders or farmers followed.
   c. Homesteaders followed by farmers.
   d. Correct as is

5. a. Also, them
   b. However, those
   c. In addition, those
   d. Correct as is

6. a. weren't any
   b. were not no
   c. wasn't no
   d. Correct as is

# The Scarlet Ibis (page 592)

# Selection Test

**A.** Read each statement from the narrator of this story and think about the theme it suggests. For each statement, write notes explaining what it reveals about the narrator or what he learned from the event it describes. Then, write a theme suggested by the statement or the event. (8 points each)

| Statement | What It Reveals About the Narrator | Suggested Theme |
|---|---|---|
| 1. "There is within me . . . a knot of cruelty borne by the stream of love, much as our blood sometimes bears the seed of our destruction, and at times I was mean to Doodle." | | |
| 2. "Renaming my brother was perhaps the kindest thing I ever did for him, because nobody expects much from someone called Doodle." | | |
| 3. "But all of us must have something or someone to be proud of, and Doodle had become mine." | | |

**B.** Write the letter of the best answer. This exercise is continued on the next page. (5 points each)

_____ 1. Throughout Doodle's life, the narrator does all he can to
  a. harm Doodle.
  b. avoid Doodle.
  c. protect Doodle.
  d. change Doodle.

_____ 2. In general, how does Doodle respond to the narrator's efforts to push him beyond what Doodle thinks he can do?
  a. angrily
  b. willingly
  c. fearfully
  d. fearlessly

3. Doodle's response to the scarlet ibis reveals his
   a. sensitivity.
   b. fear of dying.
   c. desire to be "normal."
   d. determination to survive.

4. Why does the narrator run away from Doodle during the storm at the end of the story?
   a. He knows that Doodle is about to die.
   b. He wants to encourage Doodle to run faster.
   c. He realizes that Doodle "lies" better than he does.
   d. He wants to punish Doodle for failing.

**C. Words to Know.** Write the letter of the best answer. (4 points each)

1. If a plane's departure is <u>imminent</u>, it will take off
   a. very soon.          b. on schedule.          c. without danger.

2. A person with <u>doggedness</u> is one who shows
   a. responsibility.          b. good instincts.          c. determination.

3. To <u>reiterate</u> a promise is to
   a. break it.          b. say it again.          c. take it seriously.

4. If you stand <u>precariously</u> on a cliff, your footing is
   a. solid.          b. shaky.          c. relaxed.

5. Today, it would be <u>heresy</u> to say that the earth is
   a. flat.          b. polluted.          c. overpopulated.

**D.** Answer **one** of the following questions based on your understanding of the story. Write your answer on a separate sheet of paper. (20 points)

1. Think about how the scarlet ibis symbolizes Doodle. In what ways is Doodle like the scarlet ibis? Explain at least **three** ways in which they are alike.

2. How does the narrator's pride affect his relationship with Doodle? Why does it have this effect?

**E. Linking Literature to Life.** Answer the following question based on your own experience and knowledge. Write your answer on a separate sheet of paper. (16 points)

In what kinds of situations do you think pride is a mostly positive force? In what kinds of situations do you think it is a mostly negative one? Explain.

# Lineage/The Courage That My Mother Had (page 608)

## Selection Open-Book Test

**A.** Think about why Walker chose to use alliteration in "Lineage" and what is suggested by the alliteration in each of the lines below. Circle the letter of one line you wish to discuss. Then follow the directions to fill in each box below. (26 points)

    a. "They moved through fields sowing seed."
    b. "They touched earth and grain grew."
    c. "With veins rolling roughly over quick hands"

| Name the repeated initial consonant sound. | Circle one or more words in the list below that you think describe that sound. You may jot down your own word or words instead or in addition to these. |
|---|---|
| | explosive       harsh       rolling<br><br>gentle       hissing       sharp<br><br>growling       popping       soothing |
| **What things, feelings, and ideas are suggested by the alliteration?** | |

**B.** Write the letter of the best answer. This exercise is continued on the next page. (8 points each)

_____ 1. Which of the following is **most** emphasized by the title of "Lineage"?
    a. the speaker's straightforward manner
    b. the speaker's strong tie to his or her ancestors
    c. the rows of grain planted by the grandmothers
    d. the end of an era in the speaker's family's history

_____ 2. In the first stanza of "Lineage," the speaker conveys the idea that hard work can bring
    a. boredom.
    b. financial reward.
    c. joy and well-being.
    d. troubles and sorrows.

3. In the last line of "Lineage," the speaker reveals a feeling of
   a. pride.
   b. inferiority.
   c. self-hatred.
   d. contentment.

4. In "The Courage That My Mother Had," which of the following **best** describes the speaker's attitude toward the golden brooch?
   a. guilty
   b. scornful
   c. resentful
   d. appreciative

5. In "The Courage That My Mother Had," Millay uses repetition for effect or emphasis in
   a. line 3.
   b. line 4.
   c. lines 7 and 10.
   d. lines 7 and 12.

6. In **both** poems, the speakers
   a. wish they were living in the past.
   b. say they are very like their ancestors.
   c. recall words spoken by their ancestors.
   d. feel they lack certain qualities their ancestors had.

**C.** Answer **one** of the following questions based on your understanding of the poems. Write your answer on a separate sheet of paper. (15 points)

1. In each poem, what is the speaker's attitude toward his or her ancestors? How does each speaker feel that he or she compares with the ancestors? Support your answer with details from the poems.

2. Compare the images each speaker uses to express his or her ancestors' best qualities. How are the images similar?

**D. Linking Literature to Life.** Answer the following question based on your own experience and knowledge. Write your answer on a separate sheet of paper. (11 points)

Think about qualities that you admire in the important adults in your life. What one quality would you most want to "inherit"? Why?

# My Papa's Waltz/Grape Sherbet (page 613)

# Selection Open-Book Test

**A.** Think about the imagery used in each poem and how the images contribute to its mood and tone. For each of the images listed below, write notes in the boxes describing what sense(s) the image appeals to and what feelings it suggests. (8 points each)

| Image | Sense(s) It Appeals To | Feelings It Suggests |
|---|---|---|
| **"My Papa's Waltz"**<br>1. "The whiskey on your breath" | | |
| 2. "My right ear scraped a buckle." | | |
| **"Grape Sherbet"**<br>3. "swirled snow, gelled light" | | |
| 4. "like salt on a melon that makes it sweeter" | | |
| 5. "The diabetic grandmother /<br>stares from the porch" | | |

**B.** Write the letter of the best answer. (5 points each)

_____    1. Which lines from "My Papa's Waltz" best support the idea that the
speaker's experience was pleasant?
    a. lines 3–4            c. lines 11–12
    b. lines 5–6            d. lines 13–14

_____    2. What is the rhyme scheme of "My Papa's Waltz"?
    a. *aabb*               c. *abab*
    b. *aaab*             d. *abba*

_____    3. Which word best describes the tone of lines 1–16 in "Grape Sherbet"?
    a. sarcastic          c. peaceful
    b. solemn            d. exuberant

_____    4. In "Grape Sherbet," what did the speaker do "that morning"?
    a. went to a parade      c. ran through a cemetery
    b. made ice cream        d. played in the snow

**C.** Answer **one** of the following questions based on your understanding of the selection. Write your answer on a separate sheet of paper. (20 points)

1. In "My Papa's Waltz," the speaker says, "Such waltzing was not easy." Why do you think that waltzing with his father was difficult for the speaker? Support your ideas with details from the poem.

2. "Grape Sherbet" begins with the words "The day? Memorial." Describe how the poem itself could be considered a memorial.

**D. Linking Literature to Life.** Answer the following question based on your own experience and knowledge. Write your answer on a separate sheet of paper. (20 points)

Both of these poems describe memories of a father. Think about your father or someone else who is important to you. What memories would you include in a poem about your father or another person? What do those memories mean to you?

# Marine Corps Issue (page 618)

# Selection Test

**A.** Each box on the left describes a suspenseful moment in the story. In each box on the right, write notes explaining what makes that moment in the story suspenseful. (10 points each)

| | |
|---|---|
| 1. Johnny listens as his father and a friend from the Marine Corps drink whiskey and talk about their experiences in Vietnam. | **What makes it suspenseful?** |
| 2. Johnny sneaks into his parents' bedroom while his father is in the shower and takes the key to his father's boxes. | **What makes it suspenseful?** |
| 3. While he's looking through the contents of the second box, Johnny hears the back door of the house open and close. | **What makes it suspenseful?** |

**B.** Write the letter of the best answer. This exercise is continued on the next page. (5 points each)

_____ 1. The **main** reason that Johnny keeps his research on the war in Vietnam a secret is that he wants to
a. gain power over his father.
b. avoid causing his father pain.
c. make his father proud of him.
d. surprise his father with his knowledge.

_____ 2. When Johnny first considers opening the boxes, he feels torn between his desire to understand his father's past and his
a. fear about his father finding out.
b. fear of what he'll find inside the boxes.
c. wish to forget about Vietnam altogether.
d. hunch that the boxes may contain little of interest.

3. The father's margin notes in *Escape and Torture* suggest that he
   a. wrote the manual.
   b. tortured people during the war.
   c. was trained to torture people.
   d. was tortured as a prisoner of war.

4. Johnny and his father are alike in all of these ways **except** that his father
   a. enjoys baseball.
   b. has a hot temper.
   c. has secrets that trouble him.
   d. becomes physically violent when he's angry.

**C. Words to Know.** Write the letter of the best answer. (4 points each)

1. A person who shows <u>vulnerability</u> is
   a. sensitive.          b. hardworking.          c. intelligent.

2. To change your <u>demeanor</u>, you need to work on how you
   a. dress.              b. act.                  c. think.

3. <u>Deprivation</u> is something one would be **most** likely to experience while
   a. eating out.         b. on a diet.            c. fixing dinner.

4. An <u>agitated</u> person is **most** in need of
   a. confidence.         b. energy.               c. peace and quiet.

5. You might experience <u>trepidation</u> about a test if you
   a. enjoy challenges.   b. are well-prepared.    c. haven't studied.

**D.** Answer **one** of the following questions based on your understanding of the story. Write your answer on a separate sheet of paper. (15 points)

1. What does Johnny risk by communicating with his father about his father's experience in Vietnam? What does he gain?

2. How do the flashback scenes contribute to your understanding of the relationship between Johnny and his father?

**E. Linking Literature to Life.** Answer the following question based on your own experience and knowledge. Write your answer on a separate sheet of paper. (15 points)

Is the Vietnam War a significant event for your generation, or is it simply something that happened in the past to the previous generation? Support your opinion.

# Unit Four: All in the Family

# Part One Open-Book Test

**A.** Write the letter of the best answer to each question. (5 points each)

_____ 1. In "The Scarlet Ibis," Doodle's fate is foreshadowed by the
　　　　　　a. sudden appearance of the screech owl.
　　　　　　b. storage of his go-cart.
　　　　　　c. death of the scarlet ibis.
　　　　　　d. calm before the storm.

_____ 2. "Lineage" and "The Courage That My Mother Had" both concern
　　　　　　a. the strength of women who lived in the past.
　　　　　　b. how parents spoil their children.
　　　　　　c. the relationships of women to their husbands.
　　　　　　d. how difficult life was in the past.

_____ 3. The speakers of "My Papa's Waltz" and "Grape Sherbet" both describe
　　　　　　memories of
　　　　　　a. dancing.　　　　　　　　　c. war.
　　　　　　b. their fathers.　　　　　　d. past holidays.

_____ 4. To Johnny, the narrator in "Marine Corps Issue," what did the three locked
　　　　　　boxes represent?
　　　　　　a. his childhood　　　　　　c. his father's past
　　　　　　b. fond memories　　　　　　d. lost opportunities

**B.** Think about how images are used in the poems in this part to convey ideas and feelings about relationships. Choose **one** image from the poems in this part. In the boxes below, write the title of the poem and the line or lines that contain the image. Then describe the ideas and feelings that the image conveys about the relationship in that poem. (20 points)

| Title of Poem: | |
|---|---|
| **Image** | **What the Image Conveys About the Relationship** |
| | |

**C.** Answer **two** of the following essay questions. Write your answers on a separate sheet of paper. (20 points each)

1. Choose **one** relationship described in these selections that suffers from communication problems. Why do the problems exist? Describe the communication problem and explain its causes.

2. All of these selections deal in some way with the idea of love in family relationships. Choose **two** families described in the selections and tell which family you think is more loving. Support your opinion with details from the selections and your own ideas.

3. Most of these selections concern a child's view or memory of a parent. Choose **two** of the selections that you want to discuss. Compare and contrast the views of a parent presented in each selection. Then, discuss which view you think is more admiring, and why.

**D.** Most of these selections focus on relationships between children and their older relatives. In the boxes below, write the names of people involved in a relationship in **one** selection you want to discuss. Then write notes describing some things that tie the older and younger person together or that they have in common, and some things that separate the older and younger person or that create conflict in their relationship. (20 points)

| People Involved/Selection: | |
|---|---|
| **Things That Bring Them Together** | **Things That Separate Them** |
| | |

## *from* **Black Boy (page 654)**

# Selection Test

**A.** For each passage of dialogue, write notes in the boxes on the right telling what the dialogue reveals about the people. (16 points each)

| | |
|---|---|
| 1. "Where's my story?" I asked.<br>"It's in galleys," he said.<br>"What's that?" I asked; I did not know what<br>galleys were.<br>"It's set up in type," he said. "We're publishing it."<br>"How much money will I get?" I asked, excited.<br>"We can't pay for manuscript," he said.<br>"But you sell your papers for money," I said with logic.<br>"Yes, but we're young in business," he explained.<br>"But you're asking me to *give* you my story, but you<br>don't *give* your papers away," I said.<br>He laughed.<br>"Look, you're just starting. This story will put your name<br>before our readers. Now that's something," he said. | ➡ Wright<br><br><br><br><br><br>➡ Wright's editor |
| 2. "Did you really write that story?" they asked me.<br>"Yes."<br>"Why?"<br>"Because I wanted to."<br>"Where did you get it from?"<br>"I made it up."<br>"You didn't. You copied it out of a book."<br>"If I had, no one would publish it."<br>"But what are they publishing it for?"<br>"So people can read it."<br>"Who told you to do that?"<br>"Nobody."<br>"Then why did you do it?"<br>"Because I wanted to," I said again. | ➡ Wright<br><br><br><br><br><br>➡ Wright's classmates |

**B.** Write the letter of the best answer. This exercise is continued on the next page.
(6 points each)

_____ 1. Which of the following does Wright pour into the writing of *The Voodoo of Hell's Half-Acre?*
   a. his emotions
   b. his life experiences
   c. his philosophy of life
   d. his literary knowledge

_____ 2. Which of the following would Wright **most** probably say that the
educational system of the state of Mississippi gave him?
a. a solid background in reading and writing
b. a set of challenges and limits to overcome
c. the solid belief that he was inferior to whites
d. the encouragement to believe in his dreams

_____ 3. At the end of the selection, Wright uses a metaphor to compare his life
at that time to a train
a. going nowhere.         c. running right on schedule.
b. chugging up a mountain.    d. running dangerously out of control.

**C. Words to Know.** Write the letter of the best answer. (4 points each)

_____ 1. People are considered <u>naive</u> by those who believe themselves to be more
a. honest.           b. talented.          c. sophisticated.

_____ 2. A principal who <u>relents</u> on the school dress code makes it more
a. rigid.            b. relaxed.           c. detailed.

_____ 3. Scientists <u>speculate</u> about whether life exists
a. after death.      b. in the Arctic.      c. on the moon.

_____ 4. If you do something <u>intuitively</u>, you do it without being
a. rude.             b. taught.            c. effective.

_____ 5. An <u>articulate</u> person makes good use of
a. words.           b. hours.            c. dollars.

**D.** Answer **one** of the following questions based on your understanding of the selection.
Write your answer on a separate sheet of paper. (15 points)

1. What do you think are Wright's chief motives for writing *The Voodoo of Hell's Half-Acre?* What might be his main motives for trying to get the story published? Does he achieve what he set out to accomplish?

2. Wright says, "Had I been conscious of the full extent to which I was pushing against the current of my environment, I would have been frightened altogether out of my attempts at writing." Describe "the current" of Wright's environment. Why might it have frightened him away from writing?

**E. Linking Literature to Life.** Answer the following question based on your own experience and knowledge. Write your answer on a separate sheet of paper. (15 points)

What does your environment encourage you to aspire to? If you were to choose different goals, how do you think people in your environment would react? Explain.

# Daughter of Invention (page 663)

# Selection Test

**A.** The passages below contribute to the narrator's characterizations of her father and mother. Read each passage. Then, write notes describing what you learn from the passage about the character of the mother or father and about the narrator's perspective. (10 points each)

| Passage | What You Learn About the Character | What You Learn About the Narrator's Perspective |
|---|---|---|
| 1. "My mother would wave us out of her room. 'The problem with you girls . . .' I can tell you right now what the problem always boiled down to: We wanted to become Americans and my father—and my mother, at first—would have none of it." | | |
| 2. "The minute my father saw my mother and me, filing in, he put his paper down, and his face brightened as if at long last his wife had delivered a son, and that was the news we were bringing him." | | |
| 3. "His eyes glared at me, then shifted to my mother, accusingly. In barely audible Spanish, as if secret microphones or informers were all about, he whispered, 'You will permit her to read *that*?'" | | |

**B.** Write the letter of the best answer. This exercise is continued on the next page. (5 points each)

_____ 1. The narrator's parents came to America to
   a. improve their economic situation.
   b. get a better education for their children.
   c. live where women had more opportunities.
   d. escape from a repressive government.

2. The narrator and her sisters had some problems at school because
   a. other students were prejudiced against them.
   b. they preferred speaking English to Spanish.
   c. they had a sour attitude toward living in America.
   d. none of them liked to read.

3. Reading Walt Whitman's poems opened a door to the narrator's
   a. sentimental nature.          c. religious beliefs.
   b. feelings of rebellion.       d. love of language.

4. The narrator's father bought her an electric typewriter mainly to
   a. help her improve her schoolwork.
   b. make amends and show how much he truly cared about her.
   c. put a stop to what he saw as a bad attitude.
   d. celebrate the success of the speech she gave.

**C. Words to Know.** Write the letter of the best answer. (4 points each)

1. If you provoke someone, you cause him or her to
   a. feel grateful.        b. defend you.        c. feel angry.

2. Which of the following would most likely be a plagiarist?
   a. a writer              b. a pharmacist       c. a dictator

3. Which of the following are innumerable?
   a. the pyramids of Egypt  b. the world's oceans  c. the stars in the sky

4. A tentative statement is
   a. inconsiderate.        b. hesitant.          c. persuasive.

5. Someone who is insubordinate shows
   a. respect.              b. disobedience.      c. timidity.

**D.** Answer **one** of the following questions based on your understanding of the selection. Write your answer on a separate sheet of paper. (15 points)

1. Which speech do you think would have been better for the teacher's day address—the speech the narrator wrote or the speech her mother wrote for her? Why?

2. How did the father's past in the Dominican Republic affect his behavior in America? Provide examples from the selection.

**E. Linking Literature to Life.** Answer the following question based on your own experience and knowledge. Write your answer on a separate sheet of paper. (15 points)

The narrator's mother gave up speaking Spanish with her daughters when she moved to America. Do you feel that this was the right thing to do? Why or why not?

# A Voice/The Journey (page 680)

# Selection Open-Book Test

**A.** In each poem, the poet's diction, or word choice, helps the reader understand the external pressures on the main character ("you") and to experience the character's intense feelings. For each poem, note words and phrases that communicate these outside pressures and the feelings they evoke in the character. (20 points each)

| Poem | Outside Pressures | Character's Feelings |
|------|-------------------|----------------------|
| 1. "A Voice" | | |
| 2. "The Journey" | | |

**B.** Write the letter of the best answer. This exercise is continued on the next page. (5 points each)

_____ 1. When the speaker's mother in "A Voice" was a child, she **generally**
   a. felt uncomfortable speaking English.
   b. liked giving speeches in public.
   c. disliked being on stage with everyone looking at her.
   d. avoided speaking Spanish.

_____ 2. In "A Voice," the speaker learned from her mother to
   a. use formal Spanish.
   b. win speech contests.
   c. avoid being the only Mexican.
   d. speak up for herself.

_____ 3. In "The Journey," the "you" of the poem left a situation that
   a. made many demands on him or her.
   b. helped his or her unique strengths blossom.
   c. he or she had hoped would last forever.
   d. made it clear that no one cared about him or her.

_____   4. In "The Journey," the speaker suggests that the "you" of the poem was
          a. terribly confused.
          b. lacking in courage.
          c. uncaring and hurtful.
          d. right to leave.

**C.** Answer **one** of the following questions based on your understanding of the selection. Write your answer on a separate sheet of paper. (20 points)

1. Compare the two poems. In which one do you feel as if you know the "you" of the poem better? Why?

2. Choose three examples of figurative language—simile, metaphor, or personification— in these poems. Describe the feeling or mood conveyed by each example.

**D. Linking Literature to Life.** Answer the following question based on your own experience and knowledge. Write your answer on a separate sheet of paper. (20 points)

Think about a time when you became aware of a weakness in someone you admired or looked up to. How did the realization make you feel? Did it change your view of the person? Explain.

# Only Daughter (page 694)

# Selection Test

**A.** Think about the ideas about life and human nature that Cisneros expresses in the selection. In the box at the top, note what you think the theme of the selection is. In each box at the bottom, note a detail from the selection that supports the theme. (20 points)

| Theme |
| --- |
|  |

| Note a detail that supports this theme. | Note a detail that supports this theme. |
| --- | --- |
|  |  |

**B.** Write the letter of the best answer. This exercise is continued on the next page. (6 points each)

_____ 1. As a child, growing up as the only daughter in a family of six sons made Cisneros feel
    a. lucky.
    b. lonely.
    c. secure.
    d. superior.

_____ 2. Cisneros worries that her father views her writing as
    a. trivial.
    b. boring.
    c. depressing.
    d. overemotional.

_____ 3. More than anything else, Cisneros wants her father to feel
    a. proud of her.
    b. sorry for treating her badly.
    c. humbled by her achievements.
    d. at peace with their relationship.

_____ 4. When Cisneros's father says, "Use this, and not this," he means that he
wants his children to
a. pursue a profession like his.
b. make raising a family their chief occupation.
c. find more rewarding work than he has found.
d. follow their own dreams, whatever they may be.

_____ 5. At the end of the selection, Cisneros's father's reaction to her story
suggests that he feels
a. proud.          b. puzzled.          c. shocked.          d. embarrassed.

**C. Words to Know.** Write the letter of the best answer. (4 points each)

_____ 1. An anthology is a good place to look if you want to find something to
a. eat.                    b. wear.                    c. read.

_____ 2. If you embroider your story, you make it more
a. detailed.              b. humorous.              c. to the point.

_____ 3. A person who experiences trauma **most** probably needs to go
a. home.                  b. to a restaurant.        c. to a hospital.

_____ 4. Nostalgia is something that adults are likely to feel toward their
a. childhood.             b. weaknesses.            c. strengths.

_____ 5. When you fulfill a goal, you
a. set it.                 b. work toward it.         c. achieve it.

**D.** Answer **one** of the following questions based on your understanding of the selection.
Write your answer on a separate sheet of paper. (15 points)

1. Think about how Cisneros responds to her father's ideas about what she should
become. How do his ideas make her feel? How do they affect the decisions she
makes about her education and occupation? Support your answers with details
from the selection and your own ideas.

2. How might Cisneros's experiences as "the only daughter" and "only a daughter"
affect her as a writer? Support your ideas with details from the selection and your
own ideas about writers.

**E. Linking Literature to Life.** Answer the following question based on your own
experience and knowledge. Write your answer on a separate sheet of paper. (15 points)

Why do you think the need for approval is important in many people's lives? Give at
least two possible reasons.

# *from* The House on Mango Street (page 701)

# Selection Test

**A.** Each vignette in this selection gives you important information about Esperanza's life and also conveys a tone that reveals her attitude. For each vignette, write notes that describe what aspect of her life the vignette tells about and what the attitude or tone of the vignette is. (10 points each)

| Vignette | What It Tells About | Attitude or Tone |
|---|---|---|
| 1. "The House on Mango Street" | | |
| 2. "My Name" | | |
| 3. "Papa Who Wakes Up Tired in the Dark" | | |
| 4. "A Smart Cookie" | | |
| 5. "Mango Says Goodbye Sometimes" | | |

**B.** Write the letter of the best answer. This exercise is continued on the next page. (5 points each)

_____ 1. Esperanza thinks that a woman born in the Chinese "year of the horse" will be
    a. unlucky.        c. sad.
    b. strong.       d. full of hope.

_____ 2. How did the narrator feel when she saw the house her parents bought on Mango Street?
    a. pleased       c. excited
    b. furious       d. discouraged

_____ 3. Esperanza's mother quit school because she
    a. was ashamed of her clothes.
    b. wasn't expected to do well.
    c. didn't understand English.
    d. needed to work.

_____ 4. Esperanza tries to ease the pain she feels about her life by
        a. making fun of her own name.
        b. asking her father to tell her about life in Mexico.
        c. singing opera with her mother.
        d. making her life into a story.

**C.** Answer **one** of the following questions based on your understanding of the selection. Write your answer on a separate sheet of paper. (15 points)

1. Why does the narrator dislike her name, and how does the last vignette in the selection, "Mango Says Goodbye Sometimes," let the reader know that "Esperanza" is the right name for the narrator after all?

2. Describe Esperanza's parents based on what you learned about them in the selection.

**D. Linking Literature to Life.** Answer the following question based on your own experience and knowledge. Write your answer on a separate sheet of paper. (15 points)

    Think about your own hopes for the future. Do they involve leaving or staying in your community? What would you like the answer to be when friends and neighbors ask, "What ever happened to [you]?"

# On Writing The House on Mango Street (page 711)

# Selection Test

**A.** The voice in this selection is different from the voice of Esperanza in *The House on Mango Street*. Read the passages below to remind yourself of these two voices. Then answer the questions about each voice, below. (10 points each)

**Voice 1: Esperanza's voice in *The House on Mango Street*:**
"I like to tell stories. I tell them inside my head. I tell them after the mailman says, Here's your mail."

**Voice 2: Cisneros's voice in "On Writing *The House on Mango Street*":**
"I remember I was trying to write something that was a cross between fiction and poetry—like Jorge Luis Borges' *Dream Tigers,* a book whose stories read like fables, but with the lyricism and succinctness of poetry."

| Question | Voice 1 | Voice 2 |
|---|---|---|
| 1. What do you notice about the writing style? | | |
| 2. What is the tone of the writing? | | |
| 3. What do the style and tone tell you about the narrator/writer? | | |

**B.** Write the letter of the best answer. This exercise is continued on the next page. (5 points each)

_____ 1. Cisneros noticed that none of the books assigned to her in graduate school
    a. were interesting to her.
    b. featured houses like those she had lived in.
    c. included insights that would help her write.
    d. could help her understand her "otherness."

_____ 2. Which sentence best describes the voice of the narrator in *The House on Mango Street*?
    a. It was carefully crafted by the author.
    b. It came naturally to the author.
    c. It was almost like a foreign language to the author.
    d. It was taken directly from her earlier writing.

_____ 3. Cisneros became angry because she believed that
      a. no one cared about her.
      b. her professors were insulting her.
      c. she wasn't as smart as everyone else.
      d. her education had been a lie.

_____ 4. Which sentence best describes the vignettes in _The House on Mango Street?_
      a. They tell the story of the author's childhood.
      b. They are entirely fictional.
      c. They combine the author's own and other people's stories.
      d. They focus on the lives of her students.

**C. Words to Know.** Write the letter of the best answer. (4 points each)

_____ 1. When something evolves, it
      a. loses strength.     b. changes gradually.     c. turns around.

_____ 2. Your presumptions about something are things you
      a. assume are true.     b. plan to do.     c. already know.

_____ 3. If a person ingests something, he or she
      a. disregards it.     b. remembers it.     c. takes it in.

_____ 4. A project's inception is its
      a. detailed plan.     b. beginning.     c. desired outcome.

_____ 5. An affirmation of an idea is something that
      a. disproves it.     b. expands it.     c. supports it.

**D.** Answer **one** of the following questions based on your understanding of the selection. Write your answer on a separate sheet of paper. (15 points)

1. In what sense did Cisneros's writing become a "quiet revolution" while she was in graduate school? Explain.

2. How did the two halves of the author's life—her community activist self and her writer self—meet and merge after the publication of _The House on Mango Street?_ Give examples of how she realized that this had happened.

**E. Linking Literature to Life.** Answer the following question based on your own experience and knowledge. Write your answer on a separate sheet of paper. (15 points)

Cisneros says that "anger, when it is used . . . nonviolently, has power." Do you agree with this statement? Why or why not? What other examples of this principle have you observed in life or literature?

# Unit Four: All in the Family

# Part Two Open-Book Test

**A.** Write the answer to each question on the lines. (5 points each)

1. In "Daughter of Invention," why did the father object to the daughter's speech?

_____

_____

2. In "A Voice," what did the speaker learn from her mother?

_____

_____

3. In "Only Daughter," what does Cisneros mean when she says she was *"only a daughter"*?

_____

_____

4. What is the narrator's tone in the vignettes from *The House on Mango Street?*

_____

_____

**B.** Many of these selections concern problems that the writers faced. Choose **one** person or character you want to discuss. In the boxes below, write the name of the person or character and the selection. Then write notes describing the problem the person faces as a writer, why that problem exists for the person, and how that problem is solved or why it isn't solved. (20 points)

| Person or Character/Selection: | |
|---|---|
| **The Problem** | **Reasons for the Problem** |
| | |
| **How is the problem solved, or why isn't it solved?** | |
| | |

**C.** Answer **two** of the following essay questions. Write your answers on a separate sheet of paper. (20 points each)

1. Choose **one** selection in which the writer expresses negative opinions or judgments about the society or culture in which he or she grew up. Explain what the writer criticizes the society or culture for, and why.

2. Choose the **one** character in these selections that you admire most. Explain what you admire about that character, and give at least **three** reasons for your choice.

3. All of these selections deal in some way with the theme of becoming independent from one's family. Choose **two** people described in the selections that you want to discuss. Compare and contrast what they want to accomplish, what independence means to them, and how successful they are in becoming independent.

**D.** In many of these selections, a person has a special talent, goal, or characteristic. In the boxes below, write the name of **one** person you want to discuss. Then write notes describing what makes the person special; how other people react to the person's talent, goal, or characteristic; and how the person's life seems to be affected by that reaction. (20 points)

| Person/Selection: | | |
|---|---|---|
| **What makes the person special?** | **How do others react to this person?** | **How does this reaction affect his or her life?** |
| | | |

# Full Circle (page 742)

# Selection Test

**A.** Plot is an especially significant element of a detective story. For each of the elements of the plot listed on the left, make notes that describe an example from the story. (5 points each)

| | |
|---|---|
| **1. Exposition** → | |
| **2. Rising Action** → | |
| **3. Rising Action** → | |
| **4. Rising Action** → | |
| **5. Climax** → | |
| **6. Falling Action** → | |

**B.** Write the letter of the best answer. This exercise is continued on the next page. (6 points each)

_____  1. The narrator's immediate reaction to the accident is one of
      a. wild panic.
      b. unemotional calm.
      c. efficient excitement.
      d. stunned bewilderment.

_____  2. Mrs. Spurrier wants the narrator to investigate her daughter's death because she
      a. thinks the police are involved in a cover-up.
      b. thinks the narrator knows something important.
      c. doesn't trust the police to investigate thoroughly.
      d. blames the police for not protecting her daughter.

_____  3. Mrs. Spurrier's reason for thinking that Caroline was killed by someone who knew her is that
      a. Caroline had many enemies.
      b. someone had been bothering Caroline.
      c. the shot was fired through the passenger-side window.
      d. a random shooting would not have occurred on a highway.

_____ 4. The **main** reason Lt. Dolan gives the narrator the witness list is because
   a. he thinks she might help solve the case.
   b. he usually cooperates with her investigations.
   c. he doesn't want to use police time on the case.
   d. Caroline's mother has pressured him to cooperate.

_____ 5. The narrator cracks the case with information she receives from
   a. Judy Layton.
   b. Terry Layton.
   c. Mrs. Spurrier.
   d. the photographer.

**C. Words to Know.** Write the letter of the best answer. (4 points each)

_____ 1. If you harass people, you
   a. thank them.          b. pester them.          c. delight them.

_____ 2. You might be described as being sullen if you are
   a. pouting.             b. laughing.             c. complaining loudly.

_____ 3. A person who is egotistical is **most** likely to be described as being
   a. moody.               b. dishonest.            c. stuck-up.

_____ 4. Which of the following might police officers be assigned to dispel?
   a. a crime              b. a crowd               c. the mayor

_____ 5. You are **most** likely to be wary when you are
   a. anxious.             b. relaxed.              c. distracted.

**D.** Answer **one** of the following questions based on your understanding of the story. Write your answer on a separate sheet of paper. (10 points)

1. What obstacles does the narrator face while investigating Caroline's death? What personal qualities does the narrator have that help her to overcome the obstacles? Support your answer with details from the story.

2. The writer concludes the mystery neatly and efficiently with Terry Layton's death at the end. Did you find this ending satisfying or not? Explain your answer.

**E. Linking Literature to Life.** Answer the following question based on your own experience and knowledge. Write your answer on a separate sheet of paper. (10 points)

Do you think that being a detective would be a rewarding job? Explain your answer.

# Wasps' Nest (page 759)

# Selection Test

**A.** In each excerpt below, underline words or phrases that help build the suspense of "Wasps' Nest" by foreshadowing or suggesting something mysterious or ominous. Then, in the boxes on the right, note what the underlined words foreshadow or suggest. (6 points each)

| Excerpt | What does this suggest? |
|---|---|
| 1. "Who has been murdered?" <br> "As yet," said Hercule Poirot, "nobody." | |
| 2. Again Poirot looked at him, and again an indefinable something made Harrison uneasy. | |
| 3. "I mean," said Poirot, and his voice had a new note in it, "that a man may conceal his hate till the proper time comes." | |
| 4. Once outside on the road, . . . his face became grave and troubled. . . . he almost seemed on the point of returning. | |
| 5. There was, perhaps, something a little sinister in the stillness, like the lull before a storm. | |

**B.** Write the letter of the best answer. This exercise is continued on the next page. (5 points each)

_____ 1. Why did Claude Langton purchase cyanide of potassium?
   a. He wanted to kill Harrison.
   b. He planned to kill himself.
   c. Harrison asked him to buy it.
   d. He planned to use it in his garden.

_____ 2. From this story, what can you infer about washing soda?
   a. It looks like cyanide of potassium.
   b. It has a distinctive flavor.
   c. Poirot had to sign the poison book to buy it.
   d. People use it to kill wasps.

_____ 3. What was Harrison's primary feeling toward Langton?
   a. friendship          c. fear
   b. admiration          d. jealousy

_____ 4. What did Harrison think would happen by nine o'clock, when Poirot
   returned?
   a. The wasps would be dead.
   b. Langton would be dead.
   c. He himself would be dead.
   d. Both he and Langton would be dead.

**C. Words to Know.** Write the letter of the best answer. (4 points each)

_____ 1. A <u>languorous</u> day creates a mood that is
   a. lively.              b. irritable.          c. lazy.

_____ 2. An <u>absurd</u> idea is
   a. nonsensical.        b. original.           c. controversial.

_____ 3. Something done <u>resolutely</u> is done with
   a. evil intent.        b. determination.      c. caution.

_____ 4. To <u>slacken</u> one's pace is to make it
   a. more regular.       b. slower.             c. quicker.

_____ 5. Someone who speaks <u>impersonally</u> speaks in a manner that is
   a. very intense.       b. compassionate.      c. unemotional.

**D.** Answer **one** of the following questions based on your understanding of the selection. Write your answer on a separate sheet of paper. (15 points)

1. Summarize what Poirot already knew before he went to John Harrison's house for the first time. What did he think Harrison was planning? What did Harrison do or say to confirm Poirot's suspicions?

2. Why does Harrison believe that Poirot's visit might actually help him succeed in his plan? What does he say to trick Poirot, and how does Poirot trick Harrison instead?

**E. Linking Literature to Life.** Answer the following question based on your own experience and knowledge. Write your answer on a separate sheet of paper. (15 points)

   Imagine you have been told that you have only a short time to live. How would this affect the way you behaved in the present? Would you try to "settle scores" with people who have angered you? Why or why not?

# Trifles (page 770)

# Selection Test

**A.** Read the two excerpts below. For each excerpt, write notes in the boxes explaining what you can infer about the character from what he says and why this particular statement is ironic. (15 points each)

| 1. **Sheriff.** I suppose anything Mrs. Peters does'll be all right. She was to take in some clothes for her, you know, and a few little things. We left in such a hurry yesterday. | |
|---|---|
| **What You Can Infer About the Sheriff** | **Why This Statement Is Ironic** |
| | |

| 2. **County Attorney.** Oh, I guess they're not very dangerous things the ladies have picked out. | |
|---|---|
| **What You Can Infer About the County Attorney** | **Why This Statement Is Ironic** |
| | |

**B.** Write the letter of the best answer. This exercise is continued on the next page. (6 points each)

_____ 1. At the farmhouse, the County Attorney is looking **mainly** for clues about
   a. the murder weapon.
   b. a motive for the crime.
   c. evidence of an intruder.
   d. how the crime could have been committed.

_____ 2. Mrs. Hale suggests that the cheerless atmosphere in the Wrights' home is due **mainly** to
   a. poverty.
   b. bad housekeeping.
   c. Mr. Wright's personality.
   d. Mrs. Wright's personality.

_____ 3. The play suggests that Mrs. Hale restitches Mrs. Wright's sewing on the quilt piece in order to
   a. show that she can do it better.
   b. help Mrs. Wright get the quilt completed.
   c. protect Mrs. Wright from critical comments.
   d. destroy evidence that Mrs. Wright was emotionally upset.

_____ 4. What do Mrs. Peters and Mrs. Hale come to believe is particularly meaningful about Mr. Wright's death?
   a. the method used to kill him
   b. the place where he was killed
   c. the time of day at which he was killed
   d. the coldness of the house after his death

_____ 5. Why does Mrs. Peters try to hide the box the women have found?
   a. It upsets her.
   b. She wants to protect Mrs. Wright.
   c. She doesn't want the men to laugh at her.
   d. She is afraid it will give the men the wrong idea.

**C. Words to Know.** Write the letter of the best answer. (4 points each)

_____ 1. Which occupation is **most** likely to require a person to be covert?
   a. a spy          b. a busboy          c. an evangelist

_____ 2. If you were preoccupied when a teacher asked you a question, he or she would be most likely to say,
   a. "Louder, please."     b. "That's correct."     c. "Pay attention."

_____ 3. If you are abashed, your most likely response would be to
   a. look confused.     b. pass out.          c. blush.

_____ 4. If you are speaking facetiously, you are trying to be
   a. humorous.          b. believable.        c. bossy.

_____ 5. You could indicate comprehension of an idea by saying,
   a. "No way!"          b. "I see."             c. "Huh?"

**D.** Answer the following question based on your understanding of the play. Write your answer on a separate sheet of paper. (10 points)

   Do you think that Mrs. Peters and Mrs. Hale are doing the morally right thing by protecting Mrs. Wright? Explain your answer.

**E. Linking Literature to Life.** Answer the following question. Write your answer on a separate sheet of paper. (10 points)

   Identify a legal action that you consider to be a crime. Why do you consider this act a crime, and what might be an appropriate punishment for it?

# The Great Taos Bank Robbery (page 787)

# Selection Test

**A.** Consider how the writer uses verbal irony to, in effect, say one thing and mean another. Read each quotation below and note what its surface meaning is. That is, restate or summarize what it would mean if the writer intended no irony. Then note what the writer is using verbal irony to suggest—that is, what the writer really means to communicate. (16 points each)

| 1. "Customers quickly noticed that the line-stander clad as a woman had a full day's growth of dark stubble bristling through his pancake makeup and that the nylons encased an unseemly growth of leg hair. They also noticed that this person's costume was remarkably chic for Taos, which is one of the few places where a man can still feel adequately dressed downtown in bib overalls." ||
|---|---|
| **Surface Meaning** | **Real Meaning** |
|  |  |
| 2. "Considering the number of officers involved and the modest dimensions of Taos it is safe to guess that at least one policeman looked almost everywhere at least once, except in the deserted house where the two had chosen to sleep." ||
| **Surface Meaning** | **Real Meaning** |
|  |  |

**B.** Write the letter of the best answer. This exercise is continued on the next page. (7 points each)

_____ 1. Which of the following people is first to know that the bank is going to be robbed?
　　　　　a. an elderly lady
　　　　　b. a police officer
　　　　　c. a bank president
　　　　　d. a newspaper editor

_____ 2. The writer suggests that, during the search for the suspects, some
residents fail to help the police because the residents
a. dislike the police.
b. have no community spirit.
c. are afraid of the suspects.
d. do not take the situation very seriously.

_____ 3. What did The Great Flood of 1935 lack that most floods have?
a. water damage        c. a declaration of emergency
b. huge amounts of water    d. a need to evacuate residents

_____ 4. The writer's **main** purpose in writing this selection was **most** probably to
a. inform.        c. persuade.
b. entertain.        d. express an opinion.

**C. Words to Know.** Write the letter of the best answer. (4 points each)

_____ 1. If you use impeccable logic you are most likely
a. right.        b. wrong.        c. confused.

_____ 2. To be in conformity with a rule means you are
a. obeying it.        b. breaking it.        c. enforcing it.

_____ 3. If you are tolerant, you could best be described as
a. unhappy.        b. ignorant.        c. open-minded.

_____ 4. An example of a dissenting opinion would most probably be
a. "I agree."        b. "You're wrong."        c. "I couldn't care less."

_____ 5. Which of the following is a normal reaction to an affront?
a. anger        b. gratitude        c. amusement

**D.** Answer **one** of the following questions based on your understanding of the selection.
Write your answer on a separate sheet of paper. (10 points)

1. Why do you think Mrs. Fish and others gather at the bank to watch the robbery?
How would you describe their attitude toward the incident?

2. What do you think prompts the people of Taos to refer to this incident as "The Great
Taos Bank Robbery"? How is it like "The Great Flood of 1935"?

**E. Linking Literature to Life.** Answer the following question based on your own
experience and knowledge. Write your answer on a separate sheet of paper. (10 points)

Do you think that living in a place where people have to be a little unusual in order to
fit in sounds like fun? Explain your answer.

# Unit Five: A World of Mysteries

# Part One Open-Book Test

**A.** Write the answer to each question on the lines. (5 points each)

1. In "Full Circle," why was Caroline's college roommate reluctant to talk to the detective?

   _____

   _____

2. In "Wasps' Nest," what did John Harrison plan to do to Claude Langton?

   _____

   _____

3. In "Trifles," what does the broken birdcage symbolize?

   _____

   _____

4. How would you describe the characters Gomez and Smith in "The Great Taos Bank Robbery"?

   _____

   _____

   _____

**B.** In many of these selections, characters are driven to do something that they ordinarily wouldn't do. On the line below, write the title of one selection and a character you wish to discuss. Then, in the boxes, describe something the character does that he or she wouldn't ordinarily do and explain why the character takes that action. (20 points)

**Selection and Character:** _____

| Action | | Reason |
|---|---|---|
| | ➝ | **Reason** |
| | ➝ | **Reason** |

**C.** Answer **two** of the following essay questions based on your understanding of the selections. Write your answers on a separate sheet of paper. (20 points each)

1. Which character in the selections in this part do you think is easiest to fool, and which do you think is most difficult to fool? Support your choices with details from the selections and your own ideas.

2. Think about the strange or unusual behavior of some of the characters in these selections. Which strange or unusual action did you find the easiest to understand, and which did you find the most difficult to understand? Support your choices with details from the selection or selections and your own ideas.

3. Think about which characters from this part are victims and which are victimizers, that is, characters who deliberately harm others. Identify a character who clearly seems to be a victim, a character who clearly seems to be a victimizer, and a character who might be considered both a victim and a victimizer. Use details from the selections and your own ideas about right and wrong to support your choices.

**D.** In several of these selections, characters use deceit or trickery to get what they want. On the line below, write the title of **one** selection and a character you wish to discuss. Then, in the boxes, write notes to answer each question. (20 points)

| **What does this character attempt to accomplish through deceit or trickery?** | **Does the deceit or trickery get the character what he or she wants?**<br><br>☐ yes   ☐ no |
|---|---|
| **Why is the character's use of deceit or trickery effective or not effective?** | |

# The Open Window (page 816)

# Selection Test

**A.** Think about the narrative point of view in this story. For each main character, the reader learns something that the character does not know. In the boxes below, write notes about what the character knows and what the reader knows that the character does not. (10 points each)

| 1. What does Mr. Nuttel know about Vera? | 3. What does Mrs. Sappleton know about Mr. Nuttel? |
|---|---|
| 2. What does the reader know about Vera that Mr. Nuttel does not know? | 4. What does the reader know about Mr. Nuttel that Mrs. Sappleton does not know? |

**B.** Write the letter of the best answer. This exercise is continued on the next page. (5 points each)

_____ 1. From the beginning of the story, the reader knows that Framton Nuttel is
   a. a self-possessed man.
   b. an avid hunter.
   c. a nervous person.
   d. a gullible visitor.

_____ 2. Why did Vera have a look of horror in her eyes when the hunters returned?
   a. She thought they were ghosts.
   b. She realized that she was traveling in time.
   c. She knew she'd be caught in a lie.
   d. She was play-acting to fool Framton.

_____    3. How did Mrs. Sappleton feel as Nuttel told her about himself?
          a. bored
          b. fascinated
          c. sympathetic
          d. puzzled

_____    4. Why did Framton Nuttel leave quickly when the hunters arrived?
          a. He was very uncomfortable in social situations.
          b. He was horribly frightened.
          c. He realized that Vera had made a fool of him.
          d. He was not invited to stay for tea.

**C.** Answer **one** of the following questions based on your understanding of the selection. Write your answer on a separate sheet of paper. (20 points)

1. Why is Vera so successful in making Framton Nuttel believe her story? Give at least **three** reasons.

2. Why, do you think, does the author choose to tell the reader more about Framton's thoughts than about Vera's? How would the story be different if the reader knew Vera's thoughts?

**D. Linking Literature to Life.** Answer the following question based on your own experience and knowledge. Write your answer on a separate sheet of paper. (20 points)

If you went away for a restful vacation, would you wish to call on people whose names were given to you by a friend or relative? Or would you rather be entirely on your own and trust that you might meet nice people? Explain.

# Sorry, Right Number (page 823)

# Selection Test

**A.** Think about how the suspense builds in this play through the use of foreshadowing—hints that something dreadful is going to happen. Some of the foreshadowed events turn out to be true, but others do not. In the boxes on the left, write notes describing examples of foreshadowing in the play. In the boxes on the right, tell what actually happens. (5 points each)

| Example of Foreshadowing | What Actually Happens |
|---|---|
| **1.** | |
| **2.** | |
| **3.** | |
| **4.** | |
| **5.** | |

**B.** Write the letter of the best answer. This exercise is continued on the next page.
(5 points each)

_____ 1. At the beginning of the play, Katie's family life seems
   a. boring.
   b. ordinary.
   c. unhappy.
   d. strangely spooky.

_____ 2. When Katie gets the mysterious phone call, her reaction is one of
   a. irritation.
   b. suspicion.
   c. immediate panic.
   d. slowly growing concern.

_____ 3. As Bill goes with Katie to Dawn's house, he is feeling
      a. fearful about his own safety.
      b. annoyed at Katie for overreacting.
      c. worried that something may be wrong.
      d. concerned about Katie's mental health.

_____ 4. Katie's feelings on her daughters's wedding day could **best** be described as
      a. numb.              c. joyous.
      b. mixed.            d. regretful.

_____ 5. Which of the following **cannot** have its normal limitations in order for the events in this play to make sense?
      a. time              c. death
      b. love              d. space

**C. Words to Know.** Write the letter of the best answer. (4 points each)

_____ 1. A person who is <u>prone</u> to violence is **most** likely to be called a
      a. bully.           b. victim.          c. peacemaker.

_____ 2. Which of the following is **most** likely to make someone react <u>bleakly</u>?
      a. a bee sting       b. good news       c. a failing grade

_____ 3. Another way of saying "in the <u>interim</u>," is to say
      a. "afterward."       b. "meanwhile."       c. "occasionally."

_____ 4. A <u>chasm</u> is **most** likely to be located in
      a. the ground.       b. a museum.       c. a leg muscle.

_____ 5. A person who relies on <u>intuition</u> depends on his or her
      a. feelings.       b. education.       c. strength.

**D.** Answer **one** of the following questions based on your understanding of the play. Write your answer on a separate sheet of paper. (15 points)

1. Why do you think Katie was unable to recognize her own voice? Give and support at least **two** reasons.

2. Describe what you think is the falling action in this play. Support your ideas.

**E. Linking Literature to Life.** Answer the following question based on your own experience and knowledge. Write your answer on a separate sheet of paper. (15 points)

If you had an opportunity to go back in time and change something that happened, would you do it? Why or why not?

# Beware: Do Not Read This Poem (page 845)

## Selection Open-Book Test

**A.** This poem has three distinct parts, as indicated in the chart below. Reread each part to look for unusual features that contribute to the poem's unique form, and note those features in the middle boxes. Then, in the boxes on the right, describe the mood conveyed by each part of the poem. (10 points each)

| Part of Poem | Notable Features | Mood |
|---|---|---|
| 1. Lines 1–18 | | |
| 2. Lines 19–43 | | |
| 3. Lines 44–50 | | |

**B.** Write the letter of the best answer. This exercise is continued on the next page. (8 points each)

_____ 1. Which of these elements is found in all three parts of the poem?
  a. mirror imagery
  b. warnings to the reader
  c. facts and statistics
  d. people disappearing

_____ 2. Which statement best describes the woman with the mirrors?
  a. She does not want other people to use her mirrors.
  b. She wants to escape from the mirrors.
  c. She rejects other people to admire only herself.
  d. She is the only one who can disappear into a mirror.

_____ 3. In lines 19–31, the imagery suggests that the poem is
          a. devouring the reader.
          b. reflecting the reader as a mirror would.
          c. being eaten by the reader.
          d. imprisoning the reader.

_____ 4. The last part of this poem implies that
          a. the woman with the mirrors will return.
          b. many people have disappeared for mysterious reasons.
          c. everyone who reads poetry is in danger.
          d. no one who disappears is really missed.

**C.** Answer **one** of the following questions based on your understanding of the selection. Write your answer on a separate sheet of paper. (20 points)

1. Compare the mirrors described in the first part of the poem with the character of the poem itself, as described in the second part. How are they alike? How are they different?

2. Imagine that this poem is a metaphor for a highly addictive drug or other substance. What parallels do you see between this poem and an addictive drug? How could the different parts of the poem be describing things that happen to people with such addictions?

**D. Linking Literature to Life.** Answer the following question based on your own experience and knowledge. Write your answer on a separate sheet of paper. (18 points)

    The speaker says, "this poem is the reader & the reader this poem." How do you see the relationship between a reader and a poem? Is a poem always the same, or is it different for each reader? Do you read every poem in the same way, or do you bring something different to each poem? Explain.

# In the Family (page 856)

# Selection Test

**A.** In this story, elements of magical realism focus on the character Clara. In the boxes on the left, note three or four ways in which she is a normal, real-world character. In the boxes on the right, note three or four ways in which her character includes aspects of fantasy. (15 points each)

| 1. Real World | 2. Fantasy |
|---|---|
| | |

**B.** Write the letter of the best answer. This exercise is continued on the next page. (5 points each)

_____ 1. The people who inhabited the mirror were
     a. for the most part, strangers.
     b. storybook characters.
     c deceased members of the family.
     d. troubled souls.

_____ 2. The family reacted to the inhabitants of the mirror with
     a. terror.          c. excitement.
     b. acceptance.     d. resentment.

_____ 3. What can you tell about the women in this family?
     a. They were expected to be highly educated.
     b. They were feisty and argumentative.
     c. They turned to the men for decision making.
     d. They took charge of household matters.

_____ 4. What drove Clara to ask Eulalia to pass the salad?
    a. curiosity               c. hunger
    b. confusion            d. a death wish

## C. Words to Know. Write the letter of the best answer. (4 points each)

_____ 1. A person who is in a state of <u>contemplation</u> is
    a. unfocused.        b. in deep thought.      c. frustrated.

_____ 2. An <u>indolent</u> person is
    a. lazy.               b. not generous.         c. careful.

_____ 3. To <u>bolster</u> a person's confidence is to
    a. undermine it.      b. ignore it.            c. reinforce it.

_____ 4. Someone who feels <u>grievously</u> wronged believes the wrong is
    a. unintentional.      b. severe.            c. temporary.

_____ 5. An <u>oversight</u> is a
    a. mistake.         b. judgment.        c. plan.

**D.** Answer **one** of the following questions based on your understanding of the selection. Write your answer on a separate sheet of paper. (15 points)

1. At the end of the story, what does the narrator think Clara will try to do? Do you think Clara will succeed? Why or why not?

2. Two characteristics of magical realism are the presence of the unexplainable and unusual humor. What is unexplainable in this story, and how has the author created humor?

## E. Linking Literature to Life. Answer the following question based on your own experience and knowledge. Write your answer on a separate sheet of paper. (15 points)

If the mirror in the story were in your house, who would be reflected there? Tell about the people who would be in the mirror and how you and the people you live with might react to the images.

# A Very Old Man with Enormous Wings (page 863)

# Selection Test

**A.** Think about the author's style in this story, particularly his use of **imagery**, **magical realism**, **tone**, and **irony**. Read each excerpt below. Then, in the boxes on the right, describe the element of style used in the excerpt and what it contributes to the overall effect of the story. (6 points each)

| Excerpt | Element of Style and Its Effects |
|---|---|
| 1. "He was dressed like a ragpicker. There were only a few faded hairs left on his bald skull and very few teeth in his mouth, and his pitiful condition of a drenched great-grandfather had taken away any sense of grandeur he might have had." | |
| 2. "On the following day everyone knew that a flesh-and-blood angel was held captive in Pelayo's house." | |
| 3. "Some visionaries hoped that he could be put to stud in order to implant on earth a race of winged wise men who could take charge of the universe." | |
| 4. "That was how they skipped over the inconvenience of the wings and quite intelligently concluded that he was a lonely castaway from some foreign ship wrecked by the storm." | |

**B.** Write the letter of the best answer. This exercise is continued on the next page. (5 points each)

_____ 1. The people who encounter the old man with wings all seem to be strangely lacking in
      a. curiosity.        c. hope.
      b. compassion.    d. religious faith.

_____ 2. What does the parish priest do when he encounters the old man?
      a. He attempts to make the old man more comfortable.
      b. He suggests that the man should take charge of the universe.
      c. He warns people that the old man may be a devil.
      d. He explains the pope's position on such creatures.

_____ 3. What do the "most unfortunate invalids on earth" who come in search of health have in common?
  a. Their ailments are absurd.
  b. They cannot stand noise.
  c. They try to feed the old man.
  d. They are patient.

_____ 4. After Elisenda gets a comfortable new house, how does she feel toward the old man with wings?
  a. grateful          c. caring
  b. frightened        d. annoyed

**C. Words to Know.** Write the letter of the best answer. (4 points each)

_____ 1. A <u>magnanimous</u> act springs from
  a. generosity.       b. contempt.        c. courage.

_____ 2. Someone who makes a <u>conjecture</u> is
  a. fooling.          b. preaching.       c. guessing.

_____ 3. If something is <u>dispersed</u>, it is
  a. given away.       b. scattered.       c. consumed.

_____ 4. When things <u>proliferate</u>, they
  a. collapse.         b. multiply.        c. burst.

_____ 5. An <u>ungainly</u> animal is
  a. timid.            b. wild.            c. clumsy.

**D.** Answer **one** of the following questions based on your understanding of the selection. Write your answer on a separate sheet of paper. (20 points)

  1. Wings are often used in literature and art as a symbol for freedom. Do the old man's enormous wings represent freedom in this story? Explain.

  2. What effect does the old man with wings have on the lives of Elisenda and Pelayo, Father Gonzaga, and other people who come to see him?

**E. Linking Literature to Life.** Answer the following question based on your own experience and knowledge. Write your answer on a separate sheet of paper. (16 points)

  Imagine encountering a very old man with enormous wings near your home. He is ailing and cannot speak your language. What would you do? How would your family and your neighbors probably react?

# Unit Five: A World of Mysteries

# Part Two Open-Book Test

**A.** Write the letter of the best answer to each question. (5 points each)

_____ 1. In "The Open Window," Vera convinced Mr. Nuttel that
    a. she was a ghost.
    b. Mrs. Sappleton's husband and brothers were dead.
    c. the spaniel would attack him because he was a stranger.
    d. Mrs. Sappleton was insane.

_____ 2. In the mysterious phone call in *Sorry, Right Number,* whose voice did Katie hear on the phone?
    a. Polly's             c. her mother's
    b. Dawn's            d. her own

_____ 3. What element of "In the Family" is left unexplained?
    a. how the narrator felt about Clara
    b. who the people in the mirror were
    c. how the people appeared in the mirror
    d. what the narrator and Clara had in common

_____ 4. Which word best describes the tone of "A Very Old Man with Enormous Wings"?
    a. ironic            c. complaining
    b. threatening     d. sympathetic

**B.** Think about the new or unusual experiences that the characters in these selections have. On the line below, write the title of **one** selection and a character you wish to discuss. In the box on the left, describe the new or unusual experience the character has. In the box on the right, explain whether the experience was positive, negative, or mixed, and why. (20 points)

**Selection and Character:** _____

| New or Unusual Experience | Was this experience positive, negative, or mixed? Why? |
|---|---|
| | |

**C.** Answer **two** of the following essay questions based on your understanding of the selections. Write your answers on a separate sheet of paper. (20 points each)

1. Choose **one** character from these selections who came to see or understand something in a new way. Explain what changed and what caused that change in his or her understanding.

2. Several selections in this part involve events that go beyond the limits of credibility. In which selection did you think the events were most believable, and in which selection did you think they were least believable? Describe the events and why you think they were believable or not.

3. Many of these selections concern images or views of death and how it affects the characters who remain after someone dies. Choose **one** of these selections. Describe the image or view of death in the selection and how it affects the characters who remain.

**D.** Several of these selections blend elements of illusion with elements of reality to communicate an important message or theme. In the boxes below, write the title of **one** selection you wish to discuss. Then write notes describing elements of reality and elements of illusion in the selection, and what theme or message the selection conveys. (20 points)

| Title: | | |
|---|---|---|
| **Elements of Reality** | **Elements of Illusion** | **Theme or Message** |
| | | |

# Book 9 *from the* Odyssey (page 893)

## Selection Test

**A.** Think about Odysseus as an epic hero. Actions taken by Odysseus are noted in the boxes on the left. For each action, make a mark in a small box to show whether you think that action is more like that of an epic hero or of an ordinary man. In each box on the right, jot down a reason for your opinion. (6 points each)

| | | |
|---|---|---|
| 1. Odysseus leads his men away from the land of the Lotus Eaters. | ☐ epic hero <br> ☐ ordinary man | |
| 2. Odysseus leads his men into Polyphemus' cave. | ☐ epic hero <br> ☐ ordinary man | |
| 3. Odysseus blinds Polyphemus. | ☐ epic hero <br> ☐ ordinary man | |
| 4. Odysseus gets his men out of Polyphemus' cave. | ☐ epic hero <br> ☐ ordinary man | |
| 5. Odysseus informs Polyphemus that he and his men have escaped. | ☐ epic hero <br> ☐ ordinary man | |

**B.** Write the letter of the best answer. This exercise is continued on the next page. (5 points each)

_____ 1. What is Odysseus' destination?
   a. home
   b. the land of the Cyclopes
   c. Olympus, where the gods live
   d. Troy, where the Trojan war is taking place

_____ 2. According to Odysseus, he is famous for being
   a. witty.                 c. kind and caring.
   b. cunning.               d. honest and straightforward.

_____ 3. Odysseus' **greatest** fear is that the Lotus will make his men
   a. ill.                   c. moody.
   b. sleepy.                d. content.

_____ 4. Which of the following **best** describes Polyphemus' attitude toward Zeus?
a. fearful          b. devoted          c. scornful          d. unconcerned

_____ 5. Which of the following helps Odysseus to defeat Polyphemus?
a. calling on the god Poseidon
b. telling Polyphemus that his name is Nohbdy
c. offering Polyphemus' prize ram as a sacrifice to Zeus
d. leaving men behind when he goes to Polyphemus' cave

_____ 6. Why, despite the wizard's prediction, is Polyphemus surprised by Odysseus?
a. Odysseus arrived earlier than he expected.
b. Odysseus was supposed to have come alone.
c. Odysseus is far more powerful than he expected.
d. Odysseus is a much smaller man than he expected.

**C. Words to Know.** Write the letter of the best answer. (4 points each)

_____ 1. What is your adversary in a volleyball game?
a. the net          b. your team          c. the other team

_____ 2. Which of the following is ponderous?
a. a scholar          b. a chandelier          c. a hippopotamus

_____ 3. What do you make when you entreat someone?
a. a request          b. an accusation          c. an agreement

_____ 4. When a person disdains help, what does he or she do?
a. offers it          b. rejects it          c. begs for it

_____ 5. Which expression does an indifferent person use?
a. "No way!"          b. "So what?"          c. "Beats me!"

**D.** Answer **one** of the following questions based on your understanding of the epic poem. Write your answer on a separate sheet of paper. (10 points)

1. What is the mood of Odysseus and his men at the end of this excerpt from the *Odyssey*? What are some reasons that they feel the way they do?

2. What can you infer from Book 9 about the civilization of the Cyclopes? What can you infer about ancient Greek civilization? Explain your ideas.

**E. Linking Literature to Life.** Answer the following question based on your own experience and knowledge. Write your answer on a separate sheet of paper. (10 points)

What, in your opinion, are the main characteristics of an effective leader? Explain your ideas.

# Book 10 *from the* Odyssey (page 916)

# Selection Test

**A.** Read the description below of Odysseus' return to his men. Then, in each box on the right, write notes about a technique used in the passage to bring the scene to life, or jot down a vivid sensory detail from the passage. (30 points)

"So I went down to the sea beach and the ship,
where I found all my other men on board,
weeping, in despair along the benches.
Sometimes in farmyards when the cows return
well-fed from pasture to the barn, one sees
the pens give way before the calves in tumult,
breaking through to cluster about their mothers,
bumping together, bawling. Just that way
my crew poured round me when they saw me come
—their faces wet with tears as if they saw
their homeland, and the crags of Ithaca,
even the very town where they were born."

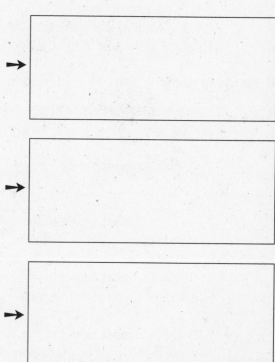

**B.** Write the letter of the best answer. This exercise is continued on the next page. (4 points each)

_____ 1. Eurylochus believes that Odysseus' behavior in the land of the
Cyclopes was
a. heroic.
b. comical.
c. reckless.
d. irritating but understandable.

_____ 2. Odysseus becomes angry with Eurylochus for
a. wanting to go home.
b. disobeying his orders.
c. questioning his judgment.
d. expecting him to be perfect.

_____ 3. What prevents Circe from turning Odysseus into a pig?
a. magic
b. his virtue
c. his reputation
d. her conscience

_____ 4. Circe encourages Odysseus to forget about all of the following **except** his
     a. duty.       b. goals.       c. values.       d. pleasure.

_____ 5. Where does Circe send Odysseus when he leaves her house?
     a. to his home
     b. to the land of Death
     c. to Olympus, where the gods live
     d. back to the land of the Cyclopes

## C. Words to Know. Write the letter of the best answer. (4 points each)

_____ 1. One would **most** expect to see people moving with <u>stealth</u> during a
     a. parade.       b. burglary.       c. marathon.

_____ 2. One would **most** expect a <u>regaled</u> audience to
     a. boo.       b. yawn.       c. laugh.

_____ 3. One would **most** expect to see <u>contenders</u> at a
     a. barbecue.       b. boxing match.       c. birthday party.

_____ 4. One would **most** expect to see <u>disconsolate</u> people at a
     a. funeral.       b. reunion.       c. wedding.

_____ 5. One would **most** expect to see <u>vile</u> people in a
     a. spy thriller.       b. home video.       c. romantic comedy.

**D.** Answer **one** of the following questions based on your understanding of the epic poem. Write your answer on a separate sheet of paper. (15 points)

1. Although Odysseus and his men are eager to get home, they spend an entire year on Circe's island. What accounts for their remaining so long? Is Odysseus at fault for staying so long with Circe? Support your answers with reference to Book 10.

2. Evaluate Odysseus' behavior in this episode of his journey. What, if any, alternatives exist for Odysseus in this episode?

**E. Linking Literature to Life.** Answer the following question based on your own experience and knowledge. Write your answer on a separate sheet of paper. (15 points)

What are some things that you think are within the power of human beings to control, and what are some things that are outside of their power? Identify at least **four** things and explain why they can or cannot be controlled by people.

# Book 12 *from* the Odyssey (page 928)

# Selection Test

**A.** Read the quotations and think about the themes they convey. Then, in the boxes below, note two themes from the *Odyssey* that each quotation supports. (20 points each)

So [Circe's] advice ran; but I faced her, saying: "Only instruct me, goddess, if you will, how, if possible, can I pass Charybdis, or fight off Scylla when she raids my crew?" Swiftly that loveliest goddess answered me: "Must you have battle in your heart forever? The bloody toil of combat? Old contender, will you not yield to the immortal gods? That nightmare cannot die, being eternal evil itself— horror, and pain, and chaos; there is no fighting her, no power can fight her, all that avails is flight."

But as I sent them on toward Scylla, I told them nothing, as they could do nothing. They would have dropped their oars again, in panic, to roll for cover under the decking. Circe's bidding against arms had slipped my mind, so I tied on my cuirass and took up two heavy spears, then made my way along to the foredeck—thinking to see her first from there, the monster of the gray rock, harboring torment for my friends. I strained my eyes upon that cliffside veiled in cloud, but nowhere could I catch sight of her . . .

Then Scylla made her strike, whisking six of my best men from the ship.

**1. What themes are emphasized or supported?**

**2. What themes are emphasized or supported?**

|  |  |
|---|---|
|  |  |
|  |  |

**B.** Write the letter of the best answer. This exercise is continued on the next page. (5 points each)

_____ 1. Circe helps Odysseus by
   a. planning his future.
   b. changing the future.
   c. revealing dangers that lay ahead.
   d. protecting him against all dangers.

_____ 2. By not plugging his own ears with wax when Odysseus sails past the Sirens, Odysseus
    a. disobeys Circe.
    b. knowingly takes a risk.
    c. takes the safest course of action.
    d. brings doom and destruction on his men.

_____ 3. Odysseus is told to sail closer to Scylla than to Charybdis so that
    a. no harm will come to Odysseus' men.
    b. Odysseus will not be harmed.
    c. harm will come to fewer of Odysseus' men.
    d. Odysseus won't be tempted to fight against fate.

_____ 4. As they approach Charybdis and Scylla, Odysseus keeps the terrified men going by
    a. begging them.
    b. threatening them.
    c. encouraging them.
    d. making fun of them.

**C. Words to Know.** Write the letter of the best answer. (4 points each)

_____ 1. If you enjoy peril, the **best** job for you would be that of a
    a. farmer.          b. comedian.          c. stunt pilot.

_____ 2. If your allowance dwindles, it
    a. gets bigger.     b. gets smaller.      c. stays the same.

_____ 3. If someone treats you abominably, you are most likely to feel
    a. hurt.            b. hopeful.           c. honored.

_____ 4. If you feel anguish, you might
    a. brag.            b. moan.              c. giggle.

_____ 5. If you had to report on a person who became famous for questing activities, the **best** choice would be
    a. Albert Einstein.    b. Susan B. Anthony.    c. Christopher Columbus.

**D.** Answer the following question based on your understanding of the epic poem. Write your answer on a separate sheet of paper. (10 points)

How important do you think Circe's role is in determining Odysseus' fate? Use details from Book 12 to support your answer.

**E. Linking Literature to Life.** Answer the following question based on your own experience and knowledge. Write your answer on a separate sheet of paper. (10 points)

What kinds of factors do you think are most important in determining what a person's future will hold? Explain your ideas.

# Books 21, 22, and 23 *from the* Odyssey (page 941)

# Selection Test

**A.** For each quotation from the *Odyssey*, identify a character and note one trait that is revealed about him or her. Then make a mark in the small box next to each characterization technique that is used in the quotation. (8 points each)

| | Who and What | How |
|---|---|---|
| 1. "Now Penelope sank down, holding the weapon on her knees, and drew her husband's great bow out, and sobbed and bit her lip and let the salt tears flow. Then back she went to face the crowded hall, tremendous bow in hand, and on her shoulder hung the quiver spiked with coughing death." | | ☐ Physical description<br>☐ Character's speech, thoughts, feelings, or actions<br>☐ Speech, thoughts, feelings, or actions of other characters<br>☐ Direct comments about the character |
| 2. "That was the way he played it, hoping inwardly to span the great horn bow with corded gut and drill the iron with his shot—he, Antinous, destined to be the first of all to savor blood from a biting arrow at his throat, a shaft drawn by the fingers of Odysseus whom he had mocked and plundered, leading on the rest, his boon companions." | | ☐ Physical description<br>☐ Character's speech, thoughts, feelings, or actions<br>☐ Speech, thoughts, feelings, or actions of other characters<br>☐ Direct comments about the character |
| 3. "'Strange woman, the immortals of Olympus made you hard, harder than any. Who else in the world would keep aloof as you do from her husband if he returned to her from years of trouble, cast on his own land in the twentieth year? Nurse, make up a bed for me to sleep on. Her heart is iron in her breast.'" | | ☐ Physical description<br>☐ Character's speech, thoughts, feelings, or actions<br>☐ Speech, thoughts, feelings, or actions of other characters<br>☐ Direct comments about the character |
| 4. "Now from his breast into his eyes the ache of longing mounted, and he wept at last, his dear wife, clear and faithful, in his arms, longed for as the sun-warmed earth is longed for by a swimmer spent in rough water where his ship went down under Poseidon's blows, gale winds and tons of sea." | | ☐ Physical description<br>☐ Character's speech, thoughts, feelings, or actions<br>☐ Speech, thoughts, feelings, or actions of other characters<br>☐ Direct comments about the character |

**B.** Write the letter of the best answer. This exercise is continued on the next page. (6 points each)

_____  1. The **main** reason that the suitors and servants don't recognize Odysseus
when he first appears is that
a. he has disguised himself.
b. he has aged 20 years.
c. he is wearing armor and a helmet.
d. Athena has made him beautiful and taller.

_____ 2. In the struggle between Odysseus and the suitors, Odysseus refuses to do all of the following **except**

    a. forgive.            c. show mercy.

    b. take aid.          d. strike a bargain.

_____ 3. In the struggle between Odysseus and the suitors, the gods appear to

    a. remain neutral.

    b. take Odysseus' side.

    c. take the suitors' side.

    d. swing their support back and forth between the two.

_____ 4. Which of the following causes Penelope to accept Odysseus as her true husband?

    a. Zeus' thunderbolt

    b. Odysseus' stringing the bow

    c. Odysseus' knowing that their bed cannot be moved

    d. the goddess Athena's making Odysseus look like his younger self

**C. Words to Know.** Write the letter of the best answer. (4 points each)

_____ 1. Another word for a throng is a

    a. mob.         b. barb.         c. sandal.

_____ 2. Children tend to be implacable when they are having a

    a. nap.         b. party.         c. tantrum.

_____ 3. Students who were in a frenzy would probably be told to

    a. speak up.         b. settle down.         c. check their work.

_____ 4. The wiliest animal in a children's story is often a

    a. fox.         b. lamb.         c. chicken.

_____ 5. Which is **most** likely to be considered an omen?

    a. a song         b. a skyscraper         c. a clap of thunder

**D.** Answer the following question based on your understanding of the epic poem. Write your answer on a separate sheet of paper. (12 points)

    Why does Odysseus feel justified in killing the suitors? Do you think he is justified? Use details from the epic poem to support your answers.

**E. Linking Literature to Life.** Answer the following question based on your own experience and knowledge. Write your answer on a separate sheet of paper. (12 points)

    If you were married to someone who left for 20 years, how do you think you would respond to his or her homecoming? Why?

# Unit Six: The Classic Tradition

# Part One Open-Book Test

**A.** Write the answer to each question on the lines. (5 points each)

1. In Book 9 of the *Odyssey,* why didn't Odysseus try to kill Polyphemus when the Cyclops killed and ate two of his men?

_____

_____

2. In Book 10, why did Eurylochus criticize Odysseus for deciding to stay on Circe's island?

_____

_____

3. In Book 12, what do the Sirens symbolize?

_____

_____

4. In Book 23, why was Penelope suspicious of Odysseus?

_____

_____

**B.** Think about the victories and defeats that Odysseus experienced during his wanderings. For each of the three events listed below, tell whether Odysseus won or lost the encounter. In the boxes on the right, explain why you think he won or lost. (20 points)

| Events: Win or Loss? | Why You Think He Won or Lost |
| --- | --- |
| 1. Polyphemus (the Cyclops) | |
| 2. The Sirens | |
| 3. Scylla and Charybdis | |

Name _____ Date _____

**C.** Answer **two** of the following essay questions based on your understanding of the *Odyssey*. Write your answers on a separate sheet of paper. (20 points each)

1. In your opinion, in which adventure does Odysseus shows his best qualities, and in which does he show his worst qualities? Use details from the selections to support your opinions.

2. Based on your understanding of the tale of Odysseus, identify at least **three** values that seem to have been important to the Greeks of Homer's time. Use details from the selections to support your ideas.

3. Identify **two** things that you would have done differently if you were Odysseus. Explain what you would have done differently, how you would have done it, and why you would have done it that way.

4. In your opinion, is Penelope an epic hero just as Odysseus is? Support your opinion with reference to the selections and to your own ideas about heroism.

**D.** Think about Odysseus as an epic hero. He displays some of the virtues or qualities that were honored in ancient Greek society, but he also displays human faults. In each box on the left, note a quality that Odysseus has and whether it is a virtue or a fault. For each quality, write notes in the box on the right describing something he does to display that virtue or fault. (20 points)

| Quality: Virtue or Fault? | How Odysseus Displays This Quality |
|---|---|
| **1.** | |
| **2.** | |
| **3.** | |

# The Tragedy of Romeo and Juliet: Act One (page 989)

# Selection Open-Book Test

**A.** Think about the conflicts that are established in Act One. Read the lines from different scenes in the boxes below. For each scene, describe the conflict or conflicts established in the scene and the main characters involved in the conflict. (10 points each)

| Scene | Conflict(s) | Characters Involved |
|---|---|---|
| **Scene 1**<br>**Tybalt.** I hate the word / As I hate hell, all Montagues, and thee. / Have at thee, coward!" | | |
| **Scene 3**<br>**Lady Capulet.** Well, think of marriage now. Younger than you, / Here in Verona, ladies of esteem, / Are made already mothers. | | |
| **Scene 5**<br>**Romeo.** Is she a Capulet? / O dear account! my life is my foe's debt. | | |

**B.** Write the letter of the best answer. This exercise is continued on the next page. (8 points each)

_____ 1. At the beginning of the play, Romeo's parents are worried about him because he
    a. is too friendly with their enemies.
    b. has involved himself with rowdy friends.
    c. seems unaccountably sad and gloomy.
    d. is too hot-tempered and quick to anger.

_____ 2. Benvolio encourages Romeo to go to the Capulet party to
    a. enjoy the company of Rosaline.
    b. see what they can get away with for sport.
    c. challenge Tybalt and other enemies.
    d. compare Rosaline with other young ladies.

_____ 3. Romeo's dream in Scene 4 foreshadows that
   a. tragic consequences will result from attending the ball.
   b. Rosaline will return Romeo's affections at the ball.
   c. Romeo's parents will punish him for attending the ball.
   d. the queen of the fairies will protect Romeo and Mercutio at the ball.

_____ 4. How does Capulet react when Tybalt first tells him that Romeo, the son
   of his enemy, has come to the party uninvited?
   a. He shakes with anger.
   b. He tells Tybalt to ignore Romeo.
   c. He doubts that it is true.
   d. He plots Romeo's downfall.

_____ 5. Judging from his behavior at the party, you can predict that Tybalt will
   a. seek revenge against the Montagues.
   b. tell Lady Capulet about Romeo as soon as possible.
   c. become more tolerant of the Montagues.
   d. question his own loyalty to Capulet.

**C.** Answer **one** of the following questions based on your understanding of the selection. Write your answer on a separate sheet of paper. (20 points)

1. Describe the reactions of Juliet's father and mother when Paris proposes marriage to their daughter. How are their opinions the same, and how are they different?

2. Describe the personalities of Romeo and Juliet as they have been presented so far. In what ways are they similar? In what ways are they different?

**D. Linking Literature to Life.** Answer the following question based on your own experience and knowledge. Write your answer on a separate sheet of paper. (10 points)

Do you believe that love at first sight is genuine love? Why or why not?

# The Tragedy of Romeo and Juliet: Act Two (page 1020)

# Selection Open-Book Test

**A.** Think about each soliloquy or aside listed below. What important information does the audience learn? In the box on the right, make notes that describe what the character reveals to the audience. (8 points each)

| Soliloquy or Aside | What Is Revealed |
|---|---|
| 1. Romeo's soliloquy in Scene 2, beginning with, "But soft! What light through yonder window breaks?" and ending with, "O that I were a glove upon that hand, / That I might touch that cheek!" | |
| 2. Juliet's soliloquy in Scene 2, beginning with, "O Romeo, Romeo! wherefore art thou Romeo?" and ending with, "Romeo, doff thy name; / And for that name, which is no part of thee, / Take all myself." | |
| 3. Romeo's aside after the first four lines of Juliet's soliloquy: "Shall I hear more, or shall I speak at this?" | |
| 4. Friar Laurence's soliloquy at the beginning of Scene 3: "The grey-eyed morn smiles . . ." | |

**B.** Write the letter of the best answer. This exercise is continued on the next page.
(6 points each)

_____ 1. Juliet's soliloquy on the balcony (Scene 2) is unlike most soliloquies because
     a. she is alone.
     b. another character overhears her and responds.
     c. it reveals thoughts she meant to keep private.
     d. she is expressing concern and worry.

_____ 2. When Romeo and Friar Laurence begin to talk, it is evident that Romeo
   a. had once planned to become a friar himself.
   b. is trying to hide his real purpose.
   c. seeks advice from the friar.
   d. has spoken with the friar before about Rosaline.

_____ 3. Mercutio is **best** described as a man of
   a. kindness.              c. sharp wit.
   b. moodiness.             d. good sense.

_____ 4. Mercutio realizes that Romeo has cast off his gloomy mood when
   a. Romeo stays away from home all night.
   b. Romeo engages in lively word play with him.
   c. Juliet's nurse arrives seeking Romeo.
   d. Romeo says that "his business was great."

_____ 5. Which sentence **best** describes the nurse?
   a. She is foolish but loyal.
   b. She is warm and comforting.
   c. She has a clever, witty tongue.
   d. She is haughty and arrogant.

**C.** Answer **one** of the following questions based on your understanding of the selection. Write your answer on a separate sheet of paper. (20 points)

1. Compare the roles of Juliet's nurse and Friar Laurence. In what ways are they similar?

2. In what sense is the nurse a foil for Juliet? Describe the ways in which her behavior helps to highlight Juliet's qualities.

**D. Linking Literature to Life.** Answer the following question based on your own experience and knowledge. Write your answer on a separate sheet of paper. (18 points)

If you were a friend to Romeo and Juliet, what advice would you give them about their hasty plan to marry? Explain.

# The Tragedy of Romeo and Juliet: Act Three (page 1044)

# Selection Open-Book Test

**A.** Each passage below contains an allusion to something outside the play. For each passage, write notes explaining what the allusion means and what the speaker suggests by using it. (10 points each)

|  | **What the Allusion Means** | **What It Suggests** |
|---|---|---|
| **Scene 1 (lines 80–81)**<br>**Mercutio.** Good King of Cats, nothing but one of your nine lives. |  |  |
| **Scene 2 (lines 1–4)**<br>**Juliet.** Gallop apace, you fiery-footed steeds, / Toward Phoebus' lodging! Such a wagoner / As Phaëton would whip you to the West, / And bring in cloudy night immediately. |  |  |
| **Scene 5 (lines 19–20)**<br>**Romeo.** I'll say yon grey is not the morning's eye, / 'Tis but the pale reflex of Cynthia's brow. |  |  |

**B.** Write the letter of the best answer. This exercise is continued on the next page. (6 points each)

_____ 1. What is the irony in the encounter between Tybalt and Romeo in Scene 1?
  a. Romeo knows that Tybalt is now his kinsman but Tybalt does not.
  b. Tybalt's anger toward Romeo is a case of mistaken identity.
  c. Romeo does not know about Tybalt's letter to him proposing a duel.
  d. Tybalt is not really intending to harm Romeo.

_____ 2. After Tybalt's death, when Juliet cries, "O Serpent heart, hid with a flow'ring face!" she is implying that
  a. Tybalt, though handsome, was like a serpent.
  b. Romeo was right to have killed the deceitful Tybalt.
  c. her own heart is like a serpent's.
  d. Romeo's seeming goodness has deceived her.

_____ 3. Both Juliet and Romeo react to the news of Romeo's banishment
by saying that
a. it is unfair.
b. he will soon be allowed to return.
c. it is no better than death.
d. they will go away together.

_____ 4. What will happen if Juliet refuses to marry Paris?
a. Everyone will learn about her secret marriage.
b. The houses of Montague and Capulet will fight again.
c. Juliet will be scorned by her friends.
d. Juliet's father will disown her.

_____ 5. How does Juliet react to the nurse's advice at the end of Act Three
regarding marriage to Paris?
a  She feels comforted and will go to confession.
b. She is furious and will no longer trust the nurse.
c. She is grateful for the advice but unconvinced.
d. She wishes she had married Paris, not Romeo.

**C.** Answer **one** of the following questions based on your understanding of the selection.
Write your answer on a separate sheet of paper. (20 points)

1. When Capulet first spoke with Paris in Act One, he said that Juliet was still too young
to wed. How has his attitude changed? How does he react when Juliet refuses to
wed Paris?

2. Compare and contrast Juliet's feelings toward Romeo immediately after she hears
he has killed Tybalt, and after she has had a few moments to reflect. Why does she
have mixed reactions?

**D. Linking Literature to Life.** Answer the following question based on your own
experience and knowledge. Write your answer on a separate sheet of paper. (20 points)

Think about the concepts of honor and revenge. Is it right to repay violence with
violence? In your answer, discuss whether killing Tybalt after Mercutio's death was an
honorable thing for Romeo to do. What other options did he have?

# The Tragedy of Romeo and Juliet: Act Four (page 1072)

# Selection Open-Book Test

**A.** Think about the uses of comic relief in Act Four. In each box on the left, write notes explaining what happened in the scene just before the comic relief and what the mood of that scene was. In each box on the right, describe what happens in the scene of comic relief and what mood it creates. (10 points each)

| What Happened Before/Mood | Scene of Comic Relief | What Happens in This Scene/Mood |
|---|---|---|
| **1.** | Scene 2: Juliet returns from the friar and promises to marry Paris. | |
| **2.** | Scene 4: The cooking scene | |
| **3.** | Scene 5: The musicians | |

**B.** Write the letter of the best answer. This exercise is continued on the next page. (6 points each)

_____ 1. In Act Four, Juliet's major goal is to
   a. repent her wrongdoing.   c. run away from home.
   b. deceive her family.   d. avoid marriage to Paris.

_____ 2. Which lines spoken by Juliet foreshadow the course of action that Friar Laurence proposes?
   a. "That is no slander, sir, which is a truth;
      And what I spake, I spake it to my face."
   b. "Or walk in thievish ways, or bid me lurk
      Where serpents are; chain me with roaring bears."
   c. "Or bid me go into a new-made grave
      And hide me with a dead man in his shroud"
   d. "Where I have learnt me to repent the sin
      Of disobedient opposition"

_____ 3. Juliet fears that if she wakes too early in the tomb, she will
  a. go insane.     c. have to marry Paris.
  b. frighten other people.  d. be disowned by her father.

_____ 4. What happens when the nurse finds Juliet on her bed?
  a. A search begins for her killer.
  b. Her parents regret their unkind words to her.
  c. Wedding plans become funeral plans.
  d. Friar Laurence sends word of her death to Romeo.

_____ 5. There is irony in Friar Laurence's consoling words about Juliet's death
  because he
  a. has never been a parent.
  b. knows she is actually alive.
  c. has never been married.
  d. caused her death.

**C.** Answer **one** of the following questions based on your understanding of the selection. Write your answer on a separate sheet of paper. (20 points)

1. What led Juliet's parents to believe that she was grieving for Tybalt's death too "immoderately"? How did this misunderstanding make Juliet's situation even worse?

2. Why does Friar Laurence want to help Juliet avoid marriage with Paris? What plan does he propose?

**D. Linking Literature to Life.** Answer the following question based on your own experience and knowledge. Write your answer on a separate sheet of paper. (20 points)

Why is keeping a secret often a very difficult thing to do? Do you think it's true that one lie often leads to another? Use examples from Act Four to help explain your views.

# The Tragedy of Romeo and Juliet: Act Five (page 1087)

# Selection Open-Book Test

**A.** Think about the events that bring Romeo and Juliet to a tragic end. Some of these events are brought about by Romeo's character flaw—his excessive emotion. Others are caused by outside factors, particularly the feud between the families. In the chart below, note two important events that resulted from Romeo's character flaw and two important events that resulted from the family feud. (15 points each)

| 1. Events Brought About by Romeo's Excessive Emotion | 2. Events Caused by the Family Feud |
|---|---|
|  |  |
|  |  |

**B.** Write the letter of the best answer. This exercise in continued on the next page. (6 points each)

_____ 1. Romeo goes to the Apothecary to
   a. get medicine for Juliet.
   b. buy poison to kill himself.
   c. get drugs to help him sleep.
   d. buy poison for both Juliet and himself.

_____ 2. What does Romeo mean when he says that he has sold the Apothecary poison?
   a. He is joking to relieve the tension of the illegal transaction.
   b. He has caused the Apothecary to do something illegal and thus has harmed him.
   c. He will tell a lie to keep the Apothecary out of legal trouble.
   d. The gold he pays the Apothecary is the cause of more men's undoing than poisons.

_____ 3. Why does Friar Laurence's plan fail?
      a. Juliet wakes too soon.
      b. Romeo does not receive the friar's letter.
      c. Paris arrives and discovers the plot.
      d. Romeo's servant hides in the churchyard.

_____ 4. Paris goes to the graveyard to
      a. put flowers on Juliet's grave.
      b. find Romeo.
      c. see whether Juliet is really dead.
      d. commit suicide.

_____ 5. In the end, the Prince declares that for Montague and Capulet, as well as for himself, the deaths of that night
      a. are evil omens.
      b. will bring a happier future.
      c. are a deserved punishment.
      d. must be avenged.

**C.** Answer **one** of the following questions based on your understanding of the selection. Write your answer on a separate sheet of paper. (20 points)

1. Which three characters from the play lie dead in the vault with Juliet? Identify each one and explain his relationship to the Capulet/Montague feud.

2. What lessons can the story of Romeo and Juliet teach? Think of at least three themes, or lessons, suggested by this play.

**D. Linking Literature to Life.** Answer the following question based on your own experience and knowledge. Write your answer on a separate sheet of paper. (20 points)

    Imagine that you are writing a Romeo and Juliet story that takes place in our time. What would the setting be? Which two opposing groups would the "star-crossed" lovers represent? Explain your choices.

# Unit Six: The Classic Tradition

## Part Two Open-Book Test

**A.** Write the letter of the best answer to each question. (5 points each)

_____ 1. In Act One of *The Tragedy of Romeo and Juliet,* which character is a foil for Romeo?
a. Rosaline    c. Juliet
b. Paris    d. Mercutio

_____ 2. In Act Three, Romeo is banished for
a. the murder of Mercutio.    c. taking Juliet from Paris.
b. killing Tybalt.    d. marrying Juliet.

_____ 3. In Act Four, Friar Laurence tries to help Romeo and Juliet by
a. telling Capulet that Paris is not worthy of Juliet.
b. sending Juliet to Mantua to meet Romeo.
c. faking Juliet's death.
d. giving poison to Paris.

_____ 4. Why were Romeo and Juliet described as "star-crossed" lovers?
a. They were too young to consider marriage.
b. The plague was threatening everyone in Verona.
c. Paris was determined to come between them.
d. Circumstances doomed them to a tragic end.

**B.** Many of the events in this play are foreshadowed by things that happen earlier. For each example below, write notes describing what event it foreshadows and what actually happens. (20 points)

| Example | What It Foreshadows | What Actually Happens |
|---|---|---|
| 1. Act One: Tybalt vows to kill Romeo. | | |
| 2. Act Two: Friar Laurence collects herbs that can be either healthful or poisonous. | | |
| 3. Act Four: Juliet tells Friar Laurence that, if he cannot help her stay married to Romeo, she will kill herself. | | |

**C.** Answer **two** of the following essay questions based on your understanding of the selections. Write your answers on a separate sheet of paper. (20 points each)

1. Think about Friar Laurence's actions in this play and his position as a man of the church. Describe what he does for Romeo and Juliet and explain whether or not you think he was right to do what he did.

2. Choose **one** of the women in this play—other than Juliet. Describe what kind of person she is, what role she plays, and how her actions affect Romeo and Juliet.

3. Think about the causes that led to Romeo and Juliet's tragic end. Explain what the causes were. Then decide who or what you think was most responsible for what happened to Romeo and Juliet and explain why.

**D.** One of the major themes of *The Tragedy of Romeo and Juliet* is that fate—rather than our own actions—determines the course of life. Choose three events from the play that you think contributed to the tragic plot. Then tell whether each event was caused by fate or by a character's actions, and write notes explaining in what ways this was so. (20 points)

| Event | Fate/Character's Actions? |
|---|---|
| | |
| | |
| | |

# End-of-Year Test

**Directions:** Read the selection below. Then answer the questions that follow.

### The Wife's Story
*Ursula K. Le Guin*

He was a good husband, a good father. I don't understand it. I don't believe in it. I don't believe that it happened. I saw it happen but it isn't true. It can't be. He was always gentle. If you'd have seen him playing with the children, anybody who saw him with the children would have known that there wasn't any bad in him, not one mean bone. When I first met him he was still living with his mother, over near Spring Lake, and I used to see them together, the mother and the sons, and think that any young fellow that was that nice with his family must be one worth knowing. Then one time when I was walking in the woods I met him by himself coming back from a hunting trip. He hadn't got any game at all, not so much as a field mouse, but he wasn't cast down about it. He was just larking along enjoying the morning air. That's one of the things I first loved about him. He didn't take things hard, he didn't grouch and whine when things didn't go his way. So we got to talking that day. And I guess things moved right along after that, because pretty soon he was over here pretty near all the time. And my sister said—see, my parents had moved out the year before and gone south, leaving us the place—my sister said, kind of teasing but serious, "Well! If he's going to be here every day and half the night, I guess there isn't room for me!" And she moved out—just down the way. We've always been real close, her and me. That's the sort of thing doesn't ever change. I couldn't ever have got through this bad time without my sis.

Well, so he come to live here. And all I can say is, it was the happy year of my life. He was just purely good to me. A hard worker and never lazy, and so big and fine-looking. Everybody looked up to him, you know, young as he was. Lodge[1] Meeting nights, more and more often they had him to lead the singing. He had such a beautiful voice, and he'd lead off strong, and the others following and joining in, high voices and low. It brings the shivers on me now to think of it, hearing it, nights when I'd stayed home from meeting when the children was babies—the singing coming up through the trees there, and the moonlight, summer nights, the full moon shining. I'll never hear anything so beautiful. I'll never know a joy like that again.

It was the moon, that's what they say. It's the moon's fault, and the blood. It was in his father's blood. I never knew his father, and now I wonder what become of him. He was from up Whitewater way and had no kin around here. I always thought he went back there, but now I don't know. There was some talk about him, tales, that come out after what happened to my husband. It's something runs in the blood, they say, and it may never come out, but if

---

1. **Lodge:** a social organization.

it does, it's the change of the moon that does it. Always it happens in the dark of the moon. When everybody's home and asleep. Something comes over the one that's got the curse in his blood, they say, and he gets up because he can't sleep, and goes out into the glaring sun, and goes off all alone—drawn to find those like him.

And it may be so, because my husband would do that. I'd half rouse and say, "Where you going to?" and he'd say, "Oh, hunting, be back this evening," and it wasn't like him, even his voice was different. But I'd be so sleepy, and not wanting to wake the kids, and he was so good and responsible, it was no call of mine to go asking "Why?" and "Where?" and all like that.

So it happened that way maybe three times or four. He'd come back late, and worn out, and pretty near cross for one so sweet-tempered—not wanting to talk about it. I figured everybody got to bust out now and then, and nagging never helped anything. But it did begin to worry me. Not so much that he went, but that he come back so tired and strange. Even, he smelled strange. It made my hair stand up on end. I could not endure it and I said, "What is that—those smells on you? All over you!" And he said, "I don't know," real short, and made like he was sleeping. But he went down when he thought I wasn't noticing, and washed and washed himself. But those smells stayed in his hair, and in our bed, for days.

And then the awful thing. I don't find it easy to tell about this. I want to cry when I have to bring it to my mind. Our youngest, the little one, my baby, she turned from her father. Just overnight. He come in and she got scared-looking, stiff, with her eyes wide, and then she begun to cry and try to hide behind me. She didn't yet talk plain but she was saying over and over, "Make it go away! Make it go away!"

The look in his eyes, just for one moment, when he heard that. That's what I don't want ever to remember. That's what I can't forget. The look in his eyes looking at his own child.

I said to the child, "Shame on you, what's got into you!"—scolding, but keeping her right up close to me at the same time, because I was frightened too. Frightened to shaking.

He looked away then and said something like, "Guess she just waked up dreaming," and passed it off that way. Or tried to. And so did I. And I got real mad with my baby when she kept on acting crazy scared of her own dad. But she couldn't help it and I couldn't change it.

He kept away that whole day. Because he knew, I guess. It was just beginning dark of the moon.

It was hot and close inside, and dark, and we'd all been asleep some while, when something woke me up. He wasn't there beside me. I heard a little stir in the passage, when I listened. So I got up, because I could bear it no longer. I went out into the passage, and it was light there, hard sunlight coming in from the door. And I saw him standing just outside, in the tall grass by the entrance. His head was hanging. Presently he sat down, like he felt weary, and looked down at his feet. I held still, inside, and watched—I didn't know what for.

And I saw what he saw. I saw the changing. In his feet, it was, first. They got long, each foot got longer, stretching out, the toes stretching out and the foot getting long, and fleshy, and white. And no hair on them.

The hair begun to come away all over his body. It was like his hair fried away in the sunlight and was gone. He was white all over, then, like a worm's skin. And he turned his face. It was changing while I looked. It got flatter and flatter, the mouth flat and wide, and the teeth grinning flat and dull, and the nose just a knob of flesh with nostril holes, and the ears gone, and the eyes gone blue—blue, with white rims around the blue—staring at me out of that flat, soft, white face.

He stood up then on two legs.

I saw him, I had to see him, my own dear love, turned into the hateful one.

I couldn't move, but as I crouched there in the passage staring out into the day, I was trembling and shaking with a growl that burst out into a crazy, awful howling. A grief howl and a terror howl and a calling howl. And the others heard it, even sleeping, and woke up.

It stared and peered, that thing my husband had turned into, and shoved its face up to the entrance of our house. I was still bound by mortal fear, but behind me the children had waked up, and the baby was whimpering. The mother anger come into me then, and I snarled and crept forward.

The man thing looked around. It had no gun, like the ones from the man places do. But it picked up a heavy fallen tree branch in its long white foot, and shoved the end of that down into our house, at me. I snapped the end of it in my teeth and started to force my way out, because I knew the man would kill our children if it could. But my sister was already coming. I saw her running at the man with her head low and her mane high and her eyes yellow as the winter sun. It turned on her and raised up that branch to hit her. But I come out of the doorway, mad with the mother anger, and the others all were coming answering my call, the whole pack gathering, there in that blind glare and heat of the sun at noon.

The man looked round at us and yelled out loud, and brandished[2] the branch it held. Then it broke and ran, heading for the cleared fields and plowlands, down the mountainside. It ran, on two legs, leaping and weaving, and we followed it.

2. **brandished:** waved in warning or as a threat.

I was last, because love still bound the anger and the fear in me. I was running when I saw them pull it down. My sister's teeth were in its throat. I got there and it was dead. The others were drawing back from the kill, because of the taste of the blood, and the smell. The younger ones were cowering[3] and some crying, and my sister rubbed her mouth against her forelegs over and over to get rid of the taste. I went up close because I thought if the thing was dead, the spell, the curse, must be done, and my husband could come back—alive, or even dead, if I could only see him, my true love, in his true form, beautiful. But only the dead man lay there white and bloody. We drew back and back from it, and turned and ran, back up into the hills, back to the woods of the shadows and the twilight and the blessed dark.

3. **cowering:** crouching or shrinking down in fear.

**A.** The following items test your understanding of the selection. Circle the letter of the response that best completes the sentence or answers the question.

1. In this story, where did the narrator first meet her husband?
   a. in Whitewater
   b. in the woods
   c. at a picnic
   d. at a Lodge Meeting

2. The narrator says at the beginning that her husband was always
   a. mysterious.
   b. cruel.
   c. strange.
   d. gentle.

3. You can tell from this story that a person who is "larking along" is
   a. happy and carefree.
   b. mean and nasty.
   c. fearful and suspicious.
   d. loving and kind.

4. What was the first change the narrator noticed in her husband?
   a. He began to lose his hair.
   b. He could not stand being near their daughter.
   c. He began to smell different.
   d. He went off by himself several times without explanation.

5. According to the narrator, the kind of change that affected her husband was brought about by
   a. his mother's bloodline.
   b. eating strange foods.
   c. the changes of the moon.
   d. changes in the seasons.

6. How did the narrator's sister help when the husband changed?
   a. She killed him.
   b. She took care of the children.
   c. She moved out of the house.
   d. She talked with the narrator often.

**B.** The following items check your understanding of the way in which the selection is written. Circle the letter of the response that best completes the sentence or answers the question.

7. The first few sentences of this story suggest that
   a. the narrator's husband has divorced her.
   b. something bad has happened.
   c. the narrator's husband was a successful man.
   d. something wonderful will happen soon.

8. The mood of this story is
   a. suspenseful.
   b. lighthearted.
   c. angry.
   d. bitter.

9. What can you infer about the narrator of this story?
   a. She never loved her husband.
   b. She has a new husband.
   c. She never wanted to have children.
   d. She is a wolf.

10. Which of the following is an example of foreshadowing?
    a. The husband always left in the dark of the moon.
    b. The husband returned late and worn out.
    c. The husband led the singing in Lodge Meetings.
    d. The sister moved out.

**C.** The following items check your understanding of the way in which the selection is written. Write your response after each item.

11. What is ironic about the narrator's statement, "Lodge Meeting nights, more and more often they had him to lead the singing"?

    _____

    _____

    _____

12. What did the narrator begin to notice about her husband that caused her to become concerned that something was wrong?

    _____

    _____

    _____

13. How does the narrator's point of view in this story influence how the reader feels about the husband?

    _____

    _____

    _____

**D.** The following items check your ability to analyze and evaluate the selection. Circle the letter of the response that best completes the sentence or answers the question.

14. What happened to the husband as he stood in the sunlight?
    a. He turned into a wolf.
    b. He got lost in the woods.
    c. He changed into a man.
    d. He murdered his wife.

15. Why did the daughter look at her father and say, "Make it go away"?
    a. She did not like his smell.
    b. She wanted her bad dreams to go away.
    c. She did not want to have a father anymore.
    d. She knew he was no longer a wolf.

16. The narrator of this story feels the "mother anger" when
    a. her husband leaves.
    b. her children are in danger.
    c. her husband dies.
    d. her sister attacks her husband.

17. When the husband changes, he and the narrator
    a. decide to go their separate ways.
    b. are forced to leave the pack.
    c. have become natural enemies.
    d. become more affectionate.

**E.** The following items check your ability to analyze and evaluate the selection. Write your response after each item.

18. Why did the narrator view her husband as the "hateful one"?

_____

_____

_____

_____

19. Describe the narrator's tone in this story.

_____

_____

_____

_____

20. What is the theme of this story?

_____

_____

_____

_____

**Writing Exercise**  The following activity is designed to assess your writing ability. The prompt asks you to explain something. Think of your audience as being any reader other than yourself.

When scorers evaluate your writing, they will look for evidence that you can:

- respond directly to the prompt;

- make your writing thoughtful and interesting;

- organize your ideas so that they are clear and easy to follow;

- develop your ideas thoroughly by using appropriate details and precise language;

- stay focused on your purpose for writing by making sure that each sentence you write contributes to your composition as a whole; and

- communicate effectively by using correct spelling, capitalization, punctuation, grammar, usage, and sentence structures.

Prompt: Think about how you reacted to this story when you figured out what had really happened. How did the ending make you feel? Whom did you sympathize with most—the narrator or her husband? Write a personal response essay in which you explain your reactions to the story and your feelings about it.

Use the bottom of the page to organize your ideas. Then write your essay on a separate sheet of paper.

_____

_____

_____

_____

_____

_____

_____

_____

_____

_____

_____

_____

_____

**Revising/Editing**  The purpose of the following exercise is to check your ability
to proofread and revise a piece of writing in order to improve its readability and
presentation of ideas. Read the following paragraph. Then, for each underlined
section, circle the letter of the revision below that most improves the writing.
Or, if the section is best left as it is, circle letter *d.*

    People enjoy reading science fiction and fantasy for many reasons.

I like reading these <u>kinds of storys</u> because <u>it makes</u> me look at the world
              1.                    2.

in a different way. <u>Seeing the world in a way I had not thought of before.</u>
                                        3.

For example, several classic science fiction <u>novels, such</u> as *Brave New World*
                                        4.

and *1984,* show us visions of <u>what their future</u> might be. *Frankenstein* and
                                    5.

*Dr. Jekyll and Mr. Hyde* reflect on what it means to be a human being

and how everyone has many sides to his or her personality. Visions

of what could happen in the future or in <u>a different place gives</u> me
                                              6.

new perspectives on what is happening here and now.

1. a. kind of storys
   b. kinds of story
   c. kinds of stories
   d. Correct as is

2. a. they make
   b. it make
   c. it made
   d. Correct as is

3. a. Seen the world in a way I had not thought
     of before.
   b. Seeing the world in a way I did not think
     of before.
   c. I see the world in a way I had not thought
     of before.
   d. Correct as is

4. a. novels such
   b. novels, like
   c. novel, such
   d. Correct as is

5. a. where their
   b. why our
   c. what our
   d. Correct as is

6. a. a different places give
   b. a different place give
   c. a different place giving
   d. Correct as is

# Additional Test Generator Questions

## Contents

**To the Teacher** . . . . . . . . . . . . . . . . . . . . . . . . . . . . . . . . . . . . . . . . . . . . . . . . 179

Unit One . . . . . . . . . . . . . . . . . . . . . . . . . . . . . . . . . . . . . . . . . . . . . . . . . . . . 180

Unit Two . . . . . . . . . . . . . . . . . . . . . . . . . . . . . . . . . . . . . . . . . . . . . . . . . . . . 187

Unit Three . . . . . . . . . . . . . . . . . . . . . . . . . . . . . . . . . . . . . . . . . . . . . . . . . . . 192

Unit Four . . . . . . . . . . . . . . . . . . . . . . . . . . . . . . . . . . . . . . . . . . . . . . . . . . . . 198

Unit Five . . . . . . . . . . . . . . . . . . . . . . . . . . . . . . . . . . . . . . . . . . . . . . . . . . . . 203

Unit Six . . . . . . . . . . . . . . . . . . . . . . . . . . . . . . . . . . . . . . . . . . . . . . . . . . . . . 207

# To the Teacher

The following pages contain additional selection questions, which you may wish to use to construct tests that are customized to better meet the needs of your students. Correct responses to questions on these pages are marked with an asterisk. Read the questions and determine if any of them are appropriate for your students. Then use the Test Generator software to call up the questions and add them to your customized tests. Directions for using the Test Generator software are included in the *Test Generator User's Guide,* which accompanies the software.

# UNIT ONE

## Part One
### The Necklace
### Test Generator

1. At the beginning of the story, Mme. Loisel dreams about being
   a. loved.
   b. famous.
   c. independent.
   *d. rich and stylish.

2. Why is Mme. Loisel upset at receiving the invitation to a fancy party?
   a. She doesn't know how to behave at a fancy party.
   *b. She doesn't have the appropriate clothes to wear.
   c. She knows very few of the people who will be there.
   d. She thinks her husband will embarrass her at the party.

3. Which of the following is a clue to the surprise ending of the story?
   a. M. Loisel's suggestion that his wife pretend the necklace clasp broke
   b. Mme. Forestier's irritated response when the necklace is returned late
   c. the Loisels' finding a virtually identical necklace in another jeweler's shop
   *d. the jeweler's statement that he did not sell the necklace but only supplied the case

4. Mme. Forestier responds to Mme. Loisel's story with
   a. bored annoyance.
   *b. sympathy and dismay.
   c. anger at having been deceived.
   d. amusement at the misunderstanding.

### The Most Dangerous Game
### Test Generator

1. What does Rainsford's conversation with Whitney reveal about Rainsford's attitude toward hunting?
   a. He tends to identify with the prey.
   *b. He has no moral questions about it.
   c. He thinks it is insufficiently challenging.
   d. He thinks of it as a business, not a sport.

2. Even before he gets to the island, Rainsford knows he will find people because he
   a. sees lights.
   b. sees the mansion.
   *c. hears pistol shots.
   d. hears a man whistling.

3. Zaroff implies that his and Ivan's common race makes them both
   a. clever.
   *b. savage.
   c. English.
   d. great hunters.

4. Early in their conversation, Rainsford is made uneasy by the feeling that Zaroff seems to be
   a. insane.
   b. overly proud.
   *c. sizing Rainsford up.
   d. eager for a hunting companion.

5. Zaroff obtains most of the men he hunts from
   *a. shipwrecks.
   b. slave traders.
   c. the island's inhabitants.
   d. men who fall overboard.

6. What does the story suggest is the reason Zaroff looks away from Rainsford's hiding place in the tree?
   a. His attention is distracted.
   b. He feels sorry for Rainsford
   *c. He does not want the hunt to end so soon.
   d. He does not realize that Rainsford is in the tree.

### Where Have You Gone, Charming Billy?
### Test Generator

1. To escape his feelings of fear, Paul Berlin
   a. watched Billy Boy Watkins.
   *b. pretended he was camping with his father.
   c. stayed at the back of the string of soldiers.
   d. stayed in the center of the path.

2. What attitude toward stepping on a land mine did Paul learn in training?
   a. It can't be helped.
   b. It's a good way out of the war.
   c. You'd be better off dead.
   *d. If you're alert, you can avoid it.

3. Of the places they passed on the march, which did Paul find most appealing?
   a. the rice paddy
   b. the village
   *c. the graveyard
   d. the dirt path

4. Which of these is a symbol of hope for Paul during the march?
   *a. the sea
   b. the shadows ahead
   c. the clouds
   d. the color green

5. Which of the following best describes the cause of Paul's giggling?
   a. He never liked Billy anyway.
   b. His relief in finding a friend made him laugh.
   *c. The tension and fear inside him were out of control.
   d. He wanted to prove to everyone that he wasn't afraid.

# Marigolds

## Test Generator

1. To the black people of the narrator's hometown, the American Dream was
   a. a goal.
   *b. a myth.
   c. a reality.
   d. an excuse.

2. The narrator remembers spending most of her summer days
   *a. playing.
   b. working.
   c. reading.
   d. studying.

3. Which of the following is not a reason that annoying Miss Lottie is usually fun?
   a. It breaks up the boredom.
   *b. It hurts Miss Lottie's feelings.
   c. It involves a little bit of danger.
   d. It gets a rise out of Miss Lottie.

4. To Lizabeth, everything that is associated with or related to Miss Lottie is
   a. boring.
   *b. strange.
   c. beautiful.
   d. dangerous.

5. John Burke, Miss Lottie's son, is a symbol of
   a. Lizabeth's future.
   b. security in old age for Miss Lottie.
   c. the same things as the marigolds.
   *d. Miss Lottie's frustrated hopes and desires.

6. When the narrator ends her story saying, "And I too have planted marigolds," she is referring to marigolds
   a. strictly as flowers.
   b. as symbols of shame and regret.
   c. as symbols of poverty or imprisonment.
   *d. as symbols of hope, accomplishment, or beauty.

# Two Kinds

## Test Generator

1. The main external conflict in this story is between
   a. the mother and her past.
   b. the mother and the piano.
   c. the daughter and the piano.
   *d. the daughter and the mother.

2. The mother's attitude toward America is mainly one of
   a. patriotic pride.
   b. grief and regret.
   *c. boundless optimism.
   d. distrust and suspicion.

3. At first, the daughter's attitude toward becoming a prodigy is one of
   *a. enthusiasm.
   b. fearful doubt.
   c. disappointment.
   d. embarrassment.

4. At first, the daughter believes that if she were to become a prodigy, her problems would
   a. worsen.
   *b. disappear.
   c. stay the same.
   d. slightly improve.

5. What is the long-term effect of all of the tests that the daughter takes?
   a. They increase her intelligence.
   *b. They change her opinion of herself.
   c. They make her more respectful and cooperative.
   d. They make her more determined to become a prodigy.

6. Which of the following does the mother hold most responsible for the daughter's not becoming a prodigy?
   a. the mother's pushiness
   b. the mother's unrealistic expectations
   c. the daughter's lack of intelligence
   *d. the daughter's not trying hard enough

7. Of the following, which does the daughter fear most in her relationship with her mother?
   a. that her mother will desert her
   b. that her mother loves her too much
   c. that her mother will always be too proud of her
   *d. that her mother doesn't love her for who she is

8. The main reason that the daughter's performance at the piano recital is so awful is that the daughter
   a. tries too hard.
   b. feels too nervous.
   *c. didn't prepare well enough.
   d. is determined to humiliate her mother.

9. As an adult, the daughter sees the mother's agreement to end the daughter's piano lessons as a sign of her mother's
   a. trust in her.
   b. respect for her.
   c. concern for her.
   *d. loss of confidence in her.

10. When the mother gives the piano to the daughter, the daughter is overcome by a sense of
    a. guilt.
    b. grief.
    *c. relief.
    d. failure.

## *from* The Perfect Storm
## Test Generator

1. Who wants to stay on the *Satori* and ride out the storm?
   a. Stimpson
   *b. Leonard
   c. Bylander
   d. Moore

2. The Coast Guard's first plan for rescuing the crew was to
   a. have a helicopter pluck people from the water.
   b. use the *Tamaroa* to tow the *Satori*.
   c. lift the crew directly into the air from the *Satori*.
   *d. have the *Tamaroa* take the crew off the *Satori* by raft.

3. Who suggested using a rescue swimmer?
   *a. the helicopter pilot
   b. the commander of the *Tamaroa*
   c. the District One Command Center
   d. the crew of the *Satori*

4. Which of these techniques best helps establish this narrative as nonfiction rather than fiction?
   a. using vivid words to describe the storm
   *b. giving exact times for events
   c. using dialogue
   d. using present-tense verbs

5. Which condition was **not** a cause for concern during the rescue?
   a. the size of the waves
   b. the speed of the wind
   *c. the temperature of the water
   d. the time of the day

## The Wreck of the Hesperus
## Test Generator Open-Book Test

1. Who or what is described as being "angry" in the poem?
   a. the skipper
   b. the old sailor
   *c. the sea
   d. the ship

2. How did the skipper die?
   a. He died of despair.
   *b. He froze.
   c. He was murdered.
   d. He drowned.

3. This selection is an example of a
   a. lyric poem.
   b. sonnet.
   c. concrete poem.
   *d. ballad.

4. What happened to the ship's crew?
   *a. They were swept from the deck.
   b. They went down with the ship.
   c. They were rescued in the morning.
   d. The poem does not say.

5. The death of the skipper's daughter makes this story seem more
   a. hopeful.
   b. realistic.
   *c. tragic.
   d. playful.

## Part Two
## O What Is That Sound
### Test Generator Open-Book Test

1. All of the following help the reader decide that "O What Is That Sound" is a poem except the fact that it
   a. rhymes.
   *b. tells a story.
   c. has a strong rhythm.
   d. is arranged in stanzas.

2. Who speaks in the last stanza of the poem?
   *a. the first speaker only
   b. the second speaker only
   c. the first speaker, then the second speaker
   d. the second speaker, then the first speaker

3. Who runs away from the soldiers near the end of the poem?
   a. the first speaker only
   *b. the second speaker only
   c. both speakers
   d. neither speaker

4. By the end of the poem, it seems that the soldiers have come for
   a. the doctor.
   b. the parson.
   c. the farmer who lives nearby.
   *d. one or both of the speakers.

## Incident in a Rose Garden
### Test Generator Open-Book Test

1. The gardener views Death with an attitude of
   a. scorn.
   *b. respect.
   c. hopelessness.
   d. acceptance.

2. The gardener quits his job mainly because he
   a. thinks the master is going to die and won't need him.
   b. doesn't want to work in a place where Death lurks.
   *c. has things he wants to do before he dies.
   d. thinks he will be held responsible for the master's death.

3. As Death stands among the roses, he
   a. bends over to sniff them.
   b. offers a bouquet to the master.
   c. ignores the blossoms.
   *d. plucks them.

4. The end of the poem suggests that the master
   a. has met Death before.
   *b. is about to die.
   c. is an old friend of Death's.
   d. is prepared to die.

5. What is the theme of this poem?
   *a. Death comes to rich and poor alike.
   b. Wealthy people need not fear death.
   c. People can avoid death by running away.
   d. Roses are a symbol of death.

## The Gift of the Magi
### Test Generator

1. Della is crying at the beginning of the story because she
   a. is sad about selling her hair.
   b. has been accused of stinginess.
   c. is depressed by the gray day.
   *d. has too little money for Jim's gift.

2. Della thinks the watch fob is like Jim because it
   a. is cheerful and bright.
   *b. has quietness and value.
   c. is inexpensive yet nice.
   d. has elegance and charm.

3. When he first sees Della on Christmas Eve, Jim seems to feel
   a. angry.
   b. sad.
   *c. confused.
   d. delighted.

4. When Della first sees Jim on Christmas Eve, she
   *a. begins to chatter nervously.
   b. shouts "Merry Christmas!"
   c. begins to cry.
   d. accuses him of not loving her.

5. In the end, Della and Jim most likely feel
   a. sorry for themselves.
   *b. firm in their love.
   c. that the other is to blame.
   d. confused and upset.

## The Sniper
### Test Generator

1. Lighting a cigarette was risky for the sniper mainly because it might
   a. ignite his ammunition.
   *b. let enemies know his location.
   c. cause health problems.
   d. distract him from keeping watch.

2. The sniper's purpose was to
   a. make his neighborhood safe.
   b. learn more about his enemies.
   c. protect people in the house below.
   *d. eliminate his enemies.

3. Why did the sniper let his rifle and hat fall to the street?
   a. He no longer wanted them.
   *b. He wanted his enemy to think he was dead.
   c. He needed to lighten his load before he escaped.
   d. His wound made him lose his grip.

4. What did the sniper respect about the gunman he had killed?
   a. He was brave.
   b. He couldn't be fooled.
   *c. He was a good shot.
   d. He was honest.

5. What can you infer about many of the people fighting against each other in this war?
   *a. They had recently been in the same army.
   b. They had been enemies throughout history.
   c. They were of different religious backgrounds.
   d. They did not know what the other side wanted.

## The Possibility of Evil
### Test Generator

1. Miss Strangeworth reveals her disapproval in which of the following remarks?
   a. "Such a lovely day, isn't it?"
   b. "My grandfather built the first house on Pleasant Street."
   c. "Are those strawberries from Arthur Parker's garden?"
   *d. "How old is Her Highness now?"

2. Miss Strangeworth disapproved of the car Billy Moore's father bought because it was
   *a. too expensive.
   b. not dignified.
   c. noisy and dirty.
   d. better than hers.

3. How did Miss Strangeworth feel when some people in town wanted to put up a statue of Ethan Allen?
   a. enthusiastic
   *b. resentful
   c. proud
   d. embarrassed

4. Miss Strangeworth firmly believed that the people of her town
   a. were good at heart.
   b. could take care of themselves.
   *c. were inferior to her.
   d. liked her suggestions.

5. You can infer that the problems of Linda Stewart and Dave Harris were caused by
   a. Dave's attitude.
   b. Linda's desire to break free of her parents.
   c. Mr. Stewart's violent temper.
   *d. one of Miss Strangeworth's letters.

6. Which of these was most important to Miss Strangeworth?
   a. having friends
   b. doing good deeds
   c. writing beautifully
   *d. banishing evil

## The Censors
## Test Generator

1. According to the narrator, Juan's troubles began when he
   *a. let happiness get the better of him.
   b. tried to trick the censors.
   c. decided to visit Mariana.
   d. betrayed a confidential source.

2. After he sent a letter to Mariana, Juan worried about the censors because
   a. he had used a code he knew they would figure out.
   b. Mariana was known to be disloyal to the government.
   *c. he knew that fault would be found even where none existed.
   d. he had revealed too much information about himself.

3. How did Juan change as he worked in the Censorship Division?
   a. He made new friends.
   *b. He lost interest in everything but his job.
   c. He gained fame and wealth.
   d. He became listless and dull.

4. Juan got his first promotion by
   *a. betraying a fellow worker.
   b. working faster than anyone else.
   c. protesting unsafe conditions.
   d. discovering hidden messages.

5. Juan began to believe that his true mission in life was to
   a. become the head of the Division.
   b. make money.
   c. fool government officials.
   *d. catch enemies of the government.

6. In the end, Juan's patriotism
   a. changed to rebellion.
   *b. destroyed him.
   c. changed to terror.
   d. made him a hero.

## Annabel Lee
## The Bells
## Test Generator Open-Book Test

1. According to the speaker, who was responsible for the illness that killed Annabel Lee?
   *a. angels
   b. the speaker himself
   c. sea demons
   d. Annabel Lee's kinsmen

2. The speaker's reaction to Annabel Lee's death is characterized by
   a. religious faith.
   b. disbelief.
   c. acceptance.
   *d. bitterness.

3. The rhythm of "Annabel Lee" resembles the
   a. pace of a solemn funeral march.
   b. turbulence of a thunderstorm.
   *c. drumming of the ocean's surf.
   d. jerky rhythm of an unsteady gait.

4. The mood in the first section of "The Bells" is
   a. raucous and tense.
   *b. bright and cheerful.
   c. solemn and slow.
   d. rich and melodious.

5. Which line from "The Bells" includes an example of assonance?
   a. "Through the balmy air of night"
   b. "In a sort of Runic rhyme"
   *c. "From the molten-golden notes"
   d. "How the danger ebbs and flows"

6. Which line from "The Bells" includes an example of alliteration?
   a. "They are neither brute nor human"
   b. "In the silence of the night"
   c. "To the rhyming and the chiming of the bells!"
   *d. "*What* tale of terror, now, their turbulency tells!"

## The Cask of Amontillado
## Test Generator

1. The insult that Fortunato inflicts on Montresor
   a. concerns Montresor's home.
   b. concerns Montresor's heritage.
   c. concerns Montresor's knowledge of wine.
   *d. is not revealed in the story.

2. When Fortunato offers to judge the wine, Montresor responds by
   a. being sincerely eager.
   b. being sincerely reluctant.
   c. pretending to be eager.
   *d. pretending to be reluctant.

3. Why does Montresor tell his servants that, even though he will not return until morning, they are not to leave the house?
   a. Deep down, he wants to be stopped.
   b. He thinks he may need their help.
   *c. He knows this will make them leave.
   d. He wants them to testify that he wasn't there.

4. If Fortunato had not been under the influence of alcohol, he might have wondered why Montresor
   a. mentioned Luchesi.
   b. offered him wine.
   c. expressed concern for him.
   *d. was carrying a trowel.

5. Montresor stops working when Fortunato begins rattling his chains because Montresor
   a. is exhausted.
   b. feels remorse.
   *c. wants to listen and gloat.
   d. worries that someone will hear.

# UNIT TWO

## Part One
### Life Without Go-Go Boots
### Test Generator

1. Clothes handed down from her older cousin rarely worked out for the author because they
   a. were too big.
   b. looked like something out of a horror movie.
   c. never fit quite right.
   *d. were out of fashion by the time she got them.

2. When she thinks about the boots her mother got her for Christmas, the author
   a. feels angry about her mother's choice.
   *b. appreciates her mother's good intentions.
   c. feels embarrassed about how she looked in them.
   d. wishes she had appreciated them more.

3. How does the author's young daughter feel about clothes?
   a. She is proud of always having what is in fashion.
   *b. She is much more carefree than the author was.
   c. She is obsessed with trying to be different.
   d. She feels the same way the author did as a child.

4. From this essay, you can infer that the author now thinks go-go boots are
   *a. ridiculous.
   b. fashionable.
   c. beautiful.
   d. ordinary.

5. Why does the author imagine that the suit her friend convinced her to buy is unhappy hanging among the other clothes in her closet?
   a. It is too stiff and old-fashioned.
   b. It is the wrong color.
   *c. It is far more elegant than the rest.
   d. It is humble and threadbare.

## from Angela's Ashes
### Test Generator

1. Sister Rita disliked the poem "The Highwayman" because it
   a. was so sad.
   *b. involved sin.
   c. was about death.
   d. made no sense.

2. The Kerry nurse said many things that
   a. comforted McCourt.
   b. annoyed Sister Rita.
   *c. frightened McCourt.
   d. amused Seamus.

3. Several people suggest that receiving blood from soldiers will
   a. cure McCourt quickly.
   b. cause an infection.
   c. cost too much.
   *d. make McCourt tough.

4. In the upstairs hospital ward, McCourt is haunted by visions of
   *a. starving children.
   b. Patricia.
   c. his father.
   d. thieves.

5. Why did McCourt's mother stop visiting the hospital?
   a. She could no longer afford to come.
   b. Sister Rita feared she might catch something.
   c. McCourt was too weak to have visitors.
   *d. Sister Rita was punishing McCourt.

## Unfinished Business
### Test Generator

1. Kübler-Ross seems to feel she can do all of the following for her patients except help
   a. them accept dying.
   b. them gain peace of mind.
   *c. them survive their illnesses.
   d. their families accept that the children are dying.

2. According to Kübler-Ross, the dying little girl "could not die" because
    a. she was not sick enough yet.
    b. she held out hope that she would live.
    *c. she feared what would happen to her after death.
    d. her doctors would not let her die.

3. Kübler-Ross suggests that, when children express resentment about a dying patient, it is important to
    a. tell them how unfair this is.
    *b. help them find a way to get rid of this feeling.
    c. make them see that this feeling is not their true feeling.
    d. explain that there is nothing they can do about the situation.

4. When dealing with the families of dying children, Kübler-Ross uses drawing as a way to
    a. quickly solve these people's problems.
    *b. quickly see how these people are feeling.
    c. help the dying child deal with his or her family.
    d. change the way the family views the dying child.

## A Christmas Memory
## Test Generator

1. The relationship between Capote and those who Know Best could best be described as
    a. warm.
    b. loving.
    *c. distant.
    d. imaginary.

2. When they meet Haha Jones, Capote and his friend find that Haha is not really
    a. a giant.
    b. scarred.
    c. an Indian.
    *d. unable to laugh.

3. Capote's friend refuses to sell their Christmas tree to the mill owner's wife because
    *a. it is too special to sell.
    b. they don't need the money.
    c. they wouldn't be able to get another tree.
    d. the woman will not pay her a fair price for it.

4. As a child, exchanging homemade gifts with his friend year after year makes Capote feel
    a. furious.
    b. disappointed.
    c. embarrassed.
    *d. pleasantly satisfied.

## Song of the Open Road
## The Road Not Taken
## Test Generator Open-Book Test

1. In "Song of the Open Road," the speaker looks to the future with
    a. regret.
    *b. joy.
    c. reluctance.
    d. fear.

2. The speaker in "Song of the Open Road" emphasizes that
    a. there will always be tough decisions.
    b. he must prepare carefully for the future.
    *c. his fate is in his own hands.
    d. he can only hope for good fortune along the way.

3. In "The Road Not Taken," how does the speaker feel about the road he did not take?
    a. He feels sorry for anyone who would choose that way.
    b. He always knew it would lead him astray.
    *c. He will always wonder what might have been.
    d. He wishes he had chosen that way instead.

4. The structure of "The Road Not Taken" is characterized by
    *a. a carefully controlled rhyme scheme.
    b. an emphasis on alliteration and assonance.
    c. repeated words that lend force to the lines.
    d. a lack of rhyme or rhythm patterns.

5. The speaker of "The Road Not Taken" views the predicament of having to choose between the two roads as
    a. a reward.
    *b. a fact of life.
    c. a punishment.
    d. an annoyance.

## American History
### Test Generator

1. The black girls at Elena's school treat her with
   *a. scorn.
   b. fearful respect.
   c. friendly acceptance.
   d. careful concern for her feelings.

2. Elena's attitude toward the old couple who live in the house does not include
   a. envy.
   b. curiosity.
   c. familiarity.
   *d. superiority.

3. From what Elena can see from her fire escape, Eugene's family appears to
   a. have more fun than the old couple did.
   b. argue a great deal more than the old couple did.
   *c. spend less time together than the old couple did.
   d. spend more time at home than the old couple did.

4. To Elena, her parents' plans for the future are
   *a. fanciful.
   b. exciting.
   c. practical.
   d. intimidating.

5. Elena's attitude toward El Building could best be described as
   a. proud.
   b. loving.
   *c. ashamed.
   d. indifferent.

## Part Two
### The Beginning of Something
### Test Generator

1. When Roseanne's mother hears about Cousin Jessie's death, she is
   a. angry.
   b. relieved.
   *c. wild with grief.
   d. sad but not shocked.

2. What does Roseanne claim she felt during the month her family spent with Cousin Jessie's family every summer?
   a. worry
   *b. boredom
   c. excitement
   d. very mixed feelings

3. Which of the following is not a word Roseanne would use to describe Melissa at the beginning of the story?
   a. pretty
   b. spoiled
   c. annoying
   *d. intelligent

4. Roseanne insists on staying home from the visitation because she
   *a. doesn't want to go.
   b. doesn't have an appropriate dress.
   c. wants to take care of her little brother.
   d. wants to make things easier for her mother.

5. When Uncle Roy wants to talk in detail about Cousin Jessie's sickness and death, Roseanne's mother
   a. is irritated and feels bad about it.
   b. finds it too painful to listen to him.
   *c. listens carefully and with real interest.
   d. excuses herself to go clean the house.

6. When Roseanne knew Travis several years before, she thought he was
   *a. nice.
   b. stupid.
   c. boring.
   d. gorgeous.

7. Roseanne doesn't talk to Travis when she first sees him again because she
   a. wants to play hard to get.
   b. is annoyed that he is there.
   *c. is stunned by how good-looking he is.
   d. believes he is only there to talk to Melissa's boyfriend.

8. Which of the following is not a reason that Roseanne wants to go out with Travis?
   a. She likes him.
   b. She's never been on a date.
   c. She thinks he's good-looking.
   *d. She thinks it will make Melissa jealous.

# Young
# Hanging Fire
## Test Generator Open-Book Test

1. For answers to her questions, the girl in "Young" turns to
   a. her mother.
   b. the leaves.
   c. her father.
   *d. the stars.

2. The speaker in "Young" remembers herself as a child feeling
   *a. lonely.
   b. energetic.
   c. angry.
   d. content.

3. The speaker in "Hanging Fire" could best be described as extremely
   a. sad.
   b. generous.
   *c. insecure.
   d. bored.

4. By ending each stanza with the words "and momma's in the bedroom / with the door closed," the speaker in "Hanging Fire" emphasizes her
   a. distrust of her family.
   *b. desire for support and guidance.
   c. unrealistic expectations.
   d. attention to sensory details.

5. The phrase "a thousand doors ago" at the beginning of "Young" suggests that in growing up, the speaker has
   a. moved into a house with many doors.
   b. found many friends.
   *c. gone through many changes.
   d. kept to herself.

6. In the first stanza of "Hanging Fire," the speaker suggests that "the boy [she] cannot live without"
   a. adores her.
   b. is a jerk.
   *c. is immature.
   d. can't stand her.

7. All of the following lines from "Hanging Fire" reflect the speaker's discomfort with her physical appearance except
   a. line 2.
   b. lines 6 and 7.
   *c. lines 27.
   d. lines 28–30.

8. In "Hanging Fire," lines 19–21 mainly suggest that the speaker is feeling
   a. content.
   *b. conflicted.
   c. overjoyed.
   d. disappointed.

# The Seven Ages of Man
## Test Generator Open-Book Test

1. In Jaques's view, a man in the stage of "the lover" tends to be
   a. childish.
   *b. wistful.
   c. severe.
   d. quarrelsome.

2. You can infer that Jaques views life as
   a. exciting.
   b. fulfilling.
   c. humbling.
   *d. pointless.

3. According to Jaques, in old age a man becomes
   a. wise.
   b. noble.
   *c. babyish.
   d. demanding.

4. This speech reveals that Jaques is
   a. kind.
   b. jealous.
   c. clever.
   *d. gloomy.

5. Jaques implies that a man in the stage of "the justice" is
   *a. an old bore.
   b. a wise man.
   c. easily bribed.
   d. not truly just.

## Brothers Are the Same
### Test Generator

1. The other young men, besides Temas, are involved in the battle mainly in order to
   a. protect Temas.
   b. track and awaken the lion.
   c. carry the lion's body to the village.
   *d. guide and witness the lion's attack.

2. When Temas received the chief's spear, Medoto's reaction to Temas revealed Medoto's
   *a. scorn.
   b. respect.
   c. jealousy.
   d. amazement.

3. When Temas sees that the lion intends to attack someone other than him, he feels
   a. guilty.
   b. jealous.
   *c. relieved.
   d. resentful.

4. At what point in the story does Temas's fear leave him?
   a. When the lion crouches.
   *b. When the lion charges him.
   c. When he succeeds in killing the lion.
   d. When he reenters the village in triumph.

5. Temas's worries after killing the lion are based on concerns that
   a. he will have to fight Medoto.
   b. he will not survive his wounds.
   *c. Medoto will reveal Temas's earlier fear.
   d. his success was based on luck rather than skill.

6. This story emphasizes the Masai people's respect for
   a. loyalty.
   *b. courage.
   c. kindness.
   d. cleverness.

## Through the Tunnel
### Test Generator

1. Why does Jerry go to the crowded beach instead of the bay on the first day of his vacation?
   a. He doesn't know about the bay.
   *b. He wants to make his mother happy.
   c. There is no one at the bay to play with.

2. At first, the boys on the bay make Jerry feel
   a. unhappy.
   *b. accepted.
   c. all-powerful.

3. The boys on the bay react to Jerry's clowning around with
   a. anger.
   b. good humor.
   *c. embarrassment.

4. Jerry's efforts to prepare for swimming through the tunnel focus most heavily on
   *a. controlling his breathing.
   b. improving his swimming skills.
   c. overcoming his fear of dark, enclosed places.

5. As Jerry enters the tunnel to swim through it, his greatest feeling is one of
   *a. fear.
   b. pride.
   c. confidence.

6. When Jerry sees the other boys after his swim through the tunnel, he
   *a. ignores them.
   b. waves to them.
   c. tells them all about his accomplishment.

7. After he swims through the tunnel, Jerry's attitude toward his mother is one of
   *a. affection.
   b. superiority.
   c. embarrassment.

8. Jerry is most interested in proving something to
   *a. himself.
   b. his mother.
   c. the other boys.

# UNIT THREE

## Part One
## The Devil and Daniel Webster
## Test Generator

1. The crowd's reaction to Scratch's song is one of
   a. grief.
   *b. terror.
   c. enjoyment.
   d. bewilderment.

2. Scratch's collection box holds
   *a. souls.
   b. deeds.
   c. evidence.
   d. a list of his victims.

3. When the crowd hears the moth speak, they don't believe it is Miser Stevens mainly because
   *a. moths can't speak.
   b. it doesn't sound like Stevens.
   c. they don't know Stevens is dead.
   d. they don't believe Stevens would bargain with the devil.

4. When the neighbors realize Jabez has sold his soul to the devil, their response is to
   a. help him.
   *b. run away.
   c. attack him.
   d. turn for help to Webster.

5. Jabez made his deal with the devil for all of the following reasons except that he
   *a. was evil.
   b. was young.
   c. was horribly discouraged about his farm.
   d. couldn't afford to marry Mary.

6. Mary's quoting the Book of Ruth shows all of the following except that she
   a. loves Jabez sincerely.
   b. isn't likely to leave Jabez.
   *c. believes Jabez's soul is lost forever.
   d. is very familiar with the Christian Bible.

7. The jury is made up of
   *a. lost souls.
   b. neighbors.
   c. former lawyers.
   d. people who have escaped the devil.

8. In order to defeat Daniel Webster, the judge does all of the following except
   a. deny all his motions.
   b. deny all his objections.
   *c. refuse to let him speak.
   d. refuse to let him cross-examine the witness.

## I Have a Dream
## Glory and Hope
## Test Generator

1. In "I Have a Dream," Martin Luther King, Jr., urges his followers to
   a. work toward gradual change.
   *b. demand justice now.
   c. use any means necessary.
   d. distrust white people.

2. Which repeated phrase in King's speech has additional power because it is from a familiar patriotic song?
   a. "I have a dream"
   b. "Now is the time to"
   c. "One hundred years later"
   *d. "Let freedom ring"

3. Of the ideals expressed in "Glory and Hope," which was **not** included in "I Have a Dream"?
   a. justice for all
   b. nonracialism
   c. freedom from poverty
   *d. nonsexism

4. Both of these speeches incorporate
   *a. repeated phrases.
   b. quotations from songs.
   c. thanks to distinguished guests.
   d. references to "God's children."

5. Both speakers are convinced that
   a. dreams rarely become reality.
   *b. the struggle must continue.
   c. democracy has prevailed.
   d. justice is a privilege.

## The United States vs. Susan B. Anthony
## Test Generator

1. For some time, the writer thought Susan B. Anthony was all of the following except
   a. stern.
   *b. likable.
   c. committed.
   d. courageous.

2. Anthony bases her claim to have the legal right to vote on the
   a. Bill of Rights.
   *b. Fourteenth Amendment.
   c. newspaper announcement.
   d. Declaration of Independence.

3. After Anthony registers to vote, more than 50 other women in the city
   *a. also register.
   b. try to get her arrested and taken to trial.
   c. write letters of protest to the newspaper.
   d. demonstrate in front of the barbershop.

4. The election inspectors allow Anthony to vote after she
   a. bribes them.
   b. threatens them.
   c. persuades them of the justice of her cause.
   *d. promises to pay legal expense if they are arrested.

5. The deputy marshal who comes to arrest Anthony is all of the following except
   *a. angry.
   b. respectful.
   c. embarrassed.
   d. eager to avoid taking Anthony in charge.

6. The district attorney puts off Anthony's trial in order to
   a. punish her.
   *b. work around her lecture schedule.
   c. give her a chance to change her mind.
   d. allow the publicity around the trial to grow.

7. Anthony doesn't testify in her own behalf because she
   a. is advised not to.
   *b. isn't allowed to do so.
   c. doesn't feel that it is necessary.
   d. wants to be convicted in order to test the law.

8. The judge deprives Anthony of her rights at the trial because
   a. he doesn't like women.
   b. he doesn't like Anthony.
   c. he is strongly anti-suffrage.
   *d. the senator who got him his job is anti-suffrage.

9. The judge doesn't stop Anthony's speech at the end of the trial because
   *a. she ignores him.
   b. she threatens to sue him.
   c. he is afraid of her supporters.
   d. he realizes he has gone too far.

10. Anthony refers to the time when helping fugitive slaves was illegal in order to
    a. justify defying all laws.
    *b. justify defying unjust laws.
    c. prove that what she is doing is legal.
    d. enlist the support of the black community.

11. Anthony refuses to pay her fine for all of the following reasons except that
    a. the fine is unjust.
    *b. she has no way to get the money to pay it.
    c. she is using all her money to pay a debt she thinks is just.
    d. she wants to go to prison so she can appeal to a higher court.

## Theme for English B
## The Writer
## Test Generator Open-Book Test

1. In "Theme for English B," what does the speaker say that he or she has in common with the instructor?
   a. race
   b. religion
   *c. nationality
   d. career goals

2. In "The Writer," the speaker is
   a. giving the daughter feedback about her writing.
   b. privately reading something the daughter wrote.
   *c. secretly listening to the daughter while she writes.
   d. reading over the daughter's shoulder while she writes.

3. In "The Writer," the speaker strongly suggests that what the daughter has to write about may be
   a. dull.
   *b. painful.
   c. thrilling.
   d. humorous.

4. In "The Writer," the speaker's daughter writes
   a. steadily.
   *b. in bursts.
   c. effortlessly.
   d. in a leisurely way.

## from I Know Why the Caged Bird Sings
## Test Generator

1. What motivates Marguerite's grandmother to insist on delivering Mrs. Flowers's groceries?
   a. pride
   *b. respect
   c. insecurity
   d. ignorance

2. Why doesn't Marguerite wear a Sunday dress to Mrs. Flowers's house?
   *a. It would be disrespectful to God.
   b. It would be disrespectful to Mrs. Flowers.
   c. Marguerite doesn't want to seem too eager.
   d. Marguerite wants Mrs. Flowers to feel sorry for her.

3. When Mrs. Flowers begins reading A Tale of Two Cities, Marguerite is most surprised by
   a. the plot of the novel.
   *b. the sound of the words.
   c. the meaning of the words.
   d. Mrs. Flowers's ability to read.

4. Mrs. Flowers's general approach to changing Marguerite's behavior involves
   a. feeling sorry for Marguerite.
   b. treating Marguerite as if she is beyond hope.
   *c. treating Marguerite as if she is a gifted individual.
   d. accepting Marguerite as she is and expecting nothing of her.

5. After the visit, Marguerite is convinced that Mrs. Flowers's interest in her is motivated by
   a. pity for her.
   *b. fondness for her.
   c. admiration for her grandmother.
   d. a sense of obligation to her grandmother.

## New Directions
## Test Generator

1. When she and her husband separated, Annie Johnson's main problem was to
   a. buy a new home for her children.
   *b. find a way to make a living.
   c. cope with racial discrimination.
   d. improve her education.

2. Mrs. Johnson carried a basket of stones three miles to the cotton gin one night in order to
   *a. test her strength.
   b. see if she could find her way in the dark.
   c. make a path.
   d. impress the workers there.

3. The town's two factories "worked for" Mrs. Johnson in the sense that they provided
   a. the supplies she needed.
   b. a job that she could do at home.
   c. indoor space for cooking and selling.
   *d. customers for her business.

4. You can tell from reading this selection that
   a. Annie Johnson was the best cook in town.
   *b. no one else was selling lunch to the workmen.
   c. all of the workers were poor.
   d. Annie Johnson wanted a factory job.

5. Mrs. Johnson did not build a stall for her business until she
   a. had enough money to buy the wood.
   b. discovered a good location.
   *c. knew the customers were dependent on her.
   d. became too exhausted to walk to both locations.

## Encounter with Martin Luther King, Jr.
### Test Generator

1. When Angelou met King in person, it was clear that Angelou found him to be
   a. intimidating.
   b. funny.
   c. disappointing.
   *d. friendly.

2. For Angelou, it was most important to gain King's
   *a. respect.
   b. help.
   c. sympathy.
   d. gratitude.

3. Angelou's mother had caused Maya to worry that
   a. she could never be as famous as King.
   b. no one would accept her because of her brother.
   *c. the status of blacks could never be changed.
   d. working for King would bring nothing but trouble.

4. Of all that happened when she met Martin Luther King, Jr., what made the biggest impression on Angelou?
   a. his athletic good looks
   *b. his sadness about her brother
   c. his sense of humor
   d. his musical voice

## Part Two
### To Build a Fire
### Test Generator

1. When the man first tried to eat his lunch, he could not because
   a. his food was frozen.
   b. he couldn't unwrap the package.
   *c. his frozen beard held his mouth shut.
   d. he was shaking from the cold.

2. What does the dog appreciate about the man?
   *a. his ability to make fire
   b. his drive to keep going
   c. his comforting presence
   d. his willingness to take risks

3. The relationship between the man and his dog was most like that of
   a. two old friends.
   *b. master and slave.
   c. father and son.
   d. teammates.

4. What fatal mistake did the man make after his feet got wet?
   a. He waited too long before building a fire.
   *b. He built his fire under a spruce tree.
   c. He left his wet footgear on.
   d. He put green moss on the fire.

5. What is the basic approach to life of the man in the story?
   a. He depends on his religious faith to bring him through.
   b. He relies upon the advice of those with more experience.
   c. He plans carefully in advance to prepare for every possibility.
   *d. He feels confident that he can handle each thing as it comes.

## from Into Thin Air
### Test Generator

1. Krakauer did not stay at the summit long because he
   *a. knew he would need more oxygen soon.
   b. was disappointed with the experience.
   c. wanted to catch up with his group.
   d. wasn't thinking very clearly at that point.

2. Beck Weathers could not continue to the summit because of his
   a. frail health.
   b. need for oxygen.
   *c. poor vision.
   d. lack of climbing experience.

3. In retrospect, Krakauer seems to believe that if he had had more oxygen during his descent, he might have
   a. gotten down before the storm.
   *b. helped others survive.
   c. remembered the events better.
   d. taken better photographs.

4. When Andy Harris informed Krakauer that the oxygen bottles were empty, he was demonstrating his
   a. lack of consideration.
   b. stubborn nature.
   c. lack of experience.
   *d. growing confusion.

5. Which of the following most likely saved Krakauer's life?
   a. skillfully predicting and coping with weather conditions
   b. feeling detached from his body
   *c. compulsively memorizing the terrain on the way up
   d. tossing his pack ahead of him down the steep incline

## The Sharks
## A narrow Fellow in the Grass
## Test Generator Open-Book Test

1. In "The Sharks," how does the speaker feel about the sharks?
   a. amused
   b. terrified
   *c. annoyed
   d. fascinated

2. Before the sharks appeared, the speaker in "The Sharks" had felt
   *a. carefree.
   b. worried.
   c. reckless.
   d. cautious.

3. In "The Sharks," the image of sundown suggests a sense of
   a. beauty.
   b. the unknown.
   c. evil.
   *d. transition.

4. In "The Sharks," the line "Dark / the sharp lift of the fins" gains strength from the poet's use of
   a. internal rhyme.
   b. alliteration.
   *c. assonance.
   d. repetition.

5. How does the speaker in "A narrow Fellow in the Grass" feel toward snakes in comparison with other wild creatures?
   a. more curious
   *b. not as comfortable
   c. more focused
   d. less frightened

6. The overall structure of the poem "A narrow Fellow in the Grass" is governed by
   *a. symmetry and regular rhythm.
   b. internal and end rhyme.
   c. the rhythms of conversational speech.
   d. repetition of words and phrases.

7. Which of the following images most closely mirrors the overall impression of the "narrow Fellow" in Dickinson's poem?
   a. "Comb"
   b. "Boggy Acre"
   c. "Corn"
   *d. "Whip lash"

## My Wonder Horse/Mi Caballo Mago
## Test Generator

1. The narrator's fascination with the horse is shared
   a. by no one else.
   b. only by other boys.
   c. secretly, with his father.
   *d. openly, by all the ranch hands.

2. What has the greatest effect on the narrator's interest in the Wonder Horse?
   a. hearing stories about him
   b. having a dream about him
   *c. seeing him for the first time
   d. fantasizing about capturing him

3. The Wonder Horse stops struggling after his capture is complete because
   *a. struggle is useless.
   b. his spirit has been broken.
   c. he wants to go with the narrator.
   d. he does not realize he has been caught.

4. The narrator's triumphant return through the village with the horse is
   a. a big disappointment.
 *b. marred by the horse's fall.
   c. marred by his father's reaction.
   d. everything he dreamed it would be.

# UNIT FOUR

## Part One
### The Scarlet Ibis
### Test Generator

1. Which of the following least drives the narrator to persist in his work with Doodle?
   a. his pride
   b. his optimism
   *c. his parents' urging
   d. his love for Doodle

2. All of the following are reasonable explanations for Doodle's willingness to push himself except that he wants to
   *a. die.
   b. lead an active life.
   c. please his brother.
   d. be able to go to school.

3. The actions of Doodle's parents reveal that they expect the narrator to
   a. pick on Doodle.
   *b. love and protect Doodle.
   c. prevent Doodle from dying.
   d. be embarrassed by Doodle.

4. Doodle's "lies" reveal that he is
   a. bitter.
   *b. imaginative.
   c. not "all there."
   d. prepared to die.

5. Doodle's parents respond to his walking with
   *a. joy.
   b. terror.
   c. mild anger.
   d. worried concern.

6. Who is most affected by the death of the scarlet ibis?
   *a. Doodle
   b. Aunt Nicey
   c. the father
   d. the narrator

7. All of the following quotations foreshadow Doodle's death except
   a. " 'Dead birds is bad luck,' said Aunt Nicey, poking her head from the kitchen door. 'Specially *red* dead birds!'"
   b. "They named him William Armstrong, which was like tying a big tail on a small kite. Such a name sounds good only on a tombstone."
   *c. "Renaming my brother was perhaps the kindest thing I ever did for him, because nobody expects much from someone called Doodle."
   d. "The five o'clocks by the chimney still marked time, but the oriole nest in the elm was untenanted and rocked back and forth like an empty cradle."

### Lineage
### The Courage That My Mother Had
### Test Generator Open-Book Test

1. In "Lineage," the speaker's attitude toward the grandmothers could best be described as
   *a. admiring.
   b. accepting.
   c. complaining.
   d. disappointed.

2. In "Lineage," strength is most closely associated with
   a. age.
   b. poverty.
   c. hardship.
   *d. hard work.

3. Line 4 of "Lineage" suggests that the grandmothers
   *a. were good farmers.
   b. knew how to use magic.
   c. found their work effortless.
   d. used modern equipment and methods.

4. Alliteration is used in all of the following lines from "Lineage" except
   a. line 4.
   b. line 5.
   c. line 8.
   *d. line 10.

5. In lines 3 and 4 of "The Courage That My Mother Had," the speaker conveys the idea that the mother was
   *a. firm and strong.
   b. naturally beautiful.
   c. cold and unfriendly.
   d. hard on the speaker.

6. In "The Courage That My Mother Had," which of the following best describes the speaker's attitude toward her mother?
   a. superior
   b. resentful
   *c. admiring
   d. sorrowful

## My Papa's Waltz
## Grape Sherbet
## Test Generator Open-Book Test

1. Which line from "My Papa's Waltz" contains a simile?
   *a. line 3
   b. line 5
   c. line 9
   d. line 14

2. Lines 7 and 8 of "My Papa's Waltz" suggest that the speaker's mother
   a. found the waltzing amusing.
   *b. was displeased or unhappy about the waltzing.
   c. wished that her husband would waltz with her that way.
   d. didn't want to admit that she enjoyed the moment.

3. The tone of "My Papa's Waltz" might best be described as
   *a. bittersweet.
   b. jolly.
   c. scary.
   d. tense.

4. To the speaker of "Grape Sherbet," the sherbet represents a
   a. gravestone.
   *b. fond memory.
   c. lost tooth.
   d. sad moment.

5. Lines 18–21 of "Grape Sherbet" suggest that the grandmother looked
   a. sad.
   b. confused.
   *c. stern.
   d. amused.

6. Both poems could be described as
   a. character sketches.
   b. experiments with sound.
   c. light verse.
   *d. reminiscences.

## Marine Corps Issue
## Test Generator

1. Johnny remembers his father's style of playing handball as
   *a. fierce.
   b. gentle.
   c. awkward.
   d. effortless.

2. Johnny considers it necessary to become a noisy child because
   a. his father can't hear very well.
   *b. his father is startled by surprises.
   c. no one notices him when he's quiet.
   d. being noisy is the only thing that gets his father's attention.

3. How often does Johnny's mother speak about her experiences while her husband was in Vietnam?
   *a. never
   b. rarely
   c. frequently
   d. constantly

4. As an adult, Johnny regards his mother as
   a. harsh.
   *b. strong.
   c. helpless.
   d. emotionally distant.

5. When Johnny tells people that he is the son of a Marine Corps drill instructor, they often regard him with
   a. pity.
   *b. envy.
   c. shame.
   d. amusement.

6. The first and second boxes contain all of the following except
   a. ordinary family keepsakes.
   b. his father's military uniforms.
   c. souvenirs of his father's military service.
   *d. evidence of his father's experience as a prisoner of war.

7. Johnny almost decides not to open the third box because
   a. his fear of being caught is overwhelming.
   b. he no longer cares about his father's past.
   *c. he feels guilty about prying into his father's past.
   d. Joe almost caught him with the second box open.

8. In the last four years of his life, the father talks about his experience in Vietnam
   a. casually.
   b. constantly.
   c. only when asked.
   *d. seldom and with great difficulty.

## Part Two
### *from* Black Boy
### Test Generator

1. According to Wright, what motivates him to write *The Voodoo of Hell's Half-Acre?*
   a. poverty
   b. curiosity
   *c. boredom
   d. stubbornness

2. When Wright walks into the newspaper office to submit his story for publication, he
   a. feels shy.
   *b. feels confident.
   c. feels amazed at himself.
   d. is having second thoughts.

3. The editor of the newspaper responds to Wright with all of the following except
   a. surprise.
   *b. disapproval.
   c. amusement.
   d. seriousness.

4. Wright interprets his classmates' questions about his story as evidence of their
   a. jealousy of him.
   b. admiration of him.
   *c. disapproval of him.
   d. sense of being inferior to him.

5. Wright's grandmother objects to the publication of his story mainly because she sees it as being
   a. impractical.
   b. too showy or flashy.
   *c. disrespectful to God.
   d. an invasion of the family's privacy.

6. Wright's mother mainly worries that the publication of his story will harm his
   a. character.
   *b. reputation.
   c. development as a writer.
   d. relationship with his family.

## Daughter of Invention
### Test Generator

1. The attitude of the narrator's father toward police and others in uniform resulted from feelings of
   a. respect.
   *b. fear.
   c. anger.
   d. envy.

2. The narrator describes her mother as
   a. very homesick.
   b. obedient and subservient.
   *c. energetic and creative.
   d. rigid and strict.

3. How were the mother and daughter alike?
   a. Both loved gadgets.
   b. Both were embarrassed by their accents.
   *c. Both loved to use their imaginations.
   d. Both wanted to return to the Dominican Republic.

4. Why was it difficult for the narrator's mother to help her daughters puzzle out serious questions about their identity?
   a. She needed time for her inventions.
   b. She did not take their problems seriously.
   *c. She, too, was adjusting to life in a foreign country.
   d. She focused all her hopes on returning to the homeland.

5. When she thought about delivering the teacher's day address, the narrator felt
   *a. apprehensive.
   b. honored.
   c. popular.
   d. terrified.

6. Which of the following best describes the father's attitude toward the speech his daughter wrote?
   *a. He thought it showed disrespect for her teachers.
   b. He thought it was poorly written.
   c. He was concerned that it would reflect badly on him.
   d. He thought she was being too serious.

7. The narrator's mother got ideas for the speech she wrote from
   a. the torn-up speech of her daughter.
   b. a poetry book.
   c. the speeches she heard on American television.
   *d. a speech of her husband's.

## A Voice

## The Journey

## Test Generator Open-Book Test

1. Which lines in "A Voice" contain a simile?
   a. lines 4–5
   b. lines 17–18
   c. lines 28–29
   *d. lines 32–33

2. What do lines 9 and 10 imply about the speaker's grandfather?
   a. He was a truck driver.
   *b. He came to the United States illegally.
   c. An accident landed him in the United States.
   d. He had been an adventurer.

3. What can you tell about the main character in "The Voice"?
   a. She was timid.
   b. She didn't get along with her parents.
   *c. She was fluent in two languages.
   d. Her courage never let her down.

4. What can you tell about the main character in "The Journey"?
   *a. It took him or her quite a while to decide what to do.
   b. He or she didn't really want to leave.
   c. There was no one to give him or her advice.
   d. The journey was the easy way out.

5. In line 26 of "The Journey," what do the "sheets of clouds" probably represent?
   a. bad weather
   *b. obstacles to the person's self-discovery
   c. evil spirits
   d. feelings of comfort and security

## Only Daughter

## Test Generator

1. According to Cisneros, her father wanted her to go to college in order to
   *a. meet someone to marry.
   b. generally educate herself.
   c. develop her skills as a writer.
   d. prepare herself for a well-paying job.

2. Cisneros's brothers find the idea of her going to college
   *a. silly.
   b. insulting.
   c. admirable.
   d. disappointing.

3. Which of the following best describes how Cisneros feels about not being married?
   a. confused
   b. humiliated
   *c. unconcerned
   d. relieved

4. To Cisneros, her father and the "public majority" are alike because both
   a. support the efforts of writers.
   b. heavily depend on writers to inform them.
   *c. have little interest in what writers have to say.
   d. are more interesting in reading than generally believed.

## from The House on Mango Street
## Test Generator

1. The narrator thinks that Mexicans and Chinese are alike because
   a. both name calendar years after animals.
   *b. neither likes women to be strong.
   c. both have large families and small houses.
   d. neither adjusts quickly to life in the United States

2. Why does Esperanza dislike her name?
   a. It was her grandmother's.
   b. It means "hope."
   *c. It suggests sadness.
   d. It sounds like "silver" in Spanish.

3. How does Esperanza's mother feel about herself?
   a. She has made her life a success.
   b. She has very few interests in life.
   c. She has totally unrealistic hopes.
   *d. She let her talents go to waste.

4. Overall, the life of Esperanza's family seems to be
   *a. filled with disappointments.
   b. cheerful and energetic.
   c. building success upon success.
   d. grim and hostile.

5. Esperanza's mother believes that
   a. women should work only in the home.
   b. Madame Butterfly is a good role model.
   *c. women should get a good education.
   d. her daughter needs to have nice clothes.

6. Esperanza feels she can free herself from the house on Mango Street by
   *a. writing down her thoughts about it.
   b. remembering other houses.
   c. making plans for the future.
   d. making up a better, imaginary house.

## On Writing The House on Mango Street
## Test Generator

1. For Cisneros, what was the important first step in finding her voice?
   a. discovering authors whose work spoke to her
   b. rejecting poetic language
   c. listening to the stories of ordinary people
   *d. recognizing her "otherness"

2. *The House on Mango Street* began as a memoir, but it changed as the author added
   a. historical elements.
   b. autobiographical elements.
   *c. fictional elements.
   d. personal elements.

3. In Iowa City, Cisneros could barely speak at first because she
   a. was not entirely fluent in English.
   b. had no one to talk to.
   c. felt an urge to express herself in writing.
   *d. felt terribly out of place in the community.

4. After she finished her studies in Iowa, Cisneros felt torn between wanting to write and wanting to
   *a. do something for her community.
   b. have a big family.
   c. travel.
   d. work in the visual arts.

5. The most important type of recognition to Cisneros is knowing that she has
   a. won the praise of literary critics.
   *b. touched the lives of many different people.
   c. satisfied her need to express herself.
   d. supported herself entirely through writing.

# UNIT FIVE

## Part One
### Full Circle
### Test Generator

1. The narrator's actions at the accident scene show her to be
   a. very bossy.
   *b. very capable.
   c. easily distracted.
   d. emotionally uninvolved.

2. The police want to find the man in the blue pickup mainly because they want to
   a. arrest him for murder.
   b. arrest him for stealing the truck.
   *c. find out what he might have noticed.
   d. charge him with giving them false information.

3. Judy Layton is uncooperative because she
   a. is in a hurry.
   *b. is trying to hide something.
   c. is upset over Caroline's death.
   d. doesn't like the narrator.

4. What surprises the narrator about Ron Cagle?
   a. He is at home in the middle of the day.
   *b. He isn't the man she saw driving a blue pickup.
   c. He can't explain the mystery of the blue pickup.
   d. He hadn't noticed that his license plates were switched.

5. Terry Layton is tied to the murder by all of the following except
   a. a gun.
   b. a stolen pickup.
   c. his running away.
   *d. fingerprints at the crime scene.

### Wasps' Nest
### Test Generator

1. From the characterization in this story, you can guess that Hercule Poirot is known for his
   a. gloomy outlook.
   *b. powers of observation.
   c. fiery temper.
   d. bumbling good humor.

2. Poirot believes that Molly Deane plans to
   a. encourage a friendship between Harrison and Langton.
   b. marry Harrison.
   *c. break her engagement to Harrison.
   d. accuse Langton of murder.

3. Whose life is Poirot primarily trying to save?
   a. Harrison's
   b. his own
   c. Molly's
   *d. Langton's

4. Why does Harrison want Langton to meet with him in the garden?
   a. He wants Langton to kill the wasps.
   b. He wants to murder Langton.
   c. He hopes to convince Langton to leave Molly alone.
   *d. He wants his suicide to look like a murder.

5. In the end, Harrison is
   a. disappointed and bitter.
   *b. grateful to Poirot.
   c. angry and confused.
   d. determined to try again.

### Trifles
### Test Generator

1. Mrs. Wright is never seen on stage because she is
   *a. in jail.
   b. at Mrs. Hale's house.
   c. in a mental institution.
   d. upstairs in the bedroom.

2. The way the men behave toward Mrs. Hale and Mrs. Peters suggests that the men
   a. are suspicious of what the women might be up to.
   b. sympathize with the women's feelings for Mrs. Wright.
   c. realize that the women may have insights the men lack.
   *d. think the women are concerned with unimportant matters.

3. Mrs. Hale indicates that she feels guilty about
   a. protecting Mrs. Wright.
   *b. not visiting Mrs. Wright.
   c. not preventing Mr. Wright's death.
   d. having had unfriendly feelings toward
      Mr. Wright.

4. What do Mrs. Hale and Mrs. Peters think
   happened to the canary?
   a. A cat killed it.
   *b. Mr. Wright killed it.
   c. Mrs. Wright killed it.
   d. It died as a result of neglect.

5. As Mrs. Peters remembers her kitten and her
   homesteading experiences, she begins to
   a. realize that women can withstand any hardship.
   b. believe that hardships can, and should,
      be endured.
   c. feel that her own life was harder than
      Mrs. Wright's.
   *d. feel more and more sympathetically toward
      Mrs. Wright.

## The Great Taos Bank Robbery
## Test Generator

1. The suspects are able to elude capture for
   so long because
   a. they are careful.
   b. they are very clever.
   *c. the police search is ineffective.
   d. there are so few police officers looking
      for them.

2. The reaction of the spectators to the attempt
   to rob the bank is one of
   a. panic.
   b. boredom.
   c. contempt.
   *d. great interest.

3. The plan to rob the bank fails when
   a. Mrs. Fish calls the city editor.
   b. the city editor calls the bank.
   c. customers become suspicious.
   *d. the suspects get embarrassed and leave.

4. The suspects stay in town because they
   *a. have no money.
   b. have been injured.
   c. think they are safer in town.
   d. feel guilty about what they have done.

## Part Two
## The Open Window
## Test Generator

1. Framton Nuttel traveled to a rural area to
   a. visit the rectory.
   b. start up a new business.
   *c. improve his health.
   d. call on his sister's acquaintances.

2. According to Vera, the window was open because
   *a. Mrs. Sappleton hoped for the return of her
      husband and brothers, who had died three
      years earlier.
   b. it was a warm October day.
   c. Mrs. Sappleton preferred to go in and out
      that way.
   d. the house felt creepy and haunted when it was
      closed up tight.

3. Why was Mrs. Sappleton's conversation horrible
   to Framton?
   a. He found hunting an intolerable subject.
   *b. She spoke cheerfully of people he believed
      to be dead.
   c. He could tell she wasn't interested in him.
   d. She was the kind of person who grated on
      his nerves.

4. Framton Nuttel is portrayed as
   a. a clever wit.
   b. a self-assured young man.
   c. a person with something to hide.
   *d. a rather dull fellow.

5. Vera is remarkable for her
   a. beauty and charm.
   *b. imaginative storytelling.
   c. empathy for others.
   d. considerate hospitality.

6. In the end, the reader discovers that Framton Nuttel is
   *a. totally fooled by the story.
   b. afraid of dogs.
   c. totally lacking in manners.
   d. reckless and headstrong.

## Sorry, Right Number
## Test Generator

1. Early in the play, Katie believes that the mysterious call is placed by someone who
   *a. needs help.
   b. is trying to warn her.
   c. is trying to frighten her.
   d. is about to do something desperate.

2. Why is Katie convinced that the caller is someone in her family?
   *a. The caller's voice sounds familiar.
   b. The caller says she is a family member.
   c. Katie believes that no one else would call.
   d. Katie is the type of person who expects the worst.

3. Katie's worry about her sister is based mainly on the fact that
   a. Dawn has a baby.
   b. Dawn's phone is busy.
   c. Dawn lives in the country.
   *d. Dawn's husband is out of town.

4. All of the following add to the suspense at Dawn's house except
   a. the scratches on the door.
   b. no answer to the doorbell.
   *c. the music playing on the Walkman.
   d. Bill's feeling that a gun might be necessary.

5. After leaving Dawn's house, Bill seems to feel that Katie
   a. overreacted a little.
   b. overreacted a great deal.
   *c. behaved reasonably.
   d. imagined the phone call.

6. In the last scene of the play, which of the following would be necessary only if the play were performed on stage instead of being filmed by a camera?
   *a. Two actresses would be needed to play Katie.
   b. The viewer would have to be caught up in the plot.
   c. There would have to be two different rooms shown.
   d. The operator would have to be shown instead of only heard.

## Beware: Do Not Read This Poem
## Test Generator Open-Book Test

1. According to the speaker in this poem, how are the poem and the mirrors alike?
   a. Both offer only reflections.
   b. Both are the subject of "thriller."
   c. Both give victims a warning.
   *d. Both entrap people.

2. Which of these devices is used most in this poem?
   a. rhyme
   b. alliteration
   *c. repetition
   d. assonance

3. What does the first part of this poem describe?
   *a. a television show or movie
   b. a true story
   c. another poem
   d. a dream

4. Which word best describes the tone of lines 19–29?
   a. cheerful
   *b. threatening
   c. mysterious
   d. angry

5. The last part of the poem is quite different from the rest in that it
   a. suggests mysterious disappearances.
   b. addresses the reader directly.
   *c. provides statistics.
   d. adds suspense.

## In the Family
### Test Generator

1. The people in the mirror differ from those in the room because they
   a. cannot hear.
   *b. have less color.
   c. don't eat.
   d. show no feelings.

2. When Clara ate the salad that Eulalia passed to her, she
   a. gained magical powers.
   b. became ill.
   *c. faded and died.
   d. fainted.

3. Which sentence best describes the narrator of this story?
   *a. She accepts the extraordinary as ordinary.
   b. She has a lively imagination.
   c. She is unusually bold and fearless.
   d. She enjoys surprising people.

4. The narrator's feelings toward the people in the mirror are
   a. filled with deep emotion.
   b. tinged by guilt and regret.
   c. filled with fascination and wonder.
   *d. very matter-of-fact.

## A Very Old Man with Enormous Wings
### Test Generator

1. A recurring image in this story suggests that the house and yard are filled with
   a. bright light.
   *b. unpleasant odors.
   c. musical sounds.
   d. gentle breezes.

2. The wise neighbor woman thought that angels
   a. would bring good fortune.
   b. could save a sick child's life.
   *c. should be clubbed to death.
   d. were God's messengers.

3. Father Gonzales believed that an angel would
   a. never come to earth.
   b. seem quite human.
   c. never grow old.
   *d. understand Latin.

4. The old man's wings were
   *a. battered and infested with parasites.
   b. awkwardly attached to his body.
   c. a source of dignity and pride.
   d. generally hidden from sight.

5. How did the old man with wings change the lives of Pelayo and Elisenda?
   a. They became more generous.
   b. He confirmed their religious faith.
   *c. They became rich because of him.
   d. He saved their child's life.

# UNIT SIX

## Part One
### Book 9
### *from the* Odyssey
### Test Generator

1. Who is the narrator of this book of the *Odyssey*?
   a. Zeus
   *b. Odysseus
   c. Polyphemus
   d. a person outside the story

2. The effect of the Lotus plant on Odysseus' men is most similar to the effect of
   a. poison.
   b. medicine.
   c. chocolate.
   *d. addictive drugs.

3. Why do Odysseus and his men enter Polyphemus' cave?
   a. to kill Polyphemus
   b. to capture Polyphemus
   c. to find desperately needed food and shelter
   *d. to satisfy Odysseus' curiosity about Polyphemus

4. Polyphemus announces early on that he has no respect for Zeus. This immediately makes the situation of Odysseus and his men less
   a. dangerous.
   *b. predictable.
   c. suspenseful.
   d. complicated.

5. In exchange for the wine, Polyphemus promises to
   *a. eat Odysseus last.
   b. let Odysseus go free.
   c. sacrifice his prize ram to Zeus.
   d. spare the rest of Odysseus' men.

6. Why does Odysseus reveal his true identity to Polyphemus?
   a. His men urge him to.
   *b. He is overcome by anger.
   c. He thinks Zeus is listening.
   d. He thinks it will make Polyphemus less angry with his men.

7. By informing Polyphemus of his true name and the fact that he and his men have escaped, Odysseus clearly
   a. pleases his men.
   b. impresses his men.
   *c. endangers his men.
   d. acts to shorten his journey home.

8. In Book 9, Odysseus' greatest weakness as a leader of men has to do with
   *a. being hot-headed.
   b. being unwilling to risk lives.
   c. having a negative outlook on life.
   d. not wanting to stand out among his men.

### Book 10
### *from the* Odyssey
### Test Generator

1. Odysseus' men are afraid of the wolves and lions they meet outside Circe's house because the animals
   *a. are so tame.
   b. are so beautiful.
   c. are so ferocious.
   d. can speak like people.

2. Why does Circe turn half of Odysseus' men into pigs?
   a. They insulted her.
   b. They threatened her.
   *c. She just feels like doing it.
   d. She wants to get Odysseus' attention.

3. Circe realizes who Odysseus is when
   a. she first sees him.
   *b. he resists her drug.
   c. he goes to bed with her.
   d. he asks to leave her house.

4. After staying with Circe for a year, Odysseus is reminded of home by
   a. Circe.
   *b. his men.
   c. his own heart.
   d. Eurylochus.

## Book 12
### *from the* Odyssey
### Test Generator

1. In Book 12, Circe
   *a. helps Odysseus.
   b. hinders Odysseus.
   c. both helps and hinders Odysseus.
   d. neither helps nor hinders Odysseus.

2. The danger of the Sirens is associated with their
   *a. voices.
   b. beauty.
   c. knowledge.
   d. physical strength.

3. What is Scylla?
   a. a whirlpool
   b. a drifting rock
   *c. a six-headed monster
   d. a slippery mountain that cannot be crossed

4. Circe advises Odysseus to
   a. fight Scylla.
   b. avoid Scylla.
   c. try to bargain with Scylla.
   *d. accept the idea of losing some of his men to Scylla.

## Books 21, 22, and 23
### *from the* Odyssey
### Test Generator

1. All of the following characters aid Odysseus in his battle against the suitors except for
   a. Zeus.
   *b. Penelope.
   c. Odysseus' son, Telemachus.
   d. the servants, Eumaeus and Philoetius.

2. Suitors participating in the archery contest must first string the bow. Who succeeds in this first step?
   *a. Odysseus
   b. Telemachus, Odysseus' son
   c. Antinous, the ringleader of the suitors
   d. Eurymachus, the suitor who pleads for the suitors' lives

3. The suitors look down on Odysseus when he first appears because they think he
   *a. is an old beggar.
   b. is no longer in favor with the gods.
   c. is too weary from his journey to harm them.
   d. was wrong to leave Penelope alone for so long.

4. Penelope's initial reaction to Odysseus is one of
   a. joy.
   b. anger.
   c. shock.
   *d. distrust.

## *Part Two*
### The Tragedy of Romeo and Juliet: Act One
### Test Generator Open-Book Test

1. How does the prince react to the tensions between the Capulets and Montagues?
   a. He favors the Capulets.
   b. He favors the Montagues.
   *c. He insists that both must end their hostilities.
   d. He suggests that they join their two houses in marriage.

2. According to Romeo's parents, how has Romeo been spending his days?
   *a. pining away in a dark room
   b. picking fights with the Capulets in the town square
   c. reading and writing romantic poetry
   d. talking about love with anyone who will listen

3. When Paris states his interest in marrying Juliet, Juliet's father
   a. asks Juliet to look upon Paris favorably.
   *b. tells Paris that Juliet is still too young to marry.
   c. tells Juliet she must marry the man her parents choose.
   d. says he hopes to find a suitor more to his liking than Paris.

4. Juliet's mother and the nurse agree that
   a. the nurse's late husband was very witty.
   b. Juliet is too young to be thinking of love.
   c. a man such as Paris is unworthy of Juliet.
   *d. Juliet is old enough to be married.

5. When Benvolio and Mercutio encourage Romeo to dance at the Capulet party, they are trying to
   a. help Romeo gain Rosaline's attention.
   b. annoy Tybalt and the other Capulets.
   *c. distract Romeo from his gloomy thoughts.
   d. bring Romeo and Juliet together.

6. Which character in Act One serves as a foil for Tybalt?
   a. Romeo
   b. Juliet
   c. Benvolio
   *d. Capulet

## The Tragedy of Romeo and Juliet: Act Two
## Test Generator Open-Book Test

1. After the party at the Capulet house, Mercutio and Benvolio
   a. are worried about Romeo's interest in Juliet.
   *b. assume that Romeo still pines for Rosaline.
   c. wonder why Romeo has suddenly cheered up.
   d. feel angry because Romeo has deserted them.

2. When Romeo sees Juliet at her window, he compares her to
   a. the night.
   b. a flower.
   *c. the sunrise.
   d. a bird.

3. In the speech that begins "O Romeo, Romeo! wherefore art thou Romeo?" Juliet expresses the idea that
   a. she will seek far and wide to find her Romeo.
   b. her love for Romeo can only lead to disaster.
   c. no man's love for her can ever equal the love she feels for Romeo.
   *d. true love is more important than loyalty to a family name.

4. When Mercutio and Benvolio meet on the street the morning after the party, their conversation reveals that
   a. Tybalt is not to be taken seriously.
   *b. Tybalt has challenged Romeo to a duel.
   c. Romeo has surprised Tybalt with his boldness.
   d. Romeo has been seriously injured by Rosaline.

5. When Juliet's nurse encounters Romeo and his friends, they
   a. show respect.
   b. try to avoid her.
   *c. tease and insult her.
   d. show their surprise.

6. At the end of Act Two, Friar Laurence takes Romeo and Juliet aside to
   *a. perform a marriage ceremony.
   b. give them advice.
   c. hide them from their enemies.
   d. discover their plans.

## The Tragedy of Romeo and Juliet: Act Three
## Test Generator Open-Book Test

1. What type of remark does Mercutio specialize in when he engages in word play?
   a. proverbs
   *b. insults
   c. compliments
   d. nonsense

2. After killing Tybalt, Romeo flees to
   a. his parents' house.
   b. Juliet's house.
   *c. Friar Laurence's cell.
   d. the city of Mantua.

3. When Romeo hears he has been banished, he feels
   a. relieved.
   b. angry.
   c. frightened.
   *d. miserable.

4. What poetic device is used in Juliet's lines, "Come, civil night, / Thou sober-suited matron, all in black"?
   a. simile
   b. allusion
   *c. personification
   d. assonance

5. Friar Laurence attempts to convince Romeo that
   *a. he has many reasons to be happy.
   b. he must go to the prince and confess at once.
   c. trying to visit Juliet now would be too dangerous.
   d. even death would be better than banishment.

6. When Juliet objects to marrying Paris, her parents are
   a. worried.
   b. suspicious.
   c. sad.
   *d. angry.

7. At the end of Act Three, when the nurse tells Juliet what a wonderful husband Paris would make, Juliet feels
   a. grateful.
   *b. betrayed.
   c. puzzled.
   d. proud.

## The Tragedy of Romeo and Juliet: Act Four
## Test Generator Open-Book Test

1. Capulet wanted Juliet to be married in haste so that she would
   a. forget all about Romeo.
   *b. be distracted from grieving for Tybalt.
   c. soon be gone from his house.
   d. stop behaving in a childish manner.

2. How does Juliet feel about drinking the potion that Friar Laurence gave her?
   a. eager
   b. sad
   *c. frightened
   d. confident

3. Juliet drinks the potion mainly because she feels
   a. loyal to Friar Laurence.
   b. curious about its effects.
   c. sure it will make her feel better.
   *d. trapped by the wedding plans.

4. Juliet's father is so eager to have the wedding a day early that he agrees to
   *a. do women's work.
   b. provide the music.
   c. invite fewer guests.
   d. let Juliet choose her own clothes.

5. Paris is portrayed throughout the play as
   a. a villain.
   *b. a good man.
   c. a clumsy oaf.
   d. an old fool.

## The Tragedy of Romeo and Juliet: Act Five
## Test Generator Open-Book Test

1. At the beginning of Scene 1, Romeo is in Mantua feeling
   a. miserable and angry.
   b. fearful of the future.
   *c. optimistic and happy.
   d. impatient for change.

2. When Romeo hears that Juliet is dead, he immediately decides to
   a. kill Paris.
   b. return to his family.
   *c. kill himself.
   d. speak with the friar.

3. If Romeo had received Friar Laurence's letter, he would have
   a. waited in Mantua.
   b. gone to Verona to avenge Juliet's death.
   c. tried to change the plan.
   *d. gone to Verona to get Juliet.

4. Why does Paris attack Romeo at the tomb?
   *a. He thinks Romeo is planning some villainy.
   b. He is jealous of Juliet's love for Romeo.
   c. He is in a rage because of his grief.
   d. He hates all Montagues.

5. Which is the only thing that might be considered a "good" result of this tragedy?
   a. the death of Paris
   *b. the end of the family feud
   c. the death of Tybalt
   d. the arrest of Friar Laurence

# Writing Assessment

## Contents

**To the Teacher** . . . . . . . . . . . . . . . . . . . . . . . . . . . . . . . . . . . . . . . . 212

**Holistic Scoring Guide** . . . . . . . . . . . . . . . . . . . . . . . . . . . . . . . . . 213

**General Rubric** . . . . . . . . . . . . . . . . . . . . . . . . . . . . . . . . . . . . . . . . 215

**Writing Prompts for Assessment Practice**

Personal and Expressive Writing . . . . . . . . . . . . . . . . . . . . . . . . . . 216

Observation and Description . . . . . . . . . . . . . . . . . . . . . . . . . . . . . 217

Narrative and Literary Writing . . . . . . . . . . . . . . . . . . . . . . . . . . . 218

Informative Writing . . . . . . . . . . . . . . . . . . . . . . . . . . . . . . . . . . . . 219

Persuasion . . . . . . . . . . . . . . . . . . . . . . . . . . . . . . . . . . . . . . . . . . . 220

# To the Teacher

This section provides several different tools to help you conduct holistic evaluations of your students' writing. Holistic evaluation is a quick, guided method for evaluating writing. An evaluator reads the piece through, considers certain important features, and immediately assigns a grade. The grade may be a single rating for the entire piece of writing or a set of ratings for the different features being considered.

- **Holistic Scoring Guide** (213–214) Helps you rate papers objectively and consistently. This guide can be used to assign an overall rating after you have analyzed a paper using the General Rubric or a mode-specific rubric. To adapt to a three-point rating system, focus on the level designations (strong, average, weak).

- **General Rubric** (215) Demonstrates a multi-rating type of holistic evaluation, based on a list of major attributes of content and form that characterizes most types of writing. This rubric is useful for almost any type of writing.

- **Writing Prompts** (216–220) Available to help your students prepare for essay tests.

For guidance in evaluating your students' writing, you can refer to the scored student models and rubrics that appear in the Unit Resource Books.

# Holistic Scoring Guide

The following 6-point scale shows the features that tend to appear in a range of student papers representing various levels of accomplishment. The aim of the scale is to guide teachers in the evaluation of student papers according to a set of standards that are similar to those used in large-scale evaluations of student writing all across the country. A single student's paper may not include all the characteristics identified with any one score point, but it can be assigned a score by looking for the description that most nearly matches its features or its dominant impression. Some allowance should be made for minor errors in style, usage, mechanics, and spelling on the unit assessment, since that test does not provide time for revision.

## Level: Strong

| Exceptional — 6 points | Commendable — 5 points |
|---|---|
| A paper at score point 6 <ul><li>Has a clear and consistent focus</li><li>Has a logical organization</li><li>Uses transitions to connects ideas</li><li>Supports ideas with details, quotations, examples, and/or other evidence</li><li>Exhibits well-formed sentences varying in structure</li><li>Exhibits a rich vocabulary, including precise language that is appropriate for the purpose and audience of the paper</li><li>Contains almost no errors in usage, mechanics, and spelling</li></ul> | A paper at score point 5 has the same general features of organization and effective elaboration as a 6-point paper, but it represents a somewhat less accomplished performance. It may, for example, <ul><li>Have an organization that is predictable or unnecessarily mechanical</li><li>Lack the depth and logical precision of a 6-point paper in presenting its argument and supporting evidence</li><li>Exhibit appropriate sentence variety and vocabulary but without the control and richness of a 6-point paper</li><li>Contain a few errors in usage, mechanics, and spelling</li></ul> |

## Level: Average

| Proficient      4 points | Basic      3 points |
|---|---|
| A paper at score point 4 <br><br> • Has a fairly clear focus that may occasionally become obscured <br><br> • Shows an organizational pattern, but relationships between ideas may sometimes be difficult to understand <br><br> • Contains supporting evidence that may lack effect and so only superficially develops ideas <br><br> • Has complete and varied sentences most of the time <br><br> • Contains some errors in usage, mechanics, and spelling but which do not confuse meaning | A paper at score point 3 <br><br> • Has a vague focus and so may contain irrelevant details or digressions <br><br> • Shows an attempt at organization, but connections between ideas are difficult to understand <br><br> • Lacks important supporting evidence, or the evidence cited does not sufficiently develop ideas <br><br> • Shows little sentence variety <br><br> • Contains several serious errors in usage, mechanics, and spelling which causes distraction and some confusion about meaning |

## Level: Weak

| Limited      2 points | Minimal      1 point |
|---|---|
| A paper at score point 2 <br><br> • Has a topic but does not include any elaboration <br><br> • Lacks plausible support for ideas <br><br> • Shows limited word choice <br><br> • Contains serious and numerous errors in usage, mechanics, and spelling which leads to confusion about meaning | A paper at score point 1 <br><br> • Only minimally addresses the topic and lacks a discernible idea <br><br> • Has only a few simple sentences <br><br> • Shows minimal word choice <br><br> • May be incoherent and/or have serious errors in almost every sentence |

A paper is unable to be scored if it is
- illegible
- unrelated to the topic
- only a rewording of the prompt
- written in a foreign language
- not written at all

# General Rubric

| Ideas and Content | Weak | Average | Strong |
|---|---|---|---|
| 1. Contains an engaging introduction that identifies the topic | | | |
| 2. Develops a writing topic appropriate to the assignment | | | |
| 3. Fulfills the writer's general purpose and specific goals | | | |
| 4. States ideas clearly and elaborates on them with specific supporting details and examples | | | |
| 5. Uses vivid, precise language that is appropriate to the audience and the writing type | | | |
| 6. Includes an effective conclusion | | | |

| Structure and Form | | | |
|---|---|---|---|
| 7. Includes a well-developed introduction, body, and conclusion | | | |
| 8. Demonstrates proper and effective paragraphing | | | |
| 9. Uses a logical, effective organizational strategy consistent with the writing type | | | |
| 10. Includes transitional words and phrases to show relationships among ideas and maintain coherence within and between paragraphs | | | |
| 11. Uses a variety of sentence structures | | | |

| Grammar, Usage, and Mechanics | | | |
|---|---|---|---|
| 12. Contains no more than two or three minor errors in grammar and usage | | | |
| 13. Contains no more than two or three minor errors in spelling, capitalization, and punctuation | | | |

## Additional Comments

_____

_____

# Prompts for Personal and Expressive Writing

Imagine that you could communicate with a teenager who lived one hundred years ago. Write an informal letter to that person explaining what life is like for you. Highlight specific ways your lives might be the same and ways they might be different.

Think about a time in your life when you were afraid but acted in spite of your fear. Write an autobiographical account of your experience. Emphasize what you learned from it and how it changed you.

Brainstorm about a recent fad or style of clothing that you and your friends are enthusiastic about. Consider what makes the fad unique and why you think it enjoys such popularity. Then write a "time-capsule" entry for your journal to be read several years from now. Analyze the fad's popularity and express your opinion about it.

Think about a holiday or vacation you have spent with your family. Write a letter to a friend or relative describing your experience and the feelings associated with it.

# Prompts for Observation and Description

You've had many teachers over the years. Which one was the most memorable? Think about the qualities that make that teacher stand out. For your school newspaper, write a character sketch of that teacher.

Write a description of a familiar object for your classmates, without naming the object directly. Discuss both the object's physical appearance and the function in precise, vivid language that reveals its identity.

Recall an interesting exhibit or display that you have seen at a museum, an aquarium, a zoo, or any other place. Write a description of that exhibit for your local newspaper. Include specific sensory details to make your writing come alive.

In his poem "My Heart Leaps Up," the English poet William Wordsworth expressed his enthusiasm for the simple beauty of a rainbow: "My heart leaps up when I behold / A rainbow in the sky." Think about some phenomenon of nature that moves you. Write a description of your subject for an audience of young children. Use sensory language that will help the children share your feelings.

# Prompts for Narrative and Literary Writing

Imagine that, like a cat, you had nine lives. Write a story for your friends about one of your previous lives. Describe who you were, when you lived, and an important incident in your life.

Who is "your most unforgettable character"? Relate an episode that guarantees that this person would remain in your memory.

Think about a personal experience that taught you something about yourself, other people, or life in general. Write a narrative for your classmates describing the experience and what you learned from it.

What would you wish for if you were granted just one wish? Write a story for children about how getting your wish affects your life.

Recall a humorous incident in your life. Write a story for your school literary magazine based on this experience. Invent details if necessary to exaggerate the humor and make the characters and setting come alive for your readers.

# Prompts for Informative Writing

Imagine that the sports program at your school will be canceled next year because of budget cuts. Write a letter to your local school board that addresses this problem and proposes various realistic solutions.

Recall a time in your life when someone's friendship meant a great deal to you. Then write a composition for your school literary magazine defining friendship. Include anecdotes and personal experiences to present this abstract concept in concrete terms.

Choose a natural phenomenon that you have studied in your science class, such as thunder, the formation of stalactites and stalagmites, or the water cycle. In a presentation for grade school children, explain this phenomenon. Be sure to define any terms that may be unfamiliar to your audience.

Imagine that your school is planning an educational trip over the next holiday and that the students must choose between two destinations. Write an essay for your school newspaper in which you compare and contrast the two choices, stating the advantages and disadvantages of each.

# Prompts for Persuasion

For a national magazine, write an article arguing why parents should or should not place limits on their children's television viewing. Consider both the quality of the shows and the quantity of time spent watching them.

Think about the extracurricular activities your school offers. In what ways do students benefit from participating in these activities? In what ways might these activities be harmful? Write an essay for your school newspaper in which you support your opinion about extracurricular activities.

People place a dollar value not only on their property but on their time as well. Polls have shown, however, that the majority of American teenagers do volunteer work. Write a persuasive essay for your school newspaper explaining why teenagers should donate their time to those in need.

Your school has had a sudden increase in incidents of students bringing knives and other weapons into the school. In an effort to stop the activity, the school administration is recommending the installation of a metal detector at all doors. Do you agree with this action? Write an essay for your school newspaper supporting your position on this issue.

# Standardized Test Practice

## Contents

**To the Teacher** . . . . . . . . . . . . . . . . . . . . . . . . . . . . . . . . . . . . . . . . . . . . . . . . . 222

**To the Student** . . . . . . . . . . . . . . . . . . . . . . . . . . . . . . . . . . . . . . . . . . . . . . . . . 223

**Analogies** . . . . . . . . . . . . . . . . . . . . . . . . . . . . . . . . . . . . . . . . . . . . . . . . . . . . . 225

**Sentence Completion**
Part A . . . . . . . . . . . . . . . . . . . . . . . . . . . . . . . . . . . . . . . . . . . . . . . . . . . . . 229
Part B . . . . . . . . . . . . . . . . . . . . . . . . . . . . . . . . . . . . . . . . . . . . . . . . . . . . . 233

**Error Identification** . . . . . . . . . . . . . . . . . . . . . . . . . . . . . . . . . . . . . . . . . . . . . 237

**Error Correction** . . . . . . . . . . . . . . . . . . . . . . . . . . . . . . . . . . . . . . . . . . . . . . . 241

**Revision-in-Context**
Passage I . . . . . . . . . . . . . . . . . . . . . . . . . . . . . . . . . . . . . . . . . . . . . . . . . 245
Passage II . . . . . . . . . . . . . . . . . . . . . . . . . . . . . . . . . . . . . . . . . . . . . . . . . 247

**Critical Reading**
Passage I . . . . . . . . . . . . . . . . . . . . . . . . . . . . . . . . . . . . . . . . . . . . . . . . . 250
Passage II . . . . . . . . . . . . . . . . . . . . . . . . . . . . . . . . . . . . . . . . . . . . . . . . . 253
Passage I—Darkness at Noon . . . . . . . . . . . . . . . . . . . . . . . . . . . . . . . . 256
Passage II—Thumbprint . . . . . . . . . . . . . . . . . . . . . . . . . . . . . . . . . . . . 256

**Answer Key** . . . . . . . . . . . . . . . . . . . . . . . . . . . . . . . . . . . . . . . . . . . . . . . . . . . 323

# To the Teacher

This section provides opportunities for your students to develop strategies for performing well on standardized tests. Practice items are included for areas typically found on standardized tests: analogies, sentence completion, error identification, error correction, revision-in-context passages, and critical reading passages.

Each set of practice items explains the purpose of that particular test, provides an example, and describes specific strategies students can use to be successful. The To the Student form on the facing page provides general test-taking strategies. You may wish to duplicate this form, distribute it to your students, and discuss the strategies.

# To the Student

During the next few years you will be taking many standardized tests that evaluate your understanding of English. No matter what type of test you are facing, there are steps you can take beforehand to maximize your performance. As you work on the sample test questions in this booklet, you will begin to develop strategies that will help you perform well. You might also want to try using the following general strategies, which work for many people.

## Physical and Emotional Preparation

- Before the test get at least eight hours of sleep and eat a good breakfast and/or lunch.

- Wear comfortable clothes.

- Try to relax and maintain a positive attitude.

## Taking the Test

- When you receive the test, glance over it, noting the types of questions and the number of points to be awarded for each.

- Read and listen to directions carefully.

- Budget your time, making sure that you do not spend too much time on any single question.

- Read each question and all answer choices before answering. Many items include choices that may seem right at first glance but are actually wrong.

- Complete the questions that you can answer easily. Then go back to the more difficult items.

- Do not make wild guesses. Since points are deducted for incorrect answers on many standardized tests, random guessing can harm your score. If you can eliminate one or two of the answer choices, however, your chance of choosing the correct answer is increased.

# Analogies

**Analogies** involve pairs of related words. In many analogy questions you are given two words and are asked to find another pair of words that are related in the same way. Here is a typical question:

> MICROSCOPE : GERMS : : (A) doctor : illness  (B) shot : serum
> (C) patient : nurse  (D) vision : glasses  (E) telescope : stars

The analogy can be expressed this way: "A *microscope* is to *germs* as a _?_ is to _?_."

The following strategies can help you answer analogy questions:

- Determine the relationship expressed by the original pair of words. State that relationship in a sentence:
  "A *microscope* is an apparatus used to view and study *germs*."

- Decide which other pair of words expresses a similar relationship. Test your choice by substituting those words in your sentence:
  "A *telescope* is an apparatus used to view and study *stars*."

Here are the most common types of relationships used in analogies:

| Type of Analogy | Example |
|---|---|
| cause to effect | virus : disease : : carelessness : error |
| part to whole | finger : hand : : spoke : wheel |
| object to purpose | car : transportation : : lamp : illumination |
| action to object | dribble : basketball : : push : wheelbarrow |
| item to category | giraffe : mammal : : grasshopper : insect |
| item to characteristic | owl : nocturnal : : lion : carnivorous |
| word to synonym | accumulate : increase : : squander : decrease |
| word to antonym | cold : hot : : arctic : tropical |
| worker to creation | composer : symphony : : author : novel |
| time sequence | infant : child : : adolescent : adult |
| spatial sequence | ceiling : floor : : sky : ground |
| word to grammatical variant | go : went : : lose : lost |

Choose the letter of the pair of words that best completes each analogy.

1. JUICE : ORANGE : : (A) beef : meat  (B) apple : core  (C) pie : bakery
   (D) clouds : rain  (E) milk : cow

2. TRIGGER : GUN : : (A) ignition : car  (B) crossbow : arrow  (C) rifle : bullet
   (D) bullet : target  (E) umbrella : handle

3. CORRAL : ENCLOSURE : : (A) grass : lawn  (B) saddle : horse  (C) food : cook
   (D) boat : dock  (E) box : container

4. ACIDITY : LEMON : : (A) air : atmosphere  (B) element : fire
   (C) water : evaporation  (D) salinity : ocean  (E) sediment : mud

5. MILLION : QUANTITY : : (A) conservation : wilderness  (B) teacher : desk
   (C) anger : emotion  (D) fish : net  (E) ten : hundred

6. AUTHOR : MANUSCRIPT : : (A) book : pages  (B) writing : stories
   (C) actor : stage  (D) sculptor : clay  (E) artist : painting

7. WOOD : BENCH : : (A) cloth : suit  (B) thread : button  (C) lock : door
   (D) paper : clip  (E) glass : reflection

8. STUBBORN : YIELD : : (A) strong : bully  (B) withdrawn : socialize
   (C) eager : begin  (D) hungry : cook  (E) angry : fight

9. IMPOSE : EXPOSE : : (A) depress : express  (B) impress : depress
   (C) impress : express  (D) invade : escape  (E) expel : impel

10. NEGLECTED : SQUALID : : (A) tidiness : tidy  (B) clean : dirty
    (C) careful : forgetful  (D) sloppy : sloping  (E) neat : spotless

11. MILITANT : AGGRESSIVE : : (A) nonviolent : peaceful  (B) lazy : active
    (C) warlike : victorious  (D) selfish : generous  (E) military : civilian

12. SCISSORS : CUT : : (A) measure : ruler  (B) hammer : pound  (C) water : drink
    (D) write : computer  (E) nail : hammer

13. INTERMITTENTLY : CONTINUOUSLY : : (A) legally : legitimately
    (B) occasionally : always  (C) infrequently : seldom  (D) always : constantly
    (E) usually : generally

14. OVERWORK : STRESS : : (A) relaxation : anxiety  (B) gardening : lawn
    (C) starvation : hunger  (D) sport : leisure  (E) dreaming : sleep

15. RECALL : PAST : : (A) anticipate : prediction  (B) forget : reminder
    (C) foretell : future  (D) foresee : hindsight  (E) guess : luck

16. AGENT : ACTOR : : (A) proprietor : property  (B) lawyer : client
    (C) banker : investment  (D) employee : employer  (E) dentist : doctor

17. GENERATE : ELECTRICITY : : (A) mine : gold (B) conduct : orchestra
    (C) invent : patent (D) radiate : light (E) heat : fire

18. EXISTENCE : EXIST : : (A) assume : assumption (B) recreation : swim
    (C) painting : create (D) transportation : travel (E) domination : dominate

19. CAUSE : EFFECT : : (A) accident : car (B) snow : ice (C) spring : weather
    (D) scream : fear (E) lightning : thunder

20. HISTORY : MYTH : : (A) fact : fiction (B) truth : newspaper (C) narrative : story
    (D) moral : fable (E) science fiction : fiction

21. APPRECIATION : GRATITUDE : : (A) love : hatred (B) business : profit
    (C) advocate : supporter (D) testimony : jury (E) success : succession

22. WEAPON : ARSENAL : : (A) tool : toolbox (B) kitchen : cabinet
    (C) closet : hanger (D) gun : ammunition (E) army : warfare

23. DUPLICITY : HONESTY : : (A) fragility : delicacy (B) aggression : passivity
    (C) deterioration : recuperation (D) twin : quadruplet (E) agriculture : tractor

24. PROTEIN : NUTRIENT : : (A) food : vegetable (B) lunch : meal (C) egg : chicken
    (D) diet : hunger (E) carnivore : meat

25. MASK : DISGUISE : : (A) helmet : protect (B) ghost : appear
    (C) costume : mask (D) sword : fence (E) kidnapper : seek

26. SKIN : BODY : : (A) nail : finger (B) body : clothes (C) root : tree (D) yolk : egg
    (E) bark : trunk

27. SUN : SOLAR : : (A) planet : terrestrial (B) universe : galactic (C) moon : lunar
    (D) meteor : temporary (E) warmth : heater

28. PHYSICIAN : SYRINGE : : (A) artist : painting (B) banker : wealth
    (C) engineer : caboose (D) writer : word processor (E) teacher : grade

29. GRAPE : VINE : : (A) pear : fruit (B) cherry : tree (C) flower : pot
    (D) orchard : apple (E) root : leaf

30. PROPHET : PROFIT : : (A) emigration : immigration (B) moral : morale
    (C) flair : flare (D) verse : curse (E) learning : earning

31. YESTERDAY : TODAY : : (A) decade : century (B) day : month (C) past : present
    (D) Sunday : Saturday (E) memory : dream

32. TERMINATE : END : : (A) argue : agree (B) authorize : permit
    (C) prevent : incite (D) rain : snow (E) swim : wade

33. TRAITOR : BETRAYAL : : (A) hijacker : flight (B) consumer : product
    (C) vandal : defacement (D) artist : canvas (E) spy : investigation

34. MONKEY : AGILITY : : (A) snail : sluggishness  (B) smirk : smile  (C) stealth : fox
    (D) dog : Dalmatian  (E) robbery : thief

35. GRACE : GYMNAST : : (A) politeness : politician  (B) subtlety : spy
    (C) organization : typist  (D) predictability : magician  (E) affluence : accountant

36. MIRROR : GLASS : : (A) song : notes  (B) calendar : date
    (C) ice cream : milkshake  (D) glove : leather  (E) sofa : cushion

37. DISTILL : WATER : : (A) shred : paper  (B) exhaust : fume  (C) refine : oil
    (D) alloy : metal  (E) melt : ice

38. LIBRARY : BOOK : : (A) title : chapter  (B) sentence : paragraph
    (C) camera : film  (D) pharmacy : medicine  (E) data : computer

39. HOSPITAL : SURGEON : : (A) teacher : school  (B) courtroom : lawyer
    (C) store : shopper  (D) library : book  (E) water : duck

40. SERVITUDE : SLAVERY : : (A) king : queen  (B) latitude : longitude
    (C) limitation : restriction  (D) dependence : loneliness  (E) bandage : wound

41. CONTEMPORARY : PAST : : (A) first : last  (B) late : early  (C) ancestral : future
    (D) current : former  (E) old-fashioned : modern

42. COMPASS : NAVIGATE : : (A) pencil : educate  (B) scalpel : stitch
    (C) thermometer : convalesce  (D) odometer : travel  (E) calculator : compute

43. APERTURE : CAMERA : : (A) doorway : exit  (B) film : photograph
    (C) lips : mouth  (D) window : building  (E) fence : gate

44. BOILING : EVAPORATION : : (A) freezing : condensation  (B) eating : hunger
    (C) burning : oxidation  (D) forgetting : memorization  (E) hypothesizing : truth

45. ARM : HAND : : (A) hat : head  (B) leg : foot  (C) wrist : ankle  (D) nail : finger
    (E) bow : arrow

46. CALF : WHALE : : (A) pup : seal  (B) cow : calf  (C) robin : egg  (D) bee : drone
    (E) butterfly : caterpillar

47. TIPTOE : WALK : : (A) babble : chatter  (B) whisper : talk  (C) scurry : stroll
    (D) speak : drawl  (E) caress : strike

48. UNIFORMITY : UNIQUENESS : : (A) quantity : quality  (B) deformity : infirmity
    (C) reformation : information  (D) conformity : individuality
    (E) simplicity : directness

49. IMMODERATE : EXCESSIVE : : (A) immature : adult  (B) reasonable : irrational
    (C) immodesty : modesty  (D) immobile : stationary  (E) moderate : extreme

50. MECHANIZATION : PRODUCTIVITY : : (A) invention : discovery  (B) regulation : rules
    (C) industry : automation  (D) system : confusion  (E) organization : efficiency

# Sentence Completion

**Sentence completion** questions test your ability to understand words and to recognize relationships among parts of a sentence. You are given a sentence with one or more words missing and are asked to choose the word or words that best complete the sentence. Here is a typical question:

> The argument _____, but Aaron felt his anger _____.
> (A) proceeded . . . grow  (B) exploded . . . simmer
> (C) continued . . . diminish  (D) regressed . . . disappear
> (E) ended . . . slightly

The following strategies can help you answer sentence completion questions:

- Read the entire sentence carefully, paying particular attention to words that indicate relationships such as contrast *(but, although, however)* and similarity *(and, another, likewise)*. For example, the word *but* in the sample question is a clue that the correct pair of words will express a contrast. The correct answer is *C, continued . . . diminish.*

- Look for grammatical clues. Does the structure of the sentence require a noun? a verb? an adjective or adverb? If a verb is needed, what tense and number must it be?

- Try each of the choices in the sentence. Eliminate those that do not make sense, are grammatically incorrect, or contradict information in the sentence.

Choose the word or words that best complete each sentence.

## Part A

1. Julio was impressed with the _____ of the mountain bike.
   - (A) mediocrity
   - (B) predictability
   - (C) technique
   - (D) quality
   - (E) expense

2. The white shark we encountered while swimming was a(n) _____ to our safety.
   - (A) predator
   - (B) threat
   - (C) prey
   - (D) surprise
   - (E) inducement

3. Because of their _____ and hostility, the two apes in the zoo had to be separated.
   - (A) remoteness
   - (B) resourcefulness
   - (C) aggressiveness
   - (D) age
   - (E) playfulness

4. The _____ in the directions for preparing the dessert made several outcomes possible.
   (A) uniformity
   (B) diversion
   (C) mistakes
   (D) transcription
   (E) ambiguity

5. The flaw in the diamond was so imperceptible that several jewelers _____ it in their appraisal.
   (A) overlooked
   (B) disguised
   (C) extolled
   (D) mentioned
   (E) fixed

6. Sonia was very apprehensive about the _____ task that was facing her.
   (A) exciting
   (B) recognizable
   (C) daunting
   (D) forgotten
   (E) pleasant

7. Scientists do _____ in the laboratory to determine how new drugs might work in the human body.
   (A) recycling
   (B) practice
   (C) experiments
   (D) hypotheses
   (E) anticipation

8. The main character in the story is intense, solitary, _____ , and pessimistic, but at the same time likable.
   (A) abominable
   (B) brooding
   (C) benign
   (D) personable
   (E) sparkling

9. The company _____ huge profits from the sale of its popular new video program.
   (A) comprised
   (B) deducted
   (C) adapted
   (D) realized
   (E) lost

10. During the debate, Raphael forcefully _____ his team's position.
    (A) remembered
    (B) deduced
    (C) confounded
    (D) forgot
    (E) articulated

11. The colony's people expressed their yearning for self-government by denouncing the _____ with which the colonial power treated them.

   (A) integrity
   (B) doggedness
   (C) stealth
   (D) paternalism
   (E) comradeship

12. Lara behaves so _____ that she makes all her friends feel inadequate.

   (A) unpredictably
   (B) haughtily
   (C) spiritually
   (D) childishly
   (E) retroactively

13. To avoid muscle strain, exercise in _____.

   (A) moderation
   (B) daylight
   (C) sweat pants
   (D) company
   (E) repetition

14. Before attempting to move to the United States, Li studied its _____ laws.

   (A) dietary
   (B) traffic
   (C) unwritten
   (D) immigration
   (E) new

15. The vaulter's pole acts as a _____ to launch him over the bar.

   (A) cataract
   (B) catapult
   (C) lever
   (D) support
   (E) reminder

16. Psychologists say that it is better to express your feelings than to keep them _____ inside.

   (A) mottled
   (B) festering
   (C) expressive
   (D) discernible
   (E) perceptive

17. A good _____ to promote comprehension and retention of what you read is to skim the material first, noting main headings, and then to study the text carefully.

   (A) reminder
   (B) improvement
   (C) distraction
   (D) approximation
   (E) strategy

18. At the end of the term, we took a _____ exam covering everything we had studied.
   (A) confusing
   (B) conservative
   (C) comprehensive
   (D) corollary
   (E) commencement

19. After examining all the evidence, the detective _____ that the suspect could not have committed the burglary.
   (A) interpreted
   (B) aspired
   (C) concluded
   (D) reconciled
   (E) appropriated

20. One of the _____ for admission to a university is a high school diploma.
   (A) benefits
   (B) prerequisites
   (C) causes
   (D) deliberations
   (E) achievements

21. Traditionally, robins are said to _____ the arrival of spring.
   (A) estimate
   (B) herald
   (C) maintain
   (D) overtake
   (E) enjoy

22. Advertisements tend to _____ even the most unexciting products and make them seem desirable.
   (A) glamorize
   (B) expose
   (C) avoid
   (D) mention
   (E) correct

23. Keeping taxes low while also providing good services is a _____ problem in city management.
   (A) perpetual
   (B) prestigious
   (C) pessimistic
   (D) risky
   (E) responsible

24. The capacity for self-preservation is a(n) _____ quality of the wild dog.
   (A) tenuous
   (B) sporadic
   (C) inherent
   (D) undesirable
   (E) unconscious

25. The newcomer's _____ solution to the problem astonished all those who had been working on it fruitlessly for months.

   (A) insolent
   (B) incomprehensible
   (C) inept
   (D) ingenious
   (E) identical

## Part B

1. As a(n) _____ to shoppers with children, the shopping mall _____ a free child-care center.

   (A) reminder . . . had discouraged
   (B) authorization . . . employs
   (C) enticement . . . offers
   (D) empowerment . . . described
   (E) inspiration . . . will have planned

2. Naomi lives in a(n) _____ neighborhood; almost everyone has a similar _____.

   (A) large . . . aspiration
   (B) sinister . . . tactical
   (C) remote . . . mobility
   (D) ethnic . . . heritage
   (E) important . . . memory

3. The critic wrote with _____ about the performance, _____ that the play was not worth the price of admission.

   (A) indictment . . . ascertaining
   (B) approval . . . envisioned
   (C) exertion . . . remembering
   (D) derision . . . proclaiming
   (E) qualification . . . predicting

4. The lecture was so _____ that I could not _____ on what the speaker was saying.

   (A) interminable . . . concentrate
   (B) revealing . . . understand
   (C) stimulating . . . expanded
   (D) unexpected . . . dispute
   (E) symbolic . . . illuminate

5. Luis did not know the _____ of the rumor, but he _____ that Jorge had started it.

   (A) source . . . suspects
   (B) reason . . . knew
   (C) humor . . . hopes
   (D) probability . . . doubted
   (E) origin . . . thought

6. The delegation from the unaligned nation _____ between _____ and
   supporting the resolution.
   (A) dispute . . . approval
   (B) vacillated . . . opposing
   (C) intensified . . . restoring
   (D) questioned . . . apprehending
   (E) circumscribed . . . applause

7. _____ behavior is not _____ in the classroom.
   (A) Superlative . . . memorable
   (B) Disruptive . . . tolerated
   (C) Hostile . . . contemptuous
   (D) Mediocrity . . . important
   (E) Immature . . . suspected

8. Unauthorized or _____ use of certain common medications can be _____
   to your health.
   (A) urgency . . . acceptable
   (B) compulsive . . . restorative
   (C) immoderate . . . hazardous
   (D) lawlessly . . . tragic
   (E) immoral . . . comforting

9. The natural _____ of the buffalo was destroyed as _____ plains were brought
   under cultivation by farmers.
   (A) equality . . . luxuriant
   (B) significance . . . flooded
   (C) nutritional . . . extinct
   (D) family . . . uninhabited
   (E) habitat . . . vast

10. As Alexis descended the stairs to the subway, she _____ to be a(n) _____
    to the commuters who were trying to exit.
    (A) proved . . . obstacle
    (B) is trying . . . example
    (C) proposes . . . guide
    (D) has hoped . . . distraction
    (E) ceased . . . interruption

11. It would have been impossible for our ancestors to have _____ today's _____.
    (A) appreciating . . . progress
    (B) understood . . . comparison
    (C) envisioned . . . technology
    (D) encounter . . . ecology
    (E) realized . . . history

12. The caterpillar's _____ into a butterfly takes place _____, not abruptly.
    (A) arrangement . . . quickly
    (B) disintegration . . . absolutely
    (C) metamorphosis . . . gradually
    (D) turning . . . inevitable
    (E) assemblage . . . consequently

13. The Renaissance was a(n) _____ when the arts and sciences _____.
    (A) atmosphere . . . implode
    (B) experience . . . disagrees
    (C) government . . . consulted
    (D) era . . . flourished
    (E) fantasy . . . floundered

14. The union hoped to _____ a pay raise that would _____ three dollars an hour.
    (A) intellectualize . . . precede
    (B) compete . . . comprise
    (C) forgo . . . expose
    (D) negotiate . . . exceed
    (E) manifest . . . deny

15. The family's _____ situation was so good that they were able to _____ in a new home.
    (A) unhealthy . . . lived
    (B) debt . . . survive
    (C) financial . . . invest
    (D) domestic . . . communicate
    (E) intellectual . . . calculating

16. _____ plant growth could not be _____ by such an arid climate.
    (A) Abundant . . . supported
    (B) Perpetual . . . uprooted
    (C) Stunted . . . described
    (D) Useless . . . appreciated
    (E) Annually . . . interrupted

17. It would be nice if the world were an ideal place where everyone _____; unfortunately, this is not the _____.
    (A) communicates . . . implication
    (B) survived . . . opportunity
    (C) agree . . . reality
    (D) prospered . . . case
    (E) existed . . . intuition

18. During a(n) _____ of two previously _____ companies, new operating policies must be developed for the new entity.
    (A) shortage . . . hostile
    (B) merger . . . independent
    (C) alternation . . . commercial
    (D) examination . . . enterprising
    (E) communicating . . . construction

19. The psychologist was _____ in her analysis of a person's _____.
    (A) uncomplicated . . . finances
    (B) distinguishable . . . style
    (C) analytical . . . memorization
    (D) disapproval . . . habits
    (E) perceptive . . . character

20. It was easy to _____ laughter from the children, who were basically uninhibited and _____.
    (A) force . . . repressed
    (B) evoke . . . effusive
    (C) adopt . . . adaptably
    (D) persuading . . . hyperactive
    (E) negate . . . serious

21. The coach _____ a(n) _____ exercise program in preparation for the upcoming triathlon.
    (A) ends . . . forgivable
    (B) commented . . . leisurely
    (C) launched . . . rigorous
    (D) practiced . . . sophisticated
    (E) recommended . . . exemplary

22. Living in a(n) _____, essentially undeveloped part of the country _____ few of the creature comforts offered by modern society.
    (A) urban . . . extols
    (B) forgotten . . . establish
    (C) remote . . . provides
    (D) sedimentary . . . manifest
    (E) mountainous . . . interprets

23. The transparent lake and the cloudless sky are so _____ that they could _____ even the most troubled mind.
    (A) visionary . . . revere
    (B) serene . . . soothe
    (C) theoretical . . . approximately
    (D) glorious . . . condemn
    (E) unbelievably . . . convince

24. The criminal _____ the state border and _____ north to Canada.
    (A) crossed . . . headed
    (B) intersected . . . calculates
    (C) misses . . . sneaked
    (D) canceled . . . vanished
    (E) lengthened . . . disgruntled

25. The shy hero _____ his accomplishment, _____ saying that anyone could have done what he did.
    (A) preserved . . . unmercifully
    (B) ennobles . . . grotesquely
    (C) brandished . . . courageous
    (D) dismantled . . . urgently
    (E) minimized . . . modestly

# Error Identification

**Error identification** questions test your ability to recognize errors in standard English usage. In each sentence four words or phrases are underlined and marked with letters. You are asked to choose the underlined part that needs correction or to mark **E** if the sentence contains no error. Here is a typical question:

---

Many a music lover <u>believe</u> that <u>Mozart's</u> music is the <u>most beautiful</u> ever
            A           B                   C

<u>written</u>. <u>No error</u>
  D      E

---

The following strategies can help you answer error identification questions:

- Read the entire sentence carefully.

- Reexamine the underlined parts. Check for lack of agreement, errors in capitalization and punctuation, improper sentence construction, incorrect forms, and inappropriate word choice. In the sample question, the subject of the sentence, *Many a music lover,* is singular and therefore requires a singular verb. Since the verb *believe* is plural, the answer is **A.**

Choose the letter that indicates an error. If the sentence is correct, mark **E.**

1. Each of the <u>women</u> <u>has brought</u> <u>her</u> own <u>scissors.</u> <u>No error</u>
              A        B       C        D      E

2. <u>Having been spoke</u> in <u>biblical times,</u> Hebrew is one of the <u>world's</u> <u>oldest living</u>
       A               B                           C       D

languages. <u>No error</u>
           E

3. <u>Him</u> singing <u>"Danny Boy"</u> and other ethnic songs <u>was</u> the highlight of the
  A          B                        C

evening for my family and <u>me.</u> <u>No error</u>
                      D     E

4. Smallpox <u>was</u> <u>one of the worse diseases</u> in history, but <u>it</u>
           A         B                     C

<u>has been virtually wiped out</u> by a worldwide vaccination campaign. <u>No error</u>
       D                                           E

5. Neither Sasha nor Isabel <u>enjoys</u> mysteries; <u>neither one</u> <u>can never guess</u> <u>who</u>
                           A              B       C      D

the murderer is. <u>No error</u>
             E

6. One of the many differences between the letters of our alphabet <u>is</u> their
                                                                    A

   <u>age; for example,</u> o is <u>thousands'</u> of years old, whereas j and v <u>came</u> into
   B                          C                                            D

   the language about 1630. <u>No error</u>
                                 E

7. When each of the witnesses <u>takes</u> the witness stand, <u>he or she</u> <u>looks</u>
                               A                             B          C

   nervously at <u>we jury members</u>. <u>No error</u>
                D                      E

8. Columbus <u>Day,</u> along with certain other <u>holidays,</u> <u>are</u> now celebrated on
            A                                  B          C

   a Monday in order to create a <u>three-day weekend</u>. <u>No error</u>
                                  D                      E

9. Although <u>Captain William Kidd</u> was employed by England to fight <u>piracy,</u> he
            A                                                          B

   became a pirate <u>himself</u> and was ultimately executed by the government that
                    C

   <u>has once employed</u> him. <u>No error</u>
   D                         E

10. Neither the host nor the guests <u>have found</u> <u>Mr. Harris's sunglasses,</u>
                                     A              B

    <u>which were</u> <u>laying</u> on the kitchen table a few hours ago. <u>No error</u>
    C           D                                                 E

11. In 1981 twenty cents <u>was</u> the price of a first-class <u>stamp; by</u> 1991 the
                          A                                 B

    price <u>had risen</u> to <u>twenty-nine cents</u>. <u>No error</u>
          C              D                        E

12. Caring for contact lenses <u>are</u> <u>more difficult</u> than <u>caring for glasses, but</u>
                               A      B                        C

    contact lenses can be <u>more convenient</u> to wear. <u>No error</u>
                           D                            E

13. *War and Peace* <u>presents</u> an intimate picture of <u>Russian society</u> during
                    A                                    B

    the <u>wars with Napoleon, in fact</u> some critics have declared Tolstoy's
        C

    novel <u>the best ever written</u>. <u>No error</u>
          D                          E

14. Because the orchestra sounded <u>so beautifully,</u> <u>we chorus members</u>
                                  A                      B

    <u>were inspired</u> to perform <u>our very best</u>. <u>No error</u>
          C                              D                  E

15. The <u>Japanese beetle,</u> an insect harmful to <u>many kinds of plants,</u> <u>comes</u>
            A                                              B                      C

    to the United States <u>accidentally</u> in about 1916, carried on a plant from
                              D

    Japan. <u>No error</u>
               E

16. <u>Neither of the mice</u> <u>has found</u> <u>its way</u> through the <u>cleverly constructed</u>
          A                      B            C                          D

    maze yet. <u>No error</u>
                   E

17. Of all the <u>peanut-growing states,</u> <u>the state of Georgia</u> <u>is</u> the <u>more productive</u>.
                      A                              B                  C            D

    <u>No error</u>
        E

18. Early <u>operas</u> <u>were based</u> on myths and legends, but <u>more realistic</u>
              A            B                                          C

    subjects <u>have been becoming</u> popular in the nineteenth century. <u>No error</u>
                      D                                                      E

19. <u>My friend Huang</u> and his brother <u>claim</u> that no theme park <u>isn't</u> <u>more famous</u>
            A                              B                              C        D

    than Walt Disney World. <u>No error</u>
                                E

20. Visitors to Peru <u>learn</u> that many of its inhabitants <u>are</u> <u>Quechua Indians,</u> <u>whose</u>
                        A                                      B            C                D

    ancestors established the great Inca Empire in that mountainous country

    hundreds of years ago. <u>No error</u>
                              E

21. The <u>coach's</u> daughter <u>taught</u> <u>Mitsuo and myself</u> some basketball
            A                    B            C

    strategies that we <u>can use</u> in tomorrow's game. <u>No error</u>
                            D                                  E

22. Fossils are <u>seen</u> by <u>paleontologists scientists</u> who study ancient life
              A                           B

    <u>forms,</u> as records of <u>earlier</u> times. <u>No error</u>
     C                    D                E

23. As soon as one of the onlookers <u>shouted, "Look,</u> <u>there's</u> the stunt planes
                                          A              B

    <u>now!" everyone</u> in the crowd <u>scanned</u> the sky intently. <u>No error</u>
     C                          D                           E

24. Despite the fact that my <u>uncle and aunt's</u> new car includes <u>all sorts of</u> special
                              A                                  B

    features, it <u>doesn't handle</u> very <u>well</u>. <u>No error</u>
                  C               D      E

25. "<u>Were</u> any of the tourists surprised to hear Catalan spoken in the streets of
      A

    <u>Barcelona," Xavier asked,</u> "<u>Especially</u> since they had been told to study
             B                        C

    <u>Castilian Spanish?"</u> <u>No error</u>
             D                E

26. Petra is the <u>most highly skilled</u> player on our <u>team; nevertheless,</u> the coach
                      A                              B

    <u>doesn't expect</u> that the state champion <u>will be her</u>. <u>No error</u>
         C                                  D            E

27. Rebecca sang <u>well</u> last night, but <u>you're voice</u> sounded even <u>better</u> than
                   A                      B                    C

    <u>hers</u>. <u>No error</u>
     D      E

28. Every job applicant <u>has already</u> filled out <u>their application</u> and <u>has taken</u> <u>it</u>
                            A                       B                 C      D

    to the appropriate office. <u>No error</u>
                                    E

29. Most of the world <u>was unaware</u> of the existence of Hawaii until
                          A

    <u>Captain James Cook</u> <u>lands</u> there in <u>January 1778</u>. <u>No error</u>
            B              C              D              E

30. Although I <u>have known</u> our <u>village</u> librarian all my life, she <u>hardly never</u>
                   A              B                              C

    speaks to <u>either my brother or me</u>. <u>No error</u>
                      D                      E

# Error Correction

**Error correction** questions can appear in a variety of formats. One of the most common is the paragraph format shown below. These questions test your ability to recognize and correct errors in sentence construction, grammar, and usage.

In each paragraph certain words are underlined and numbered. You are asked to choose the correct version of each numbered word or phrase from the choices at the right or, if the original is correct, to mark **A** or **F.** Here is a typical paragraph:

---

Vast <u>ranches, which</u> breed cattle, sheep, and
1

other domesticated animals have operated

successfully for centuries. Now ranches for wild game

are becoming popular as well, especially in Africa. In

Botswana, for example, ostriches <u>are being raised</u>
2

profitably on ranches.

1. A. No change
   B. ranches, that
   C. ranches that
   D. ranches, and which

2. F. No change
   G. are rose
   H. are risen
   J. are rising

---

The following strategies can help you answer these questions:

- Read the entire paragraph carefully.

- Then reread each sentence, paying special attention to each underlined part.

- Decide whether the underlined part contains an error and, if so, which rewording at the right corrects the error. In number 1 of the example, *ranches, which* indicates that the clause following the comma is nonessential. However, the clause actually presents essential information, so it should be introduced by *that* and no comma. The correct rewording of number 1, therefore, is *C, ranches that.*

- If the underlined part is correct, select the first choice. In number 2, the underlined words are correct, so the answer is *F, No change.*

Choose the letter that indicates the best revision of the underlined word or words. If there is no error, mark **A** or **F.**

The growth of radio, television, <u>newspapers and</u>
1
other media <u>have drawn</u> many artists and performers
2
to the attention of the public. For every famous and

generously paid rock star or <u>sculptor, however,</u> there
3
are thousands of other highly talented <u>artists which</u>
4
remain relatively unknown. Perhaps no area of

artistic endeavor receives <u>as little</u> recognition as folk
5
art. This lack of widespread appreciation for the

indigenous arts is particularly sad in a country like the

United States, <u>with it's</u> rich tapestry of cultures.
6
In formal recognition of America's folk art, the

National Endowment for the Arts awards $5,000 grants

to exceptional artists who <u>have chose</u> to use
7
traditional art forms. Those honored by the program

include a Hispanic carver of saints, a Cajun fiddler, a

quilter from Missouri, <u>a Appalachian</u> ballad singer, a
8
group of African-American gospel singers, an

Ojibwa storyteller, and a Pueblo potter. One cannot

<u>help and be</u> struck by the magnificent diversity of
9
the art forms, a phenomenon <u>that reflect</u> the diversity
10
of the American heritage.

1. A. No change
   B. newspapers, and
   C. newspapers; and
   D. newspapers also

2. F. No change
   G. have drawed
   H. had drew
   J. has drawn

3. A. No change
   B. sculptor; however
   C. sculptor although
   D. sculptor and also

4. F. No change
   G. artists, which
   H. artists who
   J. artists that

5. A. No change
   B. as less
   C. less
   D. as least

6. F. No change
   G. with its
   H. with our
   J. with their

7. A. No change
   B. choose
   C. had chose
   D. will be choosing

8. F. No change
   G. a appalachian
   H. an Appalachian
   J. the Appalachian

9. A. No change
   B. help and been
   C. help, and be
   D. help being

10. F. No change
    G. that reflects
    H. which reflect
    J. which, reflect

You are their in geography class, watching the teacher
                11
point to a map of the world. Daydreaming a little. You
                                            12
gaze at the shapes on the map. Suddenly you notice

that the bulge on the East Coast of South America looks
                        13
as if it would fit neat into the indented coast of western
              14
Africa across the ocean.

   Most scientists who study the earth now believe

that, in fact, these continents were joined until about 100
    15
million years ago. They base this belief on rock layers and

fossils common to both South America and Africa. Further
         16
support is provided by the theory of plate tectonics, which

states that the outer shell of the earth always has been and

still is being constantly in motion.
     17
   According to this theory, the outer shell of the earth

is broken up into large chunks, called tectonic plates these
                                              18
move slowly on the partially molten rock that lays beneath
                                            19
them. About 200 million years ago, there was a single

landmass, called Pangaea. Over a period of 65 million years,

Pangaea broke up into two smaller masses—Gondwanaland

and Laurasia. South America and Africa were originally part of

Gondwanaland, but they too began to drift apart, eventually

arriving at its current positions on the globe.
           20

11. A. No change
    B. hey're
    C. there
    D. here

12. F. No change
    G. little you
    H. little, you
    J. little; you

13. A. No change
    B. East coast
    C. east Coast
    D. east coast

14. F. No change
    G. be fitting neatly
    H. have fitted neat
    J. fit neatly

15. A. No change
    B. that, factually
    C. that in fact
    D. that, in fact

16. F. No change
    G. in common to
    H. uncommon to
    J. commonly in

17. A. No change
    B. is having been
    C. was
    D. is

18. F. No change
    G. plates, these
    H. plates. These
    J. plates those

19. A. No change
    B. has lain
    C. lies
    D. had laid

20. F. No change
    G. it's
    H. there
    J. their

Have you ever <u>wondered? Why </u>dogs bark?
                                21

Sometimes <u>them barking</u> serves as a warning, a threat,
                  22

a greeting, or a complaint. Although barking is a

complicated communication system, dogs often seem

to bark just because they <u>feel like it.</u>
                              23

Different breeds of dogs have different barking

habits. <u>Only some bark</u> rarely, but others find it
          24

difficult to be silent. For example, <u>terriers they</u>
                                         25

tend to bark more than most other dogs. No matter

what their particular habits, however, dogs apparently

can't help <u>but bark</u>.
              26

Scientists have been investigating this noisy

phenomenon for some time; however, they have yet

to come up with a definitive explanation. Some data

suggest a link between an <u>animals' tameness</u> and its
                              27

tendency to bark. When researchers in the Soviet

Union <u>bred unusually</u> tame foxes, they found that
        28

those animals behaved, looked, and sounded <u>not like</u>
                                              29

wild foxes but like dogs! One theory proposes that

barking is a juvenile behavior, along with dependence

and tameness. According to this theory, the barking dog

is a case of <u>revolutionary</u> immaturity. The dog has
                30

simply not developed as far as its wild cousin, the

nonbarking wolf.


21. A. No change
    B. wondered why
    C. wondered, why
    D. wondered: why

22. F. No change
    G. they barking
    H. their barking
    J. those barking

23. A. No change
    B. felt like it
    C. feel about it
    D. were feeling it

24. F. No change
    G. Only, some bark
    H. some only bark
    J. Some bark only

25. A. No change
    B. them terriers
    C. terriers
    D. a terrier

26. F. No change
    G. but be barkers
    H. but being barkers
    J. barking

27. A. No change
    B. animal tameness
    C. animals tameness
    D. animal's tameness

28. F. No change
    G. not bred usually
    H. bread unusual
    J. bred unusual

29. A. No change
    B. not alike
    C. not unlike
    D. alike

30. F. No change
    G. evolutionary
    H. revolving
    J. voluntary

# Revision-in-Context

On certain tests you may find questions that provide part of the first draft of a composition and ask you to revise it. These **revision-in-context** questions ask you to make decisions about logic, organization, sentence structure, and basic English usage. The following strategies can help you perform well on these types of questions:

- Read the entire passage carefully.

- Reread the passage, noting specific problems in the composition.

- Read each question and the answer choices provided. If necessary, go back and reread the indicated portion in the context of the whole composition.

- Choose the revision that makes the intended meaning clearest and follows the rules of standard English usage.

*The passages that follow are the first drafts of students' compositions. Some of the ideas may not be well developed or precisely expressed. For each question, choose the answer that best conveys the writer's intended meaning.*

## Passage I

(1) I am physically challenged. (2) I was born with cerebral palsy. (3) I have been attending public schools since I was six years old. (4) My brother, who doesn't have cerebral palsy, was just six years old in March. (5) Physically challenged children have the same needs as any other children—education, recreation, socialization, and recognition—and the public schools can meet those needs.

(6) Today there are physically challenged children in the public schools in all fifty states. (7) It hasn't always been this way, however. (8) Physically challenged used to be sent off to private schools. (9) Then, in the mid-1970's, the federal government passed a law for physically challenged children to attend public schools. (10) The law also stated that therapy and other services should be provided in the schools.

(11) Attending public schools gives physically challenged children an opportunity to learn to their full potential. (12) These schools can provide the special help children like me need and can also challenge us to do our best. (13) At public schools, we get a chance to socialize with other physically challenged teens. (14) It was nice for me to find out that there were other teens with the same problems who can understand what you're going through. (15) We also need to interact with people who are not physically challenged. (16) Attending public schools lets us get to know the kids in our neighborhood and makes us a part of the community.

(17) Recreation is also important for physically challenged young people. (18) We need to play games and have fun like anybody else. (19) Physical education classes like adaptive PE are very helpful. (20) They allow us to do what we can and to feel good about ourselves, which we need.

(21) In conclusion, physically challenged young people are like anybody else. (22) We just want the opportunity to prove what we can do, and attending public schools helps us achieve that goal.

1. Which is the best way to combine sentences 2 and 3?
   (A) Being born with cerebral palsy, I have been attending public schools since I was six years old.
   (B) I was born with cerebral palsy: consequently I have been attending public schools since I was six years old.
   (C) Although I was born with cerebral palsy, I have been attending public schools since I was six years old.
   (D) Because I have been attending public schools since I was six years old, I was born with cerebral palsy.
   (E) I was born with cerebral palsy and, as such, I have been attending public schools since I was six years old.

2. Which sentence does not belong in this essay?
   (A) sentence 4
   (B) sentence 12
   (C) sentence 16
   (D) sentence 20
   (E) sentence 22

3. Which is the best revision of the underlined part of sentence 9?
   *Then, in the mid-1970's, the federal government passed a law for physically challenged children to attend public schools.*
   (A) a law telling physically challenged children that public schools must be attended to
   (B) a law requiring public schools to accommodate physically challenged children
   (C) a law in terms of which physically challenged children could attend public schools
   (D) a law for public schools that had physically challenged children in attendance
   (E) a law that must be attended to regarding public schools

4. Which is the best revision of the underlined part of sentence 14?
   *It was nice for me to find out that there were other teens with the same problems who can understand what you're going through.*
   (A) that are understanding of what you're going through
   (B) who could understand what I was going through
   (C) who have an understanding of where you have gone
   (D) who are standing where you were
   (E) that share your understanding of goings on

5. Which of the following best describes the student's purpose in writing this composition?

   (A) to make friends
   (B) to tell an entertaining story about growing up
   (C) to describe cerebral palsy
   (D) to educate readers about the needs of handicapped people and how they can best be met
   (E) to ask for sympathy

## Passage II

(1) The birds along the lake shore were singing in the brisk, cool morning. (2) I will never forget that clear, piercing sound and the crispness of the air. (3) These, along with many other wonderful recollections, made my Memorial Day camping trip memorable and worth sharing. (4) The trip began with a nine-hour drive along winding country roads. (5) We set up the tents and went right to bed, so we had no idea of the beauty that surrounded us. (6) When we got up in the morning, the sun had just risen over the towering mountains and was shimmering against the awesome blue lake. (7) Because we had a flat tire, we didn't arrive at the campsite until after dark. (8) As I stepped out of my tent, and noticed all the incredibly gorgeous wildlife in the area. (9) I hated to tear myself away from the scenery to cook breakfast, but I was suddenly very hungry. (10) Then I made a fire, sat down to eat, and enjoyed a wonderful feeling as the sun shone it's warmth on me. (11) It was the most peacefulest moment of my life.

(12) After eating, I went for a long hike. (13) I found a secluded spot where I dropped my fishing pole in the water and lay in the sun not even caring if I got a bite. (14) I returned to the campsite sunburned, tired, and happy. (15) I had had a long, fun-filled day. (16) I sat down in front of a crackling campfire. (17) I roasted three plump, white, sweet marshmallows. (18) As I ate them and felt the warmth of the fire, I thought of how wonderful it all has been.

6. Which sentence in the composition is out of place, and how would you
   reposition it?

   (A) sentence 1; put it after sentence 15.
   (B) sentence 7; put it after sentence 4.
   (C) sentence 8; put it after sentence 9.
   (D) sentence 12; put it after sentence 13.
   (E) sentence 18; put it after sentence 17.

7. Where would you begin a new paragraph to separate the introduction from
   the body of the composition?

   (A) no paragraph necessary
   (B) after sentence 1
   (C) after sentence 2
   (D) after sentence 3
   (E) after sentence 5

8. Which is the best title for this composition?

   (A) The Marshmallow Roast
   (B) Sunset and Sunrise
   (C) A Memorial Day to Remember
   (D) How to Camp
   (E) Birds of the Northeast

9. Which is the best revision of sentence 8?

   (A) As I stepped out of my tent, I was dazzled by a variety of wildlife.
   (B) Stepping out of my tent and I couldn't believe the wildlife.
   (C) Because I couldn't believe the gorgeous wildlife in the area, I stepped
       out of my tent.
   (D) Until I stepped out of my tent, the wildlife was incredibly gorgeous.
   (E) As I was stepping out of my tent in the area and noticing all the incredibly
       gorgeous wildlife.

10. Which is the best revision of the underlined part of sentence 10?
    *Then I made a fire, sat down to eat, and enjoyed a wonderful feeling as the sun*
    *shone it's warmth on me.*
    (A) although the sun was shining its warmth on me
    (B) after which I was shining as warmly as the sun
    (C) as the sun warmed me
    (D) as the shining sun it warmed me
    (E) until the warm sun shone down on me

11. Which is the best revision of sentence 11?

    (A) The moment of my life which was the more peaceful was that one.
    (B) In my life it was the peacefulest moment.
    (C) Until that moment I haven't known what peaceful meant.
    (D) My life, in that moment, was inundated with peacefulness.
    (E) It was the most peaceful moment of my life.

12. Which details would you include to make the scene described in this composition seem more real to readers?

    (A) accurate instructions on how to get to the camp
    (B) specific descriptions of sights, sounds, smells, and feelings
    (C) biographical facts about the writer
    (D) actual names of people and places
    (E) the year, day, and time of the camping trip

13. Which is the best way to combine sentences 15, 16, and 17?

    (A) I had had a long, fun-filled day; having sat down in front of a crackling campfire roasting three plump, white, sweet marshmallows.
    (B) Then, after a long, fun-filled day, I sat down in front of a crackling campfire and roasted three plump, white, sweet marshmallows.
    (C) I had had a long, fun-filled day, as a result of which I was sitting down in front of a crackling campfire with three plump, white, sweet roasted marshmallows.
    (D) I had had a long, fun-filled day sitting down in front of a crackling campfire roasting three plump, white, sweet marshmallows.
    (E) I sat down in front of a crackling campfire pursuant to having had a long, fun-filled day during which I roasted three plump, white, sweet marshmallows.

14. Which specific word would best replace *awesome* in sentence 6?

    (A) awful
    (B) shimmering
    (C) watery
    (D) deeply
    (E) translucent

15. Which is the best revision of the underlined part of sentence 18?
*As I ate them and felt the warmth of the fire, <u>I thought of how wonderful it all has been</u>.*

    (A) I would think of the wondrousness of the totality of all of it
    (B) I wondered about how I would think about all of this later
    (C) I accepted that this would be a wondering memory
    (D) I realized how wonderful the day had been
    (E) I thought how wonderful that this all has been

# Critical Reading

**Critical-reading** questions test your ability to comprehend written material and to draw inferences from what you read. The following strategies can help you answer these types of questions:

- Skim the entire passage quickly.

- Read the questions that follow the passage.

- Reread the passage carefully, keeping the questions you will have to answer in mind.

- Reread each question carefully. Then choose the response that best answers the question. If necessary, go back and reread the relevant parts of the passage.

## Passage I

*The following passage is from the short story "Louisa, Please Come Home" by the American author Shirley Jackson. The story is narrated by Louisa Tether, a young woman who ran away from home three years ago. She is now returning with her old next-door neighbor, Paul, to confront her family.*

I wondered if they were watching us from the window. It was hard for me to imagine how my mother and father would behave in a situation like this, because they always made such a point of being quiet and dignified and proper; . . . the front door ahead was still tight shut. I wondered if we would have to ring the
5   doorbell; I had never had to ring this doorbell before. I was still wondering when Carol opened the door for us. "Carol!" I said. I was shocked because she looked so old, and then I thought that of course it had been three years since I had seen her, and she probably thought that I looked older, too. "Carol," I said, "Oh, Carol!" I was honestly glad to see her.
10   She looked at me hard and then stepped back, and my mother and father were standing there, waiting for me to come in. If I had not stopped to think, I would have run to them, but I hesitated, not quite sure what to do, or whether they were angry with me, or hurt, or only just happy that I was back, and of course once I stopped to think about it, all I could find to do was just stand there and say,
15   "Mother?" kind of uncertainly.
She came over to me and put her hands on my shoulders and looked into my face for a long time. There were tears running down her cheeks, and I thought that before, when it didn't matter, I had been ready enough to cry, but now, when crying would make me look better, all I wanted to do was giggle. She looked old, and sad,
20   and I felt simply foolish. Then she turned to Paul and said, "Oh, *Paul*—how can you do this to me again?"

Paul was frightened; I could see it. "Mrs. Tether—" he said.

"What is your name, dear?" my mother asked me.

"Louisa Tether," I said stupidly.

25    "No, dear," she said, very gently, "your real name?"

Now I could cry, but now I did not think it was going to help matters any.

"Louisa Tether," I said. "That's my name."

1. Who is the "I" in this passage?
   (A) Carol
   (B) Louisa's father
   (C) Louisa
   (D) a girl pretending to be Louisa
   (E) Louisa's psychiatrist

2. Which pair of adjectives best describes the tone of this passage?
   (A) angry and resentful
   (B) lighthearted and humorous
   (C) warm and nostalgic
   (D) awkward and confused
   (E) detached and analytic

3. Considering that Louisa ran from home and that her family doesn't seem to recognize her when she returns, what might you infer about the relationship between them?
   (A) Louisa is an adopted child.
   (B) Louisa's family ignored her and never realized that she had run away.
   (C) Louisa's parents and sister are blind and resent the fact that Louisa can see.
   (D) Louisa had plastic surgery while she was gone because she didn't want to look like her family.
   (E) Louisa's family has never really "seen" her or known her as a person.

4. Which statement best explains the meaning of the clause "I had never had to ring this doorbell before" (line 5) in the context of this passage?
   (A) Until she ran away, she had lived in that house and could come and go freely.
   (B) She has never lost her key to the house before.
   (C) She has always used the back door, which doesn't have a bell.
   (D) She used to just knock on the door when she forgot her key.
   (E) Her parents installed the doorbell after she left home.

5. Which statement best describes why Louisa is shocked that her sister Carol looks so old (lines 6–8)?

(A) She has forgotten what Carol looks like.

(B) She has assumed that nothing and no one would have changed during the three years she was gone.

(C) Carol has been sick with worry since Louisa's disappearance.

(D) Carol has begun to look like her mother.

(E) Carol has forgotten what Louisa looks like.

6. Which statement best explains the meaning of "crying would make me look better" (lines 18–19) in the context of this passage?

(A) Tears would make her eyes glisten and sparkle prettily.

(B) Crying would show how she really felt about being home.

(C) Tears would cleanse her eyes so that she could see more clearly.

(D) She would look more like her mother, who was crying.

(E) She looks better when she is crying than when she is giggling.

7. Which phrase has the same meaning as "matters" (line 26) in the context of this passage?

(A) spiritual concerns

(B) angry feelings

(C) cares about

(D) the situation

(E) concrete objects

8. A tether is a rope or a chain used to tie something. Which statement best describes the possible significance of the author's choice of this word as Louisa's last name?

(A) It was the author's maiden name.

(B) It was chosen at random and has no significance.

(C) It suggests the complex ties that bind parents and children.

(D) It is not the same as her parents' last name and therefore proves she is not really their child.

(E) It has the same number of letters as does her first name.

9. How does Louisa's father react to her return?

(A) His reaction cannot be determined from the information given in this passage.

(B) He echoes his wife's reaction.

(C) He is indifferent.

(D) He is angry.

(E) He is overjoyed.

10. To which type of literature does this passage belong?

(A) science fiction

(B) autobiography

(C) nonfiction

(D) fantasy

(E) first-person narrative

# Passage II

*The following passage is from an article published in* Discover *magazine. It presents the results of recent research on domestic cats and their wild ancestors.*

To anyone who has stared into the deep and unwavering blankness of a house cat's eyes, or has watched his beloved pet stand motionless in the center of a room, waiting for a thought to enter its plum-sized brain—to such a person, the news will be no surprise: compared with its wild ancestor, the domestic cat

5  has about one-third fewer neurons [nerve cells]. The cat's brain has shrunk during the course of evolution, and it has shrunk by losing neurons.

[The researchers Robert Williams of the University of Tennessee at Memphis and Carmen Cavada and Fernando Reinoso-Suárez of the Universidad Autonoma de Madrid] compared the brain of *Felis catus* with that of the Spanish wildcat.

10  Spanish wildcats are living fossils—rare survivors of the species that gave rise to domesticated cats 15,000 to 20,000 years ago. While the domestic cat's line has evolved rapidly since then, the Spanish wildcat has barely changed.

Williams and his colleagues found that the domestic cat's brain is 20 to 30 percent lighter than a Spanish wildcat's brain. (Its whole body is about half the size

15  of the wildcat's body.) To find out whether the domestic cat had smaller neurons, more tightly packed neurons, or simply fewer neurons, the researchers decided to actually count the number of neurons in a small section of the feline brain—the visual pathway.

They found that the Spanish wildcat had half again as many cone cells—the

20  cells that allow for daytime and color vision—in the retina; 50 percent more signal-transmitting axons in the optic nerve; and 50 percent more cells in the lateral geniculate nucleus, a clump of neurons in the brain that sorts the signals from the optic nerve. If one extrapolates these findings to the whole brain, says Williams, this means that domestic cats have lost about a third of their neurons during

25  evolution.

The intriguing thing is that each domestic cat seems to start out with all its ancestral neurons. . . . [A large] number of the domestic cat's cells, however, die as the fetus develops. "The death of brain cells often happens in mammals," says Williams. "The human retina initially has 2.5 million ganglion cells, and then half

30  are lost. But the domestic cat makes close to a million and keeps only 160,000." If you're going to evolve a smaller brain, he adds, the cat's strategy is probably a good one: "It has a built-in flexibility. If conditions were to change rapidly in a few thousand years, an animal could take advantage and stop losing as many cells."

Why the domestic cat should want to lose brain cells in the first place,
35  however, the researchers can't say. But they warn against drawing facile
conclusions concerning the animal's intelligence. "In some respects I'm sure
a wildcat is a much more competent animal," says Williams. "But domestic
cats are much smarter at coping with humans than are wildcats—so in that
respect, a domestic cat is obviously a genius."

11. Which statement best summarizes the main point of this passage?
   (A) Wildcats would make good pets because they're so smart.
   (B) Keeping cats as pets causes people to lose their brain cells.
   (C) Mammals become less intelligent as they evolve.
   (D) Although domestic cats have lost a third of their brain cells during evolution,
       they are still smart enough to deal effectively with their environment.
   (E) Domestic cats should be returned to the wild so that they can regain their lost
       brain cells.

12. Which statement best reflects the researchers' findings?
   (A) Domestic cats have more tightly packed neurons than do Spanish wildcats.
   (B) Spanish wildcats' color vision is much better than their daytime vision.
   (C) Domestic cats have smaller neurons than do Spanish wildcats.
   (D) Domestic cats and wildcats start out with the same number of neurons, but
       domestic cats lose more of theirs as they develop.
   (E) The neurons of all cats are concentrated in their visual pathway.

13. What is the meaning of "living fossils" (line 10) in the context of this passage?
   (A) petrified animals that have been miraculously revived
   (B) animals that are hopelessly out-of-date
   (C) ancient animal species that have survived unchanged
   (D) ancient rocks that look like present-day cats
   (E) animals that feed on extinct species

14. What is the meaning of "extrapolates" (line 23) in the context of this passage?
   (A) transports to the North or South Pole
   (B) projects or extends
   (C) adds more neurons
   (D) takes out of context
   (E) exaggerates

15. Why, according to the researchers, do domestic cats lose their brain cells?

    (A) The researchers don't know.

    (B) Domestic cats don't need so many cells, because human beings take care of them.

    (C) Their wild ancestors had too many brain cells.

    (D) Their brains are too small to hold all their brain cells.

    (E) The cats don't lose the cells: the researchers counted wrong.

16. How long ago did domestic cats evolve from wildcats?

    (A) Domestic cats didn't evolve from wildcats; they're an entirely different species.

    (B) 15,000 to 20,000 years ago

    (C) 160,000 years ago

    (D) 2.5 million years ago

    (E) The passage doesn't provide that information.

17. What is the meaning of the phrase "all its ancestral neurons" (lines 26–27) in the context of this passage?

    (A) the total number of neurons in all its ancestors' brains

    (B) its oldest neurons

    (C) the same number of neurons its ancestors had

    (D) the neurons it will pass on to its children

    (E) the neurons that are related to its own

18. Which adjective best describes the tone of this passage?

    (A) disgusted

    (B) humorous

    (C) pleading

    (D) threatening

    (E) objective

19. What is the meaning of "facile" (line 35) in the context of this passage?

    (A) funny

    (B) docile

    (C) complicated

    (D) easy

    (E) misunderstood

20. Why does a researcher state that "a domestic cat is obviously a genius" (line 39) even though it has one-third fewer neurons than a wildcat?

    (A) This is a sarcastic comment that means just the opposite.

    (B) Brain cells have nothing to do with intelligence.

    (C) Domestic cats are much better at coping with humans than are wildcats.

    (D) Domestic cats perform better than wildcats on IQ tests.

    (E) Domestic cats learn to use a litter box at an early age, but wildcats never do.

*The following two passages address the issue of recognition of individual identity. The first is from the autobiographical essay "Darkness at Noon" by Harold Krents, whose life inspired the Broadway play and movie* Butterflies Are Free. *The second is the poem "Thumbprint" by the poet and playwright Eve Merriam.*

## Passage I—Darkness at Noon

Blind from birth, I have never had the opportunity to see myself and have been completely dependent on the image I create in the eye of the observer. . . .

There are those who assume that since I can't see, I obviously also cannot hear. Very often people will converse with me at the top of their lungs, enunciating each

5    word very carefully. Conversely, people will often whisper, assuming that since my eyes don't work, my ears don't either. . . .

The toughest misconception of all is the view that because I can't see, I can't work. I was turned down by over forty law firms because of my blindness, even though my qualifications included a cum laude degree from Harvard College and a

10    good ranking in my Harvard Law School class.

The attempt to find employment, the continuous frustration of being told that it was impossible for a blind person to practice law, the rejection letters, not based on my lack of ability but rather on my disability, will always remain one of the most disillusioning experiences in my life.

## Passage II—Thumbprint

15    In the heel of my thumb
are whorls, whirls, wheels
in a unique design:
mine alone.
What a treasure to own!
20    My own flesh, my own feelings.
No other, however grand or base,
can ever contain the same.
My signature,
thumbing the pages of my time.
25    My universe key,
my singularity.
Impress, implant,
I am myself,
of all my atom parts I am the sum.
30    And out of my blood and my brain
I make my own interior weather,
my own sun and rain.
Imprint my mark upon the world,
whatever I shall become.

21. Which set of adjectives best characterizes the tone of the two passages?

    (A) I—hesitant; II—angry
    (B) I—whining; II—defiant
    (C) I—angry; II—exultant
    (D) I—optimistic; II—pessimistic
    (E) I—detached; II—anxious

22. How does Harold Krents feel about "the image I create in the eye of the observer" (line 2)?

    (A) He is angry that people do not see him as a real person because he is handicapped.
    (B) He has no feelings about other people's image of him, because he can't see it.
    (C) He accepts other people's image of him.
    (D) He tries to live up to others' image of him.
    (E) He doesn't understand how other people see him.

23. What is the meaning of "not based on my lack of ability but rather on my disability" (lines 12–13) in the context of passage I?

    (A) not because he wasn't capable of doing the job, but only because he was blind
    (B) not because he wasn't capable of doing the job, but because he didn't use the ability he had
    (C) not because he was blind, but because he didn't have the ability to do the job
    (D) not because he was blind, but because he also couldn't hear
    (E) because he was blind and he also wasn't capable of doing the job

24. What is the meaning of "disillusioning" (line 14) in the context of passage I?

    (A) unreal
    (B) disgusting
    (C) disabling
    (D) unexpected
    (E) eye-opening

25. Which statement best summarizes Harold Krents's attitude toward his blindness?

    (A) He resents it and is jealous of people who can see.
    (B) He thinks that the problem is not his blindness but the fact that other people don't see him as a capable individual.
    (C) He ignores it.
    (D) He refuses to accept it and pretends that he can see.
    (E) He doesn't realize that he is blind.

26. Which statement best describes the way the speaker in passage II perceives herself?

    (A) as a large thumb
    (B) as a person stamped out of a mold
    (C) as a barometer of the weather
    (D) as a unique individual with a special contribution to make
    (E) as a person unsure of her own identity

27. What does the image of the "whorls, whirls, wheels [on my thumb] in a unique design" (lines 16–17) signify in the context of passage II?
   (A) someone squashing an insect
   (B) someone hitchhiking
   (C) the distinctiveness of every person
   (D) It was included for sound, not for meaning.
   (E) the confusion of someone going around in circles

28. What does "I make my own interior weather" (line 31) imply in the context of passage II?
   (A) The narrator lives in a climate-controlled house.
   (B) The narrator takes her temperature regularly.
   (C) The narrator determines her own destiny.
   (D) The narrator can predict the weather.
   (E) The narrator is like a reptile, whose body temperature is determined by that of its environment.

29. Which statement best characterizes the views of personal identity presented in the two passages?
   (A) I—people must not accept other people's image of them but must fight to be recognized as individuals; II—people imprint their individual personalities joyously and freely on the world.
   (B) I—people can never see themselves clearly; II—people can never really understand one another because they are so different.
   (C) I and II—people are concerned only with themselves.
   (D) I—people with disabilities aren't really people; II—everyone has some kind of disability.
   (E) I—people are blind; II—people live in their own separate worlds.

30. Which phrases from the two passages best summarize their themes?
   (A) I—"because I can't see, I can't work"; II—"of all my atom parts I am the sum"
   (B) I—"continuous frustration"; II—"I am myself"
   (C) I—"Blind from birth"; II—"What a treasure to own!"
   (D) I—"the rejection letters"; II—"whatever I shall become"
   (E) I—"one of the most disillusioning experiences in my life"; II—"thumbing the pages of my time"

# Answer Key

## Contents

### *The Language of Literature* Test Answers

Unit One . . . . . . . . . . . . . . . . . . . . . . . . . . . . . . . . . . . . . . . . . 260

Unit Two . . . . . . . . . . . . . . . . . . . . . . . . . . . . . . . . . . . . . . . . . 272

Unit Three . . . . . . . . . . . . . . . . . . . . . . . . . . . . . . . . . . . . . . . . 282

Mid-Year Test . . . . . . . . . . . . . . . . . . . . . . . . . . . . . . . . . . . . . 292

Unit Four . . . . . . . . . . . . . . . . . . . . . . . . . . . . . . . . . . . . . . . . . 294

Unit Five . . . . . . . . . . . . . . . . . . . . . . . . . . . . . . . . . . . . . . . . . 303

Unit Six . . . . . . . . . . . . . . . . . . . . . . . . . . . . . . . . . . . . . . . . . . 312

End-of-Year Test . . . . . . . . . . . . . . . . . . . . . . . . . . . . . . . . . . . 321

### Standardized Test Practice Answers

Standardized Test Practice Answers . . . . . . . . . . . . . . . . . . . . . . . . 323

# Unit One

## The Necklace
Selection Test, pp. 7–8

**A.** (8 points each) Notes will vary but should include points similar to the following:
1. Rising Action:
   a. Mme. Loisel is miserable most of the time because she thinks she deserves the "little niceties and luxuries of living," but she and her husband cannot afford them.
   b. M. Loisel obtains an invitation to a gala reception and gives his wife 400 francs with which to buy a dress.
   c. Mme. Loisel borrows a necklace from Mme. Forestier to complete her outfit.
2. Climax:
   a. Mme. Loisel has a marvelous time at the reception.
   b. When she gets home, she realizes that she has lost the necklace.
3. Falling Action:
   a. M. Loisel borrows a great deal of money to buy a replacement necklace.
   b. M. and Mme. Loisel spend ten years working themselves to the bone to repay their debt.
   c. After the debt has finally been paid, Mme. Loisel meets Mme. Forestier and tells her the whole story. Mme. Forestier reveals that the necklace she had lent her was "only paste . . . at most it was worth only five hundred francs."

**B.** (6 points each)
1. a
2. a
3. c
4. b

**C.** (12 points) Answers will vary. Students who choose M. Loisel could say that he contrasts with Mme. Loisel in that, at the beginning of the story,
   a. he is content with their life; she is not.
   b. she craves life in high society; he does not.
   c. she needs the praise and adulation of others; he does not.
   d. he is pleased with their marriage; she is not.
Students who choose Mme. Forestier could say that she contrasts with Mme. Loisel in that Mme. Forestier
   a. has all the things that Mme. Loisel wants.
   b. sees and accepts the phoniness of high society, while Mme. Loisel is in awe of it.

**D.** (4 points each)
1. c
2. c
3. b

4. b
5. a

**E.** (10 points; students should answer one of the two)
1. Answers will vary. Students could say that the immediate effects on Mme. Loisel are feelings of
   a. shock and despair that she and her husband had wasted ten years of their lives paying for a necklace that was much more expensive than the one she had borrowed.
   b. humiliation at the unnecessary steps she and her husband had taken.
   c. fury at herself for being so naive.
Students could say that long-term effects on Mme. Loisel might be that
   a. she comes to value honesty.
   b. she realizes that the appearance of wealth can be misleading.
   c. she realizes that deceit can have disastrous effects.
   d. her life becomes much easier, because Mme. Forestier will probably replace the diamond necklace with paste and give Mme. Loisel the difference in their values, which, from a moral standpoint, she owes her.
2. Answers will vary. Students could say that Mme. Loisel's troubles are caused by such character flaws as
   a. an overemphasis on wealth, glamour, and material advantages, which make her unhappy with her comfortable life.
   b. an eagerness to impress other people with shallow characteristics, such as being well-dressed.
   c. a terror of humiliation, which makes her unable to tell Mme. Forestier the truth about what had happened at a time when telling the truth would have prevented all of her difficulties.

**F.** (10 points) Answers will vary widely, depending on students' personal experiences, situations, and viewpoints. Accept any answers that address the concern of the question and are elaborated by examples or details from the literature or from life.

## The Most Dangerous Game
Selection Test, pp. 9–10

**A.** (24 points) Notes will vary widely. Possible moments of suspense and resolutions include the following:
   a. Rainsford's falling overboard; resolved by his reaching the island.
   b. Ivan's answering the door and pointing a revolver at Rainsford; resolved by Zaroff's arrival.
   c. Zaroff's finding Rainsford in the tree; resolved by Zaroff's walking away.
   d. Zaroff's approaching the Malay man-catcher; resolved by Zaroff's setting off the trap but surviving.

e. Rainsford's leaping out into the sea; resolved by his reappearing in Zaroff's bedroom.

f. Rainsford's stepping out from behind Zaroff's bed curtain; resolved by his challenging and killing Zaroff.

**B.** (6 points each)
1. c
2. a
3. d
4. b
5. c
6. b

**C.** (4 points each)
1. b
2. a
3. c
4. c
5. a

**D.** (10 points; students should answer one of the two)
1. Answers and arguments will vary but should reflect students' knowledge that Zaroff believes that
   a. God made him a hunter.
   b. humans are the ideal animal to hunt.
   c. war shows that there are instances where it is socially acceptable for humans to kill other humans without feeling guilt or remorse.
   d. the weak were put on the earth to give the strong pleasure.
   e. the humans he hunts are "scum" and thus not a loss to the world.

Students might argue against Zaroff's position by expressing a belief in the sanctity of life and the common bonds of humanity.

2. Answers will vary. Possible answers include the following:
   a. Yes. At the beginning of the story he callously dismisses the idea that animals feel pain and fear. His experience of being hunted down as if he were an animal gives him a new perspective that probably makes him more sympathetic to hunted animals.
   b. No. At the beginning of the story he says that the world is divided into "the hunters and the huntees." After being Zaroff's quarry, he then murders Zaroff, which seems to confirm his belief that it is better to be the hunter than the huntee.

**E.** (10 points) Answers will vary widely, depending on students' personal experiences, situations, and viewpoints. Accept any answers that address the concern of the question and are elaborated by examples or details from the literature or from life.

## Where Have You Gone, Charming Billy?
Selection Test, pp. 11–12

**A.** (10 points each) Notes will vary, but students could include any three inferences similar to the following:
1. Inference: Paul is interested in the night sky. Evidence: He recognizes the Southern Cross and thinks he will learn the names of the other stars he sees.
2. Inference: Paul and his father used to go camping together. Evidence: Paul pretends he is a boy again, camping with his father.
3. Inference: Paul lived in the Midwest. Evidence: He and his father camped along the Des Moines River.

**B.** (5 points each)
1. c
2. b
3. a
4. b

**C.** (4 points each)
1. b
2. b
3. c
4. a
5. c

**D.** (15 points; students should answer one of the two)
1. Answers will vary but should suggest that
   a. Paul's internal battle against fear is not going well. He is afraid, and afraid of being afraid, especially after watching Billy Boy die of fright. Even reaching the sea does not have the calming effect he was hoping for.
   b. Paul will soon be better able to stay calm. His first day was especially bad because of Billy Boy's death. Time will help him overcome his fear.

Other ideas should be supported by appropriate evidence from the story.

2. Notes will vary but should suggest that Billy Boy's death seemed ironic because
   a. Billy Boy was known as a soldier who was "tough as nails."
   b. in war a person is expected to die from combat, not a heart attack.
   c. the medic believed that Billy's wound would not have killed him.

In addition, students should note effects on Paul, such as:
   a. He had one more reason to be afraid, knowing that fear itself could kill a good soldier.
   b. He was unable to gain control of his emotional state after witnessing such a strange and unexpected death.

**E.** (15 points) Answers will vary widely, depending on students' attitudes toward military service and personal ideals and goals. Accept any answers that address both parts of the question and are elaborated by examples or details from the literature or from life.

## Marigolds

Selection Test, pp. 13–14

**A.** (12 points each) Notes will vary but should include points similar to the following:

1. a. The town is an African-American shantytown of ramshackle shacks, dirt roads, dust, and poverty, most often described as "barren."
   b. The barrenness seems to have influenced the narrator by making her feel caged in poverty, frustrated, and out of touch with surrounding communities.
2. a. The time of the story is during the Great Depression of the 1930s. The memory recounted by the narrator takes place in late summer as the days become shorter and cooler.
   b. The poverty of the Depression leads in part to the father's failure and despair because he cannot find work, and the change of seasons makes the narrator feel as if something important is coming to an end.
3. a. Miss Lottie's house is the most broken-down of all the ramshackle houses, but she has a bed of bright yellow marigolds growing in front of it.
   b. The marigolds represent some idea of hope and beauty amid the squalor, and they cause a kind of frustrated rage in the narrator, who sets out to destroy them. Her father's breakdown seems to have caused her to lose hope, and she cannot bear to be taunted by the sight of the marigolds.

**B.** (6 points each)
1. c
2. b

**C.** (4 points each)
1. c
2. b
3. c
4. a
5. b

**D.** (16 points; students should answer one of the two)
1. Answers will vary widely. Students could say that Lizabeth
   a. is in a state of emotional confusion brought to a head by overhearing her father's crying.
   b. feels scared and lonely.

In addition, students should include points similar to the following:
   a. Lizabeth herself isn't sure of her motives for destroying the marigolds.

   b. Lizabeth immediately regrets doing it because she suddenly realizes how much her action will hurt Miss Lottie.
   c. She doesn't like how guilty she feels as a result of her action.
2. Answers will vary but should reflect students' understanding that, after the marigold incident, Miss Lottie never plants marigolds again. Most students will find that this change symbolizes a more profound change in Miss Lottie's attitude toward her life. Because the marigolds seem to symbolize hope, beauty, and accomplishment, students might say that Miss Lottie's never planting marigolds again symbolizes her loss of hope and acceptance of the barrenness of her life.

**E.** (16 points) Answers will vary widely, depending on students' personal experiences, situations, and viewpoints. Accept any answers that address the concern of the question and are elaborated by examples or details from the literature or from life.

## Two Kinds

Selection Test, pp. 15–16

**A.** (8 points each) Notes will vary but should include points similar to the following:

1. The mother believed that you could be anything you wanted to be in America, and she wanted her daughter to be a prodigy. She believed that her daughter could be the best at anything she chose if she just tried hard enough.
2. The daughter resented her mother's expectations, being pushed to be something she was not interested in being when she was perfectly happy with herself as she was.
3. The mother expected her daughter to obey her wishes and demands, but the daughter had decided to follow her own mind; she was comfortable with who she was.
4. At the end, the daughter realized that there were two parts of her: the one that wanted to please and the one that was "perfectly contented" being herself. She could also be viewed as "two kinds" of a daughter: she was obedient to her mother in some ways, but she also followed her own mind.

**B.** (6 points each)
1. d
2. a
3. a

**C.** (4 points each)
1. b
2. a
3. a
4. b
5. c

**D.** (15 points; students should answer one of the two)

1. Answers will vary but could include one or more of the following points:
   a. The daughter has conflicting feelings about her mother that are reflected in the contrasting titles of the two songs.
   b. The two songs express the daughter's different experiences in dealing with her mother's desire for her to be a prodigy.
   c. The two songs communicate the narrator's inner struggle with her desire to succeed, to please her mother, and to accept herself.
2. Answers will vary but should reflect students' understanding that the mother wants her daughter to have the successful life that seems to be possible in America. Things the mother hopes being a prodigy will achieve for her daughter include
   a. fame.
   b. financial security.
   c. the American dream of a better life.
   d. an opportunity to be the best at something.
   e. an opportunity to outdo Waverly.
   f. knowledge, discipline, and obedience.
Things the mother hopes it will achieve for herself include
   a. pride in her successful daughter.
   b. an opportunity to outdo Auntie Lindo.
   c. the American dream of a better life.
   d. financial security.

**E.** (15 points) Answers will vary widely, depending on students' personal experiences, situations, and viewpoints. Accept any answers that address the concern of the question and are elaborated by examples or details from the literature or from life.

### *from* **The Perfect Storm**
Selection Test, pp. 17–18

**A.** (10 points each) Notes will vary but could include these suspenseful moments and their resolutions (students should list three):

1. a. The crew of the *Satori* is in great danger and can't tell if they have made radio contact with anyone.
   b. A Falcon jet circles above and makes radio contact with the *Satori*.
2. a. The *Satori* must be kept afloat until the *Tamaroa* arrives.
   b. By using the engine and the storm jib, the crew is able to keep the boat from getting broached by the seas.
3. a. The Avon raft that the Coast Guard sends to rescue the crew of the *Satori* is disabled in a crash with the *Satori*.
   b. Dave Moore eventually rescues the crew of the Avon raft from the water.

**B.** (5 points each)

1. d
2. b
3. a
4. d

**C.** (4 points each)
1. a
2. c
3. a
4. b
5. b

**D.** (15 points; students should answer one of the two)
1. Answers will vary but should include two mishaps and an explanation. Mishaps might include:
   a. The life rafts dropped by the H-3 explode on impact and are useless.
   b. The Avon raft is disabled before it can bring the *Satori* crew to the *Tamaroa*.
   c. After Moore decides he cannot swim to the *Satori*, a huge wave wrenches the hoist cable off the basket that is supposed to bring him up to the helicopter.
An explanation of the operation's success might include:
   a. The Coast Guard provided sufficient backup equipment and plans.
   b. The rescue personnel were committed and clearheaded.
2. Answers will vary but may include the following points:
   a. Ray Leonard is suffering a terrible loss, since he owns the *Satori* and it means everything to him. But for Dave Moore, the rescue is an opportunity to use his skills in a major rescue for the first time.
   b. Leonard has been facing the terror of the storm for many hours, but Moore has arrived fresh from the base.
   c. Leonard is in the position of being a victim, but Moore is in the position of being a hero.

**E.** (15 points) Answers will vary. Accept any answers that state a clear position and defend it by using examples or details from the literature or from life.

### **The Wreck of the Hesperus**
Selection Test, pp. 19–20

**A.** (10 points each) Notes may vary but should include points similar to the following:

1. a. Description: The skipper might be described as proud, bold, watchful, experienced, calm, scornful, overconfident.
   b. Details: "The skipper, he blew a whiff from his pipe, / And a scornful laugh laughed he."
2. a. Description: The skipper's daughter might be described as young, innocent, helpless, fearful, frightened.
   b. Details: "And her bosom white as the hawthorn

buds, / That ope in the month of May."

3. a. Description: The *Hesperus* is at sea at night during a raging winter storm with high waves, howling winds, and snow.

   b. Details: "Colder and louder blew the wind, / A gale from the Northeast." ". . . come hither! my little daughter, / And do not tremble so;"

4. a. Description: A skipper ignores warnings of bad weather and takes his daughter to sea. Because of his brashness, he loses his ship, his crew, his life, and the life of his daughter.

   b. "And a whooping billow swept the crew / Like icicles from her deck."

**B.** (5 points each)

1. c
2. a
3. d

**C.** (25 points; students should answer one of the two)

1. Answers will vary, but may include the following points:

   a. The skipper decides that he can weather the storm and thus brings doom upon the ship and everyone aboard.

   b. The skipper's young daughter makes the reader feel more emotionally involved in the story and its outcome.

   c. The old sailor gives warnings that could have saved the ship, thus shedding light on the skipper's character.

   d. The fisherman at the end gives the reader eyes to see the sad remains of the *Hesperus* and the skipper's daughter.

It is possible also to consider the sea as a character because it is personified in the poem. It is the villain of the story, angry with the skipper's defiance and laughing at the ship's sad fate.

2. Answers will vary but may include the following points:

   a. The steady rhythm of the verses is like waves against the shore.

   b. The regular patterns of rhythm and rhyme make the words and images more memorable.

   c. Figurative language makes the storm and the rocks seem almost like characters in the story rather than impersonal forces of nature.

   d. The descriptions of the corpses of the skipper and his daughter are especially vivid and touching when described in poetry.

   e. Through repetition and vivid language, the reader can almost feel the cold and wind and sleet of the storm.

**D.** (20 points) Answers will vary. Accept any answers that address both parts of the question and are supported by examples or details from the literature or from life.

**Unit One, Part One Test**
pp. 21–22

**A.** (5 points each) Answers will vary but should include points similar to the following:

1. Before she loses it, the necklace symbolizes happiness, wealth, success, worthiness, or high social status; after she loses it, the necklace symbolizes loss of hope, the shallowness of social pretense, the stupidity of false pride, impossible dreams, or the unfairness of life.

2. Billy Boy died of a heart attack, which struck Paul as funny in an odd way; he can't stop giggling because he is so terrified that he is not in control of his emotions.

3. The mother says there are only two kinds of daughter—obedient ones and those who follow their own minds. The daughter realizes that she is both, in a sense: she tries for a long time to be what her mother wants her to be, but then she realizes that she can only be herself.

4. It is nonfiction prose; it describes an event that actually happened; it is factual.

**B.** (20 points) Answers will vary. Model answers for "The Necklace" and "Marigolds" follow.

In "The Necklace," the necklace represents

   a. everything that Mme. Loisel desires—luxury, niceties, and wealth—but cannot afford.

   b. social pretense.

   c. the unfairness of life. At first, she thought life was unfair because she did not have such a necklace; then she sacrificed what little she had after losing the necklace in pursuit of her dreams.

   d. false pride.

In "Marigolds," the marigolds represent

   a. hope or beauty amid the squalor.

   b. Miss Lottie's efforts to achieve something in spite of the hardships she faces.

   c. the kind of life that the narrator does not think she will ever achieve.

   d. a reminder that everything else in the shantytown is ugly.

**C.** (20 points each; students should answer two of the three)

1. Answers will vary. A model answer for Rainsford in "The Most Dangerous Game" and Paul Berlin in "Where Have You Gone, Charming Billy?" follows:

   a. Rainsford has an external conflict: he discovers that he is the prey and not the hunter when he reaches Zaroff's island.

b. Paul Berlin has an internal conflict: he is in Vietnam on his first day of combat, and he is terrified.

c. Rainsford resolves his conflict through skill and determination by beating Zaroff at his own game.

d. Paul Berlin cannot accept the ironic death of Billy Boy Watkins and cannot gain control over his own fear. He giggles uncontrollably and endangers the rest of the soldiers. He tries using mental games, such as counting his steps, to keep himself calm; he thinks of his family back home and what he will tell them; and he looks forward to reaching the sea as a kind of protective haven. None of these attempts to master his fear works, and his conflict remains unresolved at the end.

2. Answers will vary. A model answer for "Marigolds" and "The Wreck of the Hesperus" follows:

a. In "Marigolds," the narrator loses her innocence, or her childhood. When she overhears her father break down and cry, she suddenly sees things clearly. She realizes that she is trapped in poverty and hopelessness, that her world is barren, and that she may never achieve anything better than what she has. In a sense, she also loses her pride through her "last act of childhood," when she destroys Miss Lottie's marigolds.

b. In "The Wreck of the Hesperus," the skipper loses his life, his ship, and his entire crew. What makes the loss seem more tragic, however, is the loss of his daughter, who represents youthful innocence. She trusts her father, but her father is fearless, proud, and overconfident. He scorns the warnings he receives and defies nature, and a tremendous loss results.

Students who determine that one loss is greater than the others in this part should defend their viewpoints.

3. Answers will vary. A model answer for Mme. Forestier in "The Necklace" and Toby in "Where Have You Gone, Charming Billy?" follows:

In "The Necklace," Mme. Forestier

a. lends a necklace to Mme. Loisel.

b. through her generosity, makes Mme. Loisel think that she has achieved her goal of success and social status.

c. reveals at the end that the necklace she lent was only paste.

d. makes Mme. Loisel understand that she has worked hard for ten long years to repay her, and her efforts were all for naught.

In "Where Have You Gone, Charming Billy?" Toby

a. speaks sympathetically with Paul Berlin.

b. offers friendship to Paul, who has thought about how nice it would be to get to know the other soldiers and learn their names.

c. tries to provide comfort and consolation to "the new guy" on his first day in combat.

d. teaches Paul a few lessons about staying awake, being careful and calm, being quiet, and helping others.

e. tries to help him get over the shock of Billy Boy's death.

**D.** (20 points) Answers will vary. A model answer for the narrator in "Two Kinds" follows:

The narrator learned that

a. she could not live up to the expectations of others, especially her mother; she had to be herself.

b. there were two parts of herself: the obedient part and the part that followed her own mind.

The narrator learned this lesson by

a. trying to please her mother by taking piano lessons and playing in a recital.

b. defying her mother, who wanted her to continue with the piano.

c. hurting her mother deeply by wishing she were dead, like the mother's babies who died in China.

d. playing two songs on the piano that were actually two parts of the same song.

## O What Is That Sound

Selection Test, p. 23

**A.** (15 points each)

1. Notes will vary but could include the following:

a. Like horses running.

b. Like marching.

c. Like drumming.

d. Insistent.

e. Regular, strong.

2. Notes will vary. Students could say that the rhythm makes the

a. poem suspenseful.

b. image of approaching soldiers more real or immediate.

c. reader more involved or interested in the outcome of the situation.

d. reader experience part of what the speakers are going through.

**B.** (15 points each)

1. d

2. a

**C.** (20 points; students should answer one of the two)

1. Answers will vary widely but should reflect an understanding of the action described in the poem. Most students will suggest that the soldiers are coming to take one or both of the speakers away because at least one of them

a. is a spy.

b. is a deserter.

c. is a saboteur.

d. has been avoiding enlistment.

Some students may feel that the second speaker leaves because he or she

    a. has known all along that the soldiers are coming for him or her.

    b. chooses an attempt at escape.

Other students may feel that the second speaker leaves because

    a. the soldiers are coming for the first speaker, who realizes, gradually, that he or she has been found out.

    b. the second speaker, who comes to realize what is happening, leaves so as not to come under suspicion or be punished for something he or she hasn't done.

2. Answers will vary but should reflect students' understanding that the structure is a dialogue between people involved in a close relationship, most likely spouses or lovers. The effects of this structure include the following:

    a. The gradual revelation of the nature of the relationship between the two speakers.

    b. The building of tension in the first speaker (and in the reader) as the soldiers approach and their purpose becomes clear.

    c. The perception that one speaker is unaware, confused, and increasingly frightened, while the other grasps, or knows full well, what is going on and remains calm.

In addition, students should realize that the speaker in the last stanza is the first speaker because

    a. the scene described is one viewed from inside the house, and the second speaker has evidently already left.

    b. the first line of the stanza starts like the first lines of all the other stanzas, indicating that it is the first speaker talking.

    c. the second lines of all the other stanzas are questions that the second speaker answers in the third lines, addressing the first speaker as "dear."

    d. the last stanza is a single sentence, indicating one speaker.

**D.** (20 points) Answers will vary widely, depending on students' personal experiences, situations, and viewpoints. Accept any answers that address the concern of the question and are elaborated by examples or details from the literature or from life.

## Incident in a Rose Garden

Selection Test, pp. 25–26

**A.** (16 points each)

  1. Notes will vary but could suggest that the gardener's attitude is fearful. He is old and thinks Death has come for him.

Other ideas should be supported with appropriate reference to the poem.

  2. Notes will vary but could suggest that the master's attitude is scornful or annoyed. He views Death as an unwelcome stranger on his property, a problem to be taken care of.

Other ideas should be supported with appropriate reference to the poem.

**B.** (8 points each)

  1. b

  2. d

  3. a

  4. c

**C.** (20 points; students should answer one of the two)

  1. Answers will vary but should suggest that the irony is:

    a. the gardener, whom Death has not come for, assumes that Death has come for him; while the master, whom Death has come for, does not assume that Death has come for him.

    b. the gardener, whom Death isn't interested in just yet, takes the threat of Death seriously; the master doesn't view Death as a threat, but he should.

    c. Death comes without warning to the person in the poem who least expects to die. The gardener, who is an old man, seems more likely to be the intended victim of Death.

    d. the master treats Death, who has complete control of the situation, as if he were someone who could be ordered around.

In addition, students should note a theme communicated through the irony, such as

    a. death comes when it is least expected.

    b. it is wise to show the proper respect for death.

  2. Answers will vary but may suggest that the poet intended the poem to be

    a. funny, because of the ironic twist, as well as the humorous images of Death as a Spanish waiter and connoisseur of roses.

    b. scary, because the image of the grim reaper with its skeletal grin and bony hand is frightening, and the thought that death could come to any one of us next is also frightening.

    c. thought-provoking, because it is a reminder that life is unpredictable and always ends in death. To find the meaning of life, people need to come to terms with death.

Other ideas should be supported by appropriate reference to the poem.

**D.** (16 points) Answers will vary widely, depending on students' personal experiences, situations, and viewpoints. Accept any answers that address the concern of the question and are elaborated by examples from the literature or from life.

## The Gift of the Magi
Selection Test, pp. 27–28

**A.** (8 points each) Answers will vary but should suggest that

1. Jim had sold his watch and no longer had any use for a fob.
2. Della got the treasured combs after she had cut off her hair and could no longer use them.
3. Jim had just given her the gift that she had longed for, but then, instead of accepting her gratitude, he had to comfort her.

Accept other ideas if they show a clear understanding of situational irony.

**B.** (5 points each)
1. b
2. a
3. d
4. c

**C.** (4 points each)
1. b
2. a
3. c
4. c
5. b

**D.** (20 points; students should answer one of the two)
1. Answers will vary but could include
   a. Yes, because each of them had only one possession of value and each sold that possession to get a special gift for the other.
   b. No, because they still had their love for each other and their youth and their future together.
2. Answers will vary but might include that O. Henry believes they are the wisest because
   a. their gifts were given from true love and required a sacrifice.
   b. they cared more for each other than for themselves.
   c. their happiness was in giving, not receiving.
   Opinions as to whether they agree could include:
   a. Yes, because Jim and Della embody the true spirit of Christmas, as O. Henry implies by calling them the Magi.
   b. Yes, because gifts that can easily be exchanged for something else are not true gifts of the heart; they are not as meaningful.
   c. No, because, in the end, both Della and Jim were poorer than they had been before; they had lost things of true value and gained possessions they could not use.

**E.** (16 points) Answers will vary. Accept any answers that state a clear position and defend it by using examples or details from the literature or from life.

## The Sniper
Selection Test, pp. 29–30

**A.** (5 points each) Answers will vary but could include the following suspenseful events:

1. He is shot at when he lights a cigarette.
2. An armored car stops on the street, and an old woman points to the roof where he is lying.
3. He shoots the man in the turret of the armored car and the old woman as she runs away.
4. A shot from the opposite roof hits his arm, and he can no longer use his rifle.
5. It is near dawn, and he must kill the other gunman before morning. He tricks the gunman into shooting at his cap, then shoots the other gunman with his revolver.
6. He throws his own revolver down, and it goes off, nearly hitting him.

**B.** (5 points each)
1. c
2. a
3. d
4. b

**C.** (4 points each)
1. c
2. a
3. b
4. a
5. b

**D.** (15 points; students should answer one of the two)
1. Answers will vary but could include ideas such as the following:
   a. The sniper must believe in the cause for which he is fighting, or he would not have killed three people already. The story says that he was "used to looking at death," so he has probably been in similar situations before and may not let this one influence what he does.
   b. To justify his actions, the sniper may become even more of a fanatic for his cause. He has killed three people, his brother among them; people who do such horrible things need to feel they were in the right.
   c. His fanaticism is likely to be shaken by the experiences he has had. He already had his moments of doubt when he was upset by the death of the other gunman, and now he is likely to feel much worse.
   d. Knowing he has killed his own brother may make him question the whole meaning of the war and his role in it.

2. Answers will vary. Students should note that when he looked into the face of his enemy, the sniper saw his own brother. They should recognize that this surprise ending strongly implies an antiwar message—that in all wars, if we could truly look our enemies in the face, we would see reflections of ourselves. Events from the story that might take on new meaning include
    a. the gunman's determined attempts to kill the sniper.
    b. the sniper's shout of joy when he sees he has hit his mark and the gunman is falling.
    c. the sniper's sudden feelings of remorse when the gunman's corpse falls to the ground.
    d. the sniper's wish to know the identity of the gunman who was such a "good shot."

**E.** (15 points) Answers will vary widely, depending on students' personal experiences, situations, and viewpoints. Accept any answers that address the concern of the question and are elaborated by examples from the literature or from life.

## The Possibility of Evil
Selection Test, pp. 31–32
**A.** (6 points each) Answers will vary. Possible answers include:
1. a. She stops to smile down on the baby.
   b. She seems friendly and interested in the baby.
2. a. She thinks Helen and Don Crane are too infatuated with the child.
   b. She disapproves of spoiling a child.
3. a. "That little girl is going to grow up expecting luxury all her life."
   b. She wants to let Helen know why spoiling the child is unwise.
4. a. "I've been worrying about her."
   b. Helen trusts Miss Strangeworth enough to confide in her.
5. a. She writes an anonymous letter to Helen's husband implying that the child is an idiot.
   b. She has a hidden cruel streak—even though she seems to think she is acting for the good of the town—and cannot be trusted.

**B.** (5 points each)
1. c
2. c
3. a
4. b

**C.** (4 points each)
1. b
2. a
3. b
4. c
5. a

**D.** (15 points; students should answer one of the two)
1. Answers will vary. Students should make clear that the roses are very important to Miss Strangeworth and provide a direct link to her grandparents and her mother. What the roses help to reveal about Miss Strangeworth's character include:
    a. When tourists stop to admire them, she takes the opportunity to tell about her family history, revealing her great pride.
    b. She refuses to give any away, revealing an ungenerous nature.
    c. She is very uncomfortable with the idea of her roses leaving Pleasant Street, revealing her mistrust of everything outside her sphere of control.
    d. She revels in their beauty and their fragrance, which helps the reader to understand what "living graciously" means to her.
    e. Townspeople also take pride in the roses, revealing that Miss Strangeworth is indeed highly respected and admired.
2. Answers will vary. Points of contrast between the letters and Miss Strangeworth's outward appearance include:
    a. The letters are written on cheap paper with pencil in simple block print, whereas elegance and quality are her usual style.
    b. The letters are harsh and brutally unkind, whereas she smiles and is careful to appear considerate in public.
    c. The kind of paper she uses for the letters is used by everyone in town, whereas both she and the townspeople usually take the view that she is a cut above the common folk.
    d. She usually takes pride in everything about being a Strangeworth, but she is careful to hide her identity as the writer of these letters.

In addition, students should note that Miss Strangeworth has a hidden side to her personality that could be characterized as cruel, malicious, meddling, controlling, evil—or, perhaps, mentally ill.

**E.** (15 points) Answers will vary widely, depending on students' personal experiences, situations, and viewpoints. Accept any answers that address the concern of the question and are elaborated by examples from the literature or from life.

## The Censors
Selection Test, pp. 33–34
**A.** (6 points each)
Notes will vary. The following are model answers.
1. a. This was the beginning of his unhappy fate.
   b. situational

2. a. The worker's right hand had been blown off by a letter.
   b. situational
3. a. He was actually doing harmful, base things that were not "noble" at all.
   b. verbal
4. a. The people who wrote the letters were probably completely innocent, as Juan had been when he wrote his letter.
   b. dramatic
5. a. Having forgotten his original mission, he censored the letter and was executed.
   b. situational

**B.** (5 points each)
1. c
2. b
3. d
4. b

**C.** (4 points each)
1. a
2. c
3. a
4. b
5. c

**D.** (15 points; students should answer one of the two)
1. Answers will vary but could include points similar to the following:
   a. Initially, Juan fears government censorship and plans to sabotage it—or at least protect himself and Mariana—by becoming a censor.
   b. Later, in order to keep his job as a censor, he conforms to the government's attitude and policy on increasingly deeper levels.
   c. Finally, the desire to be perfect at his job leads him to see antigovernment plots and sentiments everywhere, including even in his own innocent letter.
   Some students may say that, rather than (or in addition to) being innocently concerned with his job, Juan is caught up in the joy of censorship until he becomes as anxious and distrustful as the government.
2. Answers will vary. Examples of the absurd include:
   a. Juan writes a letter to an old friend, and, despite the fact that he knows the contents are irreproachable, he nevertheless becomes so worried about both her safety and his that he can't concentrate at work and is losing sleep.
   b. In order to avoid trouble with the censors, he becomes a censor.
   c. Although he only took the job to get around the authorities, he gets so caught up in it that he no longer cares about family, friends, food, or anything else.

d. He does to other people what he feared would be done to him.
e. Ultimately, he does to himself exactly what he feared some unknown censor would do to him and is executed.

In addition, students should note the author's point of view; for example:
   a. Governments that use such extreme measures to avoid opposition would be laughable if the results were not so tragic.
   b. Governments that go to such lengths to control people are in themselves absurd.

**E.** (15 points) Answers will vary widely, depending on students' personal experiences, situations, and viewpoints. Accept any answers that address the concern of the question and are elaborated by examples from the literature or from life.

## Annabel Lee/The Bells

Selection Test, pp. 35–36
**A.** (10 points each)
1. End Rhyme (students should indicate two examples similar to the following):
   a. sea/Lee
   b. bells/tells
   c. despair/air
   d. roar/outpour
2. Internal Rhyme (students should indicate two examples similar to the following):
   a. ever/dissever
   b. beams/dreams
   c. rise/eyes
   d. horror/outpour
3. Assonance (students should indicate two examples similar to the following):
   a. neither/demons/sea
   b. beams/me/dreams/Lee/feel
   c. rise/bright/eyes
   d. clang/clash
4. Alliteration (students should indicate two examples similar to the following):
   a. demons/down
   b. beams/bringing/beautiful/but/bright
   c. tale/terror/tells
   d. clang/clash

**B.** (5 points each)
1. c
2. a
3. b
4. d

**C.** (20 points; students should answer one of the two)
1. Answers will vary. Reasons include the following:
The speaker thought the death of Annabel Lee was
   tragic because
   a. he was very much in love with her, and she
      with him.
   b. she was so young.
   c. she was very beautiful.
   d. she didn't deserve to die.
He thinks that she died because
   a. their love was so perfect.
   b. the angels envied their love.
   c. she was the victim of the angels' jealousy.
2. Students should name at least three of the following
   differences and cite an example from the poems for
   each difference. Answers and examples will vary.
   Differences between poetry and prose include:
   a. Poetry emphasizes rhythm to a greater degree.
   b. Poetry emphasizes sound patterns to a greater
      degree.
   c. Repetition is more often used in poetry.
   d. Figurative language is used to a greater degree
      in poetry.
   e. Poetry is usually more compact: it conveys
      meaning through brief, vivid phrases.
   f. In poetry, words and images are often used
      to imply or suggest additional meanings.
   g. Poetry is more emotionally intense.
   h. Poetry often engages the senses directly rather
      than depending on rational thought.
   Students should name three of the above differences
   and cite an example for each from the poems.
**D.** (20 points) Answers will vary widely, depending on
   students' personal experiences, situations, and
   viewpoints. Accept any answers that address the
   concern of the question and are elaborated by
   examples from the literature or from life.

## The Cask of Amontillado
Selection Test, pp. 37–38
**A.** (8 points each)
1. Notes will vary. Students could make notes suggesting
   that Montresor's statement is ironic because he
   a. suggests that he is concerned about Fortunato's
      health but is actually planning Fortunato's death.
   b. pretends to encourage Fortunato not to be overly
      concerned about the severity of his cough but means,
      in fact, that Fortunato's cough has no chance to kill
      him, since Montresor will kill him first.
   c. warns Fortunato to be careful when there is actually
      nothing Fortunato can do to protect himself from a
      danger he does not suspect.
2. Notes will vary. Students could make notes suggesting

that it is ironic for Montresor to wish Fortunato a long
life while he is planning to kill him.
3. Notes will vary. Students could make notes suggesting
   that Montresor's statement is ironic because he
   a. begs Fortunato to do something that he has no
      desire for Fortunato to do.
   b. asks Fortunato to leave when he has made sure
      Fortunato cannot leave by chaining him to the wall.
**B.** (7 points each)
1. d
2. c
3. b
4. a
**C.** (4 points each)
1. c
2. b
3. b
4. a
5. b
**D.** (14 points; students should answer one of the two)
1. Answers will vary. Students who think Montresor is
   sane might say that
   a. not all murderers are insane; evil is not the same
      thing as insanity.
   b. his murder plan was well thought out, and his
      retelling of the events leading up to the actual death
      of Fortunato shows that his mind is still clear.
   c. at the time of the story, men fought duels to the
      death over small insults to one's honor and were
      considered brave and honorable, not insane.
   d. even after 50 years, he doesn't seem to feel
      any differently about the murder.
   e. he appears to have successfully functioned in
      the world for the last 50 years.
Students who think Montresor is insane might say that
   a. even after the passage of half a century, he doesn't
      seem to feel that his desire for vengeance was
      excessive or abnormal.
   b. he doesn't show any signs of remorse.
   c. his confessing his crime to "you, who so well know
      the nature of my soul," suggests that he believes
      that others will find his act completely justified if
      only they understand the kind of person he is,
      which really doesn't have anything to do with
      whether his act was justified.
   d. he seems to think that revealing the nature
      of Fortunato's "injuries" and "insult" to him
      is completely unnecessary.
   e. he killed Fortunato in a cold-blooded, premeditated
      manner while pretending sincere friendship.
2. Answers will vary. Students who believe that Montresor
   feels no remorse could support this view with such
   details as the following:

a. He begins his story with an explanation of his reasons for wanting revenge. By not asking for the reader's pity or forgiveness, he seems to show that he assumes his reader will agree with these reasons.

b. As he leads Fortunato through the vaults, Montresor seems to enjoy himself. He even drinks to Fortunato's "long life."

c. As he is imprisoning Fortunato, he doesn't seem to have any second thoughts. He shows some fear (though not remorse) when Fortunato yells, but then becomes braver and yells with him.

d. Even after 50 years, he doesn't ask for forgiveness and doesn't apologize for what he's done. Instead, he tells the story without any hint of feeling for his victim.

Students who feel that Montresor feels remorse will find it difficult, if not impossible, to provide reasonable support for this answer.

**E.** (14 points) Answers will vary widely, depending on students' personal experiences, situations, and viewpoints. Accept any answers that address the concern of the question and are elaborated by examples or details from the literature or from life.

## Unit One, Part Two Test
pp. 39–40
**A.** (5 points each)
1. d
2. b
3. c
4. a

**B.** (20 points)
Answers will vary. A model answer for "The Censors" follows.

In "The Censors," it was hard to believe or accept that
a. Juan could become so involved in his job that he forgot why he took the job in the first place.
b. Juan could censor himself and be executed just for writing a letter.

Reasons it was hard to believe or accept might include:
a. The job itself was so sinister that it is hard to imagine any normal person becoming caught up in it and wanting to excel.
b. It doesn't seem possible that anyone could become so distracted as to bring about his own execution.
c. The existence of such a censorship bureau seems absurd.
d. There is no such level of censorship in the United States.

**C.** (20 points each; students should answer two of the three)

1. Answers will vary. A model answer for "The Possibility of Evil" might include the following points:
a. The tables are turned when Miss Strangeworth receives an anonymous letter in the mail. The reader can assume that the letter is from Don Crane. Miss Strangeworth has been pointing out signs of evil in the town while everyone thought she was morally upright and respectable; the reversal reveals that she is the source of evil and not respectable at all.
b. Miss Strangeworth has been causing suspicion and personal harm in the town by sending anonymous letters to people. At the end of this story, she receives one herself, and her precious roses have been destroyed.
c. The reversal is deserved because Miss Strangeworth has appointed herself as the person responsible for rooting out any signs of evil behavior in the town and notifying people about them by writing anonymous letters. Her letters have undoubtedly caused more problems—and evil—than they have solved.

2. Answers will vary. A model answer for "The Sniper" and "The Gift of the Magi" follows:
a. In "The Sniper," justice is served because the sniper ends up killing his own brother. The story presents the sniper as a "fanatic" and describes how he kills three people. It also suggests that the war is cruel and evil beyond imagining when two brothers can be forced into a situation where they shoot at each other. Justice is served in that the sniper suffers a terrible loss for doing what he has done—just as many other people have probably suffered terrible losses grieving for his other victims. Now he must face up to what he has done and pay the consequences, and killing his own brother might be the only way to force him to do that.
b. In "The Gift of the Magi," justice is not done because Jim and Della end up with gifts they cannot use. Jim and Della seem so generous and loving that they deserve better than what they get. In a just situation, they might sacrifice their own valuable possessions to please each other and would be successful in doing so.

3. Answers will vary. A model answer for the sniper in "The Sniper" and Montresor in "The Cask of Amontillado" follows:
Both the sniper and Montresor
a. scorn their opponents.
b. feel wronged by their opponents.
c. risk their lives and their secure futures in order to satisfy deep desires.

Unlike Montresor, the sniper
- a. does not consider the outcome or result of his actions.
- b. does not believe he will suffer any consequences for his actions.
- c. finally meets his match.
- d. receives the ultimate punishment—death.

Unlike the sniper, Montresor
- a. takes on as little risk as possible in order to avoid detection.
- b. takes on risk in order to gain vengeance.
- c. gets away with his boldness and his crime.

**D.** (20 points) Answers will vary. A model answer for the speaker in "Annabel Lee" follows:
- a. The speaker is affected by the death of his love, Annabel Lee.
- b. The speaker is overcome with grief and cannot forget her, to the extent that he lies in the tomb beside her every night.
- c. Being with Annabel Lee is the most important thing in the speaker's life, as shown by his bitterness toward the angels, whom he blames for her death, and his assertion that no one, including the angels, can "dissever my soul from the soul / Of the beautiful Annabel Lee."

# Unit Two

## Life Without Go-Go Boots
Selection Test, pp. 41–42

**A.** (10 points each) Answers and notes will vary. The following are sample answers. Students should include three.
1. funny
   - a. Her choice of subject, as well as the words and images she uses throughout the essay, are humorous.
   - b. Numerous examples could be cited, such as her description of herself as a "raiment renegade" or her description of school as "two parts ABCs to fifty parts Where Do I Stand in the Great Pecking Order of Humankind?"
2. compassionate (or sympathetic)
   - a. She was appreciative of her mother's effort to do the right thing, even though she failed so miserably.
   - b. She is willing to buy her daughter the "nineties equivalent of go-go boots" if someday she asks for it.
   - c. She is disturbed about buying expensive clothes when there is so much poverty in the world.
3. nonconformist
   - a. As an adult, she ignores fashion and wears the clothes she feels comfortable in.
   - b. She wears cowboy boots instead of high heels.
   - c. She says it is more important to be valued for inward individuality than outward conformity.

Accept other adjectives if they demonstrate understanding of the essay and are supported by examples.

**B.** (5 points each)
1. c
2. b
3. a
4. d

**C.** (4 points each)
1. b
2. a
3. b
4. c
5. c

**D.** (15 points; students should answer one of the two)
1. Answers will vary. Students may note the following differences:
   - a. Fashion is decided by outside forces; style is decided by each individual.
   - b. High fashion is expensive; style doesn't have to be.
   - c. Fashion is temporary; style can last for a lifetime.

In addition, students should note that the difference was important to the author because once she was comfortable with her own style, she no longer needed to worry about being in fashion.

2. Answers will vary, but students should address the
following points:
  a. Finding your own individuality is more important
     than slavishly conforming to the dictates of fashion.
  b. What's inside a person is far more important than
     what he or she wears.
  c. Using money to buy clothes that are meant to last
     only a short time before they are out of fashion is
     not morally defensible when so many people in
     the world live in poverty.

**E.** (15 points) Answers will vary widely, depending on
students' personal experiences, situations, and viewpoints.
Accept any answers that address the concern of the
question and are elaborated by examples or details
from the literature or from life.

## from Angela's Ashes
Selection Test, pp. 43–44
**A.** (10 points each)
  1. Ireland. Notes will vary but could include:
    a. He hears people talk about the terrible crimes
       of the English.
    b. His nurse talks of people who suffered and died
       in the Great Famine.
    c. The region he lives in is poverty-stricken.
  2. Catholic. Notes will vary but could include:
    a. The hospital is run by nuns.
    b. A priest comes to perform a ritual (Extreme
       Unction) in case he dies.
    c. Hundreds of boys say prayers for him at the
       Confraternity.
    d. He is constantly urged to pray.
    e. His father is sure Saint Jude pulled him through
       the crisis.
  3. Possible problems:
    a. His father was often out of work.
    b. His family lived in poverty.
    c. Other children in the family have apparently died
       (". . . am I to lose the whole family?")
  Notes will vary but could include:
    a. He might have suffered hunger at times.
    b. He came down with typhoid.
    c. He might have wished that he owned books.
**B.** (5 points each)
  1. d
  2. b
  3. c
  4. a
**C.** (4 points each)
  1. c
  2. a
  3. b

4. b
5. a
**D.** (15 points; students should answer one of the two)
  1. Answers will vary but should include points similar
     to the following:
    a. He got his first delicious taste of Shakespeare in
       the history book Patricia gave him, and he takes
       pleasure in reciting the brief lines.
    b. The books help to forge a bond of friendship
       among McCourt, Patricia, and Seamus.
    c. Learning "The Highwayman," which Patricia
       reads to him from the next room, brings him
       great pleasure.
    d. Because of the nuns' anger over Patricia's reading
       the poem from the next room, they banish McCourt
       to a lonely and frightening upstairs ward.
    e. McCourt's wish to find out the ending of "The
       Highwayman" inspires Seamus to learn the poem
       even though he can't read, enriching Seamus's
       life and, by extension, that of his wife.
  2. Answers will vary but should emphasize the important
     emotional bond McCourt feels with his father. Evidence
     could include:
    a. When his father looks sad, it is "the worst thing in
       the world."
    b. When his father kisses him on the forehead for
       the first time in his life, he is so happy he feels
       "like floating out of the bed."
    c. The details in the memoir of his father's one visit
       to him in the hospital are very vivid and convey a
       sense of comfort and affection.
    d. Even though he cannot visit, the father sends notes
       to let McCourt know how important his recovery is.
**E.** (15 points) Answers will vary widely, depending on
students' personal experiences, situations, and viewpoints.
Accept any answers that address the concern of the
question and are elaborated by examples or details
from the literature or from life.

## Unfinished Business
Selection Test, pp. 45–46
**A.** (8 points each)
  1. Notes will vary. Students could interpret the advice
     as follows:
    a. Don't wait until it is too late to tell people how you
       feel about them.
    b. Saying nice things about a person after he or she
       has died is a poor substitute for expressing yourself
       directly to the person.
  2. Notes will vary. Students could interpret the advice
     as follows:
    a. Pay attention to the gifts a dying person can give
       the living.

b. It isn't difficult to benefit from what a dying person can show you, but you have to be willing to face the person and the facts.

c. Don't think that being around dying people is all sadness and depression.

d. Don't be afraid to deal with the dying; they have beautiful gifts to offer.

3. Notes will vary. Students could interpret the advice as follows:

a. Pay attention to what dying people concern themselves with, because this reflects what is truly important in life.

b. Don't avoid dying people, because you can learn important things from them.

4. Notes will vary. Most students will feel the main message in the selection has to do with the importance of communicating honestly with people who are dying. Students could note such ideas as the following:

a. Honest communication helps both the dying person and the people he or she will leave through death.

b. It is harmful to both the living and the dying for the living to fear honest communication with the dying.

c. The living can help the dying and the dying can help the living.

**B.** (6 points each)

1. d
2. a
3. a
4. c

**C.** (4 points each)

1. c
2. a
3. b
4. c
5. b

**D.** (12 points; students should answer one of the two)

1. Answers will vary. Possible examples include the following:

a. Failing to tell a dying person how you feel about him or her and about his or her death.

b. Failing to express your love to a dying person.

c. Failing to face the fact that a person is dying.

d. Holding a grudge.

e. Letting fear stop you from dealing with a dying person.

f. Working out a problem in a relationship with a dying person.

Students should note that any example of "unfinished business" is harmful because it makes dying harder for the dying person and grieving harder for the survivor.

2. Answers will vary. Students should indicate that the statement could be considered a paradox because it seems contradictory but is, in fact, true. They might explain by noting that

a. a person who is as compassionate and caring as Kübler-Ross surely could not enjoy watching a child die, yet she clearly loves her work.

b. the help she is able to provide to dying children and the beauty she sees in them is enough to make her enjoy working in a situation most people would see as depressing and unbearable.

c. she gets fulfillment in situations that most people view only as tragic.

**E.** (12 points) Answers will vary widely, depending on students' personal experiences, situations, and viewpoints. Accept any answers that address the concern of the question and are elaborated by examples or details from the literature or from life.

## A Christmas Memory

Selection Test, pp. 47–48

**A.** (8 points each)

1. Notes will vary, but most students will write notes suggesting that the phrase communicates

a. a sense of loss.

b. the feeling that Capote has been cut off from an important part of himself.

2. Notes will vary, but most students will write notes suggesting that the phrase communicates Capote's feelings of

a. love.

b. closeness to his friend.

3. Notes will vary, but students could note that the kites symbolize

a. freedom.

b. beauty.

c. love.

d. happiness.

e. their friendship.

f. fun.

4. Notes will vary, but students could note that the kites symbolize

a. the link between him and his friend.

b. his memories of the past.

c. Christmas.

d. freedom.

e. happiness.

**B.** (6 points each)

1. d
2. b
3. a

**C.** (4 points each)
1. c
2. a
3. c
4. b
5. a

**D.** (15 points; students should answer one of the two)
1. Answers will vary but should include points similar to the following:
   a. As a child, "fruitcake weather" is a very special, magical time of sharing both with his friend and with others.
   b. As an adult, it is a time of lost innocence.
   c. As an adult, it is a time of loving and sharing, and remembrance of the intangible gifts his friend shared with him.
2. Answers will vary but should reflect students' understanding that Capote's friend differs from "those who Know Best" in that she
   a. is childlike and not an authority figure.
   b. seems to enjoy and appreciate life much more than they do.
   c. loves Buddy and spends time with him.
   d. is more like Buddy than they are.
   e. understands and cares more about Buddy's needs.
   f. is far more generous with her time and meager resources than they are.

**E.** (15 points) Answers will vary widely, depending on students' personal experiences, situations, and viewpoints. Accept any answers that address the concern of the question and are elaborated by examples or details from the literature or from life.

## Song of the Open Road/The Road Not Taken
Selection Test, pp. 49–50

**A.** (10 points each)
1. Notes will vary but should suggest ideas similar to the following:
   a. The road represents the speaker's future, freedom, or opportunity.
   b. The road represents choice, the speaker's life path, or a decision he made that influenced his life.
2. Notes will vary but should suggest ideas similar to the following:
   a. The poem has no rhyme scheme; it is free verse.
   b. The poem's rhyme scheme is *abaab;* it is a controlled, regular rhyme scheme.
3. Notes will vary but should suggest ideas similar to the following:
   a. The speaker has set out on the road in accordance with his own free will.
   b. The speaker has come to a major life decision and must make a choice; he chooses his path by his own free will.

4. Notes will vary but should suggest ideas similar to the following:
   a. The speaker feels "strong and content," hopeful, free.
   b. The speaker feels satisfied; his life choice "made all the difference."

**B.** (5 points each)
1. a
2. d
3. b
4. b

**C.** (20 points; students should answer one of the two)
1. Answers will vary but should suggest ideas similar to the following:
   a. The speaker made an important decision that changed the course of his life; he does not regret that choice, but he will always wonder how things might have been if he had chosen differently.
   b. The speaker has always regretted that he could not try both ways; he is not unhappy with the path he chose, but he sighs because he could not try the other too.
2. Answers will vary but should include points similar to the following:
   a. "Song of the Open Road" is told from the perspective of someone just setting out; it looks to the future.
   b. The speaker in "Song of the Open Road" has undergone a change in attitude and is eager to leave old constraints behind.
   c. "The Road Not Taken" is told from the perspective of someone looking back on choices made in the past.
   d. "Song of the Open Road" is optimistic, exuberant, enthusiastic about an unknown future.
   e. "The Road Not Taken" is a bit wistful; there is a feeling that the speaker is pleased with, even proud of, the road he took, but will never stop wondering about the road not taken.

**D.** (20 points) Answers will vary widely, depending on students' personal experiences, situations, and viewpoints. Accept any answers that address the concern of the question and are elaborated by examples or details from the literature or from life.

## American History
Selection Test, pp. 51–52

**A.** (20 points) Notes will vary, but most students will write notes suggesting that the climax occurs when Eugene's mother sends Elena away from the house because
   a. Elena has been looking forward to entering the house for a long time, and Eugene's mother dashes those hopes.

b. this is the turning point in the story, the point at which Elena's happiness turns to misery.

In addition, students should draw a line connecting the box to the point in the story at which the climax occurs. Those who believe that the climax occurs as stated above should indicate that the climax occurs near the end of the story.

**B.** (6 points each)
1. d
2. b
3. d
4. d
5. a

**C.** (4 points each)
1. a
2. b
3. c
4. a
5. c

**D.** (15 points; students should answer one of the two)
1. Answers will vary but could include points similar to the following:
   a. The hopes of Americans for the future are dashed by Kennedy's assassination; the hopes of Elena for the future of her friendship with Eugene are dashed by his mother.
   b. To many people, Kennedy's death symbolized the death of innocence; Elena's innocence is destroyed by Eugene's mother's actions.
   c. Kennedy supported civil rights; Eugene's mother's rejection of Elena is racist.
2. Answers will vary but should reflect students' knowledge that both mothers attempt to discourage the relationship. In addition, students could argue that
   a. neither mother considers the individual person but only the person's race and class.
   b. Elena's mother's behavior is simply cautious and realistic, knowing as she does how white people tend to treat Puerto Ricans.
   c. both mothers believe they are being protective of their children.

**E.** (15 points) Answers will vary widely, depending on students' personal experiences, situations, and viewpoints. Accept any answers that address the concern of the question and are elaborated by examples or details from the literature or from life.

## Unit Two, Part One Test
pp. 53–54
**A.** (5 points each) Answers will vary but should include points similar to the following:
1. When she was young, Kingsolver wanted to be fashionable, and go-go boots represented her dream of achieving that goal.

2. They don't allow typhoid and diphtheria patients to communicate with each other; they are a boy and a girl; or, the nuns who run the hospital think praying is more beneficial than talking and laughing.
3. They both feel good, satisfied, or pleased about the roads or paths they have chosen.
4. The climax occurs when Eugene's mother tells Elena, the narrator, that she cannot study with Eugene.

**B.** (20 points) Notes will vary. A model answer for *Angela's Ashes* follows:
The writer's memories focus on a childhood stay in the hospital. In particular, he describes
   a. his conversations with Patricia.
   b. discovering Shakespeare and learning "The Highwayman."
   c. reading and hearing about history involving the English.
   d. conversing with Seamus.

These experiences were memorable to the writer because
   a. he was introduced to literature, especially Shakespeare and poetry.
   b. he became aware of the Irish people's feelings toward England.
   c. he became interested in a girl, perhaps for the first time, and then suffered through losing her when she died.
   d. he began to understand the value of words and stories through Seamus, who memorized poetry so he could recite it to McCourt.

**C.** (20 points each; students should answer two of the three)
1. Answers will vary. A model answer for "American History" follows.
The story expresses the insight that people are too often selfish or self-absorbed.
   The story communicates this insight through
   a. the way that the students at Elena's school react to Kennedy's assassination. They are more pleased to be let out of school early than they are saddened by the death of the president.
   b. the way that Eugene's mother treats Elena. Eugene's mother is far more concerned about her son and his relationships than she is about the effect that her actions will have on Elena
In addition, students should explain whether this insight is true to their life experiences.
2. Answers will vary. A model answer for McCourt (*Angela's Ashes*) and Capote ("A Christmas Memory") follows.
The writers are affected by hardship in similar ways in that
   a. neither is destroyed by his or her difficult childhood experiences.
   b. both go on to achieve great things in their lives.

The writers' lives are affected differently by childhood hardships in that

    a. McCourt does not seem especially bitter toward the past. The selection focuses on the positive influences he experienced during his stay in the hospital.

    b. Capote, on the other hand, seems bitter. He refers to the people in his family who separated him from his friend as "those who Know Best."

    c. McCourt is rather matter-of-fact about the hardships of his past, even when Patricia dies. He seems to have retained the good things about his past and let go of the bad things.

    d. Capote is nostalgic and sad about the hardships of his past, possibly due to his finding little love from the people in his life. He doesn't seem to have gotten on with his life as well as McCourt has.

3. Answers will vary. A model answer for the dying girl in "Unfinished Business" follows.

The girl's love and devotion to family are important to her struggle in that

    a. the dying girl's mother unintentionally pressures her not to die by letting the girl know that she prays for her to live longer. The girl is caught between her body, which is ready to die, and her parents, who aren't ready for her to die.

    b. the dying girl holds on to life because she has been taught that it is a sin to love one's parents more than God and she fears that she cannot get into heaven. This places her in a bind because, being a child, she can't help loving her parents most of all.

**D.** (20 points) Notes will vary. A model answer for "Life Without Go-Go Boots" follows.

    a. The realization is made by Kingsolver, the writer. She realizes the difference between fashion and style.

    b. As a child, Kingsolver agonized over fashion and the need to look fashionable—especially when she asked for go-go boots for Christmas. She wanted to fit in with the other kids in school.

    c. In college, she discovered that style was perhaps more important and began to develop confidence in her own individuality.

    d. As an adult, she realized the importance of being herself, following her own mind instead of trying to please others, and dressing in whatever way made her feel comfortable.

## The Beginning of Something
Selection Test, pp. 55–56
**A.** (10 points each)

1. Notes will vary. Students might write notes suggesting that Roseanne feels jealous of Melissa because Melissa

    a. is very pretty.

    b. has lots of pretty clothes.

    c. is older and has a boyfriend.

2. Notes will vary. Students might write notes suggesting that Roseanne feels dislike for Melissa because

    a. Melissa is spoiled.

    b. their mothers expect them to be friends.

    c. Melissa is just not her type.

3. Notes will vary. Students might write notes suggesting that Roseanne feels pity for Melissa because Melissa

    a. has lost her mother.

    b. will be sad for a very long time.

    c. can't find comfort in any of the things that Roseanne has been jealous of.

**B.** (5 points each)

1. d
2. c
3. b
4. b

**C.** (4 points each)

1. a
2. a
3. b
4. a
5. c

**D.** (15 points; students should answer one of the two)

1. Answers will vary. Students who say that Travis is most important might include points similar to the following:

    a. The date with Travis makes Roseanne happy enough to be generous toward Melissa.

    b. The date makes her feel more adult and able to understand the feelings of others.

    c. The date makes her understand how life can change suddenly, for good or bad.

Other choices should be supported with appropriate reasons.

2. Answers will vary. Students might say that Roseanne means that

    a. both grief and the feelings that go with intimacy are intensely personal.

    b. the feelings of grief can be made less painful by sharing them with other people, in spite of the fact that they are so personal.

    c. the feelings that go with intimacy would be diminished if they were shared with others.

**E.** (15 points) Answers will vary widely, depending on students' personal experiences, situations, and viewpoints. Accept any answers that address the concerns of the question and are elaborated by examples or details from the literature or from life.

## Young/Hanging Fire
Selection Test, pp. 57–58

**A.** (10 points each)

1. Notes will vary but should suggest ideas similar to the following:
   a. The speaker wants to remember what she felt like when she was young.
   b. The entire poem is written in the language of remembering the past.
2. Notes will vary but should suggest ideas similar to the following:
   a. No; the speaker is an adult, the main character is an adolescent.
   b. The poem begins with the words "A thousand doors ago / when I was a lonely kid"; the speaker recalls feelings and thoughts that she had when she had a "brand new body, / which was not a woman's yet."
3. Notes will vary but should suggest ideas similar to the following:
   a. anxious; insecure; worried
   b. Her "skin has betrayed" her; the boy she adores is immature; her knees are "always so ashy"; she has to wear braces; she may die before she gets a chance to grow up; she needs to learn how to dance; her room feels too small; she is feeling torn in too many directions; her mother isn't there to support her; she was unfairly overlooked for the Math Team; and she has nothing to wear tomorrow.
4. Notes will vary but should suggest ideas similar to the following:
   a. Yes.
   b. The poem begins with the words "I am fourteen"; the poem tells the ongoing thoughts of a 14-year-old girl in present tense.

**B.** (5 points each)
1. b
2. d
3. c
4. a

**C.** (20 points; students should answer one of the two)

1. Answers will vary. A model answer could include the following points:
   a. The speaker's voice in "Young" is that of an adult remembering what it felt like to be young; the speaker of "Hanging Fire" is in the throes of adolescence and is dealing with those feelings in the present.
   b. The girl in "Young" is in the midst of a long, lonely summer, while the girl in "Hanging Fire" is feeling the pressures of the school year.
   c. The girl in "Young" is noticing the sensory details of her surroundings—the feel of the clover under her, the way her house looks, how the leaves look,

how the crickets sound. The girl in "Hanging Fire" is focusing entirely on her feelings about herself and the people in her life.
   d. Both girls are conscious of their parents but feel separated from them by barriers.
   e. Both girls are aware of changes in their bodies.
   f. Both girls are filled with questions.
   g. The girl in "Young" seems to be comforted by confiding in the stars and feeling the presence of God, while the girl in "Hanging Fire" seems to be desperately seeking support but does not know where to find it.

2. Answers will vary. Students who think the poem does a good job of expressing what it is like to be 14 might say that, like many 14-year-olds, the speaker
   a. feels that life is unfair.
   b. feels anxious and adrift.
   c. feels alienated from her mother.
   d. feels pressured to measure up.
   e. is dismayed with her appearance.
   f. worries about the future.
   g. thinks about death.

Students who don't think the poem does a good job of expressing what it is like to be 14 should support that view with appropriate reasons.

**D.** (20 points) Answers will vary widely, depending on students' personal experiences, situations, and viewpoints. Accept any answers that address the concern of the question and are elaborated by examples or details from the literature or from life.

## The Seven Ages of Man
Selection Open-Book Test, pp. 59–60

**A.** (5 points each) Notes will vary but should suggest ideas similar to the following:

1. Infant
   a. helpless or dependent
   b. The infant is "mewling and puking" and is held by a nurse.
2. Schoolboy
   a. whiny or reluctant
   b. The schoolboy is "whining" and goes "unwillingly to school."
3. Lover
   a. wistful, mournful, or passionate
   b. The lover sighs "like furnace," suggesting that he is filled with a heated passion and a wistfulness in his "woeful ballad."
4. Soldier
   a. jealous, hot-tempered, foolhardy
   b. The soldier is "quick to quarrel" and seeks to establish his reputation, even if it costs him his life ("in the cannon's mouth").

5. Justice
   a. wise, judgmental, or dignified
   b. The justice is plump from eating well, but he is also "severe" and dignified ("beard of formal cut") in his pronouncements.
6. Pantaloon
   a. foolish
   b. The pantaloon begins to shrink in size, loses his manly voice, and no longer dresses with dignity.
7. Final Scene
   a. helpless or oblivious
   a. In his last age, the man reverts to childishness, loses his eyes, teeth, and taste, and finally dies.

**B.** (5 points each)
1. b
2. a
3. c
4. d
5. b

**C.** (20 points; students should answer one of the two)
1. Answers will vary. Students should include three of the ages listed below, with negative and positive points similar to those listed:
   a. Jaques describes the infant as messy and noisy; a positive view might describe the infant as innocent, cute, soft, full of wonder.
   b. Jaques describes the schoolboy as whining and unwilling to go to school; a positive view might describe the schoolboy as full of energy, curious, eager.
   c. Jaques describes the lover as sighing and woeful; a positive view might describe the lover as passionate and full of joy.
   d. Jaques describes the soldier as "full of strange oaths," quick to quarrel, and so determined to gain honor and good reputation that he would put himself in harm's way to do so; a positive view might describe the soldier as courageous, disciplined, self-sacrificing.
   e. Jaques describes the justice as well-fed, severe, prone to relating old proverbs; a positive view might describe the justice as conscientious and fair, deserving of his high station in society because of his virtue.
   f. Jaques describes the old man as a "pantaloon," implying that he is foolish, and says he has become smaller in stature and his voice is no longer manly; a positive view might describe the old man as gentle, generous, and wise, ready to give of himself rather than to prove himself.
   g. Jaques describes the last age of man as senility, when man loses all his abilities and is like an infant again; a positive view might describe the last age

as one of acceptance, peace, satisfaction with a life well lived.
2. Answers will vary widely. Students' answers should have two parts:
   a. They should name the seven ages of woman: for example, infant, schoolgirl, lover, young wife, mother, grandmother, old crone.
   b. They should write a description of any one of the ages they have named. Accept any answers that reflect an understanding of Jaques's gloomy and negative way of characterizing people.

**D.** (20 points) Answers will vary widely, depending on students' personal experiences, situations, and viewpoints. Accept any answers that address the concern of the question and are elaborated by examples or details from the literature or from life.

## Brothers Are the Same
Selection Test, pp. 61–62
**A.** (15 points each)
1. Notes will vary. Students' notes could suggest such actions and feelings as the following:
   a. They are both interested in Kileghen.
   b. They are jealous of each other's success with Kileghen.
   c. Medoto has successfully defeated a lion and Temas has not.
   d. Medoto behaves scornfully toward Temas.
   e. Temas feels insecure about his abilities and courage.
   f. Medoto worries that Temas will be more courageous than he was.
   g. Temas worries that Medoto will tell the village, particularly Kileghen, about his fear.
   h. Temas resents having his ordeal witnessed by his enemy.
2. Notes will vary. Students' notes could suggest such actions and feelings as the following:
   a. Both felt the same fear of failure.
   b. Medoto recognizes Temas's fear as similar to his own.
   c. Medoto acts to save Temas from his deepest fear.
   d. Temas admits his fear and challenges Medoto.
   e. Medoto admits his own fear.
   f. Medoto gives Temas Kileghen's belt.
   g. Temas cuts the belt in half and gives half to Medoto.
   h. Temas claims brotherhood with Medoto.
   i. Medoto helps Temas get back to the village.
**B.** (8 points each)
1. c
2. c
3. b

4. b
5. d

**C.** (15 points; students should answer one of the two)
1. Answers will vary. Students might note that what young American men face is similar to what Temas faced because they are often
   a. fearful of not measuring up.
   b. trying to impress young women.
   c. worried about what their peers think.
   d. required to be courageous.
   e. intensely concerned with their reputations.

Students might note that what young American men face is different in that
   a. it rarely involves such a specific ritual.
   b. they are not required to fight a lion.
   c. their entire future reputations are not established by succeeding or failing at one task.
   d. it is less likely to demand great physical courage.
   e. it is more likely to involve issues of responsibility.

2. Answers will vary. Students could say that Kileghen smiles the way she does because
   a. she will have an opportunity to make a decision based on other traits of importance to her.
   b. the shared belt indicates that both young men are eager to win her.
   c. the shared belt proves that both young men who desire her are admirably courageous.
   d. she has conquered both young men.
   e. much that will be interesting still lies ahead.

**D.** (15 points) Answers will vary widely, depending on students' personal experiences, situations, and viewpoints. Accept any answers that address the concern of the question and are elaborated by examples or details from the literature or from life.

### Through the Tunnel
Selection Test, pp. 63–64

**A.** (8 points each)
1. Notes will vary but could suggest that the sentence reveals that the time is
   a. spring or summer.
   b. the beginning of vacation.

Notes will vary but could suggest that the sentence reveals that the place is
   a. probably warm and sunny (because the beach is crowded).
   b. on a coast near a large body of water.
   c. a resort, vacation, or tourist area.
   d. possibly England (because the boy is English).
   e. crowded.

2. Notes will vary but could include notes suggesting ideas similar to the following:

   a. Jerry is at a symbolic turning point.
   b. Jerry must choose between being a child (following his mother) and beginning to grow up (going off on his own to the bay).

3. Notes will vary. Students could write notes suggesting that the bay
   a. symbolizes growing up—exploring new places and experiences, and facing new tests.
   b. looks dangerous from the vantage point of childhood.

4. Notes will vary. Students could write notes suggesting that
   a. the crowded beach symbolizes safety, security, and childhood.
   b. leaving the safety of the crowd is one way of maturing.

**B.** (6 points each)
1. b
2. c
3. c

**C.** (4 points each)
1. c
2. a
3. a
4. c
5. b

**D.** (15 points; students should answer one of the two)
1. Answers will vary. Students could say that Jerry shows that he is
   a. patient, in practicing his breathing exercises and not making the attempt until he's prepared.
   b. courageous, in doing something even though it's frightening.
   c. persevering, in finding the tunnel's opening, learning to use the goggles, and practicing under water even though it gives him nosebleeds.
   d. secretive, in not telling his mother what he's doing.
   e. foolhardy, in attempting something so difficult and dangerous.

2. Answers will vary but should include points similar to the following:
   a. Jerry struggles with his desire to be independent of his mother and his desire not to worry her.
   b. Swimming through the tunnel is very dangerous and Jerry's mother would probably try to stop him if she knew about his plans.

**E.** (15 points) Answers will vary widely, depending on students' personal experiences, situations, and viewpoints. Accept any answers that address the concern of the question and are elaborated by examples or details from the literature or from life.

# Unit Two, Part Two Test

pp. 65–66

**A.** (5 points each)
1. d
2. b
3. c
4. a

**B.** (20 points) Notes will vary. A model answer for the closed door in "Hanging Fire" follows:
  a. The closed door stands for the barrier, or separation, between the speaker and her mother.
  b. The speaker is 14 years old and feels anxious, emotionally tormented, and insecure about her appearance, her boyfriend, her inability to dance, her failure to make the Math Team, and death. Her mother might provide the support and guidance she needs, but the speaker feels separated or alienated from her mother ("and momma's in the bedroom / with the door closed").

**C.** (20 points each; students should answer two of the three)
1. Answers will vary. A model answer for the speaker in "Young" and Melissa in "The Beginning of Something" follows.
The speaker's communication problems involve
  a. her apparent alienation from her parents.
  b. her loneliness.
  c. her habit of expressing her questions to the stars.
Melissa's communication problems involve
  a. her inability or unwillingness to communicate her grief in words to anyone.
  b. her inability or unwillingness to let her cousin know that she needs her.
The speaker's and Melissa's communication problems are similar in that they involve
  a. confusion about what they are feeling
  b. an apparent lack of experience in expressing themselves.
  c. failing to directly communicate their feelings to those who are there to help them.
The speaker's and Melissa's communication problems are different in that
  a. Melissa is having difficulty in dealing with feelings of grief, while the speaker, as a child, had difficulties with the questions and confusion of growing up.
  b. Melissa's problems do not keep her from spending time with others and having a boyfriend, while the speaker's do.
2. Answers will vary. A model answer for Temas in "Brothers Are the Same" follows.

  a. Temas is moving from boyhood to manhood by passing his test against the lion. However, unlike the schoolboy in Jaques's monologue, he is not whining or unwilling; he looks forward to his test.
  b. In relation to his skills as a warrior, Temas is becoming a soldier. Like the soldier in Jaques's monologue, he risks his life to gain honor and reputation. He is also jealous and "quick in quarrel" when he challenges Medoto.
  c. In relation to his feelings for Kileghen, he is moving toward the stage of lover. He is not wistful or woeful yet, as Jaques's lover is, because he has not yet established a relationship with Kileghen.
3. Answers will vary. A model answer for Roseanne in "The Beginning of Something" and Temas in "Brothers Are the Same" follows.
In "The Beginning of Something," Roseanne
  a. faces emotional challenges in relating to Melissa and Travis.
  b. tries to be supportive of Melissa but gets little response.
  c. successfully experiences her first date with Travis.
  d. realizes that Melissa needs her help and friendship, and she expresses herself by helping Melissa without being asked.
  e. reaches an understanding of both Melissa and her own mother and how she can meet their emotional needs.
  f. looks forward to new challenges.
In "Brothers Are the Same," Temas
  a. faces physical and emotional challenges.
  b. overcomes his fear of failure in his test against the lion, partly because Medoto helps turn the lion toward him.
  c. overcomes the physical challenge by spearing the lion, ignoring his own pain, and using his sword to finish off the lion by himself.
  d. challenges Medoto and learns how similar their experiences have been and how wrong he has been about Medoto.
  e. refuses to accept Kileghen's choice and instead accepts a new challenge for himself.

**D.** (20 points) Notes will vary. A model answer for Jerry ("Through the Tunnel") follows.
Before the rite of passage, Jerry
  a. thinks of himself as a child.
  b. is beginning to feel unsatisfied with the relatively safe adventures and amusements of children.
  c. is dependent on his mother.
  d. is more influenced by the need not to worry his mother.
  e. is beginning to feel a strong need to prove himself.

Jerry's rite of passage involves swimming through the underwater tunnel.

After the rite of passage, Jerry
a. is more mature.
b. doesn't feel the need to prove himself.
c. is independent of his mother.
d. no longer worries about being dependent on his mother.
e. can be satisfied again with the relatively safe amusements of children.

# Unit Three

## The Devil and Daniel Webster

Selection Test, pp. 67–68

**A.** (6 points each) Notes will vary but should include points similar to the following:

1. a. Jabez is a state senator and a farmer, but he sold his soul to the devil ten years ago to achieve his success.
   b. He marries Mary, but he knows that the devil will arrive at midnight to claim him.
2. a. Mary is a pious, innocent woman who is proud of her new husband and will stand by him.
   b. Mary asks Daniel Webster for help, and she prays for her husband's deliverance.
3. a. Scratch is the devil; he has supernatural powers, and he preys on people who are greedy or weak.
   b. Scratch disrupts the wedding celebration as he arrives to claim Jabez Stone. He calls up a judge and jury of the dead and argues his case as the plaintiff.
4. a. Daniel Webster is a famous politician and a lawyer, he is a hero to the people of the town, and he is a great orator.
   b. Webster challenges the devil, argues successfully to free Jabez Stone, and throws the devil out of New Hampshire.

**B.** (6 points each)
1. a
2. d
3. c
4. b
5. c

**C.** (4 points each)
1. b
2. a
3. c
4. a
5. a

**D.** (13 points; students should answer one of the two)
1. Answers will vary. Students might say that the speech would be just as appropriate because it
   a. does not talk about Jabez's legal position.
   b. does not argue about Jabez's guilt or innocence.
   c. only appeals to the jury's love of freedom, asking them not to deprive another man of it.

Students who say that the speech would only work for someone who is fundamentally innocent should support that answer with appropriate reasons.

2. Answers will vary. Students might say that the poetic language
   a. creates a mood of unreality in which we can more easily accept characters such as the devil and the lost souls.

b. makes Scratch seem more powerful and frightening.

c. makes the bias of the courtroom more overpowering.

d. allows Webster to play with images and emotions.

**E.** (13 points) Answers will vary widely, depending on students' personal experiences, situations, and viewpoints. Accept any answers that address the concerns of the question and are elaborated by examples or details from the literature or from life.

## I Have a Dream/Glory and Hope

Selection Test, pp. 69–70

**A.** (10 points each) Notes will vary but should suggest ideas similar to the following:

1. a. Slavery in the United States was ended by the Emancipation Proclamation.

   b. Laws of racial separation (apartheid) brought internal conflict to South Africa and made South Africa an outlaw state in the world of nations.

2. a. One hundred years later, the descendants of slaves are still not free; they are crippled by segregation, discrimination, and injustice.

   b. Now South Africa has put an end to the laws of apartheid and has successfully carried out its first democratic elections.

3. a. Americans must continue the struggle for freedom and justice for all until it truly is a reality.

   b. South Africans must dedicate themselves to building a new government of peace, prosperity, nonsexism, nonracialism, and democracy; they must all work together, never allowing one group to oppress another again.

**B.** (5 points each)

1. b
2. c
3. d
4. b

**C.** (4 points each)

1. b
2. a
3. c
4. b
5. a

**D.** (15 points; students should answer one of the two)

1. Answers will vary but could include the following points:

   a. The quote expresses the principle of nonviolent resistance; King believes that blacks must not resort to violence to achieve their goals.

   b. "Soul force" is on a higher level than physical force because it means being morally right and standing up for one's beliefs, not simply using fear and physical coercion to gain power.

c. The speech itself can help people gain "soul power" because it is inspiring and speaks of admirable goals.

d. The words of the speech are moving and emotionally charged and in themselves can be used to help in the struggle to win people over by persuasion rather than physical force.

2. Answers will vary but should suggest that both envision a future in which

   a. there is justice for all.

   b. no group oppresses another.

   c. freedom reigns.

   d. no one is robbed of dignity.

**E.** (15 points) Answers will vary widely, depending on students' personal experiences, situations, and viewpoints. Accept any answers that address the concern of the question and are elaborated by examples or details from the literature or from life.

## The United States vs. Susan B. Anthony

Selection Test, pp. 71–72

**A.** (10 points each) Examples will vary. A model answer follows.

1. a. Anthony and three other women went to the barbershop on West Street, where voters for the Eighth Ward were being registered.

   b. "It was bad enough for a bunch of women to barge into one sacred male precinct—the barbershop—but to insist on being admitted to another holy of holies—the voting booth—was absolutely outrageous."

The reactions of the men in the barbershop are examples of opinions.

2. a. "With the U.S. marshal at her side, Susan was brought before the federal commissioner of elections, William C. Storrs."

   b. "Susan couldn't help being amused at Keeney's embarrassment."

3. a. "By the afternoon of June 18, the case of *The United States* vs. *Susan B. Anthony* was ready to go to the jury."

   b. "But Susan, who must have been taking delight in his consternation, kept on talking."

**B.** (4 points each)

1. a
2. d
3. d
4. c
5. a

**C.** (4 points each)

1. c
2. c
3. a
4. a
5. c

**D.** (15 points; students should answer one of the two)

1. Answers will vary. Students might say that Anthony is shown to
   a. be courageous, as evidenced by her willingness to face ridicule and even prison for what she believes in.
   b. be clever, as evidenced by her interpretation of the Fourteenth Amendment and her taking advantage of the invitation to register to vote.
   c. have a strong personality, as evidenced by her effect on the people she deals with.
   d. be honorable, as evidenced by her determination to pay off her publishing debt and to pay the fines owed by the election inspectors who had let her vote.
   e. possess a sense of humor, as evidenced by the pleasure she seems to derive from playing with the sexist attitudes of the men she encounters.
2. Answers will vary. Students might say that Anthony's decision is right because
   a. the old interpretation of the law was wrong and needed to be challenged.
   b. her action had a powerful symbolic meaning.
   c. she received a great deal of positive publicity for her cause from the action and the trial that followed.
   d. she harmed no one in her rebellion against the law.

Students who think Anthony's decision was wrong should support that answer with appropriate reasons.

**E.** (15 points) Answers will vary widely, depending on students' personal experiences, situations, and viewpoints. Accept any answers that address the concerns of the question and are elaborated by examples or details from the literature or from life.

## Theme for English B/The Writer

Selection Test, pp. 73–74

**A.** (14 points each)
1. Notes will vary widely, depending on the emotions students choose.

Possible ideas to be suggested by students' notes include the following:
   a. Wonder, confusion, or worry. The speaker wonders about the truth of the instructor's statement, "let that page come out of you— / Then, it will be true," and other things about his or her own identity and ability to know the truth at such a young age.
   b. Loneliness or alienation. The speaker is the only African American in the class. He or she considers that the instructor may not "want to be a part of" him or her, suggesting a possible conflict or communication problem between the speaker and the instructor.

   c. Amusement or enjoyment. The speaker's inventive theme and imaginative way of communicating with the instructor suggests that he or she enjoys the creative process.
2. Notes will vary widely, depending on the emotions students choose. Possible answers to be suggested by students' notes include the following:
   a. Frustration or discouragement. The daughter's writing pace is uneven. She successfully produces the right words, then stops, then starts again, only to stop.
   b. Joy. Finding the right words is a matter "of life or death," and when they do come, the daughter will find great release from her creative burden.

**B.** (6 points each)
1. b
2. a
3. d

**C.** (12 points each)
1. Notes will vary widely but could suggest ideas similar to the following:
   a. The daughter carries "the stuff of her life" that goes into her writing—her success, dreams, disappointments, and limitations—just as a ship carries a cargo.
   b. Just as a cargo might be varied and heavy or light, so might the daughter's accumulated life experiences and her experiences communicating her thoughts on paper.
   c. Just as a cargo's journey might be easy or difficult, so might the daughter's life as a writer.
2. Notes will vary widely but could suggest ideas similar to the following:
   a. Just as the starling is trapped in the room, the daughter is trapped by her difficulty expressing herself on paper.
   b. Both the starling and the daughter struggle against limitations imposed by their inadequate experiences.
   c. Both are exhausted by their efforts and need to regain strength in order to approach their problems again.
   d. Just as escape comes to the starling, the daughter may have a similar experience when she successfully completes her creative endeavor.

**D.** (15 points; students should answer one of the two)
1. Answers will vary widely, but students may point out that the speaker could probably teach the instructor about
   a. being a student new to New York.
   b. life in the South.
   c. life in Harlem.
   d. being an African American.
   e. being a young person.
   f. what the two of them have in common.

Students may point out that the instructor could probably teach the speaker about

- a. his or her life experiences.
- b. being a white American.
- c. being an older person.
- d. being a teacher.
- e. English.
- f. communicating one's ideas and life experiences through writing.

2. Answers will vary but should include points similar to the following:
   - a. Expressing ideas and feelings in precise, fresh language is a matter "of life or death" to the daughter because she is a writer.
   - b. The speaker reaffirms the original wish but harder now, for he or she realizes the difficulties inherent in the creative process.

**E.** (15 points) Answers will vary widely, depending on students' personal experiences, situations, and viewpoints. Accept any answers that address the concern of the question and are elaborated by examples or details from the literature or from life.

### *from* **I Know Why the Caged Bird Sings**
Selection Test, pp. 75–76
**A.** (15 points each)

1. Notes will vary, but students could write notes suggesting that, like the bird, Marguerite
   - a. feels deeply.
   - b. has no one who understands her.
   - c. has no one with which to share her feelings.
   - d. is imprisoned (by the past, by racism).
   - e. remains hopeful.
   - f. very much wants to reach out and communicate with others.
   - g. wants to be saved from her imprisonment.
   - h. has been badly hurt and abused.
   - i. knows little of the world outside of her cage (hometown).
2. Notes will vary, but students could write notes suggesting that the visit
   - a. gives her self-confidence.
   - b. opens up the world of language to her as a means of self-expression.
   - c. relieves her emotional pain.
   - d. helps her to see that there is more to the world than her hometown.
   - e. helps her to lead a more fulfilling life.
   - f. shows her that an African American can lead a dignified life and achieve a great deal despite racism.

**B.** (5 points each)
1. d
2. d

3. b
4. d

**C.** (4 points each)
1. b
2. c
3. a
4. c
5. a

**D.** (15 points; students should answer one of the two)
1. Answers will vary but could include points similar to the following:
   - a. Marguerite appreciates being acknowledged as an individual and not just someone related to other people.
   - b. It is important to her because it means that she is liked, she is growing up, and she has worth as an individual.
   - c. It helps her heal her damaged self-esteem.
2. Answers will vary, but students could note that Mrs. Flowers encourages Marguerite to
   - a. read books and listen to them being read.
   - b. memorize and recite poetry.
   - c. appreciate language and literature.
   - d. be tolerant of illiteracy.
   - e. respect country wisdom and common sense.
   - f. develop her intellect.

In addition, students should recognize that Mrs. Flowers feels that developing these qualities is important because doing so will

- a. give Marguerite self-confidence.
- b. deepen her love of learning.
- c. make her more sensitive, aware, expressive, and articulate.
- d. more fully engage her in the world around her.
- e. help her to lead a richer, fuller life.

**E.** (15 points) Answers will vary widely, depending on students' personal experiences, situations, and viewpoints. Accept any answers that address the concern of the question and are elaborated by examples or details from the literature or from life.

### **New Directions**
Selection Test, pp. 77–78
**A.** (10 points each) Notes will vary but should suggest ideas similar to the following:

1. a. choose our own path in life; go in a new direction if the path we are on doesn't feel right.
   b. Annie Johnson's decision to end her marriage and start her own business exemplifies this principle.
2. a. determination and hard work; ability to be dependable in providing a service people want.
   b. Mrs. Johnson had to work very hard in difficult conditions to succeed; she provided something

people wanted and established loyal customers by being totally dependable, regardless of the weather.

3. a. you may need to create your own opportunity.

   b. No one offered Mrs. Johnson a job or agreed to help her set up a business; she had to figure out what to do and how to do it on her own.

**B.** (5 points each)

1. c
2. d
3. b
4. c

**C.** (25 points; students should answer one of the two)

1. Answers will vary but could include the following points:

   a. At first she carried everything she needed, walked several miles each day, and made meat pies outside the factories at lunchtime.

   b. After she was sure that the workers depended on her for lunch, she set up a stall between the two factories.

   c. The stall grew into a store that provided many things.

   d. Based on her approach to business, she probably added new products and services whenever she noticed that her customers wanted something that she could provide.

2. Answers will vary but could include the following points:

   a. Mrs. Johnson did not expect others to take care of her; she was self-reliant.

   b. She had few skills and few resources, but she was able to figure out how she could use what she had to provide a service people would pay for.

   c. Personal qualities that helped her succeed included patience, determination, dependability, a willingness to put up with discomfort and inconvenience, a clear sense of her goal, a strong body, and a willingness to work hard.

**D.** (25 points) Answers will vary widely, depending on students' personal experiences, situations, and viewpoints. Accept any answers that address the concern of the question and are elaborated by examples or details from the literature or from life.

### Encounter with Martin Luther King, Jr.

Selection Test, pp. 79–80

**A.** (10 points each) Notes will vary but should suggest that

1. a. she expected him to look taller and older.

   b. he was shorter than she imagined and younger looking, reminding her of a popular school athlete.

2. a. she expected him to have a "church way of talking," like a preacher.

   b. she was surprised by his easy friendliness, his interest in her background, and his understanding.

3. a. she worried that his disapproval of Bailey's criminal behavior might make her lose her job or his respect.

   b. he showed genuine sorrow and concern about Bailey's fate; he did not blame Bailey but sympathized with him.

**B.** (5 points each)

1. b
2. c
3. d
4. c

**C.** (25 points; students should answer one of the two)

1. Answers will vary but could include the following points:

   a. King's role as leader of the civil rights movement was a very serious one; humor would usually be inappropriate in discussing the life-and-death issues he was concerned with.

   b. In his public appearances, it was important that he be taken seriously because he was emphasizing the importance and the urgency of social change.

   c. He could not afford to allow people to take him lightly because that would encourage the very attitude he was trying to discourage: that the civil rights movement was just a passing fad and things would soon go back to "normal."

   d. As a private person, he was free to let his sense of humor show because the people around him already took the principles he stood for seriously.

   e. The change in King's manner of speaking when Levison came to tell him it was time to get back to work exemplifies the difference between the private and the public self: a change from a casual conversational tone to a more eloquent and preacherly manner.

2. Answers will vary but could include the following points:

   a. King wanted to keep young men like Bailey from ending up in prison.

   b. He believed that Bailey had turned to crime because of social conditions; the disappointments young black men face often cause desperate acts.

   c. He said that it was because of people like Bailey that they must fight and win the struggle for civil rights.

   d. He also expressed his belief in redemptive suffering—which Angelou did not entirely accept— i.e., that Bailey's suffering would redeem him.

**D.** (25 points) Answers will vary widely, depending on students' personal experiences, situations, and viewpoints. Accept any answers that address the concern of the question and are elaborated by examples or details from the literature or from life.

## Unit Three, Part One Test
pp. 81–82

**A.** (5 points each) Answers will vary but should include points similar to the following:

1. He appeals to each juror's memory of when he was a man who enjoyed and fought for freedom.
2. Anthony felt that the trial was unjust because she was not tried by a jury of her peers and was not given a jury verdict. She also believed that the Fourteenth Amendment gave her the right to vote. If she could get the judge to send her to jail, she would have the right to appeal and perhaps take her case to the U.S. Supreme Court.
3. Marguerite felt that she was respected and liked by an important person; it made her feel important and determined to follow Mrs. Flowers's suggestions.
4. Angelou is respectful and modest; appreciative of the accomplishments and examples set by others; strong-willed and accomplished in her own right; compassionate toward others.

**B.** (20 points) Notes will vary. A model answer for Annie Johnson in "New Directions" follows.
What makes her unusual:
  a. She does not ask for help from anyone.
  b. She establishes and builds up her own business and takes care of her children.
  c. She accomplishes these things in a cultural environment that does not encourage self-reliance or entrepreneurial spirit in either women or blacks.
How others react to her:
  a. The workers at the factory come to depend on her and become steady customers.
  b. Angelou herself reacts to Annie Johnson with respect and admiration for what she has accomplished.

**C.** (20 points each; students should answer two of the three questions)

1. Answers will vary. A model answer for Nelson Mandela in "Glory and Hope" follows.
Mandela criticizes the culture he grew up in by
  a. calling the system of apartheid an "extraordinary human disaster."
  b. describing how South Africa tore itself apart in a "terrible conflict."
  c. describing how South Africa was spurned and isolated from the rest of the world because of its actions.
  d. referring to the need to build a new society that does not have the problems of the old, namely a society of "peace, prosperity, nonsexism, nonracialism and democracy."
  e. implying that blacks in South Africa had never been granted democratic rights, justice, work, food, and basic human dignity.

2. Answers will vary. A model answer for *The Devil and Daniel Webster* and "The United States vs. Susan B. Anthony" follows.
Daniel Webster
  a. struggled to achieve victory over the devil.
  b. struggled to achieve freedom for Jabez Stone and the other citizens of New Hampshire.
  c. risked his reputation and his life by challenging the devil.
  d. was rewarded by victory over the devil and even greater admiration from the people.
  e. managed to achieve freedom for Jabez Stone and, metaphorically, threw "the Devil" out of New Hampshire.
Susan B. Anthony
  a. struggled to attain the right to vote for women.
  b. struggled to attain equality for women and equal treatment under the law.
  c. risked her reputation, her freedom (she could have been imprisoned for a long time), and the respect of many men who opposed her.
  d. was rewarded by the attention she and her case received, the achievement of an important step in a larger struggle for equality, and the respect and support of a larger number of both women and men than she had had before.

3. Answers will vary. A model answer for Martin Luther King, Jr., in "I Have a Dream" and Marguerite in *I Know Why the Caged Bird Sings* follows.
Martin Luther King, Jr.,
  a. lived in a country where slaves had been emancipated but were still not free; where blacks lived with segregation and other forms of racial discrimination; where blacks lived in hardship and poverty and were seething with discontent.
  b. could have continued to accept and live with these injustices, but instead he became a leader in the struggle for civil rights.
  c. called for a nation in which all people would live in freedom and be treated equally.
  d. preached nonviolent protest in a world where violence had often been used to achieve other goals.
Marguerite
  a. was a shy, quiet person who read all the time but had no self-confidence and did not express herself.

b. took a different direction after visiting with Mr. Flowers, who made her feel important and liked.

c. developed an appreciation of literature, language, and poetry and—by implication, since she became a writer—developed an ability to express herself in ways that could move, impress, and influence others.

**D.** (20 points) Notes will vary. A model answer for "The United States vs. Susan B. Anthony" and "Encounter with Martin Luther King, Jr." follows.

In "The United States vs. Susan B. Anthony":

a. Margaret Truman "meets" Susan B. Anthony in her evaluation of Anthony's life.

b. By examining Anthony's life, Truman changes her view of Anthony and comes to appreciate what she accomplished.

c. Truman develops an admiration for Anthony's courage, her outspokenness, and her determination in pursuing her goals.

In "Encounter with Martin Luther King, Jr.":

a. Maya Angelou meets Martin Luther King, Jr.

b. After meeting King, Angelou feels a new compassion for her brother Bailey, who is in prison.

c. She feels hope that the struggle for civil rights might succeed, despite her mother's views that the lives of blacks would not change because whites would never change.

d. She feels inspired to continue the struggle with more determination.

e. She feels greater admiration and respect for King after seeing private aspects of his personality and experiencing his warmth and compassion.

## To Build a Fire
Selection Test, pp. 83–84

**A.** (10 points each) Answers will vary widely. The following examples are model answers.

1. a. There was an "explosive crackle" as the man's spit froze in the air before it could fall to the snow.
   b. hearing and sight
   c. This image contributes to the mood of harshness and extreme danger.

2. a. ". . . speech would have been impossible because of the ice muzzle on his mouth."
   b. hearing and sight
   c. This image suggests a sense of isolation, aloneness, and quiet.

3. a. The snow "grew like an avalanche, and it descended upon the man and the fire, and the fire was blotted out!"
   b. sight, and perhaps hearing and touch
   c. This image suggests a sense of abrupt shock and desperation.

**B.** (5 points each)
1. b
2. d
3. c
4. a

**C.** (4 points each)
1. a
2. c
3. c
4. b
5. a

**D.** (15 points; students should answer one of the two)

1. Answers will vary, but could include that the man might have survived if he had
   a. traveled with a partner.
   b. brought along dry socks and moccasins.
   c. kept a big fire burning and waited out the cold snap next to it.
   d. gone along with the rest of the group rather than taking the roundabout way.

2. Answers will vary but could suggest that the man's name is unnecessary because we never will know anything about his background or family, and the man's anonymity emphasizes the theme of man against nature. The reader may feel
   a. more detached from him.
   b. more likely to think of him as a kind of "everyman."

The story supports these attitudes in ways such as the following:

a. It focuses only on the situation at hand, not on interesting or private thoughts the man might have about family and friends; the man is not nice to his dog and has no imagination and thus seems to be an unsympathetic person whom the reader doesn't really want to know.

b. The story devotes itself to vivid images of the circumstances and conditions, and the man's fate is controlled by these conditions.

**E.** (15 points) Answers will vary widely, depending on students' personal experiences, situations, and viewpoints. Accept any answers that address the concern of the question and are elaborated by examples or details from the literature or from life.

## from Into Thin Air
Selection Test, pp. 85–86

**A.** (10 points each) Answers will vary but should include points similar to the following:

1. a. Circled phrases: fire off, quick shots.
   b. These phrases suggest that the author felt impatient, anxious, a sense of urgency.

2. a. Circled words: overwhelmed, disturbingly, suffocation.

b. The author felt a heightened concern for his own safety, a sense of vulnerability, an awareness of the seriousness of his situation.

3. a. Circled words: dicey, fatiguing, safely, lunged, sprawled.

   b. He felt tension and intense concentration, followed by enormous relief; he was safe at last and totally spent.

**B.** (5 points each)
1. b
2. d
3. b
4. c

**C.** (4 points each)
1. b
2. a
3. c
4. c
5. a

**D.** (15 points; students should answer one of the two)
1. Answers will vary but could include the following points:
   a. He started down before many of the others.
   b. He was closer to camp when the storm hit than those he left behind.
   c. He had oxygen for part of the descent.
   d. He had memorized the terrain on the way up.
   e. He did not use up time and energy helping others.
Students should also include a statement about how he felt: e.g., guilty, remorseful, sad about the fate of his companions.

2. Answers will vary but could include the following points:
   a. He didn't celebrate or enjoy the summit because he was worried about getting a fresh oxygen bottle.
   b. His thinking became fuzzy and confused.
   c. He hallucinated.
   d. He moved slowly.
   e. He became extremely exhausted.
   f. He didn't fully recognize or properly respond to other people's distress.

**E.** (15 points) Answers will vary widely, depending on students' personal experiences, situations, and viewpoints. Accept any answers that address the concern of the question and are elaborated by examples or details from the literature or from life.

## The Sharks/A narrow Fellow in the Grass
Selection Test, pp. 87–88
**A.** (20 points each)
Notes will vary but should include points similar to the following:

1. "The Sharks":
   a. In the beginning, the mood is ominous and threatening. Words: "dark"; "sinister."
   b. In the middle, the mood is nostalgic, looking back at past happiness when life was carefree and daring. Words: ". . . won't we play in it any more?"; "I liked it"; "enough waves to fly in on"; "dared to swim out of my depth."
   c. In the end, the mood returns to ominous and threatening. Words: "sheen of copper stills the sea"; "dark"; "sharp."

2. "A narrow Fellow in the Grass":
   a. In the beginning, the poem is mysterious but not scary, like a riddle. Words: "narrow Fellow"; "you may have met Him—did you not"; "A spotted shaft is seen."
   b. In the middle, the mood continues to be mysterious or puzzling, but with hints of something a little unpleasant. Words: "Boggy"; "too cool"; "Whip lash"; "wrinkled"; "was gone."
   c. In the end, the poem suggests an instinctive feeling of sudden fear. Words: "tighter breathing"; "Zero at the Bone."

**B.** (5 points each)
1. c
2. b
3. a
4. b

**C.** (20 points; students should answer one of the two)
1. Answers will vary. Students might suggest turning points and evidence such as the following:
   a. The poem might represent a transition from the innocence of childhood to the more confusing and threatening time of adolescence. This is supported by the fact that the speaker has "dared to swim out of my depth" for the first time and by the suggestive word "innocent," describing the sharks' arrival. Soon the "sea becomes sinister," and sharks seem to be everywhere, with their sharp, dark fins.
   b. The sharks might represent difficulties in life, obstacles to be overcome, dangers to face, or perhaps even boys who are attracted to a young woman.
   c. The poem might represent a transition from the carefree existence of a vacation to the frustrations and perhaps serious problems of everyday life. This is supported by the phrase "the last day," by the happy description of playing in the sea prior to the sharks' arrival, and by the image of a sunset that gives the speaker a clear view of the threatening and ominous sharks lurking a short distance away.

2. Answers will vary. Students might note such similarities and differences as the following:
   a. In both poems, the creature makes the speaker uncomfortable.
   b. Both creatures appear unexpectedly.
   c. Both creatures seem cool and unfriendly.
   d. The snake disappears quickly; the sharks stay.
   e. The snake is alone; the sharks are in a group.
   f. The encounters with snakes are occurrences that repeat; the encounter with sharks is a single event.

**D.** (20 points) Answers will vary widely, depending on students' personal experiences, situations, and viewpoints. Accept any answers that address the concern of the question and are elaborated by examples or details from the literature or from life.

## My Wonder Horse/Mi Caballo Mago
Selection Test, pp. 89–90
**A.** (10 points each)
1. Notes will vary. Students may say that what the passage literally describes is that
   a. the horse neighs loudly.
   b. the horse looks alert.
   c. the way the horse stands makes him look proud.
   Students may say that the writer's style contributes to the description in that it
   a. helps the reader to see and hear the horse.
   b. emphasizes specific details about the horse.
   c. contrasts the wild horse with his calm surroundings.
   d. suggests how it might feel to see such a horse.
   e. makes the horse seem majestic.
   f. communicates a sense of the horse's spirit.
2. Notes will vary. Students may say that what the passage literally describes is that
   a. the Wonder Horse reacts strongly to being lassoed.
   b. the Wonder Horse struggles.
   c. the struggle lasts long enough to exhaust the narrator.
   d. the Wonder Horse pulls hard on the rope.
   e. the Wonder Horse tramples a wide area of snow in his struggle.
   Students may say that the writer's style contributes to the description in that it
   a. helps the reader imagine the sight of snow being flung through the air.
   b. helps the reader hear and see the effects of the rope rubbing against the narrator's gloves and saddle.
   c. emphasizes the motion involved in the struggle.
   d. suggests the excitement the narrator experiences.
   e. communicates how desperate and determined the narrator feels.

**B.** (8 points each)
1. d
2. c
3. b
4. d
**C.** (4 points each)
1. a
2. c
3. b
4. c
5. a
**D.** (14 points; students should answer one of the two)
1. Answers will vary. Students may say that the narrator is inspired by the horse because
   a. he has heard many stories about the horse.
   b. others have tried and failed to capture the horse.
   c. he found the horse magnificent when he saw him.
   d. the horse is virtually unattainable.
   e. not much is known about the horse.
   Students may say that, to the narrator, the horse represents
   a. freedom, in that the horse cannot be captured.
   b. power, in that the horse rules his band and defeats those who try to capture him.
   c. pride, in that the horse appears defiant.
   d. beauty, in that the horse is magnificent in appearance.
   e. a challenge, in that no one has been able to defeat him.
   f. a way to achieve manhood, in that capturing the horse would require the skills that are traditionally thought of as belonging only to adult men.
2. Answers will vary. Students may say that the narrator is changed in that
   a. he realizes that he is capable of meeting the challenge of capturing the horse.
   b. he experiences both a mature sense of accomplishment and what he thinks of as a childish sense of exhilaration.
   c. he discovers that he doesn't want victory at the expense of the horse's defeat.
   d. he learns to empathize with the horse, instead of merely thinking of his own needs.
   e. he learns that his fantasy of the horse is more valuable to him than the reality of possessing the horse.
   f. he realizes that holding the horse captive would destroy what he admired about the horse in the first place—the horse's freedom.

**E.** (14 points) Answers will vary widely, depending on students' personal experiences, situations, and viewpoints. Accept any answers that address the concern of the question and are elaborated by examples or details from the literature or from life.

# Unit Three, Part Two Test

pp. 91–92

**A.** (5 points each)

1. b
2. d
3. a
4. c

**B.** (20 points) Notes will vary. A model answer for the man in "To Build a Fire" follows.

The unexpected challenge was

    a. extreme cold.
    b. falling through the ice.
    c. wasting his matches.
    d. having snow fall on his fire.

The challenge was unexpected because

    a. the man did not expect it to be as cold as it was.
    b. he thought he was prepared for what he expected to be a short trip.
    c. he was not worried about his ability to survive.
    d. he thought he was being careful enough to avoid ice traps.
    e. he had plenty of matches for the trip he had planned.
    f. he underestimated the importance of traveling with a companion.

**C.** (20 points each; students should answer two of the three)

1. Answers will vary. A model response for "To Build a Fire" follows.

The man in "To Build a Fire" faces the most difficult problem because

    a. the temperature is unbelievably cold.
    b. he is traveling alone, so there is no one to help him.
    c. there is little light because the sun never rises at that time of year.
    d. he is relatively new to the region and does not have enough experience.
    e. he downplays or disregards much of the advice he has received.
    f. he is in a life-and-death situation; if he makes a mistake, he will die.

2. Answers will vary. A model answer for the author of *Into Thin Air* and the narrator of "My Wonder Horse" follows.

In *Into Thin Air*,

    a. Krakauer, the author, strives toward the goal of reaching the summit of Mt. Everest—and returning safely.
    b. he reaches the summit but does not stay long because he is nearly out of oxygen.
    c. he returns safely but has to overcome several dangerous obstacles on the way, and some of his comrades do not survive.
    d. Afterward, Krakauer seems to regret several aspects of his experience, particularly not helping others along the way.

In "My Wonder Horse,"

    a. the narrator strives to catch—and keep—the Wonder Horse.
    b. he does manage to catch the Wonder Horse and brings it back to the ranch.
    c. he fails to keep his prize, as the Wonder Horse escapes.
    d. Afterward, the narrator feels proud that he successfully captured the horse. He feels a combination of sorrow and happiness when he discovers that it has escaped: sorrow because he no longer has the horse, happiness because he realizes that the horse should remain free.

3. Answers will vary. A model answer for the speaker in "The Sharks" and the speaker in "A narrow Fellow in the Grass" follows.

    a. The speaker in "The Sharks" encounters sharks while swimming in the ocean; the speaker in "A narrow Fellow" encounters a snake.
    b. The speaker in "The Sharks" views the encounter with annoyance because she can no longer play in the water; the speaker in "A narrow Fellow" views the encounter with a sense of curiosity and admiration, followed by fear.
    c. In "The Sharks," the speaker is disappointed that the sharks have arrived because she had swum out farther than ever before, and she had to stay out of the water after seeing the sharks. In "A narrow Fellow," the speaker wonders at the remarkable appearance of the snake and how it vanishes so quickly, but also admits that he has never seen a snake without feeling a touch of fear ("Without a tighter breathing / And Zero to the Bone").

**D.** (20 points) Notes will vary. A model answer for "To Build a Fire" and *Into Thin Air* follows.

In "To Build a Fire,"

    a. the voice of experience is an old-timer the man had met earlier at Sulphur Creek.
    b. the old-timer advised the man never to travel alone in such cold temperatures and told him about the problems he would likely encounter, such as ice traps, the effects of numbing cold, and the essential need for fire.
    c. the old-timer's advice was a positive influence, but the man did not pay enough attention to his advice until it was too late. He tried to follow parts of the old-timer's advice in taking care of himself, but he admitted at the end, just before he died, that "You were right, old hoss; you were right."

In *Into Thin Air,*

a. the expedition guides represent the voice of experience.

b. the guides told all the climbers what to do at different stages; for example, Rob told Beck to wait where he was until Rob returned from the summit, and Andy Harris told the author that the oxygen tanks were all empty when they were not.

c. in the author's view, the guides were a negative influence because the climbers "had been specifically indoctrinated not to question our guides' judgment." The guides probably should have provided more oxygen, should have recognized that a storm was coming, and should have been more concerned about their clients' safety rather than the number of people they managed to get to the top. The author suggests that he survived in spite of the guides because he had had significant experience in such situations before; but, if it were not for the guides' attitudes, he might have been able to help some of the guides and other climbers survive.

# Mid-Year Test
**pp. 93–100**

**A.** 1. b
2. d
3. a
4. b
5. d
6. a

**B.** 7. b
8. b
9. c
10. a

**C.** Answers may vary but should include points similar to the following:

11. In the first half, the mood is tense and suspenseful as the moment of the hanging approaches. The mood in the second half might be described as sad, or perhaps desperate, since the reader already knows that Wolfer Joe will betray Annie.

12. Barney Gallagher is first resentful or irritated: he does not like the fact that Wolfer Joe yawns at him and later laughs. He speaks to Joe "half-admiringly," though, and Joe earns his "grim respect." At the end, Barney is puzzled and reflective when he hears Joe's final words.

13. Wolfer Joe might be described as ruthless, bold, amoral, cold, cruel. He is an outlaw who has been running from the law for a long time, he has killed at least two men, and he has always expected to die for his crimes.

**D.** 14. d
15. a
16. c
17. c

**E.** Answers may vary but should include points similar to the following:

18. Doubt made Joe wonder if Annie would show up and whether she really loved him. Suspicion made him wonder why Annie would want to go with him and if Annie would someday betray him to the law.

19. To Wolfer Joe, Annie was naive, innocent, loving, faithful, and too young or ignorant to know what was good for her. "He saw not the girl but her patience." He was angry with her for being a "damn little fool."

20. Answers will vary, depending on students' personal experiences, situations, and viewpoints. Joe's act was one of the only virtuous things he ever did. On the surface, it seemed to be a heartless betrayal of an innocent girl, but Joe knew that he was no good for Annie. "Running off with a man she don't hardly know!" Joe "saw love by the fire, and he could not endure looking for fear he might see it end." He betrayed Annie to save her from a fate she did not deserve.

## Writing Exercise Scoring Guide

**4** An **exceptional** paper:
- Has a clear and consistent focus
- Has a logical organization
- Uses transitions effectively to connect ideas
- Supports ideas with details, quotations, examples, and/or other evidence
- Exhibits well-formed sentences varying in structure
- Exhibits a rich vocabulary, including precise language that is appropriate for the purpose and audience of the paper
- Contains almost no errors in usage, mechanics, and spelling

**3** A **proficient** paper:
- Has a relatively clear and consistent focus
- Has a logical organization, although it may be unnecessarily mechanical
- Uses some transition words and phrases to connect ideas, but they do not always clarify connections effectively
- Supports ideas with details, quotations, examples, and/or other evidence
- Exhibits some variety in sentence structures
- Uses vocabulary that is appropriate for the purpose and audience
- Contains a few errors in usage, mechanics, and spelling

**2** A **basic** paper:
- Has a fairly clear focus that may occasionally become obscured
- Shows an organizational pattern, but relationships between ideas may sometimes be difficult to understand
- Contains supporting evidence that may lack effect and so only superficially develops ideas
- Has complete and varied sentences most of the time
- Contains several errors in usage, mechanics, and spelling which cause distraction and some confusion about meaning

**1** A **limited** paper:
- Has a topic but does not include any elaboration, or it only minimally addresses the topic and lacks discernible ideas
- Has only a few simple sentences
- Contains little or no plausible support for ideas
- Shows limited word choice
- Contains numerous and serious errors in usage, mechanics, and spelling which cause confusion about meaning

A paper is unable to be scored if it is
- illegible
- unrelated to the topic
- only a rewording of the prompt
- written in a foreign language
- not written at all

## Revising/Editing
1. b
2. a
3. c
4. d
5. b
6. a

# Unit Four

## The Scarlet Ibis
Selection Test, pp. 101–102

**A.** (8 points each) Notes will vary but should include points similar to the following:
1. a. The narrator realized that he was sometimes cruel and mean to his brother, as he was when he took Doodle to see his own casket.
   b. Suggested Theme: We hurt those we love the most.
2. a. The narrator realized that he took Doodle for granted and never expected much from him; he also realized that some of the other things he did for Doodle were less than kind.
   b. Suggested Theme: People often become what we expect them to be.
3. a. The narrator realized that much of what he did for Doodle was done for selfish reasons or pride, because he was "ashamed of having a crippled brother."
   b. Suggested Theme: We sometimes do things that seem well-intended, but we do them for the wrong reasons.

**B.** (5 points each)
1. d
2. b
3. a
4. d

**C.** (4 points each)
1. a
2. c
3. b
4. b
5. a

**D.** (20 points; students should answer one of the two)
1. Answers will vary. Students could say that the scarlet ibis and Doodle
   a. die tragically.
   b. appear similar in death—the blood on Doodle's neck and chest match the red color of the bird.
   c. are innocent victims of forces beyond their control.
   d. are physically similar—both have long, thin necks and legs.
   e. have traveled long distances—one in miles, one in years—at risk to their lives.
   f. are rare, exotic, special, and vulnerable.
   g. don't fit in with their surroundings.
2. Answers will vary but should reflect students' understanding that the narrator's pride cements his relationship with Doodle. In addition, answers should include points similar to the following:
   a. The narrator's pride results in his forcing Doodle to do things that Doodle otherwise would not have accomplished. The narrator doesn't want to be embarrassed by his brother's being different, so he forces him to try to become "normal." As a result, Doodle comes to trust him and look up to him.
   b. The narrator's pride results in his not always considering Doodle's best interests and refusing to recognize Doodle's limitations. As a result, Doodle suffers more from the relationship than does his brother.

Some students may blame the narrator's pride for killing Doodle because it leads the narrator to push Doodle beyond his capabilities and to cruelly abandon him.

**E.** (16 points) Answers will vary widely, depending on students' personal experiences, situations, and viewpoints. Accept any answers that address the concern of the question and are elaborated by examples or details from the literature or from life.

## Lineage/The Courage That My Mother Had
Selection Test, pp. 103–104

**A.** (26 points) Notes will vary. Students who choose line *a* could write notes suggesting ideas similar to the following:
   a. Repeated sound—*s.*
   b. Words—*gentle, hissing, rolling, soothing.*
   c. The alliteration suggests the graceful movement of the grandmothers and the quiet, steady action involved in sowing seeds.

Students who choose line *b* could write notes suggesting ideas similar to the following:
   a. Repeated sound—*gr.*
   b. Words—*explosive, harsh, gentle, growling, popping.*
   c. The alliteration suggests that the plants seem to pop up suddenly and effortlessly because of the grandmothers' magical or miraculous abilities.

Students who choose line *c* could write notes suggesting ideas similar to the following:
   a. Repeated sound—*r.*
   b. Words—*gentle, growling, rolling, soothing.*
   c. The alliteration suggests calluses and dryness from hard work outdoors, the delicate skin of old age, and the grandmothers' grace and energy.

**B.** (8 points each)
1. b
2. c
3. b
4. d
5. b
6. d

**C.** (15 points; students should answer one of the two)
1. Answers will vary. Students might make points similar to the following:

a. Both speakers admire and respect their ancestors.

b. The speaker of "Lineage" believes that he or she does not have the strength, cheer, and wisdom the grandmothers have.

c. The speaker of "The Courage That My Mother Had" believes that he or she does not have the courage the mother had.

d. Both speakers wish that they were more like their ancestors.

2. Answers will vary. Students might say that the key image

a. in "Lineage" is of strength and sturdiness.

b. in "The Courage That My Mother Had" is of rocklike courage, which also suggests moral strength.

c. in both poems connects the speakers' ancestors to nature—earth, fields, seed, onions, clay, and granite.

Other answers should be supported with appropriate reasons and details from the poems.

**D.** (11 points) Answers will vary widely, depending on students' personal experiences, situations, and viewpoints. Accept any answers that address the concern of the question and are elaborated by examples or details from the literature or from life.

## My Papa's Waltz/Grape Sherbet
Selection Test, pp. 105–106
**A.** (8 points each)
Answers will vary but should include points similar to the following:

1. a. smell, and perhaps touch

   b. The image suggests a feeling of being overwhelmed, made dizzy, or repelled by a strong smell.

2. a. touch

   b. The image suggests a feeling of pain or discomfort.

3. a. sight, touch

   b. The image suggests coolness, lightness, brightness.

4. a. taste

   b. The image suggests contradictory feelings of bitterness and sweetness or sadness and happiness.

5. a. sight

   b. The image suggests sternness and intolerance, or perhaps the inability to share in pleasure (because the woman is diabetic and can't eat sweets).

**B.** (5 points each)

1. b
2. c
3. d
4. c

**C.** (20 points; students should answer one of the two)

1. Answers will vary. Students should include some of the following points:

a. The whiskey on his father's breath was overpowering.

b. The waltzing was wild and uncontrolled.

c. His mother was made unhappy by the waltzing.

d. His mother's feelings conflicted with his father's feelings.

e. The waltzing was physically uncomfortable, even painful at times.

f. The father was under the influence of alcohol, making his behavior unpredictable.

2. Answers will vary. Students might suggest that the poem is a memorial to

a. a special day long ago.

b. the special qualities of the speaker's father.

c. the innocence or exuberance of childhood.

d. the sensory experiences that make up our memories.

**D.** (20 points) Answers will vary widely, depending on students' personal experiences, situations, and viewpoints. Accept any answers that address the concern of the question and are elaborated by examples or details from the literature or from life.

## Marine Corps Issue
Selection Test, pp. 107–108
**A.** (10 points each)

1. Notes will vary, but students could write notes suggesting that the moment is suspenseful because

a. Johnny is eavesdropping on his father's conversation about something that is deeply painful to his father.

b. there is some risk that Johnny's father will catch him.

c. Johnny's father is drinking, which is very unusual for him.

d. Johnny's father cries, or perhaps giggles, about his deformed hands.

e. Johnny's father opens the secret boxes that are usually kept closed and locked.

2. Notes will vary, but students could write notes suggesting that the moment is suspenseful because

a. there is a strong possibility that Johnny will be caught by his father or mother.

b. the time available to take the key is extremely limited.

c. the plan to take the key and open the boxes is a violation of his father's privacy.

d. Johnny's father has a tendency to become violent during stressful situations.

3. Notes will vary, but students could write notes suggesting that the moment is suspenseful because

a. the sound of the door is startling.

b. Johnny (and the reader) fears that it's his father coming.

c. in a brief length of time, Johnny has to replace all the items that he removed from the box, close it, lock it, rearrange the items on top of it, and come up with a believable story as to what he's doing.

**B.** (5 points each)
1. b
2. a
3. d
4. d

**C.** (4 points each)
1. a
2. b
3. b
4. c
5. c

**D.** (15 points; students should answer one of the two)
1. Answers will vary widely, but students might point out that Johnny risks
   a. upsetting his father.
   b. bringing up painful, perhaps unbearable, memories for his father.
   c. his father's refusal to speak with him about Vietnam.
   d. provoking his father's temper.
Students might point out that Johnny gains
   a. a deeper understanding of his father's life.
   b. a closer relationship with his father.
   c. profound respect for his father.
   d. his father's recognition that Johnny loves and cares for him.
2. Answers will vary widely, but students might point out that the flashbacks
   a. provide images of Johnny's earliest experiences with his father.
   b. show the father's past violent behavior and help the reader understand the sense of danger that Johnny feels when he takes the key and looks in the boxes.
   c. indicate how distanced Johnny (as a child) feels from his father, and how far he must reach out in order to build a feeling of connection with him.
   d. show the enormous difference between Johnny's relationship with his father when he's a child and his relationship when he's a young adult.
   e. help the reader to comprehend the courage it takes for Johnny to reach out to his father.
   f. help the reader to comprehend the courage it takes for the father to share his experience with Johnny.

**E.** (15 points) Answers will vary widely, depending on students' personal experiences, situations, and viewpoints. Accept any answers that address the concern of the question and are elaborated by examples or details from the literature or from life.

**Unit Four, Part One Test**
pp. 109–110
**A.** (5 points each)
1. c
2. a
3. b
4. c

**B.** (20 points) Notes will vary. A model answer for an image from "My Papa's Waltz" follows.
The image of the boy's clinging to his father's shirt while the father beats time on his head conveys the idea that the relationship is
   a. slightly dangerous.
   b. slightly insecure for the boy.
   c. loving and close.
   d. fun-loving.

**C.** (20 points each; students should answer two of the three)
1. Answers will vary. A model answer for Johnny and his father ("Marine Corps Issue") follows.
Johnny and his father have never really been close because his father was away during most of Johnny's early childhood. Johnny and his father do not seem to communicate about anything important, particularly his father's past.
The communication problems between Johnny and his father are caused by
   a. the father's traumatic experiences in Vietnam and his inability or unwillingness to share them with his family.
   b. Johnny's unwillingness to upset his father by asking him about his experiences in Vietnam.
   c. Johnny's concealment of his investigation of his father's past.
   d. the father's inability to communicate feelings of love.
2. Answers will vary. A model answer for the families in "The Scarlet Ibis" and "Grape Sherbet" follows.
In "The Scarlet Ibis,"
   a. the family members relate to one another with love and affection.
   b. the family members relate to one another with concern and worry.
   c. the family members take interest in the opinions and hopes of one another.
   d. the family members take responsibility for one another's happiness and well-being.
   e. the elder brother (the narrator) sometimes torments his younger brother and pushes him to do things that are extremely difficult for him.
In "Grape Sherbet,"
   a. the speaker expresses love for her father, but he has died.

b. the speaker implies that the whole family loved the father and has fond memories of the days he made grape sherbet.

c. the love among family members may have been unspoken while the father was alive.

d. the speaker has come to understand the family relationships more deeply since the father's death ("Now I see why / you bothered, / father").

e. the "diabetic grandmother" mentioned in the poem, who is probably part of the same family, does not seem to be involved in the excitement and joy felt by the rest of the family.

For the reasons listed above, most students will find that the family in "The Scarlet Ibis" is more loving.

3. Answers will vary. A model answer for "The Courage That My Mother Had" and "My Papa's Waltz" follows.

In "The Courage That My Mother Had," the speaker

a. admires her mother's courage.

b. treasures the golden brooch that her mother left her.

c. wishes that her mother had bequeathed her courage instead of the brooch.

In "My Papa's Waltz," the speaker

a. has mixed feelings associated with a memory of dancing with his father.

b. suggests criticism of his father in mentioning the whiskey on his breath, the discomfort or displeasure he caused the mother, and his clumsiness ("every step you missed").

c. implies the pain his father caused him ("My right ear scraped a buckle"; "You beat time on my head").

d. suggests that he loved or admired his father anyway ("Still clinging to your shirt").

For these reasons, most students will find that the speaker of "The Courage That My Mother Had" is more admiring of a parent than the speaker in "My Papa's Waltz."

**D.** (20 points) Notes will vary. A model answer for Johnny and his father ("Marine Corps Issue") follows.

Things that bring them together include the following:

a. Johnny's investigation of his father's experiences in Vietnam

b. their love for each other

c. Johnny's pride in his father

d. their love for baseball

e. talking about Vietnam

Things that separate them include the following:

a. the father's inability or unwillingness to discuss his experiences in Vietnam

b. the psychological effects on the father of his experiences in Vietnam

c. the secrets they keep from each other

d. the family's desire to protect the father by not talking about Vietnam

*from* **Black Boy**
Selection Test, pp. 111–112

**A.** (16 points each)

1. Notes will vary widely but could suggest that the dialogue reveals that Wright

   a. was confident, straightforward, and honest.

   b. knew very little about the newspaper business.

   c. was intelligent and logical.

   d. stood up for himself and wasn't intimidated easily.

   e. expected to be paid for his work.

Students might write notes suggesting that the dialogue reveals that the editor

   a. was businesslike.

   b. was wise, honest, straightforward, and caring.

   c. had a sense of humor.

2. Notes will vary widely but could suggest that the dialogue reveals that Wright was

   a. honest, confident, and straightforward.

   b. logical.

   c. different from his classmates.

   d. considered odd by his classmates.

   e. patient with others.

   f. not embarrassed.

Students might write notes suggesting that the dialogue reveals that Wright's classmates were

   a. puzzled by Wright's behavior.

   b. curious about Wright.

   c. suspicious of Wright.

   d. used to people being predictable.

   e. naive about writers and writing.

   f. close-minded.

**B.** (6 points each)

1. a

2. b

3. d

**C.** (4 points each)

1. c

2. b

3. a

4. b

5. a

**D.** (15 points; students should answer one of the two)

1. Answers will vary. Students might identify the following as motives for writing the story:

   a. Boredom.

   b. The desire to express pent-up emotions.

   c. The need to explore his new awareness of himself.

Students could identify the following as motives for trying to get the story published:

   a. The desire for recognition or to be seen as someone special.

   b. The desire to fit in or be accepted by his classmates.

c. The desire to become less isolated.

d. The desire to make money.

In addition, students should include points similar to the following:

a. The experience does give Wright a better understanding of himself and an outlet for expressing pent-up emotions.

b. The experience doesn't gain Wright the admiration and acknowledgment that he hopes for; in fact, it bothers and offends others, isolating him even more than he was before.

c. The newspaper doesn't pay Wright for his story, but it does offer him a paying job and the chance to learn to write.

2. Answers will vary. To describe "the current" of Wright's environment, students might use words and phrases similar to the following:

a. A small town in Mississippi.

b. Racist, Jim Crow.

c. Stifling, limiting.

d. Suspicious, hostile.

e. Dangerous, deadly.

f. Encouraging conformity, discouraging creativity and individuality.

g. Strict religious household or background.

This environment might have frightened him away from writing because

a. writers need to use their imagination.

b. African Americans weren't generally thought in the South at that time to be capable of being writers.

c. African-American writers, by their very existence, threatened the Southern way of life at that time.

d. writing, therefore, could be a lonely, dangerous enterprise for African Americans in the South at that time.

**E.** (15 points) Answers will vary widely, depending on students' personal experiences, situations, and viewpoints. Accept any answers that address the concern of the question and are elaborated by examples or details from the literature or from life.

## Daughter of Invention

Selection Test, pp. 113–114

**A.** (10 points each) Notes will vary but might incorporate ideas such as the following:

1. a. At first her mother didn't want to help her daughters become more American, but she accepted American ways before her husband did.

b. The narrator was annoyed by her parents' resistance to American ways and resented their lack of support.

2. a. The narrator's father is proud of her and wants to be supportive of her endeavors.

b. The narrator understands that her father loves her. She also realizes that, although her father loves his daughters, he would have liked to have had a son to "complete" the perfect Hispanic family.

3. a. The father has a strict sense of propriety; while he may support his daughter in some things, he is close-minded if she doesn't conform to his ideas of what is right.

b. The narrator feels the intensity of her father's anger but is also aware that there is a history of fear and persecution at the root of it.

**B.** (5 points each)

1. d
2. a
3. b
4. b

**C.** (4 points each)

1. c
2. a
3. c
4. b
5. b

**D.** (15 points; students should answer one of the two)

1. Answers will vary. Students might choose either speech and defend their choice by citing reasons similar to the following:

a. Her own speech would have been better, since it was an expression of her own feelings; delivering her mother's speech was hypocritical and dishonest; writing the speech had made the narrator feel as if she had found her own voice in English, and she would have been proud and happy to deliver the speech.

b. Her mother's speech was more appropriate to the occasion, since her own speech might have been viewed as rebellious and insulting; the occasion was meant to express appreciation for the teachers and was not meant to be an opportunity for expressing her own ideas; delivering the speech her mother wrote for her brought approval, while her own speech might have caused controversy and disapproval.

2. Answers will vary but might include the following points:

a. It was traditional for men to dominate and for women to be subservient in the Dominican Republic; this made the independent behavior of his wife and daughters difficult for him to accept.

b. The Dominican Republic was a dictatorship and a police state in which any expression of dissatisfaction could be a cause for arrest.

c. Her father had witnessed violence and injustice; the dictator had killed his brothers and friends.

d. Because of these experiences, her father had learned to fear police and anyone else in uniform; for example, he jumped at the sight of a black Volkswagen because the dictator's police drove black Volkswagens.

e. His traditional values, as well as his fears, made him overreact when his daughter wrote a rebellious speech that she planned to deliver at the school assembly on teacher's day.

**E.** (15 points) Answers will vary widely, depending on students' personal experiences, situations, and viewpoints. Accept any answers that address the concern of the question and are elaborated by examples or details from the literature or from life.

## A Voice/The Journey

Selection Test, pp. 115–116

**A.** (20 points each)

Notes will vary but might include words and phrases such as the following:

1. a. Pressures: "lights [were] unrelenting"; "eyes [were] unrelenting"; "language forbidden at home"; "fight with the neighbors."
   b. Feelings: "couldn't hide / wanted to hide"; "eyes were pinpricks"; "breath stuck in your throat / like an ice-cube."
2. a. Pressures: "voices shouting . . . bad advice"; "tug at . . . ankles"; "'Mend my life!' / each voice cried"; "their melancholy / was terrible"; "a wild night."
   b. Feelings: "tremble"; "wind pried / with . . . stiff fingers"; "felt the old tug"; "stars . . . burn / through . . . sheets of clouds"; "slowly / recognized"; "strode"; "determined."

**B.** (5 points each)

1. b
2. d
3. a
4. d

**C.** (20 points; students should answer one of the two)

1. Answers will vary. Students will probably agree that they know the "you" of "A Voice" better. Reasons might include:
   a. The character in "A Voice" is given a clear identity; the poem tells many facts about her life.
   b. The speaker of "A Voice" is the daughter of the main character and communicates her feelings about her mother as well as her mother's feelings.
   c. The character in "The Journey" remains mysterious; the poem does not reveal his or her identity.
   d. In "A Voice" the character's problem is clearly defined; in "The Journey," the poem does not make clear exactly what the character is running from.

e. "A Voice" provides concrete sensory information about the external world; "The Journey" appears to use descriptions of the external world as metaphors for an internal struggle.

Accept student responses in which he or she relates personally to the "you" in "The Journey" if the student supports the answer with references to the poem and examples from his or her own life.

2. Answers will vary. Students should choose three of the following examples and offer explanations similar to those provided:
   a. Simile: "Lights on the stage unrelenting / as the desert sun" communicates the intensity of the character's self-consciousness.
   b. Simile: "He walked slow / as a hot river" suggests that the father is someone who has a quiet self-control and holds his passions in check.
   c. Simile: "An aunt in Mexico, spunky as a peacock" conveys the sense of a bright and lively person.
   d. Metaphor: "Their eyes were pinpricks" conveys the intense discomfort the character feels.
   e. Simile: "felt your breath stick in your throat / like an ice-cube" conveys the feeling of being frozen, stuck, suffocating.
   f. Simile: "Your breath moves / through the family like the wind / moves through the trees" conveys the sense that the mother's influence is ever-present, gentle, and inspirational for her family.
   g. Personification: "the wind pried / with its stiff fingers at the very foundations" reinforces a threatening and gloomy mood.

**D.** (20 points) Answers will vary widely, depending on students' personal experiences, situations, and viewpoints. Accept any answers that address the concern of the question and are elaborated by examples or details from the literature or from life.

## Only Daughter

Selection Test, pp. 117–118

**A.** (20 points) Notes will vary widely. A model answer for one possible theme includes the following ideas:
   a. Theme: with determination, hard work, and belief in oneself, it is possible to overcome great obstacles.
   b. Support: Cisneros goes to college to study writing, even though her father believes she should only be in search of a husband.
   c. Support: Cisneros finds success as a writer, even though her father believes that she wasted her college education.

Other themes should be supported with appropriate details from the selection.

**B.** (6 points each)
1. b
2. a
3. a
4. c
5. a

**C.** (4 points each)
1. c
2. a
3. c
4. a
5. c

**D.** (15 points; students should answer one of the two)
1. Answers will vary widely. Students could say that his ideas make her feel
   a. rejected because she wants to be so much more than a wife.
   b. saddened or depressed because writing is so important to her and so unimportant to him.
   c. alienated or lonely in that the differences between their ideas of who and what she should be build a barrier between them.

In addition, some students will probably say that his ideas affect her educational and occupational decisions very little because
   a. they do not stand in the way of her dreams.
   b. her father approves of her going to college and studying something as "unimportant" as writing because these things won't prevent her from getting a husband.

Other students may feel that his ideas affect her educational and occupational decisions a great deal because she
   a. follows his advice by choosing to work with her mind instead of her hands.
   b. achieves the hopes and dreams he sets for his children by finding success in a rewarding occupation.

2. Answers will vary widely. Students may include points similar to the following:
   a. From playing alone a good deal of the time in her childhood, she develops an appreciation for being alone to think and read—experiences and capabilities especially important to writers.
   b. From standing up to her father and brothers, she gains determination to prove that she can achieve more than they expect of her.
   c. Her father's and brothers' disinterest in her writing prepares her for the general public's disinterest in her writing.
   d. From her strong need to win her father's approval, she drives herself to achieve success as a writer.

**E.** (15 points) Answers will vary widely, depending on students' personal experiences, situations, and viewpoints. Accept any answers that address the concern of the question and are elaborated by examples or details from the literature or from life.

### *from* **The House on Mango Street**
Selection Test, pp. 119–120
**A.** (10 points each)
Notes will vary but should be consistent with the following:
1. a. tells about the places Esperanza's family has lived
   b. Tone: frustrated; disappointed
2. a. tells about Esperanza's personality and that of her great-grandmother
   b. Tone: determined; strong-willed
3. a. tells about Esperanza's father
   b. Tone: sad, loving
4. a. tells about Esperanza's mother
   b. Tone: filled with regret, but also nurturing hopes of a better future
5. a. tells about Esperanza as storyteller and writer; Esperanza's hopes
   b. Tone: pain, hope, and determination

**B.** (5 points each)
1. b
2. d
3. a
4. d

**C.** (15 points; students should answer one of the two)
1. Answers will vary but should include some of the following points:
   a. Her name is long and has too many letters.
   b. It connotes sadness and waiting.
   c. It reminds her of the songs on her father's Mexican records that sound like sobbing.
   d. At school, people say her name in a way that sounds ugly to her.
   e. She has no nickname, like her sister's.
   f. She does not think it reflects her true self.
   g. She hopes that she will go away to find success and that she will return, bringing hope to those she left behind.

2. Answers will vary but should include some of the following points about Esperanza's parents:
   a. They dreamed of having a wonderful house.
   b. They were very poor and did not achieve their dream.
   c. Papa had to get up very early for work and was often tired.
   d. Papa was very sad when his own father died.
   e. Mother can sing opera and knows how to fix a TV.

f. Mother would like to go to a ballet or a play, but she doesn't even know which subway train to take to get downtown.

g. Mother likes to draw and does needlework.

h. Mother wants Esperanza to have the success she didn't have.

**D.** (15 points) Answers will vary widely, depending on students' personal experiences, situations, and viewpoints. Accept any answers that address the concern of the question and are elaborated by examples or details from the literature or from life.

## On Writing The House on Mango Street
Selection Test, pp. 121–122

**A.** (10 points each) Notes will vary but should incorporate ideas such as the following:

1. Style:
   a. short sentences, easy words
   b. long sentences, hard words; reference to another author and book
2. Tone:
   a. straightforward, direct, conversational, unsophisticated
   b. complex, layered, academic
3. What the style and tone tell about the narrator/writer:
   a. child or childlike speaker; unsophisticated, not highly educated
   b. mature writer; sophisticated, highly educated, thoughtful

**B.** (5 points each)
1. b
2. a
3. d
4. c

**C.** (4 points each)
1. b
2. a
3. c
4. b
5. c

**D.** (15 points; students should answer one of the two)

1. Answers will vary but should include points such as the following:
   a. She didn't want to sound like her classmates.
   b. She didn't want to imitate writers she had been reading.
   c. She searched for the ugliest subjects she could find.
   d. She was determined to write the kind of book she had never seen.
   e. Each week she did the opposite of whatever she learned in the class readings.
2. Answers will vary. Students might note that
   a. people who could barely afford books were buying her book because it meant a lot to them.

b. she was getting letters from all kinds of people saying that her book told their story.

c. people were bringing her well-worn "raggedy" copies of her book to sign.

d. when she realized how her writing could touch the lives of the people she wanted to help, her writer self and her community activist self became the same person.

**E.** (15 points) Answers will vary widely, depending on students' personal experiences, situations, and viewpoints. Accept any answers that address the concern of the question and are elaborated by examples or details from the literature or from life.

## Unit Four, Part Two Test
pp. 123–124

**A.** (5 points each) Answers will vary but should include points similar to the following:

1. The father thought the speech was disrespectful; his daughter praised herself instead of the teachers; he worried that it might cause trouble.
2. The speaker learned how to speak up, or to express herself.
3. She was considered inferior to her brothers and, in her father's view, was destined to become someone's wife.
4. The tone is at times sad, angry, and resentful.

**B.** (20 points) Notes will vary. A model answer for Cisneros in "On Writing *The House on Mango Street*" follows.

   a. The Problem: She needed to find her own voice and her own subject.
   b. Reasons for the Problem: Cisneros could not relate to the books she was reading in graduate school; she could not write about "normal" Americans because she was not one; she felt alienated by an "otherness"; and the books she read did not provide an adequate model for what she wanted to write.
   c. How the problem was solved: Cisneros found her voice by writing in the language of the street, which she was familiar with, and not in the language of academics. She found her subject by writing about her own life, combined with other people and situations she knew or encountered at different times in her life. She created her own form of literature, starting out by writing a memoir and adding fictional elements to present a series of vignettes.

**C.** (20 points each; students should answer two of the three)

1. Answers will vary. A model answer for "Only Daughter" follows.

Cisneros criticizes Mexican (or Mexican-American) culture for
- a. being "macho."
- b. failing to value women.
- c. failing to treat women and men equally.

Cisneros criticizes Mexican culture for these things because she
- a. was raised with Mexican cultural values.
- b. was isolated in her family as the only daughter.
- c. feels that she has never been valued as a worthy individual by her father and brothers.
- d. wants to be loved and respected for who she is, not for how well she lives up to her father and brothers' stereotype of women.

2. Answers will vary. A model answer for the narrator in "Daughter of Invention" follows.

The narrator
- a. struggles with her own confusion to find her own voice.
- b. writes a speech that reflects who she is and what she feels.
- c. achieves honors in school even though she is learning a new language.
- d. presents a speech in her second language and it is well received.
- e. maintains a close relationship with her mother, despite their differences.
- f. expresses appreciation for her mother's creativity and inventiveness, even though she makes fun of her mother in an affectionate way.
- g. expresses an understanding of her father's perspective, even though he ripped up a speech she was proud of and made no secret of the fact that he had wanted a son.

3. Answers will vary. A model answer for the narrator in "Daughter of Invention" and Cisneros in "Only Daughter" follows.

Both the narrator and Cisneros want to become independent by
- a. expressing themselves in their own voice.
- b. being recognized as worthy and valuable people, even though they are females in cultural situations where males are valued more.
- c. pursuing their own visions of success.

The narrator is less successful than Cisneros in that
- a. her father still dominates the household and her life.
- b. her father tears up the speech she has written.
- c. her mother convinces her and helps her to write a new speech and deliver it.
- d. the new speech reflects her father's values and not her own.

Cisneros is more successful than the narrator in that
- a. she pursues her own goals of going to college and becoming a writer.
- b. she does not pursue finding a husband, which is what is expected of her.
- c. she becomes a writer and has her stories published.
- d. she shows a story to her father, who appreciates her talent and wants to give out copies of the story to their relatives.
- e. she stands up for herself when her father refers to her as one of his "seven sons."

**D.** (20 points) Notes will vary. A model answer for Wright (*Black Boy*) follows.

Wright's special characteristic is that he is an African-American writer in the South during the Jim Crow era. Other people tend to react to this fact with
- a. suspicion.
- b. worry.
- c. fear.
- d. anger.
- e. disgust.

This reaction
- a. isolates him within his community.
- b. teaches him not to trust others.
- c. angers and surprises him.
- d. makes him feel lonely and misunderstood.
- e. doesn't stop him from continuing to write.

# Unit Five

## Full Circle

Selection Test, pp. 125–126

**A.** (5 points each) Notes will vary widely. Possible answers for each element follow.

1. Examples of exposition include the description of
   a. rush hour traffic.
   b. the narrator's old car.
   c. the narrator's job.

2–4. Examples of rising action include
   a. the accident on the highway.
   b. the news of Caroline's death.
   c. Caroline's mother's belief that her daughter was murdered.
   d. the narrator's discovery that the man in the blue pickup gave false information.
   e. the shift manager's description of Caroline's problem with an old boyfriend.
   f. Judy Layton's mysterious lack of cooperation.
   g. the narrator's discovery of the blue pickup's license plate number.
   h. the narrator's finding the missing pickup in the Layton garage.

5. Reasonable descriptions of the climax include
   a. the narrator's discovery of the pickup in the Layton garage.
   b. Terry Layton's attempt to escape.
   c. Terry Layton's crash on the highway.

6. Examples of falling action will vary depending on what students have identified as the climax. Possible examples include
   a. the narrator's pursuit of Terry Layton.
   b. Terry Layton's crash.
   c. Terry Layton's death.
   d. the aftermath of the crash.
   e. the narrator's revelation that she has kept Caroline's picture.
   f. the narrator's philosophizing.

**B.** (6 points each)
1. c
2. c
3. b
4. a
5. d

**C.** (4 points each)
1. b
2. a
3. c
4. b
5. a

**D.** (10 points; students should answer one of the two)
1. Answers will vary. Students may say that the narrator faces such major obstacles as
   a. a lack of witnesses to the shooting itself.
   b. police regulations about giving out information.
   c. a false identity for the man in the blue pickup truck.
   d. few leads on how to track down the man in the blue pickup truck.
   e. sketchy information about the man who'd been harassing Caroline.
   f. Judy Layton's unwillingness to talk.

Students may say that the narrator is able to overcome these obstacles because she is
   a. good at building relationships. She is able to get information from the police clerk, Lt. Dolan, and the photographer because she has established good relationships with them.
   b. methodical. She systematically interviews Caroline's co-workers, friends, roommate, professors, and the witnesses. She goes back over the evidence, eventually discovering the license plate number of the blue pickup truck in a photograph.
   c. determined. She continues to pursue the case despite difficulties.
   d. observant. She notices Judy Layton's evasive behavior.
   e. intuitive. She looks in the Layton garage because she has a hunch.

2. Answers will vary. Students who think the ending was satisfying may say that
   a. justice demands an eye for an eye.
   b. Terry Layton's death is his punishment for killing Caroline.
   c. it is fitting that Terry Layton dies on the spot where he killed Caroline.
   d. Caroline's family will be spared the pain of a trial.

Students who think the ending was not satisfying may say that
   a. although Terry Layton behaved in a suspicious manner, it is not certain that he, in fact, killed Caroline.
   b. the full facts of the case, including Terry's reason for killing Caroline, will never be known.
   c. Terry Layton does not have to face his accusers and realize the consequences of his actions.
   d. it doesn't seem believable; it's all too neat and convenient.

**E.** (10 points) Answers will vary widely, depending on students' personal experiences, situations, and viewpoints. Accept any answers that address the concern of the question and are elaborated by examples or details from the literature or from life.

# Wasps' Nest

Selection Test, pp. 127–128

**A.** (6 points each) Answers will vary. Underlined words and what they suggest might be:

1. a. murdered, as yet, nobody
   b. A murder is planned but not yet carried out, or someone will be murdered.
2. a. indefinable something, uneasy
   b. Harrison isn't sure what Poirot is suggesting but it concerns him.
3. a. conceal his hate till the proper time
   b. The motive for the planned crime is a concealed hate.
4. a. grave, troubled, point of returning
   b. Poirot is worried that something could go seriously wrong.
5. a. sinister, lull before a storm
   b. Something bad is about to happen.

**B.** (5 points each)

1. c
2. a
3. d
4. c

**C.** (4 points each)

1. c
2. a
3. b
4. b
5. c

**D.** (15 points; students should answer one of the two)

1. Answers will vary. Summaries could include the following points:

Poirot knew that
   a. Harrison probably has a fatal disease.
   b. Molly is engaged to Harrison but actually loves Langton.
   c. Harrison has asked Langton to purchase cyanide, a deadly poison.
   d. Langton is coming to visit Harrison at 8:30.

Poirot thinks that Harrison is planning to
   a. commit suicide using the cyanide.
   b. set up his suicide so that it will appear that Langton has murdered him.

Harrison confirms Poirot's suspicions by
   a. pretending he knows nothing of the cyanide purchase.
   b. lying about the time that Langton will be coming.

2. Answers will vary but might include the following points:
   a. Harrison believes that Poirot can be useful as a witness against Langton.

b. He pretends to be surprised about Langton's purchase of cyanide so that Poirot will not suspect his own part in the purchase.
   c. He says that Langton is arriving at nine o'clock so that Poirot will "discover" the corpse while Langton is on the scene.
   d. Poirot actually knows more than he has revealed.
   e. Poirot substitutes the poison in Harrison's pocket with a harmless substance in order to thwart the plan.

**E.** (15 points) Answers will vary widely, depending on students' personal experiences, situations, and viewpoints. Accept any answers that address the concern of the question and are elaborated by examples or details from the literature or from life.

# Trifles

Selection Test, pp. 129–130

**A.** (15 points each) Notes will vary but should include points similar to the following:

1. What you can infer about the Sheriff:
   a. He trusts his wife, Mrs. Peters.
   b. He underestimates his wife.
   c. He does not believe his wife is capable of deceit.
   d. He does not think his wife is capable of uncovering evidence or anything else of importance.

Why this statement is ironic:
   a. His wife does deceive him by doing something that is not "all right."
   b. She does uncover evidence, and she does not reveal it to him.

2. What you can infer about the County Attorney:
   a. He has a superior attitude toward the women.
   b. He believes they are interested only in small, unimportant things.
   c. He thinks they are too simple and uncomplicated to try to trick him and are incapable of understanding something that he doesn't understand.

Why this statement is ironic:
   a. He is not as bright and perceptive as he thinks he is.
   b. He is unable to reach the insights the women have reached.
   c. He is incapable of finding the evidence he needs to convict Mrs. Wright, and he never even considers that the women have already found it.

**B.** (6 points each)

1. b
2. c
3. d
4. a
5. b

**C.** (4 points each)
1. a
2. c
3. c
4. a
5. b

**D.** (10 points) Answers will vary. Those students who think the women are morally right to protect Mrs. Wright might say that
  a. Mr. Wright had been harsh and cruel for years.
  b. he had "killed" the happiness she enjoyed as a young woman.
  c. he brutally killed the only thing that gave her any happiness.
  d. he drove her to a state of mental illness, and her murderous action was a result.
  e. the men who would most likely make up the jury would not be capable of understanding why Mrs. Wright had done what she did.
  f. there is no reason to think that Mrs. Wright poses a risk to anyone else.

Students who think the women are morally wrong to protect Mrs. Wright might say that
  a. it is never right to kill someone (or, it is right only in cases of self-defense).
  b. there are other ways to deal with horrible people besides murdering them.
  c. her husband did not deserve to die for killing the canary.
  d. the women are in a position of trust, and they are violating that trust.
  e. the women are destroying evidence, which is a felony and which makes them function as judge and jury.
  f. murder is a terrible crime that society has decided must not be tolerated; the women's actions disregard society's needs.
  g. it is not up to individuals to decide when justice has been served in a crime as serious as murder.
  h. just because one likes, or sympathizes with, another person's situation does not mean that whatever that person does is all right.
  i. the women are responding, at least in part, to the men's condescending, dismissive attitude; they are banding together to protect "one of their own," which would surely be tempting in this situation but is not necessarily morally right.

**E.** (10 points) Answers will vary widely, depending on students' personal experiences, situations, and viewpoints. Accept any answers that address the concern of the question and are elaborated by examples or details from the literature or from life.

## The Great Taos Bank Robbery

Selection Test, pp. 131–132

**A.** (16 points each)
1. Notes will vary. Students could make notes indicating that the surface meaning of the first quotation is that
  a. the bank customers are quick to notice inconsistencies in the appearance of this man.
  b. the man's clothing is more stylish than is normal in Taos.
  c. bib overalls are considered adequately fashionable attire in Taos.

Students could make notes indicating that the real meaning of the first quotation is that
  a. the man dressed in women's clothes looks completely absurd.
  b. the man is a total fool to think his attire would mislead anyone for an instant.
  c. an observer would have had to be blindfolded not to notice that the man is a man and not a woman.
  d. the normal attire for a Taos resident is far from fashionable.
  e. the most fashionable person in town is a man with hairy legs who is wearing a dress and makeup.

2. Notes will vary. Students could make notes indicating that the surface meaning of the second quotation is that
  a. Taos is small.
  b. there are many police, and the search is thorough.
  c. it is an unfortunate and odd coincidence that the one place that is not searched is the place where the suspects are sleeping.

Students could make notes indicating that the real meaning of the second quotation is that
  a. Taos is tiny.
  b. any reasonable search could cover all of Taos thoroughly.
  c. the search is bungled.
  d. the police fail to look in the most obvious place a fugitive would be—an abandoned house.
  e. the police spend their time and energy looking in all the places the suspects would not logically be.

**B.** (7 points each)
1. a
2. d
3. b
4. b

**C.** (4 points each)
1. a
2. a
3. c
4. b
5. a

**D.** (10 points; students should answer one of the two)
1. Answers will vary. Students may say that Mrs. Fish and the others gather to watch the robbery because
   a. they're hoping to witness something thrilling.
   b. excitement is rare in small towns, especially in Taos.
   c. a robbery would provide something interesting to talk about.
   d. an exciting event would be historic in Taos, and they want to witness it.

Students may describe the observers' attitude toward the incident as
   a. interested.
   b. anticipatory.
   c. curious.
   d. excited.
   e. fearless.

2. Answers will vary. Some students may say that people refer to this incident as "The Great Taos Bank Robbery" because they want to
   a. relish the excitement that the incident caused.
   b. remember that it was a significant event in the history of Taos, even if it wouldn't be considered significant in a large city.
   c. create a sense of drama about the history of their small town.
   d. feel that Taos is a place where major events occur.
   e. portray Taos as an interesting and impressive place.

Others may take a different view, saying that people refer to the incident this way because they want to
   a. poke fun at the event.
   b. show how safe life in Taos is (in that a completely harmless incident is the biggest "bank robbery" ever to have occurred there).
   c. poke fun at the police and other authorities.

Students may say that this event is similar to "The Great Flood of 1935" in that
   a. there was no actual robbery, just as there was no actual flood.
   b. a minor event has become, in this town, a Great Event.

**E.** (10 points) Answers will vary widely, depending on students' personal experiences, situations, and viewpoints. Accept any answers that address the concern of the question and are elaborated by examples or details from the literature or from life.

### Unit Five, Part One Test
pp. 133–134
**A.** (5 points each) Answers will vary but should include points similar to the following:
1. Her brother was the one who shot Caroline, and she probably knew it; she did not want to reveal what she knew about her brother.

2. He planned to frame Langton for his murder, which was actually going to be a suicide.
3. The birdcage represents Mrs. Wright's life; she was "caged up" with John Wright, but the "bird" (her spirit, happiness, singing) was dead.
4. Gomez and Smith might be described as incompetent, bungling, foolish, silly, incapable of pulling off a robbery.

**B.** (20 points) Notes will vary. A model answer for Mrs. Wright in "Trifles" follows.

Mrs. Wright is driven to murder her husband because
   a. he killed the only source of joy in her life, the canary.
   b. once the canary is dead, nothing really matters anymore.
   c. her only chance for happiness lies in being free of her husband.
   d. there is no other means of obtaining justice for the type of crimes he has committed against her.
   e. her mental state convinces her that murdering her husband is a reasonable course of action.

**C.** (20 points each; students should answer two of the three)
1. Answers will vary. A model answer for Sheriff Peters in "Trifles" and the narrator in "Full Circle" follows.

The Sheriff is easily fooled because
   a. his wife, whom he trusts, is one of those who fools him.
   b. his disregard for women and their interests leads him to assume that his wife and Mrs. Hale could not possibly possess helpful insights or information.
   c. he doesn't think of the women who fool him as being capable of outwitting him.
   d. the women easily hide the damning evidence from him.
   e. his trust in his wife leads him to relax his police standards, thereby allowing the evidence to be removed from the house.
   f. he doesn't possess the insight into women, their situation in life, and their needs and desires that one would need in order to understand Mrs. Wright's motivation for murder.

The narrator in "Full Circle" isn't easily fooled because she is
   a. a detective experienced in solving mysteries.
   b. determined to do whatever it takes to find the murderer.
   c. smart, crafty, resourceful, methodical, observant, and intuitive.
   d. able to turn to other resourceful people for information she needs to crack the case.

2. Answers will vary. A model answer for strange or unusual actions in "Full Circle" and "The Great Taos Bank Robbery" follows.

It is easy to understand why Caroline's roommate, Judy Layton, acts strangely because
- a. she knows that her brother was the one who shot Caroline.
- b. she is protecting her brother.
- c. even if she wanted to reveal what she knew, she might have been afraid of what her brother would do to her.

It is difficult to understand Mrs. Fish's unusual behavior in "The Great Taos Bank Robbery" because
- a. she knows the robbery is going to happen, but she calls the news editor instead of the police.
- b. she watches the activity in the bank but does not try to stop it.
- c. she sees the two bank robbers but does nothing to help the police catch them.

3. Answers will vary. A model answer for Caroline Spurrier in "Full Circle," John Harrison in "Wasps' Nest," and Mr. Wright in "Trifles" follows.

Caroline Spurrier is a victim in that she
- a. is murdered.
- b. has done nothing wrong.

John Harrison is a victimizer in that he
- a. plans to frame Langton for murder.
- b. knows that Langton will be blamed for his death.
- c. wants to break up the romance or marriage between Langton and Molly Deane.

Mr. Wright is both a victim and a victimizer in that he
- a. is brutally murdered by his wife.
- b. seems to have made his wife's life miserable.
- c. seems to have cruelly and deliberately killed the only source of joy in his wife's life, her canary.

**D.** (20 points) Answers will vary. A model answer for John Harrison in "Wasps' Nest" follows.

John Harrison attempts to
- a. frame Langton for murder.
- b. keep Langton from marrying Molly Deane.
- c. kill himself.

Harrison's deceit does not get him what he wants, or thinks he wants.

His deceit is ineffective because
- a. Poirot prevents him from carrying out his plan.
- b. Poirot takes the cyanide from Harrison's pocket and replaces it with sodium carbonate, a harmless cleaner.
- c. Poirot confronts Harrison with the details of everything he had planned to do, and Harrison confesses.
- d. Harrison ends up thanking Poirot for saving him from himself.

## The Open Window
Selection Test, pp. 135–136

**A.** (10 points each) Notes will vary but should include points similar to the following:
1. What Mr. Nuttel knows about Vera:
   - a. She is about 15 years old and seems very self-possessed.
   - b. She tells a touching story about her aunt's tragedy.
   - c. She explains the relationship between the open window and the tragedy.
   - d. She seems genuinely worried about her aunt's state of mind.
2. What the reader knows about Vera:
   - a. Vera is very clever and imaginative.
   - b. She knows that the men have gone out hunting and will soon return.
   - c. She has invented the entire tragedy for the sake of telling a good story. "Romance at short notice was her specialty."
3. What Mrs. Sappleton knows about Mr. Nuttel:
   - a. Mr. Nuttel has been referred to her by a friend.
   - b. He is in the area for a restful vacation.
   - c. He has some mental and physical maladies, and he insists on talking about them.
   - d. He flees in great haste when the hunters return.
4. What the reader knows about Mr. Nuttel:
   - a. Vera has told him a fabricated story about the tragedy that befell the hunters a year ago.
   - b. He thinks that Mrs. Sappleton is deluded; she expects the hunters to return through the open window, but he believes they are dead.

**B.** (5 points each)
1. c
2. d
3. a
4. b

**C.** (20 points; students should answer one of the two)
1. Answers will vary but might include the following points:
   - a. Vera knows that Framton Nuttel is ignorant about her aunt's actual circumstances, so he will not know if she is telling the truth.
   - b. She uses what she knows about the actual situation to make her fantasy totally credible.
   - c. She includes many details that she knows he will see are accurate. For example, the hunters will soon return, they will come through the open window, they will be covered with mud from the bog, one will have a white coat, they will have a spaniel with them, and one will say, "Bertie, why do you bound?"

d. She successfully uses her tone of voice and facial expressions (such as her expression of sympathy for Mrs. Sappleton and the look of horror in her eyes when she sees the hunters) to convince Nuttel of her sincerity.

2. Answers will vary but might include the following points:
   a. The author wants the reader to be taken in by Vera's story just as Framton Nuttel is taken in.
   b. There would be no surprise ending if we knew Vera's actual thoughts.
   c. The story would lose its suspense, its irony, and its humor if Vera's thoughts and the actual nature of her story were revealed earlier in the story.

**D.** (20 points) Answers will vary widely, depending on students' personal experiences, situations, and viewpoints. Accept any answers that address the concern of the question and are elaborated by examples or details from the literature or from life.

## Sorry, Right Number
Selection Test, pp. 137–138

**A.** (5 points each) Examples of foreshadowing will vary but might include the following:
1. a. Bill worries that he is going to have a brain tumor.
   b. He has a heart attack.
2. a. Katie says that sending Polly away to school was not a good idea and she often sounds very unhappy.
   b. Polly has had a wonderful day and is quite happy.
3. a. The phone call suggests that someone in the family is in trouble.
   b. It turns out to be Katie's voice from five years later, and someone—Bill—was in trouble, but nobody knew it.
4. a. Dawn's phone is off the hook, she lives in a remote area, and her husband is away.
   b. Dawn is sleeping peacefully when Katie and Bill arrive.
5. a. In the movie *Ghost Kiss,* a dead man walks out of a crypt.
   b. Just a little later, Bill dies.

**B.** (5 points each)
1. b
2. c
3. c
4. b
5. a

**C.** (4 points each)
1. a
2. c
3. b
4. a
5. a

**D.** (15 points; students should answer one of the two)
1. Answers will vary. Possible reasons that Katie was unable to recognize her own voice include the following.
   a. No one would expect to hear his or her own voice on the phone.
   b. Most people don't recognize their own voice when they hear it as others do.
   c. Katie was feeling guilty and worried about Polly and assumed it must be her.
   d. The voice was very upset and the speaker was crying, which made it harder to recognize.
   e. Katie only heard the voice say a few words.
2. Answers will vary. Most students will feel that the falling action occurs after the recorded voice tells Katie that the number is no longer in service and includes
   a. the old Bill and Katie talking after the mysterious call.
   b. the present-day Katie realizing that it had been her own voice on the phone trying to warn her of Bill's impending death.

Support for this idea could include the fact that
   a. the level of suspense drops dramatically when Katie hears the recorded voice; it is at this point that all hope of changing the past is lost.
   b. the loose ends of the play are tied up when the mysterious phone call is explained.

Other answers should be supported with appropriate reasons and references to the play.

**E.** (15 points) Answers will vary widely, depending on students' personal experiences, situations, and viewpoints. Accept any answers that address the concern of the question and are elaborated by examples or details from the literature or from life.

## Beware: Do Not Read This Poem
Selection Test, pp. 139–140

**A.** (10 points each) Notes will vary but might include points such as the following:
1. a. Features include: invented spellings and abbreviations ("abt an ol woman," "self w/"), unconventional capitalization, missing punctuation.
   b. The mood might be described as mysterious, suspenseful.
2. a. Features include: increasingly erratic punctuation, no capitalization, emphasis of certain words and phrases through repetition ("this poem has his . . ."), nonstandard grammar ("this poem aint got no manners"), continued use of abbreviations ("yr legs").
   b. The mood is menacing, threatening, insistent, very personal.

3. a. Features include: unusual line breaks and spacing (especially in the last two lines), use of numerals, little punctuation, no capitalization.

   b. The mood might be described as poignant or sad, or students might feel it is ironic or humorous (since it implies that the reader might become one of the missing).

**B.** (8 points each)
 1. d
 2. c
 3. a
 4. b

**C.** (20 points; students should answer one of the two)
 1. Answers will vary but might include the following points:
    a. The mirrors and the poem both entrap people.
    b. The poem "is the reader" as a mirror reflection is the person reflected.
    c. Both catch their victims unaware.
    d. The mirror took its victims without warning, but the poem is giving a warning.
    e. The imagery used to describe how the poem captures its victim is that of hunger and eating, while people simply disappear into the mirror.

 2. Answers will vary but might include the following points about people with drug or alcohol addictions:
    a. They tend to become absorbed in themselves and shut others out, as the woman with the mirrors does.
    b. They often disappear from the normal life of the community, and they may drag others away with them, as the woman in the mirror does.
    c. Their addictions constantly tempt them, no matter how much they are warned of the danger, and they slip more and more into the grip of the addiction, as the poem warns will happen to the reader.
    d. At some point, they and their addiction seem to be inseparable and indistinguishable, as the poem and the reader are one.
    e. They may die as a result of the addiction, or simply disappear from the lives of family and friends like the "missing persons" in the last part of the poem; either way, they leave "a space in the lives of their friends."

**D.** (18 points) Answers will vary widely, depending on students' personal experiences, situations, and viewpoints. Accept any answers that address the concern of the question and are elaborated by examples or details from the literature or from life.

## In the Family
Selection Test, pp. 141–142
**A.** (15 points each)
 1. Notes will vary. Students should include three or four points about Clara in the real world, such as the following:
    a. She is bolder and more determined than the other members of the family.
    b. She was one of the first female dentists in the country, but she never practiced dentistry.
    c. She joined the women of the family in embroidering sheets and waiting for a suitor, but she never married.
    d. She vacations at the beach each summer.
    e. She makes many of the family's decisions.

 2. Notes will vary. Students should include three or four points about Clara in the fantasy world, such as the following:
    a. She greeted Gus, who was in the mirror.
    b. She arranged the mirror so that the living family and the people in the mirror ate together each day.
    c. She asked Eulalia to pass the salad from the mirror to her.
    d. She ate the "spectral salad."
    e. After her death, she appeared in the mirror.
    f. She tried to lure the narrator into the mirror world.

**B.** (5 points each)
 1. c
 2. b
 3. d
 4. a

**C.** (4 points each)
 1. b
 2. a
 3. c
 4. b
 5. a

**D.** (15 points; students should answer one of the two)
 1. Answers will vary but should suggest that Clara is trying to lure the narrator into the mirror world. Opinions will vary. Possible reasons include:
    a. Yes, Clara will succeed because the narrator is not trying very hard to resist. The narrator chose to sit right next to the mirror even though she knew it was a "bad step," and she continues to sit there even though she knows that Clara is just waiting for her to slip up.
    b. No, Clara will not succeed because the narrator is completely aware of her tricks; the narrator knows what the result will be, so she is not likely to fall into the trap.

 2. Answers will vary, but could include:
    a. It is unexplainable that a mirror could show reflections of dead people instead of the living people standing before it.
    b. It is unexplainable that dead people in a mirror could eat and carry on as if living.

c. It is unexplainable that people could become accustomed to having a mirror that shows reflections of deceased relatives instead of the living people in the room.

d. The contrast between the matter-of-fact tone and the bizarre events creates the unusual humor.

**E.** (15 points) Answers will vary widely, depending on students' personal experiences, situations, and viewpoints. Accept any answers that address the concern of the question and are elaborated by examples or details from the literature or from life.

### A Very Old Man with Enormous Wings

Selection Test, pp. 143–144

**A.** (6 points each) Notes will vary but might include points similar to the following:

1. Imagery. It presents the angel as a pathetic old man and suggests that any sense of grandeur normally associated with angels does not apply to this man.

2. Tone or magical realism. The matter-of-fact tone of this excerpt suggests that angels are commonplace and the appearance of one should not really excite anybody.

3. Tone or magical realism. The tone of this excerpt emphasizes the absurdity of the situation: that an angel could be "put to stud" like a racehorse, or that an old man with wings might be capable of solving the world's problems.

4. Irony or tone. This excerpt says that Pelayo and Elisenda "intelligently" determined who the man was, but a better word might be "foolishly." The irony in this excerpt suggests that they really did not know what they were talking about.

**B.** (5 points each)

1. b
2. c
3. a
4. d

**C.** (4 points each)

1. a
2. c
3. b
4. b
5. c

**D.** (20 points; students should answer one of the two)

1. Answers will vary. Students will probably agree that the wings in this story do not represent freedom. In fact, one of the ironies of the story is that the old man's wings actually keep him from being free for most of the story. Students may include the following points:

a. The old man's wings get in his way; he can't get up because he is impeded by them.

b. His wings make him a freak to be gawked at; because of them he is locked up as a captive and a prisoner.

c. Only at the very end do the wings allow the old man to escape, and even then, he is not gloriously soaring, but only struggling to stay aloft.

2. Answers will vary. Students may include the following points:

a. The old man at first seems to cause nothing but trouble for Pelayo and Elisenda, but they soon figure out how to become rich from people's interest in seeing him.

b. Father Gonzaga is worried and confused by the strange creature and is anxious to get a judgment from his superiors on how to treat him. The old man is simply a burden to him, which is ultimately relieved when the people lose interest.

c. People who come to see the old man expect miracles from him, but the only miracles that occur seem absurd and even mocking or insulting: a blind man gets new teeth; a leper's sores sprout sunflowers. For the most part, people are curious, but they are not changed. Ultimately, they are disappointed rather than amazed.

**E.** (16 points) Answers will vary widely, depending on students' personal experiences, situations, and viewpoints. Accept any answers that address the concern of the question and are elaborated by examples or details from the literature or from life.

### Unit Five, Part Two Test

pp. 145–146

**A.** (5 points each)

1. b
2. d
3. c
4. a

**B.** (20 points) Notes will vary. A model answer for Katie in *Sorry, Right Number* follows.

Katie's unusual experience

a. involves a supernatural experience with time and the telephone. She receives a phone call from herself that originates in the future.

b. negatively affects her because it doesn't save her husband's life, makes her feel as if there was something she could have done to save her husband's life, gives her hope and then destroys it, and forces her to relive her husband's death.

**C.** (20 points each; students should answer two of three)

1. Answers will vary. A model answer for *Sorry, Right Number* follows.

Katie came to see that
   a. the voice on the phone was her own.
   b. the person she should have been worrying about was her husband, not her daughter, her sister, or her mother.

How Katie came to her understanding:
   a. After figuring out that Polly, her sister Dawn, and her mother were all okay, she found her husband dead in his study.
   b. Her daughter Polly was married on the same day Bill died, five years later.
   c. As she was sitting in his study thinking of him, she picked up the phone.
   d. She spoke the words into the phone that she had heard five years earlier.

2. Answers will vary. A model answer for "The Open Window" and "In the Family" follows.

The events in "The Open Window" were most believable because
   a. Vera is a mischievous but convincing character.
   b. she invents a story of the supernatural, but nothing supernatural actually happens.
   c. the narrator describes Framton Nuttel as a rather weak-minded, nervous individual with mental and physical problems, so his gullibility is quite credible.

The events in "In the Family" are least believable because
   a. a group of dead relatives exist in a mirror, but they move around and eat food as if they are real and alive.
   b. Eulalia, who is dead, passes a salad through the mirror, and Clara eats it.
   c. Clara dies from eating the salad and takes up residence in the mirror, acting much like she did when she was alive.

3. Answers will vary. A model answer for *Sorry, Right Number* follows.

The image or view of death suggests that
   a. death comes suddenly and without warning.
   b. there is seldom anything we can do to avoid or prevent it, no matter how hard we try.

How it affects the people who remain:
   a. Katie, in particular, feels a deep sense of guilt.
   b. She feels that she should have done something to prevent Bill's death.
   c. She feels a deep sense of loss for "the big guy," and she still loves and misses him five years later.
   d. The play does not reveal how the three children at home felt about the loss of their father, but it does suggest that Polly was not affected too deeply (she did not even remember that the day of her wedding was the same day that her father had died).

**D.** (20 points) Answers will vary. A model answer for "A Very Old Man with Enormous Wings" follows.

Elements of reality might include the
   a. presence of crabs in the house after a storm.
   b. stench of different odors.
   c. presence of chickens in the chicken coop.
   d. natural tendency of people to gawk at oddities.
   e. reaction of the priest, who thinks the angel might be an agent of the devil and decides to check with his superiors.
   f. decision made by Elisenda to charge admission and use the proceeds to build a new house.

Elements of illusion might include
   a. the old man's wings.
   b. how the old man arrives and later flies away.
   c. the miraculous, if inappropriate, "cures" of the invalids.
   d. the freak with the traveling circus that is part spider and part girl.

The theme or message concerns different views of angels (or the supernatural, miracles, or the inexplicable) and how people react to them. Possible theme statements: People do not accept or believe what they cannot understand. People use unusual events or people for their own purposes.

# Unit Six

## Book 9 *from the* Odyssey
Selection Test, pp. 147–148

**A.** (6 points each)

1. Notes will vary. Most students will suggest that Odysseus' action is like that of an epic hero in that he
   a. displays loyalty and responsibility toward his men.
   b. doesn't give in to the temptation of easy happiness and contentment.

   Students who feel that Odysseus' action is more like that of an ordinary man might suggest that he
   a. does what any captain of a fleet would do in that situation.
   b. doesn't feel tempted himself to try the Lotus.

2. Notes will vary. Some students will suggest that Odysseus' action is like that of an epic hero in that he
   a. leads his men into unknown dangers.
   b. acts with courage.
   c. ensures that no more men are endangered than is necessary to make the mission a success.

   Students who feel that Odysseus' action is more like that of an ordinary man might suggest that he
   a. is driven by curiosity.
   b. is foolish to court danger simply to satisfy his curiosity.
   c. doesn't think through the risks versus the rewards.
   d. doesn't put the safety of his men ahead of his curiosity.

3. Notes will vary. Some students will suggest that Odysseus' action is like that of an epic hero in that he
   a. acts to save the lives of his men at great risk to himself.
   b. attacks a being far more powerful than himself.
   c. attacks in self-defense only after more reasonable alternatives have been tried.

   Students who feel that Odysseus' action is more like that of an ordinary man might suggest that
   a. his attack on the drunk, sleeping Polyphemus is cowardly or requires little courage.
   b. anyone in his situation would take desperate measures; there is nothing to lose.

4. Notes will vary. Most students will suggest that Odysseus' action is like that of an epic hero in that his plan is
   a. cunning.
   b. courageous.
   c. daring.

   Students who feel that Odysseus' action is more like that of an ordinary man should support that view with an appropriate reason.

5. Notes will vary. Some students will suggest that Odysseus' action is like that of an epic hero in that it
   a. is daring.
   b. displays a sense of fairness; Polyphemus has a right to know who has blinded him and stolen his livestock.
   c. reveals Odysseus' strong sense of pride.
   d. reveals Odysseus' sense of outrage over what Polyphemus did to Odysseus' men.

   Students who feel that Odysseus' action is more like that of an ordinary man might suggest that it
   a. endangers his men without purpose.
   b. may anger Poseidon and lead him to punish not only Odysseus but also his men.
   c. reflects anger and pride, very human qualities that an epic hero should rise above.

**B.** (5 points each)

1. a
2. b
3. d
4. c
5. b
6. d

**C.** (4 points each)

1. c
2. c
3. a
4. b
5. b

**D.** (10 points; students should answer one of the two)

1. Answers will vary. Students could say that Odysseus and his men are feeling
   a. relieved and grateful to the gods for having survived the confrontation with Polyphemus.
   b. regretful and sad about the loss of their companions.
   c. yearning for the home that they haven't seen in almost twenty years.
   d. hopeful for their eventual homecoming.
   e. wary or frightened about the possibility of Polyphemus' prayer being answered.
   f. mentally and physically exhausted by their long journey and its hazards.

2. Answers will vary. Students might infer that the civilization of the Cyclopes is rough, brutal, backward, or primitive because the Cyclopes
   a. live in caves.
   b. have no culture or arts.
   c. have no system of government or justice.
   d. live apart from, and show little concern for, each other.
   e. have no customs or interest in their history.
   f. do not know about farming.
   g. deal out arbitrary, brutal "justice."

In contrast, students might infer that the civilization of the Greeks is complex, forward-thinking, or modern because the poem suggests that the Greeks

    a. have customs, culture, and arts.
    b. have a government and justice system.
    c. have close, sociable ties to each other.
    d. are interested in their history.
    e. know about farming.
    f. know about seafaring.

Some students may feel quite differently about these civilizations, noting that the Cyclopes civilization

    a. keeps its people at home.
    b. reflects the desires of its people.
    c. doesn't destroy the environment.

These students might also note that the Greek civilization

    a. sends men off to distant lands to make war on each other.
    b. encourages men to take advantage of people less knowledgeable or "advanced" than they.
    c. harms the environment.

**E.** (10 points) Answers will vary widely, depending on students' personal experiences, situations, and viewpoints. Accept any answers that address the concern of the question and are elaborated by examples or details from the literature or from life.

## Book 10 *from the* Odyssey

Selection Test, pp. 149–150

**A.** (30 points) Notes will vary widely. Among the many points that students could suggest are the following:

    a. The use of an epic simile to describe how the men respond to Odysseus' return.
    b. The strong appeal to the senses of hearing and touch in the epic simile.
    c. The comparison of the men's response to Odysseus to the response of calves to their mothers.
    d. The use of the words weeping, despair, tumult, and bawling to describe the men's reaction to Odysseus.
    e. The lines "their faces wet with tears as if they saw/their homeland."
    f. The strong appeal to the sense of sight in the same lines.
    g. The use of the phrase "even the very town where they were born" to emphasize the depth of the men's response to Odysseus.

**B.** (4 points each)

1. c
2. c
3. a
4. d
5. b

**C.** (4 points each)

1. b
2. c
3. b
4. a
5. a

**D.** (15 points; students should answer one of the two)

1. Answers will vary but should reflect students' understanding that Odysseus and his men stay so long because
    a. they are weary and sick of battling the sea and landing in foreign, dangerous places.
    b. Circe's island is a tropical paradise, where life is easy, the food and drink are plentiful, and beautiful nymphs wait on the men.

Opinions concerning Odysseus' role in the men's staying so long will vary widely. Students who find fault with Odysseus may note that

    a. he stays of his own free will; that is, no magic is used to force him to stay.
    b. the men over whom he has power have the sense to know that it is long past time to leave.
    c. he has been choosing pleasure over his duty, goals, and values.

Students who don't find fault with Odysseus may feel that

    a. he deserves some time away from his troubles.
    b. the time on the island is necessary to restore the men's will to withstand the troubles that lay ahead of them.
    c. Circe appears to have put some sort of spell over him. It is not like Odysseus to ignore his duties.

2. Answers will vary widely. Students who feel favorably toward Odysseus might include points similar to the following:
    a. Odysseus is courageous in challenging Circe after she turns his men into pigs. He could have deserted the men and left the island as Eurylochus recommended, but that would have been cowardly.
    b. Odysseus is wise to remain on the island for a lengthy period. He could have chosen to leave immediately, but that would have put his men—who are nearly at the end of their ropes—back into the path of danger. Their bodies and souls are desperately in need of rest and replenishment.

Students who feel less favorably toward Odysseus might include points similar to the following:

    a. Odysseus is foolhardy to challenge Circe after she turns his men into pigs. Eurylochus is right about Odysseus: he takes too many chances with his men's lives. The alternative choice (leaving the island immediately with the remaining men) is the one that a man focused on achieving his goal would have chosen.

b. By remaining on the island for such a long period, Odysseus gives in to his baser instincts. He loses sight of his goals as well as his virtue for the sake of momentary pleasure. Such behavior is beneath that of an epic hero, who would have scorned Circe's charms and left the island immediately after rescuing his men.

**E.** (15 points) Answers will vary widely, depending on students' personal experiences, situations, and viewpoints. Accept any answers that address the concern of the question and are elaborated by examples or details from the literature or from life.

## Book 12 *from the* Odyssey
Selection Test, pp. 151–152

**A.** (20 points each)
1. Notes will vary but should suggest themes similar to two of the following:
   a. It is in human nature never to give up.
   b. It is in human nature to fight against one's fate.
   c. Some things in life cannot be denied, changed, or defeated.
   d. The gods, not humans, control human destiny.
   e. Human beings are wrong to think themselves gods.
   f. Evil cannot be defeated.
2. Notes will vary but should suggest themes similar to two of the following:
   a. People are who they are; others cannot change them.
   b. It is better to remain in the dark about things that are outside one's control.
   c. Fear is a powerful force in life.
   d. Danger brings out both the best and worst in people.
   e. Danger strikes when one least expects it.
   f. There is no avoiding death.
   g. The gods, not humans, control human destiny.

**B.** (5 points each)
1. c
2. b
3. c
4. c

**C.** (4 points each)
1. c
2. b
3. a
4. b
5. a

**D.** (10 points) Answers will vary widely due to individual beliefs about fate but should reflect students' understanding that Circe
   a. describes the dangers that lie ahead of Odysseus.
   b. gives Odysseus reasonable advice to help him

make appropriate decisions and take appropriate action in various situations.
   c. informs Odysseus of the repercussions of giving in to certain temptations and attempting to take certain actions.
   d. doesn't control or plan Odysseus' future.
   e. can affect Odysseus' fate only by informing him about will happen if he and his men take certain actions.

**E.** (10 points) Answers will vary widely, depending on students' personal experiences, situations, and viewpoints. Accept any answers that address the concern of the question and are elaborated by examples or details from the literature or from life.

## Books 21, 22, and 23 *from the* Odyssey
Selection Test, pp. 153–154

**A.** (8 points each)
1. Notes will vary. Most students will say that the quotation reveals that Penelope is one of the following:
   a. Strong, tough.
   b. Sensitive.
   c. Extremely loyal.
   d. Proud.
These qualities are revealed through the character's speech, thoughts, feelings, or actions.
2. Notes will vary. Some students will say that the quotation reveals that Antinous is one of the following:
   a. Haughty, conceited, too proud.
   b. Foolish, stupid.
   c. Disrespectful, ill-mannered.
   d. A troublemaker, a bully.
   e. Doomed, about to die.
These qualities are revealed through direct comments about the character and, possibly, through the character's speech, thoughts, feelings, or actions.
Other students will say that the quotation reveals that Odysseus is one of the following:
   a. Skillful, powerful.
   b. Vengeful, unmerciful.
   c. Wronged.
These qualities are revealed through direct comments about the character, and, possibly, through the character's speech, thoughts, feelings, or actions.
3. Notes will vary. Some students will say that the quotation reveals that Penelope is one of the following:
   a. Strong.
   b. Cold-hearted, hardened.
   c. Wary, cautious.
   d. Unemotional, cool-headed.

These qualities are revealed through the speech, thoughts, feelings, or actions of other characters. Other students will say that the quotation reveals that Odysseus is one of the following:
  a. Demanding.
  b. Honest, straightforward.
  c. Bitter, hardened.
  d. Unemotional, cool-headed.
These qualities are revealed through the character's speech, thoughts, feelings, or actions.
  4. Notes will vary. Most students will say that the quotation reveals that Odysseus is one of the following:
  a. Emotional, sensitive.
  b. Loving.
  c. Grateful, appreciative.
  d. Suffering, in emotional pain.
  e. Satisfied, comforted.
These qualities are revealed through direct comments about the character and, possibly, through physical description and the character's speech, thoughts, feelings, or actions.

**B.** (6 points each)
  1. a
  2. b
  3. b
  4. c

**C.** (4 points each)
  1. a
  2. c
  3. b
  4. a
  5. c

**D.** (12 points) Answers will vary. Students could note that Odysseus feels justified in that the suitors
  a. have taken advantage of his absence to plunder his home and insult his wife and son.
  b. have disobeyed the wishes of the gods and shown disrespect by breaking the rules of hospitality.
  c. are greedy, cruel, bullying, and cowardly.
Students who believe that Odysseus' behavior is justified might say that
  a. his actions are brave and heroic; the suitors far outnumber him and his helpers.
  b. the suitors deserve to die because they are greedy, cruel, bullying, and cowardly.
  c. the suitors have been all too happy to take advantage of his absence; having to suffer upon his return is fair play.
  d. he has the right to defend his home, property, and family.
Students who don't feel that Odysseus' behavior is justified might say that

  a. his behavior is repulsive, noting that he overreacts and that his violence is as barbaric as Polyphemus' actions.
  b. the suitors plead for forgiveness and offer restitution.
  c. the suitors haven't killed or physically harmed anyone; their punishment goes far beyond their crime.
  d. his actions are motivated only by pride and a desire for vengeance.

**E.** (12 points) Answers will vary widely, depending on students' personal experiences, situations, and viewpoints. Accept any answers that address the concern of the question and are elaborated by examples or details from the literature or from life.

## Unit Six, Part One Test
pp. 155–156

**A.** (5 points each) Answers will vary but should include points similar to the following:
  1. Odysseus and the rest of his men would be trapped in the cave because they would not be able to move the boulder blocking the cave entrance.
  2. Eurylochus thought Odysseus was daring but foolhardy; he suspected that Odysseus had been bewitched; or, he remembered that the last decision Odysseus made led to the loss of several men in the land of the Cyclopes.
  3. They represent temptation, or the seductive power of women to distract men and lead them astray.
  4. She had endured many trials for 20 years and had to be on guard at all times; she wondered if he was really a man since he had just killed 100 men and obviously had help from Athena.

**B.** (20 points) Notes will vary widely, depending on students' interpretations of the outcomes of Odysseus' struggles. Possible answers follow.
  1. Students who think that Odysseus won the struggle against Polyphemus might note that Odysseus
    a. blinded Polyphemus.
    b. came up with a plan that rescued most of his men.
    c. stole all of Polyphemus' livestock.
Students who think that Odysseus lost this struggle might point out that Polyphemus
    a. killed several of Odysseus' men.
    b. brought the wrath of Poseidon, who doomed Odysseus' men to death and Odysseus himself to a long and tragic voyage home.
  2. Odysseus won the struggle against the Sirens because he
    a. followed Circe's instructions.
    b. plugged the ears of his oarsmen.
    c. arranged to listen to the Sirens' song without greatly endangering himself and his men.

3. Students might argue that Odysseus lost the struggle against Scylla and Charybdis because
   a. he had little choice but to sail near Scylla's den.
   b. nothing could prevent Scylla from taking his men.
   c. Scylla killed six of his men.
Students might argue that Odysseus won the struggle because
   a. he did the best he could under the circumstances.
   b. he lost only six men to Scylla; if he had taken a different course of action, he might have lost all his men.
   c. he kept his men rowing and working hard to get as many men as possible through the twin troubles.

**C.** (20 points each; students should answer two of the four)
1. Answers will vary widely. A model answer follows.
   In the Scylla and Charybdis adventure, Odysseus' best qualities are revealed; he
   a. shows good leadership under adversity.
   b. is unwilling to bow to fate's demand that six of his men die.
   c. rallies his men to keep rowing, despite his own dread of what lies ahead.
   d. is devastated by the death of his men.
In the Polyphemus (Cyclops) adventure, Odysseus' worst qualities are revealed when
   a. he endangers his men by leading them to Polyphemus' cave for no purpose other than to satisfy his curiosity.
   b. he allows his temper to get the best of his judgment.
   c. he endangers his men by revealing their location when he taunts Polyphemus.
   d. his pride leads him to reveal his identity to Polyphemus, bringing the wrath of Poseidon down on Odysseus and his men and dooming them to a long, perilous journey, which ends with the death of all of Odysseus' men.
2. Answers will vary but could include some of the following points:
   a. Loyalty and faithfulness, as shown by the trust Odysseus' men put in him despite the poor judgment he sometimes showed, such as when he stayed on Circe's island for an entire year.
   b. Patriotism, love of family, and perseverance, as shown by the determination of Odysseus and his men to return to their homeland.
   c. Courage, as shown by Odysseus and many of his men during their adventures.
   d. Cleverness and intelligence, as shown by Odysseus' imaginative trickery in outwitting Polyphemus.

e. Hospitality, as shown by Odysseus' remarks to Polyphemus about the treatment owed to guests and Circe's treatment of Odysseus and his men.
f. Faith in and respect for the gods, as shown by Odysseus' sacrificing Polyphemus' prize ram to Zeus and Polyphemus' being defeated by Odysseus after scorning Zeus.
Other ideas should be supported with appropriate details from the selections.
3. Answers will vary widely but should discuss any two of Odysseus' actions from the *Odyssey*. A model answer for one action students might discuss includes the following points:
   a. Odysseus took several of his men with him to satisfy his curiosity about the Cyclops.
   b. Odysseus should have weighed the danger of satisfying his curiosity and decided against it. He should have stayed on his ship or, at the very least, not have taken any of his men into Polyphemus' cave.
   c. It would have been better if he had stayed on the ship because he gained little of importance from exploring Polyphemus' cave, lost several of his men, and earned Poseidon's wrath.
4. Answers will vary. Possible answers include the following:
   a. Penelope is as heroic as Odysseus is, facing her own challenges with seemingly superhuman qualities that symbolize human achievement far beyond that of one person. Her loyalty to Odysseus surpasses that of ordinary human experience. She also displays extraordinary patience with the suitors, extraordinary hospitality to her guests, and extraordinary cunning in determining whether Odysseus is her true husband.
   b. Penelope, despite her qualities, does not measure up to the description of an epic hero as one who participates in great and dangerous adventures, victories over enemies, and difficult journeys.
   c. Penelope never had the chance to become an epic hero. She had to tend to the matters of home and family while Odysseus wandered for 20 years. While her handling of home and family is honorable and extraordinary, it is not typical of an epic hero.

**D.** (20 points) Notes will vary. A model answer includes the following points:
   a. Cunning.
   b. Virtue.
   c. Odysseus uses Polyphemus' flock to smuggle himself and his men out of Polyphemus' cave.

## The Tragedy of Romeo and Juliet: Act One
Selection Test, pp. 157–158

**A.** (10 points each) Notes will vary but should include points similar to the following:
1. a. The conflict established here is the hateful feud between the Capulets and the Montagues.
   b. Tybalt and Benvolio are involved in this fight, but the conflict involves all the members and servants of both families.
2. a. Lady Capulet wants Juliet to marry Paris, but Juliet has not really thought about marriage and shows little interest in Paris.
   b. Juliet, Lady Capulet, and Nurse are involved in the conversation, which involves Paris.
3. a. Romeo has met and fallen in love with Juliet and has just discovered her identity. She is a Capulet and he a Montague, so their relationship is ill-fated from the beginning.
   b. Romeo is talking with Benvolio. The conflict mainly involves Romeo, Juliet, and Tybalt, who represents the Capulets.

**B.** (8 points each)
1. c
2. d
3. a
4. b
5. a

**C.** (20 points; students should answer one of the two)
1. Answers will vary but could include the following points:
   a. Juliet's father thinks Juliet is still too young to marry, but Juliet's mother thinks she is old enough.
   b. Juliet's parents both think that she should have a say in whether she wants to marry Paris or not.
   c. Juliet's mother is more eager to put forward Paris's suit than Juliet's father is.
   d. The mother urges Juliet to look favorably upon Paris; the father encourages Paris to look favorably upon all the young ladies at the festivities, not just Juliet.
2. Answers will vary but could include the following points:
   a. Romeo is completely absorbed in thinking about love before he meets Juliet; he is in despair because the object of his desire has rejected him.
   b. Juliet, who is only 13 years old, has apparently given little thought to matters of love and marriage until her mother bids her to consider it.
   c. Both Romeo and Juliet are smitten with love when they first meet.
   d. Romeo and Juliet equal each other in their witty verbal exchange, and both seem comfortable with touching hands, kissing, and letting each other know their feelings during this first encounter.

**D.** (10 points) Answers will vary widely, depending on students' personal experiences, situations, and viewpoints. Accept any answers that address the concern of the question and are elaborated by examples or details from the literature or from life.

## The Tragedy of Romeo and Juliet: Act Two
Selection Test, pp. 159–160

**A.** (8 points each)
1. Notes will vary but should indicate that Romeo reveals how completely lovestruck he is over Juliet.
2. Notes will vary but should indicate that Juliet loves Romeo even though he is a Montague. If he could shed his name, she would be his.
3. Notes will vary but should indicate that Romeo reveals that he is listening to Juliet's words and trying to decide whether to speak to her.
4. Notes will vary but should indicate that the audience gains information about the setting (time of day, etc.) and learns about Friar Laurence's expertise in herbal lore; he knows how to use plants as medicines and as poisons.

**B.** (6 points each)
1. b
2. d
3. c
4. b
5. a

**C.** (20 points; students should answer one of the two)
1. Answers will vary but might include the following points:
   a. Both know of Romeo and Juliet's plan to marry.
   b. Both agree to assist Romeo and Juliet in secret.
   c. Both briefly question the sincerity of Romeo's love, but both are convinced it is sincere.
   d. Both want to protect Juliet by making sure that Romeo is serious about her.
2. Answers will vary but might include the following points:
   a. The nurse's size and age contrast sharply with Juliet's youthful beauty.
   b. The nurse uses crude language and mundane imagery in contrast to Juliet's fine phrases and elaborate metaphors.
   c. The nurse's attempts at using big words and at imitating the habits of a gentlewoman only make her seem foolish and clumsy in contrast to Juliet's natural grace and the exquisite poetry of her speech.
   d. The nurse's grumbling complaints and her wish to rest rather than talk immediately about Juliet's plans are in sharp contrast to Juliet's extreme impatience and eagerness at the nurse's return.

**D.** (18 points) Answers will vary widely, depending on students' personal experiences, situations, and viewpoints. Accept any answers that address the concern of the question and are elaborated by examples or details from the literature or from life.

## The Tragedy of Romeo and Juliet: Act Three
Selection Test, pp. 161–162
**A.** (10 points each)
1. Tybalt was the name of a cat in stories of the time, and cats were thought to have nine lives. Mercutio suggests that he is going to kill Tybalt by taking one of his lives.
2. Phoebus was the god of the sun, which traveled across the sky in a chariot, and Phaëton was a reckless driver of the sun's chariot. Juliet wishes that the sun could be driven faster to the West. She wants night to come sooner so she can be with Romeo.
3. Cynthia was a goddess associated with the moon, hence the moon itself. Romeo knows he must leave before dawn but does not want to go, so he pretends that the light in the sky is from the moon and not the sunrise.

**B.** (6 points each)
1. a
2. d
3. c
4. d
5. b

**C.** (20 points: students should answer one of the two)
1. Answers will vary but might include the following points:
   a. Capulet now wishes to have Juliet wed Paris as soon as possible.
   b. He tells Paris that Juliet must bow to his will in this matter, but previously he said that his will was only part of her consent and that Paris must win her heart.
   c. Juliet's father flies into a rage when she says she will not marry Paris and uses cruel and insulting terms to describe her.
   d. He insists he will force her to the church to marry Paris whether she wants to or not; if she refuses, he will disown her and she can die in the streets for all he cares.
2. Answers will vary but might include the following points:
   a. At first she thinks that he is the opposite of what he had seemed to be, that his innocent looks deceived her, that he is truly evil at heart (a "beautiful tyrant," a "fiend angelical," a "wolvish-ravening lamb").
   b. When the nurse criticizes Romeo, Juliet changes

her tune and jumps to her husband's defense, realizing that he must have killed Tybalt in self-defense; she becomes glad he killed Tybalt because otherwise Romeo himself would be dead.
   c. She proclaims Romeo's banishment a far greater grief than her cousin Tybalt's death.

**D.** (20 points) Answers will vary widely, depending on students' personal experiences, situations, and viewpoints. Accept any answers that address the concern of the question and are elaborated by examples or details from the literature or from life.

## The Tragedy of Romeo and Juliet: Act Four
Selection Test, pp. 163–164·
**A.** (10 points each) Notes will vary but should include the following points:
1. a. Juliet has threatened to kill herself and has agreed to a desperate plan. The mood is serious and foreboding.
   b. Juliet returns from the friar feigning a cheerful mood; her father becomes jovial and merry. The mood is mixed because Capulet has become excited and cheerful, but the audience knows that Juliet is insincere.
2. a. Juliet has just taken the potion that Friar Laurence prepared for her after a lengthy soliloquy in which she expressed her confusion and fright. The mood is suspenseful and serious.
   b. Capulet, Lady Capulet, Nurse, and the servants are merrily preparing for the wedding banquet, jesting with one another as they finish the preparations. The mood is happy and optimistic.
3. a. The family has discovered Juliet's body, assumes that she is dead, and sadly prepares for her funeral. The mood is solemn and melancholy.
   b. The servant Peter banters with the musicians who were hired to play at the wedding in a lighthearted, teasing way. The mood is lighthearted.

**B.** (6 points each)
1. d
2. c
3. a
4. c
5. b

**C.** (20 points; students should answer one of the two)
1. Answers will vary but might include the following points:
   a. When Juliet learned the circumstances of Tybalt's death, she grieved for him; but she also realized

that she and Romeo would now be separated,
and this was the greater cause of her grief.

  b. As she wept inconsolably for Romeo, she gave
her mother the impression that it was Tybalt
she grieved for.

  c. To distract her from this weeping and grieving
over her cousin's death, Juliet's father decided
she should be married at once.

  d. The marriage plan created a new and even greater
problem for Juliet: she could not explain the reason
for her refusal, nor could she agree to her parents'
plan.

  e. Because of her parents' plan for her, Juliet is forced
to take desperate action.

2. Answers will vary but might include the following
points about Friar Laurence:

  a. He knows that Juliet is already married to Romeo,
thus marriage to Paris would be a sin.

  b. He is a friend to Romeo and wants to do what he
can to secure Romeo's happiness.

  c. He proposes that Juliet drink a potion that will
make her seem to be dead for 42 hours.

  d. He says he will send a letter to Romeo explaining
the plan.

  e. He proposes to be in the tomb, with Romeo, when
Juliet awakes from her drug-induced sleep, and to
help the two escape together to Mantua.

**D.** (20 points) Answers will vary widely, depending on
students' personal experiences, situations, and viewpoints.
Accept any answers that address the concern of the
question and are elaborated by examples or details
from the literature or from life.

### The Tragedy of Romeo and Juliet: Act Five
Selection Test, pp. 165–166

**A.** (15 points each)

1. Notes will vary, but might include two of the following
points:

  a. Romeo's excessively emotional character caused
him to woo and marry Juliet very quickly and
impulsively.

  b. It caused him to kill Tybalt after Mercutio's death.

  c. It caused him to kill himself when he learned of
Juliet's death.

2. Notes will vary, but might include two of the following
points:

  a. The family feud caused Romeo and Juliet to keep
their love and marriage a secret.

  b. It caused Tybalt to attack Romeo and his friends.

  c. It caused the prince to punish Romeo with
banishment.

  d. It caused Juliet and Friar Laurence to take
desperate measures so that Juliet could remain

true to her secret marriage when her parents
had arranged a different marriage for her.

**B.** (6 points each)

  1. b
  2. d
  3. b
  4. a
  5. c

**C.** (20 points; students should answer one of the two)

1. Answers will vary. Students should name Tybalt,
Romeo, and Paris, and might include the following
points:

  a. Tybalt is Juliet's cousin, aligned with the Capulets,
and bent on fighting with the Montagues.

  b. Romeo is the heir of the Montague house. As
Juliet's husband, he is secretly aligned with the
Capulets as well as the Montagues.

  c. Paris is related to the prince. He is an innocent
victim who is involved in the feud only because
of his love for Juliet, a Capulet.

2. Answers will vary but might include ideas such as the
following:

  a. The love of two young people can transcend the
prejudices and hatred of their parents.

  b. Acting out of hatred and prejudice can only lead
to bad ends.

  c. Forcing people to hide their true passions leads
to a web of lies and misunderstandings and,
ultimately, disaster.

  d. It is dangerous to embark on a risky endeavor
(such as Romeo and Juliet's secret marriage)
too quickly.

  e. People often understand the foolishness of their
beliefs and actions only after they have resulted
in disaster.

**D.** (20 points) Answers will vary widely, depending on
students' personal experiences, situations, and viewpoints.
Accept any answers that address the concern of the
question and are elaborated by examples or details
from the literature or from life.

### Unit Six, Part Two Test
pp. 167–168

**A.** (5 points each)

  1. d
  2. b
  3. c
  4. d

**B.** (20 points) Notes will vary but should include points
similar to the following:

  1. a. Tybalt's vow foreshadows his fight with Romeo.
    b. Instead of killing Romeo, he is slain.

2. a. This foreshadows the friar's well-intentioned use of herbs to fake Juliet's death.
   b. His use of herbs leads to the deaths of both Romeo and Juliet.
3. a. This foreshadows Juliet's willingness to commit suicide if she is separated from Romeo.
   b. When death takes Romeo from her, Juliet does, indeed, kill herself.

**C.** (20 points each; students should answer two of the three)

1. Answers will vary widely. A model answer follows.
   a. Friar Laurence counsels Romeo and agrees to perform the marriage.
   b. He marries Romeo and Juliet in secret.
   c. He conspires with the nurse to keep the marriage a secret.
   d. He fakes Juliet's death by giving her poison and conceals his plans from Juliet's family.
   e. He tries to get word to Romeo in Mantua but his plan fails.

Students who think that Friar Laurence was right in his actions might give these reasons:
   a. His goal was to end the feud between the families.
   b. He was a friend of Romeo's and wanted to help him.
   c. He could see that Romeo and Juliet were passionately in love and wanted to consecrate the marriage before they did something irresponsible.
   d. He thought he would succeed and everything would turn out all right.

Students who think that Friar Laurence was wrong in his actions might give these reasons:
   a. He was helping two people who were probably too young to make such decisions.
   b. He was a man of the church who should have exemplified virtue and honesty, but instead he was dishonest and deceitful.
   c. The prince, the Capulets, and the Montagues all trusted him as a representative of the church, but he did not act in a trustworthy way.
   d. He should have told Romeo and Juliet's parents about what was going on; he might have been able to prevent their tragic end.

2. Answers will vary. A model answer for Lady Capulet follows.

Lady Capulet
   a. convinced Juliet that she should begin thinking about marriage (even though she was only 13 years old).
   b. recommended Paris as the man she should marry, even though Juliet had no interest in him.
   c. agreed with her husband, after Tybalt's death, that Juliet must be forced to marry Paris or be disowned.

Lady Capulet pressured her daughter throughout to marry Paris. After Juliet had already married Romeo, the pressure from her mother (and father) made the situation untenable and drove Juliet to take desperate measures.

3. Answers will vary. Causes should include several of the following:
   a. Romeo was impulsive and excessively emotional.
   b. Juliet was too young to act responsibly.
   c. The Capulets and Montagues hated each other and would not have accepted their love or allowed their marriage.
   d. Romeo killed Tybalt, a Capulet, and was banished from Verona.
   e. Juliet's parents pressured her to marry Paris.
   f. Friar Laurence conspired to conceal the whole affair.
   g. The presence of a plague kept Friar John from reaching Mantua.
   h. Balthasar told Romeo that Juliet was dead.

Students might argue that the person or thing most responsible for the tragedy was Friar Laurence, the family feud, Romeo, or fate. The student's judgment should be supported with evidence from the play.

**D.** (20 points) Events and notes will vary. A model answer follows:

Event A: Romeo and Juliet falling in love. This was caused by fate, because you cannot always choose with whom you fall in love, even when the person is not a practical choice.

Event B: Tybalt's murder of Mercutio. This was caused by Tybalt, not fate. Tybalt was a hot-headed and argumentative person, which caused him to fight with Mercutio in the first place.

Event C: Juliet's suicide. This was not caused by fate, but by Friar Laurence's poor judgment in giving Juliet the sleeping potion in the first place and by Juliet's own decision to take her life.

# End-of-Year Test

**pp. 169–177**

**A.** 1. b
   2. d
   3. a
   4. d
   5. c
   6. a

**B.** 7. b
   8. a
   9. d
  10. a

**C.** Answers may vary but should include points similar to the following:

11. This is ironic because it appears at first to describe a man who goes to "Lodge" meetings and sings, but it actually describes a wolf that goes out with the pack and howls.

12. Responses might include: She noticed that he began to smell strange, that he tried to wash off the smell when he thought she wasn't looking, that he evoked an awful reaction from his own daughter, that he stayed away from his daughter.

13. The narrator describes her husband tenderly and affectionately in the first part of the story. Her point of view makes the reader like the husband but wonder what he did wrong. Just as the reader comes to expect the worst, the narrator describes her husband in hateful terms and reveals that he has become a human. This leaves the reader somewhat confused about how to feel toward him.

**D.** 14. c
  15. d
  16. b
  17. c

**E.** Answers may vary but should include points similar to the following:

18. The narrator viewed her husband as the "hateful one" because he had turned into a man. Humans have always feared wolves and tried to kill them. Her instinctive fear and hatred of humans took over. She knew he would "kill our children if he could."

19. For most of the story, the narrator's tone suggests an almost casual acceptance of what has happened ("Well, so he come to live here"). Toward the end, the tone suggests disappointment in how things have turned out, or perhaps a wistful desire that things might have been different (". . . if I could only see him, my true love, in his true form, beautiful. But only the dead man lay there white and bloody").

20. Answers may vary widely. Accept any reasonable statement of theme. Examples: Being different will

not be tolerated. Members of a group distrust outsiders. We fear, or hate, those who are different from us.

## Writing Exercise Scoring Guide

**4**   An **exceptional** paper:
- Has a clear and consistent focus
- Has a logical organization
- Uses transitions effectively to connect ideas
- Supports ideas with details, quotations, examples, and/or other evidence
- Exhibits well-formed sentences varying in structure
- Exhibits a rich vocabulary, including precise language that is appropriate for the purpose and audience of the paper
- Contains almost no errors in usage, mechanics, and spelling

**3**   A **proficient** paper:
- Has a relatively clear and consistent focus
- Has a logical organization, although it may be unnecessarily mechanical
- Uses some transition words and phrases to connect ideas, but they do not always clarify connections effectively
- Supports ideas with details, quotations, examples, and/or other evidence
- Exhibits some variety in sentence structures
- Uses vocabulary that is appropriate for the purpose and audience
- Contains a few errors in usage, mechanics, and spelling

**2**   A **basic** paper:
- Has a fairly clear focus that may occasionally become obscured
- Shows an organizational pattern, but relationships between ideas may sometimes be difficult to understand
- Contains supporting evidence that may lack effect and so only superficially develops ideas
- Has complete and varied sentences most of the time
- Contains several errors in usage, mechanics, and spelling which cause distraction and some confusion about meaning

**1**   A **limited** paper:
- Has a topic but does not include any elaboration, or it only minimally addresses the topic and lacks discernible ideas
- Has only a few simple sentences
- Contains little or no plausible support for ideas
- Shows limited word choice
- Contains numerous and serious errors in usage, mechanics, and spelling which cause confusion about meaning

A paper is unable to be scored if it is
- illegible
- unrelated to the topic
- only a rewording of the prompt
- written in a foreign language
- not written at all

## Revising/Editing

1. c
2. a
3. c
4. d
5. c
6. b

# Standardized Test Practice
# Answer Key

**Analogies**
1. E
2. A
3. E
4. D
5. C
6. E
7. A
8. B
9. C
10. E
11. A
12. B
13. B
14. C
15. C
16. B
17. D
18. E
19. E
20. A
21. C
22. A
23. B
24. B
25. A
26. E
27. C
28. D
29. B
30. C
31. C
32. B
33. C
34. A
35. B
36. D
37. C
38. D
39. B
40. C
41. D
42. E
43. D
44. C
45. B
46. A
47. B
48. D
49. D
50. E

**Sentence Completion**
**Part A**
1. D
2. B
3. C
4. E
5. A
6. C
7. C
8. B
9. D
10. E
11. D
12. B
13. A
14. D
15. B
16. B
17. E
18. C
19. C
20. B
21. B
22. A
23. A
24. C
25. D

**Part B**
1. C
2. D
3. D
4. A
5. E
6. B
7. B
8. C
9. E
10. A
11. C
12. C
13. D
14. D
15. C
16. A
17. D
18. B
19. E
20. B
21. C
22. C
23. B
24. A
25. E

**Error Identification**
1. E
2. A
3. A
4. B
5. C
6. C
7. D
8. C
9. D
10. D
11. E
12. A
13. C
14. A
15. C
16. E
17. D
18. D
19. C
20. E
21. C
22. B
23. B
24. E
25. C
26. D
27. B
28. B
29. C
30. C

**Error Correction**
1. B
2. J
3. A
4. H
5. A
6. G
7. B
8. H
9. D
10. G
11. C
12. H
13. D
14. J
15. A
16. F
17. D
18. H
19. C
20. J
21. B
22. H
23. A
24. J
25. C
26. J
27. D
28. F
29. A
30. G

**Revision-in-Context**
1. C
2. A
3. B
4. B
5. D
6. B
7. D
8. C
9. A
10. C
11. E
12. B
13. B
14. E
15. D

**Critical Reading**
1. C
2. D
3. E
4. A
5. B
6. B
7. D
8. C
9. A
10. E
11. D
12. D
13. C
14. B
15. A
16. B
17. C
18. E
19. D
20. C
21. C
22. A
23. A
24. E
25. B
26. D
27. C
28. C
29. A
30. B